# SOPHIA HOUSE

*A Novel*

MICHAEL D. O'BRIEN

# SOPHIA HOUSE

## *A Novel*

I bring, I bring,
Poor mother, father's bones from the fire,
A weight not light, because of woes.
I put my all in a little space.

Childless, childless!
And I am wretched, bereft of my poor father,
I shall be orphaned in a barren home,
Not cherished in my father's hands.

They are gone, they are no more; *oimoi*, my father!
They are gone.

Euripides, *Suppliants*

IGNATIUS PRESS    SAN FRANCISCO

Cover art: *The Rescuer*, by Michael D. O'Brien

Cover design by Roxanne Mei Lum

© 2005 Ignatius Press, San Francisco
All rights reserved
ISBN 1–58617–039–2 (HB)
ISBN 1–58617–104–6 (PB)
Library of Congress Control Number 2004115170
Printed in the United States of America ∞

*For those whose sacrifice is hidden in the heart of God,*
*those whose "small" choices shift the balance of the world*

# Contents

# *Preface*

Numerous people are to be thanked for their contributions to this book, some living, some dead. I am indebted to the Russian filmmaker Andrei Tarkovsky, whose *Andrei Rublëv* germinated the idea for the imaginary script composed by Pawel Tarnowski. Nor can I forget the painter Georges Rouault. His faith, creativity, and love of his family have ever been an inspiration to me. The little role he plays in this tale is of course fictional, yet in no way inconsonant with his personality and writings. By the same token, Pablo Picasso's brief appearance is also fictional, though his utterances (so antithetical to the spirit of Rouault) are extracts from his manifestos on art.

Other aspects of the story are drawn from the lives of real people. With the fragments of their experience I have tried to form a portrait, as if in the assembly of a mosaic—Byzantine, complex, more than the sum of its parts. Stand too close to it and the image blurs. Focus on a single component and the part becomes the whole, throwing all into misinterpretation. Stand back, find proportion, locate the range of vision, and the portrait emerges. It is my hope that through the lives depicted here the face of Christ will be visible.

# *Prologue*

New York, October 1963

The fat lady lay sweating and puffing on the floor of the dressing room. She was surrounded by five men: one of them the Israeli politician she had sought, the politician's assistant, and three bodyguards. Two of the bodyguards held her to the floor while the third carefully picked through her purse and found identification.

"Ewa Poselski," he said, "Miami, Florida."

"Anything else?" said the politician. "What is she? Political? Religious?"

"Driver's license. Employee I.D. card—says she's a ticket-taker at a place called Funworld."

"No weapons, sir", said another bodyguard. "No explosives. No chemicals."

They helped the old woman to her feet. Her lime-green dress was pinned with a sparkling glass heart. She reeked of sweet perfume.

"How did you get in here?" demanded Lev the assistant, shaking her arm roughly.

"I walked in", she said. Her accent was thick. European. "No one stopped me."

"What do you mean, no one stopped you! The hall is full of guards."

"The angel guided me."

"The angel guided you", Lev mimicked with heavy sarcasm.

The woman nodded toward the politician. "After his talk I

came up the back steps to the stage. Then down here to this room for the actors, yes."

"*Poylish?*" said the politician.

She nodded, "*Tak.*"

"Why do you want to see me?"

"The angel told me to speak to you."

The three bodyguards and Lev laughed. The politician smiled.

"Should we take her out, sir?"

"Yes. Gently, please. Don't hurt her. And tell the manager of the Coliseum I want a word with him."

"Angel or no angel, you'd better give that guy hell", said Lev. "She's just a crank, but what if some of your real enemies got through?"

The politician hesitated, eyeing the woman. "What did you wish to say to me?"

"I know who you are", she said.

"Five thousand people out there tonight know who I am."

Lev smirked. "This is a very important man in Israel. His name is—"

"Oh yes, I know the name that is in the television news", she replied in a low voice, keeping her eyes on the politician; there was no hatred in them, only tears. "You are the man who prosecutes war criminals for your government."

She told him what everyone else knew: his public name, his exact position in the ministry, and the fact that probably soon he would be the deputy prime minister.

"Then why do you say such a thing as you just said?" the politician asked carefully.

"That I know your real name?"

"Yes, that."

"Because I do know your real name."

The bodyguards begged for permission to escort her out.

He silenced them with a glance.

He told her his public name. She shook her head and looked at him.

"You can leave us", he said to the others. They stared at him perplexed, then went out. Lev went last, casting an irritated look over his shoulder.

When the door had closed behind them, he asked the woman, "Why do you think you know me?"

"You were in Warsaw during the war. Your family is dead."

"It is a matter of public record that I am a Polish Jew. It would take little effort to find out that my family died in the Shoah. This does not make you a prophet. As for the matter of another name—ah, madam, about that you are quite mistaken."

"I am only an old woman. But an angel has spoken to me and guided my steps. I know you as if you are my own son, for I have thought about you for twenty years."

"Who are you?"

"I am nobody."

"Then what brought you to me? I do not believe in angels."

"I think you should."

"Answer me."

"I bring you a letter and a gift from one who loved you."

Now the man's face became an impervious wall.

"Loved me?"

"Yes, loved."

A cold bitterness washed across his features.

"Love is an illusion", he said in a tone of indifference.

She shook her head, staring at him, unblinking.

He closed his eyes as if to erase her stupid watering eyes from his mind.

"I have seen into the souls of more men than there are in your Florida—in your Funworld. And I tell you that love cannot overcome death."

"Poor boy," she sighed, "poor, poor boy."

She began to weep openly, and he hated it.

13

"Tell me, for the sake of curiosity, what you think my real name is."

"You are David Schäfer."

The politician looked momentarily stunned, then his face went blank.

"How do you know this name?" he demanded.

"Ah, then it is true. I have found you."

He stared at her. Only a handful of people on earth had known his real name, and almost certainly they were dead. There was no way she could know who he was, but somehow she did know. How? And more importantly—why?

He went to the door and pulled it open. Three guards tumbled in.

"Tea", he said to them. "Bring us tea."

He turned to the woman and said, as if speaking to a fabulous creature in which he did not yet believe, "A glass of tea?"

# SANCTUARY

# I

Warsaw, September 1942

His heart beating like a snared rabbit, he squirmed past the wire of the gate and was out. The guards saw him, of course, as he knew they would, but he dove into the crowd on the sidewalks and hoped they would hesitate an instant before firing. Though he could not run fast because of his hunger, he was able to bob and weave through the pedestrians, under a horse cart, and around a corner before the first shots echoed against the apartment buildings.

The crowd scattered; there were screams, the sound of a horse's mad whinny, running jackboots, and more shots. Gentiles stared at him astonished, parting left and right as he plunged into a main thoroughfare. He tore off the arm band and threw it wide into the crowd, where the star floated down and landed like an embarrassment. Hands tried to grab him in passing, but he was like Moses fleeing the land of bondage. Two walls of human figures crashed in behind him, covering Pharaoh's chariots.

His heart boomed in his chest and his side ached; his breath tore out of him in agonized gasps. He had his youth on his side and adrenaline—for he knew that this was the run of his life. Moreover, his pursuers were not sleek SS but older and heavier Wehrmacht sentries. A cold rain was falling, making the sidewalks treacherous. A bullet whined on the concrete at his heels. The soldiers were through the crowd, yelling in their harsh German, "*Halt! Halt!*"

Another bullet spattered chips of stone onto his coat as he wheeled around a corner into an avenue. He was heading east toward Stare Miasto now, the medieval core of the city, close by the banks of the Vistula. Block after block, past bombed or standing buildings, past a blur of people on the sidewalks, past stalls of tinsmiths and rag merchants, he ran blindly. First this way, then that, east, then north, then east again. Finally, utterly spent, he turned into a narrow side street of ancient three-story buildings in various degrees of ruin. Reaching its end, he found it blocked by a high wall. Frantic now, he gasped in a high, terrified voice, "*Sh'ma Yisrael, Adonai Eloheino, Adonai Echad . . .*"

One of the shop doors along the street was more deeply recessed than the others, and into its shadows he now threw himself. Peering around the bricks, he saw the soldiers at the mouth of the street shaking an old woman. She pointed in the direction where he had run.

"Hear, O Israel, the Lord our God, the Lord is One", he stammered, waiting for them to come.

Without warning, the door opened behind him. He stumbled backward and fell inside. A small bell swung above the head of a man who was staring at him from the dim interior of the shop. In a glance the man understood the situation, heard the boots of the soldiers clomping on the cobblestones, and pulled the rabbit farther inside.

"Up those stairs, quickly", he said, pointing to the back of the room. The boy ran through a maze of floor-to-ceiling shelves loaded with books, found the staircase, and scrambled up frantically, leaving a trail of wet shoe prints. Staring through the dusty panes of the display window, the shopkeeper watched the soldiers working their way along the street toward him, banging on every door, smashing those that were locked, and entering each one. It would take them a few minutes to arrive at his door. Losing no more time, he wiped the floor with a rag, and when the trail had been erased he seated himself at the sales desk by the front entrance. When the soldiers threw open the door with a bang, he looked up from a book, met their eyes over the rim of his spectacles, and asked politely in German, "*Ja, mein Herr?*"

"Bookseller," one barked, "have you seen a Jew boy run this way?"

"*Nein, mein Herr.*"

"*Da ist keiner hier!*" said the other soldier.

"*Wir haben gesehen.*"

"*Komm, wir gehen!*"

When they had gone at a gallop on their chase, the bookseller permitted his hands a slight tremble, and he exhaled. He glanced around the shop and uttered a prayer of thanks that it had been deserted when the boy burst in. *Why did I do it?* he asked himself. *Why such a decision, made without careful consideration of all the factors?*

He stood, and stared at the floor, seeing nothing. For a few moments he slipped into the state of distraction or withdrawal that family members referred to as his "spells", and that was in fact his place of retreat whenever life became too absurd. When the shadows of the soldiers ran past the window, retracing their steps out of the street, his eyes began to focus again.

*Yes, go*, he thought bitterly. *Go and play your role in the Wagnerfest!*

Pawel Tarnowski was not old, though his shoulders were slightly stooped, as if from decades of hovering over volumes of tiny script. He was a sturdy man in his early thirties, with brown eyes and un-Slavic black hair, deep black, which his father once called "a little incident with the Tartars". He was tall and broad-shouldered, but he did not move as one might expect from a man so well proportioned. He shuffled, as if he were twenty or thirty years older.

"Trouble", he muttered aloud. "Trouble, trouble."

He went to his private writing desk in the alcove at the back of the shop and sat down. The worktable beside it was piled high with the litter of broken-spined volumes that he was rebinding, and with strips of leather, glue-pots, tissue-covered packets of gold leaf, prewar literary magazines, unpublished manuscripts, and a graveyard of abandoned tea cups. Before him on the desk stood a wicker basket stuffed with correspondence, the letters stamped from Paris, Berlin, Krakow, New York, and Florence. The bookseller did not especially relish the contents of these letters; it was the envelopes themselves that he passionately loved as touchstones of a broader, more cultured world—the multicolored stamps, the fading violet, cream, and blue of the paper, the striped borders. For the most part they contained inquiries from ungifted writers about his publishing house, *Zofia Press*. He had managed to get three titles into print before the Germans came.

He stared at the street door and thought, *Someday they will leave. Someday paper and truth will no longer be a problem.* Yes, then it would be possible to make beautiful books once more, to walk beside the Vistula River under the flowering trees, thinking of Chekhov, to sit at outdoor cafés, drink Turkish coffee, smoke those terrible French cigarettes, and discuss Kafka or Dante with sympathetic people. On that day he would reply to the letters. And he would be answered by those who had survived. In the meantime it was enough to have the envelopes waiting in promise of the future.

He had been reworking a letter to Kahlia when the boy burst in with terror on his face and a mouth open without explanations. A Jew. Now their troubles were spilling over into his life, as if he didn't have enough of his own.

"What am I going to do?" he whispered.

*Time*, he thought. *Time eases the beating of the heart, dries the perspiration, washes out the toxin of fear.* To distract himself, he stared at a sheet of vellum paper on the desk before him.

Forcing himself to concentrate, he picked up a straight pen, the long green one, his favorite, and dipped the nib into a well of purple ink. This action hooked his eyes and would not let them go. He lifted the nib from the ink, and watched a drop roll slowly toward the point. *All human actions proceed from thought*, he mused, *and this drop of ink is the subsidiary act played by forces I have set in motion.*

The bead formed an oval as it paused at the tip, then hung suspended for a micro-instant before falling. It splashed on the vellum. A star, a violet nova, like the messages that angels let fall to earth from above.

He blinked and shook himself.

*Write!* he commanded. *Write! Push out death with the face of the one you love.*

12 September 1942, Warsaw

My Kahlia,

I do not know where you are at this moment. Nor can I know if one day, when this war is over, you will return with the glorious good news that you did not marry a nobleman or a professor. Of course, you could not have known my heart, for we never spoke. Yet so much was said when, at our first meeting, you glanced across the salon of the music faculty and saw me. I beheld the briefest pause in your look, then your eyes turned back to the score you were playing as if you had seen nothing. Even so, I know that you held an image of me within you.

I went to the university today and pinned another message to the door of the room that was your father's office. Then I went down the hall to the salon. They have stolen the piano, and there are bullet holes in the walls. Do you remember how the Goldberg Variations fused us together on the night of our first and last meeting, just before the darkness fell? Never have I heard a musician play with such sensitivity. I knew then that we were to become one soul. Had the world been different we would have been introduced and befriended each other and never permitted a parting. Perhaps the adagio tempo betrayed my sense of reality, for the future I foresaw has not come to pass.

When they arrested the professors, I hoped that you had somehow escaped the fowler's net. I cannot believe that you have been captured. Surely it is only a matter of time until you return. Until then I worry desperately over your fate.

I will write soon,

Pawel

He locked up, pulled the shades on all the windows, turned off the desk lamp and the overhead globes, and went to the storeroom. A mouse scurried across the floor in front of him. He opened the door to the staircase and ascended with a heavy tread.

On the landing of the second floor, he skirted a stack of wooden crates that contained more books, the remainder of an estate sale that he had not bothered to examine. They were an irritant to him, because he had invested good money in them only to find after opening a few that they were worthless things. He had intended to transport them all to the attic, where they would provide at least a little insulation against the cold. Most of the boxes were already up there, but he had not found sufficient energy to complete the task. He sighed, and entered the apartment. The rooms were as bleak as ever. The kitchen light bulb was burned out, so he lit a paraffin lamp, then went to the electric hot plate and got it warming up under a kettle. As he waited for it to hiss, he peered out the window overlooking the street. Far across the rooftops he could see dirty smoke hovering above the ghetto, from which direction there came occasional gunshots.

The apartment was of the same dimensions as the ground floor shop: a narrow rectangle about five meters wide by eight meters long. On this level it was divided into a front kitchen, a parlor, a toilet closet, a room containing a zinc wash tub, and a bedroom at the rear. The ceilings were four meters high, covered with plaster ornaments, yellowed badly and crumbling off in bits and pieces. The once elegant ivory wallpaper—embossed with *fleurs de lis*—was spotted and torn in many places. The few pieces of furniture, however, were of fine quality, and there were some oil paintings as well. Most of these were saccharine landscapes painted by Polish competents of the previous century. They brooded under a patina of age and smoke, their varnish badly crackled. The lack of regular heat during the winters since 1939 had not helped. He did not care about them overmuch, but he was worried about a small painting of flowers he had bought in Paris during his brief attempt to be an artist. In order to make this extravagant purchase, he had gone without meals for three weeks, surviving on scraps, enjoying the romance of starvation for art's sake only during the first two days. It had been painted by an Italian, an obscure member of a sub-branch of the Impressionists, and was cheap in comparison to a Monet or a Picasso. He thought it the best thing in the room, though it was, perhaps, the worst—pretty and banal. A Greek icon of Saint Michael of the Apocalypse hung beside it, brilliant red and indigo blue, its gold so aged it looked like liquid rosewood poured over amber. He kissed it, made the sign of the cross slowly, then bowed toward his bedroom, in the corner of which hung a small wall-shrine containing other icons. A red votive candle flickered there.

While the tea was steeping, he cut black bread, cheese, and several slices from a blood sausage that was turning green. His cousin Marysia—Masha, they called her—had brought it to him from the farm at Mazowiecki late in the summer. He had desired to wolf it down on the spot but had resisted the impulse. He was now grateful for that moment of self-control.

"Eat", Masha had said, placing the sausage atop a sack of

onions, potatoes, beets, and a summer squash. The kitchen table sagged under this bounty. Her son staggered in, bearing a large turnip.

"I will keep the meat for later", Pawel had said. "Winter is coming."

"Eat it now. It will spoil and then it will be wasted."

He sliced small pieces for the three of them, and when young Adam asked for more, his mother slapped his hand.

"Uncle Pawel will need this food", she scolded. She called him "uncle", though he was in fact the son of her mother's brother. Masha's father was peasant stock from Belorussia. Pawel's family was descended from the landed middle class, from the south, near the Carpathians.

"Matka, there is lots of food", cried the boy.

The woman shrugged and apologized to Pawel with her eyes.

"For us on the farm there is enough food, though the Germans take much of it. He is too little to understand, Pawel. In there," she nodded toward the ghetto, "they are living on a few pounds of bread and vegetables a month. I hear there are many deaths. Children abandoned, starving, begging. They are shooting people, too. They won't permit us to give food."

She sighed. "When I bring produce into the Old Town market, I come by way of the ghetto walls and throw in a few root vegetables. There is much energy in starch, you know."

Masha. Masha the Good, as homely as her squash.

"It won't be so easy to bring you things from now on. Since July, when the trains began taking all those people away, we are always watched. The entrances to the city are dangerous."

"Why do you take such risks, Masha? I am very grateful for your help, but . . . why do you do it?"

"You are family."

"You don't do this for Bronek and Jan."

"Bronek and Jan have wives to look after them."

"And more mouths to feed."

She looked down. Then up at him with her "serious" expression—the charming scold.

"Pawel, why don't you get married? There are hundreds of fine girls in Warsaw who would marry a man like you. Remember when you were little, when you Tarnowski brothers would spend the summer at our farm. All the girl cousins were in love with you—Pawel the Beautiful. Sweet Pawel. Little Pawelek. Now you are Big Pawel."

Her eyes filled with tears.

"You are such a good man!"

She kissed his cheeks and then, after hesitating, she kissed him on the lips. In a rush she left with the little boy. He had not seen them since.

Onto a tray he now placed a silver pot of steeping tea, china cups, linen napkins, the slices of green meat and black bread, and a bowl of mashed turnip. He carried the tray into his bedroom and entered the closet. At the back, behind a curtain, there was an unlit staircase that led to the attic, and this he climbed slowly and carefully to keep the tea from spilling.

The attic had the same dimensions as the lower floors, but it was not divided into rooms. It was wood-paneled and smelled of old varnish. He rarely went up to the top floor. It was empty, save for a few trunks and the crates of worthless books. At the far end was a brick chimney, and beside it a gable window that allowed access to the slate-covered roof. There, crouching between two crates, was the fugitive—a young man, hardly more than a boy.

Pawel shuffled across the bare wooden floors, muttering to himself about the dust. The visitor stared at him and rose slowly to his feet.

"Would you like to eat?" Pawel asked.

Mistrust was written in bold letters across the fugitive's face. Indeed, his eyes were stricken with a kind of terror Pawel had not seen before. He himself was familiar with many species of fear—in fact, it was his chief affliction—but he had not yet encountered the kind felt by hunted animals.

Pawel sat on a battered trunk and gestured the other to do likewise. He placed the tray between them.

"Eat", he said diffidently, as if what had occurred was of no great consequence.

"*Dziekuje!* Thank you", the boy replied meekly. He was shivering, his clothing exuding the odor of a damp unwashed body, and worse, for the dominant smell was that of a sewer. The hand that reached for the food was pale blue. He studiously avoided the sausage but gobbled the other food. Between each bite, he glanced up furtively at his benefactor.

Pawel observed him with furrowed brow.

"Is some of this for you?" the boy murmured, flushing red.

"No, it is all for you", said Pawel, though hunger was indeed gnawing at him.

"I cannot eat this", the boy said, pointing at the sausage.

Pawel reached for it a little too quickly and bit a large chunk from one end.

"What is your name?" he asked between more bites.

"My name is David Schäfer. And you, sir?"

"My name is Pawel Tarnowski."

"*Witam*, I greet you, Pan Tarnowski."

"*Witam.*"

"I wish to thank you for rescuing me from . . . them."

"It is what anyone would do", Pawel shrugged.

The boy greeted this with a dubious look.

"They are evil!" he burst out in a harsh whisper. "They are from the *sitra ahra*!"

"What is the *sitra ahra*?"

"It is the *other side*, the domain of darkness."

"The domain of darkness? What do you mean?"

"The demonic powers in the spiritual realm."

"The Germans are men, not devils. They are under the influence of evil."

They regarded each other for some moments, as if across a void.

"Why do you help me?" the boy murmured. "I am a Jew."

"I can see you are", Pawel replied, pointing to the fringes of a prayer shawl, which hung below the hem of the felt jacket.

The boy removed a skullcap from his pocket and placed it on his head. There was not much hair, merely a skim of dark fuzz.

"I could not wear this as I ran."

"You must have run a long way. Muranow district is many blocks west."

"I came out the northeast gate at Nalewki Street. A cart was going through the sentry post. I squeezed past it."

"You took a great chance. Few people get away from the Germans."

"If I remained in the ghetto, I would certainly die."

"You speak Polish without an accent", Pawel said.

Swallowing the last of the food, the fugitive turned his eyes to the floor and mumbled something that Pawel could not hear.

"What did you say?" he prompted.

"I said, language is a gift."

"A gift?"

"Without it we cannot think."

"I agree", said Pawel, looking at the boy curiously. "What other languages do you speak?"

"Yiddish, of course. I also read Hebrew and German—and English with a little effort. You?"

"Polish, French, German—and Russian with a little effort."

The boy's eyes flickered at him, then looked away.

"A glass of tea?" Pawel asked. He filled a cup and pushed it into the visitor's hands. The tea was gone in a gulp. He poured another. And another.

"How old are you?" Pawel asked.

"Seventeen."

Then the boy began to tremble violently. He bent over and hid his face in his arms. Pawel was suddenly without any idea of what to do.

He muttered the nonsense sounds by which he had been consoled as a child, and which surged up from memory. He almost touched the boy's shoulder to give it small pats, but drew his hand back without it's being seen. It was soon over, and the visitor was now doubly embarrassed.

"I must escape", he breathed, drying his eyes on a sleeve.

"Where would you go? Do you have family?"

"All Jews are in the ghettos. Or in resettlement camps. My father and mother, my brothers and sisters, are almost certainly dead."

"My mother and father—they too are dead", muttered Pawel weakly, realizing only after he had spoken that in the great democracy of death there were hierarchies of grief.

The other did not respond.

"Perhaps you should return to the ghetto", Pawel suggested uncertainly.

The boy's face told him that this was impossible, in fact, unthinkable. Surprised that his host did not understand the obvious, he said warily, "The ghetto is slow death. The camp is swift death."

"What will you do?"

"I will walk south and go over the Carpathians."

"It is more than three hundred kilometers to the mountains, and then if you get over them the Germans are on the other side. They have taken everything in Europe and are in Africa and Asia also. There is no place to go."

At this the boy turned away and stared at the window.

"They have won. They will devour everything."

"I do not believe they can win the war. At some point they will be beaten back."

"How long?"

"I don't know."

"I must try to think. Will you please hide me for a few days while I think?"

Pawel stared at him, then nodded.

## 2

Pawel Tarnowski was not a man of exceptional intelligence, nor was he gifted with any outstanding talent, although many people considered him to possess both, an assumption they had made from his reflective and taciturn temperament and his occupation as a bookseller. His chief quality (he would have called it a curse) was a sensitivity to the complexity of life. He felt, moreover, that his life was of little value to anyone. His mother and father had loved him as best they could, but they were gone. His two older brothers were not unconcerned about him, but he was a burden to them, and always had been. They were so much more bold, so successful in everything they did. They were married. He was not. They were strong and aggressive personalities, while he was painfully shy, a fault he overcame daily, but only with great determination. It had not always been so.

His earliest memory was of snow. Snow falling from the sky over Warsaw, falling down into his open eyes, his laughing mouth. He was two years old then, perhaps three. His arms were lifted high above his head to invoke the outpouring of the heavens.

Yes, it was like that. Incense went up, light came down. Light above, darkness below. And whenever the darkness was above, at night or during the dreariest days of winter, the angels sent snow as a sign. Don't forget, Pawelek, they seemed to say. We're here. We give you these stars as messengers.

Then Papa went away. He was gone for years and years, it seemed. Priests and other important people sometimes came to visit Mama. Uncle Tadeusz visited now and then, brought money, made Mama cry with gratitude.

In the beginning Pawel often demanded to know when Papa would return, but gradually learned not to ask, because it always made Mama cry when he did. It was a different kind of crying, not gratitude.

So he asked his brothers. Bronek was eight, very old. Jan was older still, ten. They knew many things that Pawel did not know. Sometimes Jan would reply, "When the Russians let him go. Now stop being a baby." Bronek would say the same thing, and underline it with a hard punch on Pawel's arm so he would not forget. "Leave Mama alone, you stupid. Can't you see it makes her sad when you ask for Papa?"

No letters came from him, no messages, no little gifts such as he used to give Pawel before he went away. The carved wooden airplane with four wings, all red, with a metal propeller that twirled on its pin. The magnifying glass for watching the tiny circus under wet leaves in the Saski Gardens. The blue marble, swirling with clouds like a planet. Because these were broken or lost, Papa's face faded.

During the summers, Uncle Tadeusz paid for train tickets for everyone. Sometimes, not often, they went to the cousins' farm at Mazowiecki in the flatter countryside east of Warsaw. Without fail, however, every August they went south to the Tatras, to the farm in the mountains where his grandfather had once been rich and now was poor. Grandfather was old with white hair, jolly sometimes, more often not. He jingled with the many religious medals of saints that he wore under his fancy linen shirt, even when he was stacking hay or shoveling manure from the goose shed. He liked the boys to call him Ja-Ja, though only Jan and Bronek did so. Pawel admired Grandfather, but did not know how to talk with him—he was so very big and mighty, sometimes kind, sometimes fierce, but always imposing.

Babscia was as old as Grandfather, though softer, with eyes that looked fondly at Pawel and often smiled. She smelled of lavender and sage, a sweet-sour scent that was her own—no other person had such a smell. She prayed the rosary with Pawel each night as he slipped toward dreams under the blue quilt with his name *Pawelek* and a heart and a cross stitched onto it. The wind poured through the window at the foot of the bed, the curtains billowing, the night larks calling to each other, the stars beyond counting and very bright, like snowflakes.

Deep were the sleeps of that house, sweet were its dreams, though Pawel would sometimes awake in the dark, alone in the alcove room where he slept, a little frightened by the sad songs of the owls in the cherry grove, and the lingering memory of tales of the cinnamon bears that Grandfather had hunted in the forest long ago when he was young. Or wolves chasing children across the winter snowdrifts. But such small frights were not many, and he always quickly fell asleep again.

Sometimes he dreamed of Papa. Sometimes he remembered. There was, for example, the most wonderful memory. Long ago, just before Papa went off to fight in the war against the Russians, he had taken Pawel onto his lap, all dressed in his soldier's clothes, with the double-headed eagle on his breast. Papa held him and kissed his cheeks, gave him a ginger candy to suck.

"*Dziecko*, my child", Papa whispered. "*Mój synu*, my little son."

Then while they were resting together like that, he put a lump of red tissue paper into Pawel's hands.

"For you, for you", Papa breathed into his ear, holding him tightly.

Gleefully Pawel tore open the paper and found inside of it a brass sculpture. It was a tiny knight slaying a dragon. He turned it this way and that, dribbled sugar juice on it when he kissed it, made Papa laugh.

"How old are you, my son?" Papa asked.

Pawel held up five fingers. "Twooo", he said.

"That's right, you're two", Papa said. "I must go away now,

Pawel, and I must fight like this brave knight. If the battle goes well, I will be back when you are—" and he held up three fingers.

*   *   *

But three fingers came and went, then four fingers. Winters and summers. New leaves and old leaves. Ice and fire.

When he was five he ran away to the Saski Gardens, all by himself. That day, Mama was at the market buying greens and fish for lunch. Jan and Bronek were minding him. They started to quarrel and fell to wrestling in the bedroom. It made Pawel laugh, because they looked so much like squirrels chasing each other up and down the stone fence behind the barn at Zakopane. First one was the chaser, then the other, and whenever one caught the other they would pummel with their fists, their platinum hair flying, faces red with rage, throwing each other to the ground, knocking over furniture, crying, slapping, yelling, jumping up, and chasing through the apartment all over again.

Pawel soon tired of watching this and went to the parlor, where he lay down in a pool of sunshine to play with the angel shapes he had been cutting out of newspaper all morning. Wishing suddenly that Papa were there to stop Jan and Bronek from fighting, he returned to the bedroom and from under his pillow pulled the brass carving of the knight and dragon. Narrowly escaping a wild punch from Bronek, he ran to the front door and went out into the hall. From the other apartments came the sounds of families playing or fighting. The air was misty with the scent of boiling cabbage.

He skipped down the staircase to the street entrance and out onto the sidewalk. There he bumped into two other tenants of their apartment block, a man and a woman arguing, gesturing intensely. Pausing to observe this for a while, he soon lost interest and decided to find a quieter place to play with his angels. Going by sense more than by memory, he walked north on their street, singing its letters—*z-i-e-l-n-a*—as he went. Reaching a larger avenue—*k-r-o-l-e-w-s-k-a*—he turned right onto it and sang its letters, too. A little farther along, he crossed over into the trees and grassy stretches of the Saski Gardens.

For hours he walked its pathways, picked flowers for Mama, sat down under chestnut trees and watched their spiky green fruit sway in the breeze. It was too early in the year for them to begin dropping onto the ground, but he hoped it would happen soon, so that he could collect enough to take to Zakopane to make a giant rosary. He would ask Grandfather to drill holes in the brown chestnuts, beg some string, put it all together, and give it to Great-Uncle Nicholas for a Christmas present.

He took the paper angels from his pocket, and when a gust of wind made the trees sway and sigh, he let the angels go up into the air and spread out over the city. After that he sat down in the shade of a lime tree, holding the brass carving of the knight and dragon, talking to the knight, reminding him to be very, very brave. He thought of Papa, imagining what they would say to each other, the places they would go together, the feel of his arms. He stretched out on the grass and dozed for a while, awakening when flies buzzed on his face. He saw that his pants were dirty and wet because he had rolled off the grass onto the damp black soil of a rose bed.

He looked around for his knight and dragon but could not find them. He could think no more about this because a woman's sob startled him. Looking up, he saw Mama striding along the walkway, coming toward him at great speed, Jan and Bronek trotting behind, worried looks on their faces.

Oh, there was a swat and a hug and tears and scolding! Mama angry and happy all at once, brushing the wet garden dirt from his pants and shirt. Jan and Bronek staring at their feet, because they were in trouble for losing him.

\*   \*   \*

That August they went to Zakopane as usual—a fine clear-sky summer. He forgot to collect chestnuts and so did not make the rosary for Great-Uncle Nicholas. He also forgot where he had lost the brass sculpture of the knight and dragon. He missed it greatly because he was in the habit of talking to the knight as if he were Papa, feeling certain that somewhere out in the world, far to the east, Papa heard his voice. Pawel did not think of him as much as he used to, and the memory of the sculpture faded.

At Zakopane he played in the attic with Grandfather's lead soldiers and the Christmas ornaments, the glass angels who could fly up and down, from heaven to earth and back again, as the golden dust fell through the air like messages. He was so happy there in the attic, or chasing the ducks into the pond, or romping in the fields and mountain paths above the house. It seemed there was always a sun, bigger than a Warsaw sun, with the white peaks all around, higher than church steeples. It was good, it was all good, the pine-scented air, the blood in his cheeks, the singing of insects in the hayfield, and the feel of heat on his legs as he skipped and danced along the dusty path that led from the farmhouse through the birch woods to the palace where Grandfather had been born.

Once, on a whim, without anyone else knowing, he walked there alone, just to see it up close. He knew this was forbidden, because Grandfather said the new owners did not like intruders, though of course *they* didn't mind intruding on Grandfather whenever they wished, without a calling card or a warning, when it was time to collect the rent on the old bailiff's house where Grandfather and Babscia now lived. Pawel went to take a peek at the palace anyway, feeling that this would not be a wrong thing to do because it had once been theirs, and maybe it still was, because houses did not forget the people who had lived in them. The landlord and his family were away that day, and all the palace servants had become invisible as well. Bronek had told him about the servants, how they were not real, could appear and disappear at will, for they had been created out of nothing by a secret magic spell known only to the new land-lord. And so there was no one to stop Pawel from standing on tiptoes to peer through a window. He saw no memories or magical things on the other side of the glass. Yet he was fasci-nated by the way light poured into the house from its many tall windows, playing across the crystal chandeliers and the deer antlers on the wall. He did pause at the sight of a bearskin rug with large open jaws, but realizing it was not alive, he smiled and skipped along home again.

Life was play—yes, everything was playing. Even suppers with Grandfather and Babscia were a kind of playing. Though Mama said he was supposed to use his best manners with them, he knew that in their house no one would scold him for snapping a piece of sizzling sausage between his teeth, grinning, dribbling, making everyone laugh, and that he could drink many glasses of crushed Spanish lemons and oranges in soda water, a luxury Grandfather could not do without, because he had once been rich and now was poor.

"Why is a *tenant* a bad thing?" Pawel once asked, interrupt-ing a worried conversation between Babscia and Mama.

"It is not a bad thing," Mama explained calmly, "just a smaller thing than being a count."

"It would be best not to say *tenant* around your grandfather", added Babscia.

"Does he not like it, Babscia?"

"It makes him sad, Pawelek."

Each year it was the same. Summer was always too short. They had only just arrived when it was time to take the train back to Warsaw, back to the gray apartment block on Zielna, the autumn rains, the trees waving goodbye to their leaves, his breath making clouds on the glass of the kitchen window that overlooked the wall beyond which Jewish people lived. Long days poring over the picture books that Uncle Tadeusz lent, while Bronek and Jan were at school, because they were older, and always would be. The cats in the alleyway growing fat, then thin, then fat again; the ice breaking up on the Vistula, the river freezing over once more; bells ringing for Christmas, for Easter, for all Sundays, for morning prayers and evening prayers, for deaths, for births; and all the while he was steeped in the silence through which messages dropped continuously as snow, as dust, as seed from the invisible gardens above.

*　　*　　*

When he was six years old, the fear began. It happened, strangely enough, at the end of the usual summer at Zakopane, at a time when rumors began to spread that the Russians were releasing prisoners. Everyone was very happy—especially Mama. Only Great-Uncle Nicholas was not. More than usual he made himself drunk on cherry kirsch. He swore a great deal, no matter how much Grandfather and Babscia told him not to.

"It would be wise", said Mama to her three boys after sitting them down on a stone wall out of earshot of the house, "to stay away from Great-Uncle for a while."

"But why, Mama?" Bronek protested. "He's so nice."

Great-Uncle Nicholas was their favorite Zakopane relative, for he sang hilarious songs and told stories and did magic tricks. When no other adults were looking, he liked to unbutton his fly and challenge the boys to a peeing contest. Best of all, he popped his glass eye and let it drop into his hand, tossed it up in the air, caught it in his mouth, and reinserted it into the hollow pink cavern of his eye socket before any grownups noticed.

"A secret, boys", he would whisper. "Our little secret. Tell no one and there will be more secrets."

And so three sets of eyes squinted with anticipation, their bodies gleefully contracting with the thrill of conspiracy.

"Great-Uncle is so nice", they all agreed. "The nicest."

37

Now Mama's face became strained and dark, though her voice remained gentle. "He was", she said carefully, "not always so nice. And we don't want him to be like that again."

She would explain no more.

The two older brothers retired to the hayloft, where they could piece together the bits of information. Only because he promised to say nothing was Pawel permitted to listen.

"Great-Uncle was a soldier", said Jan, who liked to read thick books and think about things. "Maybe he killed too many people, or the wrong ones."

"It's not that", Bronek tossed his head in a superior way. "I overheard Ja-Ja and Babscia talking about it. He was a teacher once, after he was a soldier. He was master of a great school, far away."

Eyes grew round at this astonishing news. Teachers were subjects of profound respect. The boys revered several in their acquaintance.

"He was *not* a teacher", Jan said with a scowl of disbelief. "See how wild and naughty he is when he is drunk. No teacher is ever like that."

"Stupid", Bronek scowled. "It is because he was wild they made him go home."

"But he has always been home", piped Pawel.

His brothers eyed him disdainfully.

"Not always", said Jan, pondering dates and events. "I remember when he came to live with Ja-Ja and Babscia. I was little then, like you. Babscia told us he had returned from working in another country—"

"It was not another country", Bronek interrupted. "It was a prison."

"Babscia does not tell lies", Pawel protested.

"Everybody tells lies," said Bronek, "if they don't want you to know about a really bad thing."

"Papa is in prison. Is it a really bad thing?"

"That's different", Bronek said. "Papa is in prison because he is good. Great Uncle was in prison because he was bad."

"Is he still bad?"

"Mama thinks—" said Jan.

"Mama thinks he might be bad again", said Bronek.

"Still, he is nice", said Jan.

"And so funny", said Bronek, remembering many hilarious moments.

"We should do what Mama says", Pawel offered.

"Grownups are always worrying about everything", Bronek shrugged and jumped to his feet, dismissing the subject altogether.

* * *

A week later, the news came. Papa was in a camp in Belorussia and would be arriving in Warsaw by military train within two days. Mama, Grandfather, Babscia, and Uncle Tadeusz hurried to catch the train from Zakopane to the city. There they would meet Papa and immediately bring him to Grandfather's house.

Mama wanted all the boys to accompany her to meet Papa, but Uncle Tadeusz said this would be a foolish waste of money, considering that they would be bringing Papa straight back to Zakopane. The father should be reunited with his sons in the ancestral home, he said. Everyone but Mama agreed that this was true. There was nothing to be done about it.

In the absence of the grownups, Ludmilla the maid, who was a pleasant country woman of rough manners, cooked for the boys and made sure they kept out of trouble. Great-Uncle was more drunk than usual, asleep in the hayloft—no need to worry about him. During that first day, the three brothers delighted in their newfound freedom.

Early on, Jan and Bronek shook off the little tag-along, disappeared into the woods, and returned only for meals. Three times a day Ludmilla scolded them, stuffed them full of bread and butter, kielbasa sausage, and goat cheese, and clicked her tongue hopelessly over them.

After lunch, when Pawel found himself alone with her in the big scullery, she sat him on her knees and pushed almonds into his mouth, stroked his hair and cheeks, kissed him, and sighed and sighed.

"Oh, what a beautiful child you are, my Pawelek! Och, so pretty!" This made him squirm, for beautiful and pretty were words reserved for women and sunsets. Still, she was very nice and told him all about her grandchildren, who had gone to Czestochowa to find work, and about her husband who had died of bad lungs, and about the Mother of God of Czestochowa who had two big slashes on her face from the time evil men had tried to destroy her icon at Jasna Gora, and didn't they regret it, didn't they fall dead on the spot. She made many signs of the cross, and fed him more almonds until he was bloated and was finally able to struggle from her arms.

It was a wonderful feeling, this freedom to go wherever he wanted in the house. Into the lavender-sage closet, into the boxes of Christmas ornaments in the attic, into the jar of almonds in the pantry when Ludmilla was washing dishes, into the desk drawer in Grandfather's study where the war medals were kept, into the goose yard, where he ran this way and that, flapping his wings to chase the lady geese until an old gander began to bite his bare legs. He avoided the barn where the dangerous horse lived, of course, but he was very brave when it came to leaping into the pond to chase the goldfish. It didn't matter if his shorts and shirt were all wet; it was so hot his clothes dried in the sun before anyone noticed.

After supper, the clock in the hallway chimed eight times. Ludmilla wiped her hands on her apron and said she was going home.

"Now off you go—put on your night clothes", she said in her most severe voice, which no one took seriously. "Put yourselves to bed, or Baba Yaga the witch will snatch you and never again will you lay eyes on your poor Papa."

"We will," said Jan and Bronek, tossing their white hair and their dancing eyes, "we will!"

"And where is that old Nicholas?" she murmured distractedly. "Well, no matter. He's sleeping."

Tying a kerchief about her gray hair she growled, "Now be good. If you are not good I will sell you to the Jews. They'll make a blood pudding of you soon enough, you scamps."

"We'll be good! We'll be good!"

And so they were. The older boys were so exhausted by a day crammed full of running and leaping that they went up to their bedroom and fell instantly asleep.

Pawel, who had spent much of his day in more reflective activities, continued to sit on the high kitchen stool, gazing about, listening to the sounds a house makes when everyone is gone. Old timbers creaked, the clock struck nine bells, a moth fluttered around the oil lantern. He blew at it with the breath of his mouth so it would not be burned, but it came back again. When it fizzled and snapped in the flame he felt a lump of sorrow in his throat. He desired, suddenly, to see the stars.

Jumping to the floor, he went out the kitchen door into the garden. There he lay down by the fish pond and looked far up until it seemed that the stars were singing as they flowed across the sky. All the insects were singing too, and night birds added their own special notes. He thought it would be a lovely thing to sleep outside, something he had never done before, though he was troubled a little by the thought of cinnamon bears and mountain wolves. But it was not a great fear. Papa was coming home soon, though it was difficult to remember what he looked like. Maybe Papa would like to jump into the pond with him and together they would chase the goldfish. They would laugh together, and then they would always remember each other's faces.

The night offered only a hint of relief from the day's heat. He could not recall it ever being so hot. Sweat ran down his brow and stung his eyes with salt. Runnels of it tickled his ribs. His shirt was soaked at the collar and waist. Even his bare feet were damp. On an impulse he walked into the pond and splashed around for a time. The water was warm. The fish nibbled his toes. The floating lilies exuded their perfumes. Refreshed, he waded out and stood dripping on the grass.

From behind, two furry arms grabbed him around the ribs and lifted him high. He shrieked in terror, because he knew that bears and witches do this to lost children. He screamed and kicked until he was put down on the ground, and he heard the huge voice of Great-Uncle Nicholas laughing.

"Ho-ho-ho, Pawelek", said Great-Uncle. "My little mouse. So frightened you were. But see, it is only me. I will not harm you."

Pawel felt great relief. Slowly he stopped gasping, his heart ceased its painful thumping.

"Oo, see, you are all wet," said Great-Uncle, falling clumsily to his knees, "all wet, all wet, little black princeling. Oo, now, let Uncle dry you."

He pressed Pawel to his great chest, which was hairy and bare and smelled of kirsch. Pawel did not like the feeling of it and wanted to pull away, but it was, after all, his uncle, who was nice.

"Noo, noo", the old man whispered, unbuttoning Pawel's shirt, holding him close, the crook of his arm around the base of Pawel's spine.

"I want to go to bed, Uncle", Pawel stammered. "I want to go inside and sleep."

"Yes, yes, you should go to bed, but you are all wet."

Confused and feeling uneasy, he let himself be undressed. He did not like it. Mama was the one who always did this, before plunking him into a hot bath with his toy boats. The big rough hands, with swift and gentle motions, now removed everything. Pawel began to tremble. He felt a whimper rise in his throat.

"There, now you will dry", said Great-Uncle, his fingertips playing all over Pawel's body, even the most private places.

"I don't like it!" Pawel wailed.

"It's just playing", said Great-Uncle. "Don't you like to play? Let's play."

Pawel screamed and squirmed away. Great-Uncle lost his grip on the slippery body, and Pawel ran from him. Into the kitchen, up the staircase, into the little cubby bedroom, under the covers, trembling, trembling. Curled in a ball, fists clenched over his eyes, he began to cry. It was dark; no one had lit the candles. He was glad it was dark because he could hide in it, he could hide his tears because that was babyish, and if Bronek or Jan heard him, they would mock and call him names.

"Bad, bad", he sobbed. Though what he meant by this he did not know. He felt only that people who are drunk should not be frightening, should not pretend they are bears, should ask the mother before removing the child's clothing, should not grab and hold you so you cannot take a step back from them. They should not breathe fumes in your face that make you sick. It all swam together, all the shoulds and should-nots. After a while he stopped crying and began to feel sympathy for Great-Uncle. He wondered if he had hurt his feelings. In the morning he would say he was sorry to the old man. He fell asleep.

In the night he had a bad dream. He always thought of it as a dream, though in later years it seemed to him it was something that might have happened in the strange country between waking and dreaming. Of this he could never be sure. Yet the memory of it grew with the passage of time, not like other dreams, which always faded. It grew like a tiny snake that bores a hole ever deeper into the earth, making no noise, wriggling silently, emerging only when it is hungry.

It was night. Total darkness, no stars. He lay curled in a ball, knees drawn up under his chin, his clenched fists covering his face. In this position he floated on the waters of the fish pond, beside the cherry trees; he knew it was the pond because his body was dripping with water and he smelled the rotting cherries. Clouds wrapped him all around to hide his nakedness. He was very small, and very sorry for the hurt he had caused someone.

Hands peeled the clouds from his body. Large hands, rough to the touch but moving gently, stroked his limbs in the dark. He could not see whose hands they were. He wondered if it was Papa returning. The hands turned him onto his back, pulled his limbs from their knots, straightened them. The hands played, gently at first, then more firmly. Whenever Pawel whimpered, the hands ceased their motion, and he drifted away on a layer of cloud, or the water rippled beneath him. The hands resumed their play, and then he felt lips touching his chest. He tried to cry out, but a bear loomed from the darkness, a roaring beast, its jaws open wide to devour him, though it was a bear like no other, for its single eye glared red at him. The cry froze in his throat. He thrashed, but the bear pinned his limbs to the cloud. Once again he began to scream, but a hairy paw clamped over his mouth, cut off his breath. Immobile now, he could do nothing to resist the paws that played and played until finally the weight of the bear fell upon him totally and he was crushed out of existence.

## 3

Other dreams, other memories. A thin man as gray as a corpse walking up the lane surrounded by Mama and Babscia, Grandfather, and Uncle Tadeusz. The thin man stopping, gazing at the farmhouse with a look of faint recognition, his eyes like holes, his mouth an angled slit.

Jan and Bronek running down the lane, hurling themselves upon him, laughing, shouting, Papa, Papa, Papa, babbling breaking forth from all mouths, young and old. Papa going down on his knees to embrace his sons, Papa groaning.

Only Pawel remained apart, his face a mask, staring at his feet.

"Come, Pawelek," Mama cried, "it is your Papa. Come, give him a kiss."

Pawel turned and bolted away as fast as his legs could carry him, up the hill toward the trees of the thicker forest. As he went past the pond he began to spurt tears. His feet skidded on the black cherries scattered on the ground, and he fell. He hid his face in his clenched fists, and screamed. He screamed and screamed until his throat was raw, and the smell of kirsch was vomited out of his soul, though it instantly began to seep in again.

Hands seized him and lifted him high. He kicked and thrashed. Other hands pried his fists from his face, and he saw that the thin gray man was holding him, his stubbly chin trembling, grief darker than night pouring from the wells of his eyes.

"Oo, oo, my Pawelek", soothed Mama, taking him from Papa and holding him against her bosom. "Why this fuss now? What's the matter? What's the matter?"

"He does not know me", said Papa in a dead voice, and turned away.

"He is frightened", laughed Great-Uncle who had come teetering from the barn. "It was the wolves that howled last night."

"There weren't any wolves howling last night", said Jan.

"You were sleeping", growled Great-Uncle, "and did not hear them."

* * *

And so life resumed. In the city there were no bears. No wolves. The bad dream came and went. Papa sat in the kitchen most days, staring at the wall, or reading newspapers. Jan and Bronek forced him to be their Papa, made him smile, dragged him to the park and the zoo. But Pawel would not let himself be touched by Papa, would not look at him except secretly.

* * *

School began. He was frightened by the bullies, by the roaring streetcars, by a teacher who hit him on the knuckles with a long pointed stick whenever he forgot he was in class and let his eyes fly out through the window to rise like a swallow on the wing, up into the safer clouds.

He learned to read and write. He began to read books, like Jan and Bronek. He preferred to be alone, or to rest in Mama's arms in the parlor in the evening.

"He does not like me", Papa whispered to Mama once when they thought he was asleep.

"He does not yet know you", Mama replied. "One day he will know you and love you."

"Love . . ." said Papa, trailing off, staring at the wall.

* * *

Another year went by and Papa was all well again. Though he remained thin, he could now tussle with the older boys, one on

46

each arm, chinning themselves on his bulging muscles. In time Pawel allowed himself to be hoisted onto Papa's shoulders and carried through the park or to Mass. He was frightened by this, certain that Papa would drop him, that he would smash on the sidewalk like an egg, and then all the rotten smell would come out and they would have to sweep him up and throw him on the autumn fire where the chestnut leaves are burned. But Papa did not drop him. Nor did they speak with each other. Though Papa sometimes looked at him, and he at Papa.

\* \* \*

Papa went to work as a clerk in a law office. There was more food, many lovely feasts. Sometimes Pawel laughed, and whenever that happened everyone commented, stroked him, cooed over him, and there was happiness in the apartment. Even Papa smiled, and from across the room offered his hand, begging with his eyes that Pawel would come to him. But he did not. He went to his bedroom and read a book, under the safer sheets.

He learned that a certain kind of silence was power. People flowed around it like a river around an island. It made some people stay away. And though it made others come too close, trying to get inside, they eventually gave up.

\* \* \*

When he was eight he had a good summer at Zakopane. There was a wonderful adventure with Grandfather. They went down a deep well together, carrying a sword, pretending they would kill a dragon that lived at the bottom. It was frightening, but they survived. After that he called Grandfather Ja-Ja. This made Grandfather very happy. Toward the end of summer Great-Uncle died, choking on a chicken bone.

"It is for the best", Pawel heard Babscia whisper to Grandfather as they walked from the grave.

"He was my brother", Grandfather said. "He was not always like that."

"Not always what he became."

"It devoured everything, everything."

And for the first time in his life Pawel saw a strong old man break down and sob uncontrollably.

\* \* \*

In the months following the adventure of the well and the death of Great-Uncle, Pawel's bad dreams declined in number and nearly ceased altogether. An abiding sadness took their place. In elementary school his marks were the highest of his class, every year until he graduated, for unlike other boys his interests were not scattered in a variety of activities. He had discovered in books a seemingly limitless realm into which he could plunge at will, leaving behind the dreariness of his world. Each new book opened a gateway into others, exposing inexhaustible riches of knowledge.

From childhood onward, he also developed an interest in art. Sometimes he drew with pencil on the cast-off sheets of paper that Papa brought home from the office. Whenever he drew birds or clouds, he felt happy. It felt like flying. It was a kind of language, though he knew very little of its vocabulary. It was also like a bridge from the island, spanning the noisy waters of people, who were always speaking with their mouths, always moving.

Of course, he moved as well. He walked miles each day, always alone: on streets, in parks, sometimes crossing the great bridge over the Vistula at the end of Jerozolimski Avenue, east through the zoological gardens in Praga as far as the vast Catholic cemetery, then back again into the city on the Gdansk bridge, finally wandering through the cemetery of the Jews near Muranow district. Here was no luxuriant garden of crucifixes, madonnas, and angels, but a stark, overcrowded city of the dead. Devoid of imagery, its unembellished headstones proclaimed in Hebrew letters this people's fierce loyalty to the realm of the word.

They puzzled him, the Jews. He did not dislike them, as some people did. Their strange ways intrigued him. They played and grew and studied and died just as all men did. He made drawings of their children busy at sidewalk games, their youths ever bearing their bundles of books, their men carrying giant candles through the streets on holy days.

His own religious belief gave him his only moments of peace. After long solitary rambles he would often enter a church and sit in the back pew, resting in the silence, for God was silent, too. Here also messages fell through the air, glowing golden on cataracts of light that poured from the high windows. Lingering incense, dust motes, small feathers. There was Holy Communion as well, which was the deepest and most silent peace. And confession. Confession was sometimes troubling for him, though not in the same way that it was for Jan and Bronek, who had become obsessed with girls. For him the trouble lay in the absence of sin. Whenever a priest probed, wondering perhaps if the penitent was withholding, Pawel's mind went blank. There was never anything to tell, other than his feelings of dislike for certain persons, usually those who wished to pry inside his thoughts.

Even so, despite these islands of light, as the years progressed he felt the darkness growing. He still suffered from nightmares on occasion and struggled against a weight of depression that came and went. For months on end he felt nothing, only numbness, which he told himself was better than depression.

The nightmares were not unusually disturbing. Often they contained a snake that turned into a bear or a bear that turned into a snake, or a snake that turned into a dragon and then into a bear. Sometimes he awoke from such dreams and remembered his childhood fright beside the fish pond at Zakopane, but did not attribute much significance to it. During his waking hours, at the oddest moments, it came to mind for no reason, and whenever that happened he felt a sudden stab of terror, or disgust, or rage. But because these feelings had no obvious cause, he could not blame anyone but himself. As he advanced in years, the dream told him that he was not entirely well in his mind, that he sometimes confused memories with dreams, the real with the unreal. This, combined with the other troubles of his unfolding life, helped convince him that he was a frightened person, a weak person. Thus was shame added to his guilt.

Was he guilty? Surely it was so, because the dream showed him there was badness in his thoughts.

Throughout the years of gymnasium, his marks continued to be high. This was because he did little else but read books. He excelled in the study of languages especially, learning French without much effort and German with a modicum of strain; his foray into English was brief, however, for he found this language so full of contradictions that it was difficult not to hold it in contempt. At the age of sixteen he discovered the university library, which contained more and better books than the public library. In addition, the different faculties had their own particular collections. No one seemed to notice his presence, or if they did, he was unworthy of note, for there were hundreds of young people going in and out of the buildings day and night. He did not try to borrow books, which would have unmasked his intrusion into that sacred space. He read until closing hour each night and walked home with thoughts brimming, weighing arguments, the shape of the world expanding in his consciousness.

He was mesmerized by the novels of Kafka, a Czech, who expressed so well what Pawel had come to know about life. The stories were bleak. The style was lucid, serene; the subject matter, terrifying—man's dilemma, the self imprisoned in a hostile, incomprehensible universe. He was also drawn to other writers whose vision was warmer. The Russian Gogòl, for example. A story about an overcoat, about people used as things, the revenge of the dispossessed. He had hesitated at first to read a Russian, but he thought that it would be helpful to know a little about the people who had harmed his family. After that came Dostoevsky. Here were Kafka's clear eyes, but deepened by a vision of Christ dwelling among the suffering, with them, in them. He did not know what to make of this but absorbed it nonetheless.

Then Tolstoy. *War and Peace* in a rather pedestrian Polish translation. He assumed it was about the futility of politics and ambition, the absurdity of military posturing, as if genius in battle was the defining factor of a nation's character. Perhaps, too, it was about love, though the love was ever tinged with tragedy, with unfairness. *Anna Karenina*, a woman betrayed, sexual passion, despair, suicide. Despair especially seemed to be the reigning ethos of the times. Writers of all nations were preoccupied with it. Why? Pawel was not sure, yet he wondered if his own feelings marked him as a person belonging to an elevated class. Perhaps he would become a writer. As the years went on, and his relentless journey through eighteenth- and nineteenth-century literature progressed, he knew only that, unlike his parents and brothers, he was not a person suited to the life of the bourgeoisie.

He explored philosophy as well. A few of Plato's dialogues, which interested but did not satisfy. Kierkegaard's parables, which intrigued and beckoned. Beckoned where? Into what new corner of the maze? Here again was that sense of northern bleakness, yet beneath its brooding shadow, Kierkegaard revealed certain principles at work in the universe that could not be dismissed out of hand. There was, of course, God. Pawel believed in God. Though it did seem odd that so many modern writers did not. By this time the rapture of his childhood devotions had entirely evaporated, leaving only an abstract conviction that what he had been taught about Christ was true. Even so, this rational assent did not seem to connect to his emotions. As time went on, his inner life continued to alternate between numbness and surges of raw feeling.

At Mass once, he noticed a girl and fell instantly in love with her, the first time he felt such a thing. She was kneeling before an icon of the Mother of God, her face enraptured. She remained immobile for a long time, hands clasped in front of her, beseeching silently. He watched all the while. He longed to know her name and to speak with her. This was a startling impulse, and he recoiled from it. It was enough to love from a distance.

There were more disturbing impulses that arose, infrequently at first. As the periods of depression and anguish increased—the anguish was inexplicable, it had no source, no object—he would drift off to sleep each night imagining the gardens above from which golden seed sometimes fell. These musings had an uncanny power to dissolve the anguish, scatter the depression. During his adolescence, figures appeared in the imagining, in that state he looked forward to each night—half-waking, half-sleeping. Sometimes it was Papa before he went to prison, young, strong, his face smiling. Papa would sweep him up in his arms and hold him against his chest, gently, without imprisonment. Pawel could fly from his arms whenever he wanted, like a dove or a swallow, and he could return to his arms as he wished. He could rest his ear against the great heart booming within, and warmth came from it, a radiance of peace and surest safety.

At other times, Papa's face dissolved and different faces took his place, though the love remained constant. The face of a teacher at school, the face of a young priest, the face of an athlete he once saw running along the pathways of the park. More and more he thought of such men and longed to know them.

He sometimes drew their faces, with precision, feeling himself becoming them as he drew. And he drew the rough structures of their bodies, not so precise, though volatile, latent with power, with meaning. What the meaning was, he could not say. The uneasiness that accompanied a flush of heat soon prompted him to desist from this sort of dreaming, though the longing it had opened up within him did not cease. It had no form, no name.

In prayer and in art he did not feel as alone as he usually did. It was like the father's embrace, the friend's embrace. But there was no person involved other than himself. His father had long ago given up trying to embrace him. He had no friends.

At some point along the way he purchased a beginner's set of oil paints. All the Zakopane family had died by then, leaving only the cousins at Mazowiecki. There one summer he made his first real painting—wildflowers. Papa laughed at this poor attempt and said it was girlish, said when are you ever going to be like your brothers, and Mama hushed him. For a moment Papa's eyes regained their haunted look, the just-released-from-prison look, though that was years past.

In secret, then, he painted more and more, on heavy brown paper, on cloth, on pieces of wood. These, as well as countless scraps of drawings, filled boxes beneath his bed. No one knew about it, because Jan and Bronek were no longer living at home. Both were apprenticed elsewhere, and the bedroom was now entirely his own.

When it came time for Pawel to choose an occupation or enter university, Papa took him into the parlor and said they must discuss the future. He wanted Pawel to become an engineer. Pawel could think of no reason to refuse. He applied to the university and was accepted on the strength of his high marks in gymnasium. It soon became obvious that this was a mistake, for his textbooks were practically incomprehensible, lectures a torture. He spent most of each day in the library, reading literature and philosophy. At night he painted. By the end of the year he had failed his courses so miserably that it added yet another weight to Papa's disappointments.

Then he pondered the possibility of a religious calling. He applied at a monastery in Silesia and was accepted. Of that period he later recalled only a state of perpetual exhaustion, the stone cell where he slept on a plank bed, and the head of a boiled rabbit, which a kitchen monk once served to him in broth. There was bread, and constant prayer, both of which were dry. Within six months the superiors told him that he did not have a monastic vocation.

He returned to Warsaw and worked for three years as a groundskeeper at the Saski Gardens, hoping to save enough money for a journey to Western Europe and training in art. Throughout that time he continued to read and paint, becoming ever more uncommunicative. All the while a great anger brewed within him: anger at the state of the world, anger at his fearfulness and weakness, anger at his cherished-hated solitude. His unhappiness, he was sure, was the fault of his upbringing—the insensitivity of his family. There was even anger at God, though in the beginning this was infrequent.

Toward the end of his final month in the gardens, there occurred an incident so minor, so insignificant, that it could easily have slipped from his memory. Yet it rose in his mind as a kind of signpost on the desert of those years and never completely faded.

Winter. He was shoveling snow from the Saski walkways. Though the sky was thinning, a few white flakes spun down. So large were those landing on the sleeves of Pawel's coat, they were visible to the eye as chariot wheels, the spokes radiating from labyrinthine crystals.

Looking up, he saw strolling toward him a herd of black-clad creatures, two adults and six children. Jews. Moreover, they were the ultraorthodox Jews who called themselves the Hasidim. The patriarch of the family was pointing to bare trees, the empty paths, the dry fountain, speaking all the while in an odd Germanic language, of which Pawel understood not a word. A short, gray-bearded man, he approached without a greeting or a nod, ceased speaking altogether, and busied himself adjusting a prayer shawl that dangled below the hem of his coat. His wife, a diminutive rotund woman in a waxed wig, glanced at Pawel with a guarded look and gestured with a fluttering hand that the children should stay together. In a moment they had passed on.

The youngest child, a boy about six years of age, took up the rear. He stopped a few paces from Pawel and looked back. There was in his stance, in the whole expression of body and personality, some rare mixture of energy and repose. He would have been an unusual child in any race, for his face was not only physically beautiful but angelic in disposition as well. On it there was no hint of caution or reserve as there had been on the faces of the other members of his family. His eyes were black, yet in no way opaque, for they were mysteriously transparent, radiating openness and delight.

Catching Pawel's eye, he lifted his arms to the sky. Tilting his head back, he stuck out his tongue and caught a snowflake on its tip. Then he performed a little joy-dance, hopping from one foot to the other. Pigeons dropped from nearby buildings and swooped down around him, landing near his feet, coo-cooing.

Pawel smiled. It seemed many years since he had last smiled.

"*Schneeflocke!*" the child cried, laughing.

The mood was broken by a shrill cry from the mother, who had noticed the boy's absence: "*Dovidl!*"

The boy raised a butterfly hand at Pawel and waved. Then he turned on his heels and trotted toward his family.

\*   \*   \*

Pawel was convinced that the only way to become a stronger person was to sever all ties to the past that had made him what he was. In order to succeed in this, he had to ensure that the inhabitants of his old world would not have access to his new one. Thus, in his early twenties he departed for France.

He left his parents a cryptic note, saying only that he would be traveling in Europe for some time, pursuing his interest in art. He did not again write to them and did not notify them of his location; nor did he permit himself any reflection on what effect his sudden disappearance would have on them. He intended no hurt by this. He was certain that he was relieving them of an embarrassment.

A great terror afflicted him as he stared out the glass windows of the train that carried him into the west: city after city, castles and factories, fields and battlefields, page after page of historical tragedy and glory becoming flesh before his eyes. As never before, he felt his insignificance, the microscopic dimensions of his little self, his little aspirations. More than once he had to resist a mad impulse to bolt from the carriage at stations along the way, to turn back—no, to crawl back into the safer womb of his known world. Yet the desperate need to escape his origins impelled him forward.

Arriving in Paris, Pawel's fears were diluted by surges of exhilaration, as if he were now larger than he had supposed, striding into a broader world, a cosmopolis containing unlimited possibility. Here at last, he felt sure, he would find his destiny. He took up lodgings in a *pension* on the Left Bank of the Seine, a small room under the eaves of a seventeenth-century stone tenement, and went searching in the streets for the next leap forward.

To his dismay, he found that no college of art would consider his applications. This was a shock, because he had assumed that the raw desire to paint was sufficient to open doors to the higher realms. The gatekeepers of those pantheons were not impressed by his earnest declarations; they wanted evidence, but he had nothing to show by way of drawings or painted sketches.

He had burned it all before he left Warsaw, one of many rash things he had done in order to destroy the connections to his past. He had brought with him only the hunger to make beauty. And thus, he decided to remain in Paris and do just that. He would be a "primitive". He would bypass the academic world and find a master with whom he could apprentice, and if worse came to worse, he would simply teach himself.

In his room under the eaves his fears subsided, soothed by the cooing of pigeons outside the casement window and the sidewalk games of the children playing below in the street, giggling and crying as children did everywhere. There was the baker at the corner who delivered bread on his bicycle, the baguettes bundled under his arm like firewood, singing as he squeaked along the block at six o'clock each morning: *Pain et vin, pain et vin*, bread and wine, bread and wine. And the elderly woman on the floor below, who sang love songs that reverberated through the upper rooms at all hours. There were the bells of the city churches, a concertina playing melancholic tunes in a bistro half a block away, overheard conversations on the sidewalk, gossip and laughter and heated debates over the minutiae of politics. It was all so fresh, so reassuring, so far from the stultifying social constraints of Warsaw. Laconic as always, he made no friends and spoke only to those who sold him what he needed for survival.

As he settled into his new home, he continued his longstanding habit of night reading. During his first year in Paris, he read Molière and Racine in the original French, grateful now for the effort he had made to study the language in gymnasium. He also read Dante and Boccaccio, attracted by the light-filled Italian mind, but certain that their world now lay irrevocably in the past. He forged his way through *Das Kapital* and *Mein Kampf*, also Plato's *Republic*. Hitler's book was the easiest to understand, though from the first chapters Pawel sensed a view of life antithetical to his own. *Is the only antidote to oppression a violent aggression?* he wondered. Surely there were other ways—art, for instance, was neither passive nor aggressive. If people had beauty in their lives, they would learn to create, not destroy.

During the daylight hours he painted. His subject matter was undistinguished—the Seine, the monuments, the human scenes in parks. He visited museums constantly, soaking up thousands of images, entranced most of all by the sweetness of Impressionism. He also observed numerous professional artists, champions of various styles. He eavesdropped on their conversations in galleries and cafés, read their philosophies in catalogs at art exhibits. Throughout all that first year, and well into the second, he kept an eye open for a suitable master under whom he might apprentice.

He met Picasso at a sidewalk bistro once, lingering almost by accident on the edge of a group of young painters who wished to ask the great man questions about art. They seemed to revere him—it was almost worship. Picasso observed their adulation with a cold twinkling of his eyes, amused but contemptuous. He emanated power, radical independence, authority of some undefined sort. A protean being. Picasso shrugged off the young artists' questions and dropped a few Olympian sayings by way of compensation.

"Art is war", he said. "Art is an instrument for attack and defense."

Noticing Pawel, he made a pencil sketch of his face on a napkin, smiling sardonically as with swift strokes he captured the likeness perfectly. He did not respond to Pawel's tentative probe, his Polish mouth still struggling over French words, his face too naked with longing as he stammered his request.

"W-w-would you ever c-c-consider accepting an apprentice, sir? I would v-v-very much like to find—"

Acting as if he had not heard, the Spaniard snorted and showed the drawing to a buxom woman seated beside him. "*Hermoso?*" he said, as if Pawel were not there.

"*Hermosa*", the woman replied, making Picasso smirk, then laugh. He put the end of the napkin to the flame of a candle, and as it flared, lit her cigarette with it. He threw the ruins of the drawing to the ground and crushed it into ashes with his heel. That done, they rose from the table and, without a word of farewell to the assembled devotees, ambled away along the street arm in arm.

This little incident offered Pawel a few days of reflection. In the end, however, he did not know what to make of it. He had seen a number of Picasso's early realist works in museums and commercial galleries and loved them. He had also seen some of the artist's cubist work. He was not attracted to the latter, was disturbed by the distortion, but had to admit that it was revolutionary, even brilliant. Though his admiration was dampened, it was in no way demolished.

During this time Pawel ceased attending Mass, stopped praying altogether. There seemed no point to participating in a faith that was locked in the past. By contrast, the new culture was vitally alive, dominated by the young, who were fervently exploring original ways of thinking. If the atmosphere was irradiated with cynicism and heroic despair, it did not repel Pawel. Indeed he was very drawn to it. He had suffered from a personal sense of hopelessness about the world, and it seemed that these gifted people had struggled with the same thing and risen above it through their art.

He had come to Paris in search of his destiny as an artist, and during the early part of this pilgrimage he still believed that here he would surely find a mentor who would show him the path. But with the passing of months he began to realize that no one was interested in him. He discovered that there were ten thousand young men and women in the city searching for the same savior. They had all come hoping to be adopted by Picasso.

He learned, moreover, that he had little talent. People smiled politely over his paintings. Not a single gallery would exhibit them. Impressionism is dead, they said.

"And so", he asked himself in a candid moment, staring at his reflection in a gallery window, "what is a mediocre Polish Impressionist in Paris of nineteen thirty-two to do?"

When the money ran out he searched for work. He was taken on as a gardener at the estate of a Russian princess named Sonia Ogolushov. It was there that he met Father Photosphoros, a Russian Orthodox monk who had fled the Bolsheviks with the princess and her husband and come with them to Paris in 1921. They had managed to bring out a lot of their wealth or else had put it in French banks before the Revolution. Photosphoros lived in a stone carriage house—they called it "the hermitage"—at the back of the property. He celebrated the Divine Liturgy in the large chapel in the main house. On Sundays Pawel would go quietly into the garden below the chapel window and sit with his head against the wall, listening to the exiles singing.

With money in his pocket again, he purchased more books than he had time to read, better paints and canvas, and the valuable little Italian painting of flowers. This latter expense, however, cost him a good deal more than francs. Never realistic about time or resources, he obtained it three weeks before his next payday and only after the fact realized that he would have to forgo a certain amount of food. The sacrifice was worth it, for the *fiori* lit his dark room like a window ever open on a sun-filled land. Man does not live on *pain et vin* alone, he reasoned.

For several months, he soaked in the fading splendor of the tsarists, though of course he moved only on the edges of their life, catching the crumbs that fell from their table. He studied the Russian language in the evenings, telling no one, hoping one day to surprise his employers by conversing with them in their native tongue. He was convinced that, because his family had once belonged to the upper classes, they would recognize him as one of their own. He wished to impress them by showing himself to be a young man of learning and culture, in addition to the noble blood flowing through his veins—though it was centuries old and no titles clung to him.

One day Father Photosphoros passed him as he was pruning the hedges, and said in his abrupt, almost rude, manner, "You! What are you doing in a corrupt city like this? Go back to Poland!"

He spoke in French. In the same language, Pawel replied, "Father, I wish to be an artist."

The priest snorted, "An artist! That devil Hitler is an artist. There are lots of artists in hell!"

Pawel's confidence in contemporary art had been faltering for some time. His confidence in his own skills was hanging by a thread. In the days that followed, however, it came to his mind that his failures might be God's way of directing him to a more spiritual form of painting. Did he still believe in God? Yes, it seemed he did—a little. He wondered if he should become an icon painter. He tried to pray again, but as usual heaven was silent.

Father Photosphoros lived alone and painted icons in his hermitage. He was quite old, with a long brushed beard down to his waist, and a jeweled icon of Christ on a chain around his neck. He had painted the icon himself. Pawel went to him at his hermitage and asked to apprentice in the art of icon painting.

"What! You? Paint icons?" the old priest bellowed with a scowl and an abrupt gesture. "You just want to make *money*!" He spat the last word out. Pawel felt as if he had been kicked. Photosphoros beckoned him into the room where he worked. Walking slowly with the aid of a cane, he led the gardener past a wooden table on which lay a painted marvel, a partly completed icon of the Mother of God. Cerulean blue. Iridescent purple. Ocher.

Photosphoros stopped before a shrine in the corner of the

room on which there stood a large icon of Christ Pantocrator. Cobalt blue. Cadmium red. Gold with filaments of titanium white.

"This is the burning bush!" he barked. "You must remove your shoes."

*I must take off my shoes, like Moses*, Pawel thought. He bent and began to untie his laces, but when the priest saw this he tore at his beard in exasperation. He had not meant it literally. He threw his cane on the floor and bowed low in profound reverence before the icon. Pawel thought he had dropped the cane, so he bent and picked it up for him. Photosphoros grabbed it from his hands and furiously threw it down again.

"Look", he said, getting control of his mood. He bowed again to the icon, touched the floor, and made a sign of the cross. "When a Russian does this, it means something, but for a Westerner it means *nothing*!"

"Can you not teach me?" Pawel begged.

Photosphoros threw up his hands.

"Teach you? Ha! You are a Pole! You are a Catholic too, no doubt. You are unteachable."

"*Pazhalusta*, please", Pawel stammered, switching from French to Russian. "I want to learn. Perhaps if you would speak to the princess, if you could tell her about me—"

"The princess?" Photosphoros growled. "Speak to the princess? Listen, what kind of ambitious fool are you?"

Photosphoros sat down heavily, bending over, face in one hand.

"Begone!" He waved Pawel away with the other hand. "Leave me!"

Stricken, Pawel backed out the doorway. Alone in the garden, he wrestled with dark thoughts that quickly spun from confused hurt to discouragement and then plunged into feelings of despair. Why had this Christian priest treated him this way? If the best of men—a mystic, a monk—had looked into his soul and recoiled, then it must be that even God did not want him.

*If God does not want me, then everything I have been taught about him is false,* Pawel thought. *Maybe there is no God. Maybe this is just another absurd incident in a meaningless world.*

He left the princess' service that very hour. It seemed to him the end of everything. After a few days of brooding and weeping in his darkened room, hungry and without a *sou* in his pocket, he went searching for work. In the brighter *quartiers*, however, there were no available jobs, and even the sweatshops of the working-class districts would not have him. One evening, upon returning to his room from another day's fruitless search, he found a remnant of his belongings piled on the sidewalk. The concierge had sold practically everything he owned to meet the unpaid rent. In recent months, he had foolishly overpaid for many minor extravagances—the *fiori*, a Russian language course, the finest sable brushes—presuming upon his future good fortune. Now there would be no future. He had presumed, as well, upon his landlady's patience, and in this too he was proven wrong. When he knocked on her door and protested, then pleaded for leniency, she evicted him with screams and rude gestures. He left with only the clothes on his back and the little Italian painting of flowers, which she had not been able to sell. And so, clutching the *fiori* beneath his jacket as if it were life itself, he began his descent into the regions where the lost people live, feeling that he belonged nowhere, or that if he belonged anywhere it was surely with the others who belonged nowhere.

During the following week he wandered aimlessly through the meanest *arrondissements* searching for a *pension* that would take him in on credit. None would. He slept under bridges and on park benches. He knocked on a thousand doors looking for work. But there was none. He begged for food at churches and convents, and thus survived on the kindness of those who

63

themselves had little to give. There were so many beggars like him asking for help, and there was seldom enough for all. He could not bear to push himself forward ahead of the elderly, the cripples, and the children of the poor.

One day, utterly exhausted, he came to a bridge and crossed it halfway. Leaning over the railing, he saw that the Seine would be a fitting river in which to die. *O Paris, Paris*, he cried, *you who create and destroy, how many geniuses have you drowned in your waters!*

But in the cry of protest there was an affirmation. He realized that he wanted to live.

It came to him that he should go back to the house of the princess and beg to be taken on again. How it would sting his pride, he thought, but a man must eat, must he not? He recalled with longing the leftover dishes the kitchen maids had sometimes let him have after the parties the princess and her husband gave for their friends. He would sit in the potting shed eating the crusts of saffron bread and spicy *plav*, which were specialties of the Armenian cook. How thoughtlessly he had consumed it! How, even as he ate, he had resented their wealth and their waste! Little did he know during those fat years how easily food disappears from the world.

When he knocked at the gate, he was informed by the doorkeeper that a new man had already been hired. No, there are no other jobs here, he said. Do you think jobs grow on cherry trees? No, the princess will not see you. No, there will be no more charity, no more free meals, no more indulging young fools who abandon their duties without so much as a day's notice or a by-your-leave! And worst of all, he said, the princess is very distressed that her Dutch bulbs were left unplanted and many are now ruined, all because of an insolent fly-by-night. Begone!

So Pawel continued to sleep behind bushes and under bridges. By then it was November and the nights became bitter.

Ice formed on the puddles. He caught a chill. He walked about the city day after day, looking for any kind of employment, looking for miracles, but found none. There were many men like him on the streets, even veterans from the Great War, some of them still young, missing an arm or a leg, begging or selling pencils. Women also were on the streets, some of them trying to sell themselves. This dismayed him more than anything else, horror and anguish twining into a spiral that revolved within him constantly.

He was sitting on a park bench one morning, beating the aches out of his limbs, when he noticed a man stop in midstride and stare at him.

"You", he said. "Do you want work?"

"Yes, please, monsieur", Pawel replied.

"I see that your clothing is paint-spattered. Are you a house-painter?"

"No, monsieur."

"You are familiar with artistic work, perhaps?"

"I am an artist."

The man did not reply to this, but a look of amusement and cynicism emanated from his eyes.

"I am the master of a painting academy", he said. "I need a servant. Are you willing to sweep the floor, clean brushes, and do any other chores I may have for you?"

"Yes, of course", Pawel said eagerly, trying to calm the trembling of his hands.

"I mean *anything*? I can't hire someone who makes . . . difficulties."

"Anything."

"You are not French. Your accent tells me that you are from the east. Ukrainian? Czech? Polish?"

"I am a Pole."

"Do you have a criminal record?"

"No, monsieur."

"I thought not", the man said with an odd little smile. Pawel puzzled over the look of intense interest he fixed upon him.

"I can pay you a few *centimes* a day and let you sleep on a cot in the janitor's room."

"Thank you, monsieur."

"Are you hungry?"

"Yes, monsieur."

"*Tiens*, I will give you dinner also. Come!"

Abruptly, he turned and strode away, beckoning Pawel to follow. Sick and weakened by the nights spent out in the elements, he had to struggle to keep up. Yet he felt such relief—no, it was closer to elation. He knew that he would probably have a hard day of work ahead, but he would have food. He resolved to persevere until night, when he could rest at last. The thought of sleeping in a warm place was ecstasy.

The academy was situated on the third floor of a warehouse. Pawel barely made it up the stairs and arrived at the landing to find the master engaged in an irritable exchange with the man who was his assistant. They conversed in French, and he overheard the word *modèle* repeatedly. Apparently the regular model used by their life-drawing class had failed to appear for work.

"Just as I expected", said the master with a cold laugh. "But as you know, I am always prepared. *Voilà!*"

He pulled Pawel forward and showed him to the assistant, who looked him up and down with distaste.

"I suppose one corpse is as good as another, Henri", he said.

They led him into a small office, beyond which he saw a large open room with skylights, and fifteen or twenty students encircling a central stage. Their easels resembled a bay full of old sailing ships.

"I need a model today", said the master.

"A model?" Pawel murmured.

"Yes, a nude for my students to study."

"Oh", he stammered. "That is not possible."

66

The master pointed to a dressing-screen by the studio door.

"Strip and go out onto the stage. You have five minutes."

"But there are women out there!"

Both the master and his assistant stopped short and laughed.

"Listen, are you a child?" the master said. "Those are professionals out there. You don't need to be embarrassed. You will be *nude*. That is quite a different thing from nakedness."

"I do not know this difference, monsieur. Please, give me anything else to do. I will scrub the toilet with my bare hands if you wish. But it is against my nature to be immodest."

"Is it against your nature to starve, you idiot? Do as I say or get out of my establishment instantly!"

Pawel stood quaking before them. Every muscle in his body cried out for rest, and waves of fever washed through him. He longed to lie down. His head reeled. His belly ached as it never had before.

"Well?" the master snapped.

He did not know why he decided as he did. Hunger? Fatigue? Hunger blunts the sharp edges of sensitivity. So does exhaustion. But that alone could not explain it. Perhaps he felt the cumulative effect of all the acts of depersonalization the Parisians had inflicted upon him. He was a beggar, a parasite, like the prostitutes below on the street. If his last dignity had been torn away, why should he hide with scraps of cloth what was not there . . . his privacy, his lost being, his self. Were these not mere words?

Fighting an overwhelming dread, he went behind the screen and slowly removed his clothing. He desired to scream, to retch, to run swiftly into the safer dark, but he longed more for the promised dinner.

When he was completely naked, his feet cold and white on the wooden floor, the assistant came behind the screen and tossed a bathrobe at him. Pawel hid himself in it. The assistant looked at Pawel's neck and feet and made an ugly sound.

"You stink", he said.

He thrust a washcloth and a bar of soap at Pawel, and pointed to a jug of water and a basin. When he had cleaned himself he stood mutely, without knowing what to do next. The assistant told him to put on the robe, then he pushed him through the studio door. It took an eternity to walk to the stage—each step was purchased with an act of the will. When he was a child, and even as a young man, he had felt a morbid terror of nakedness before the eyes of others. To overcome this now required the greatest effort he had made in his life up to that point. It seemed to him that the world had been flattened down into a realm of objects. He was an object about to be used by other objects. All shape, all form, all color were draining away, leaving only a knot of despair within him.

Then the master snapped at him, "Take that damn thing off!" Some of the students laughed.

Pawel dropped the robe and stood facing them. He saw only their eyes, assessing and judging, piercing and devouring. He felt as if death itself had taken him. He had never experienced an agony like it.

"*Mes enfants terribles*," the painting master said, "I bring you a treat. Rembrandt sends you the Polish Rider. A black Pole, *nu*! Defeated in battle, stripped by the conquerors. *Magnifique, n'est-ce pas?*"

"Very fine, Henri", one said. "A perfect torso surmounted by a noble, sensitive head."

"The torso is reminiscent of Rodin's *The Age of Bronze.*"

"Yes, the same extraordinary harmony of form, the athlete's body, a runner approaching the finish line as the exhausted beast."

"Yet", said another, "the face is like Renoir's bust of *Paris.*"

Throughout the morning Pawel struck the poses they demanded, alternating between standing and seated positions, changing every twenty minutes. He kept his sanity only by repeating his name to himself. Over and over, his name, his meaningless name. Resolving to endure this unspeakable morning, he would wait until the students went for lunch, demand a few coins, and leave. Then, for one day at least, he would eat. He might choose to drown himself or he might walk toward Poland or he would . . . he would . . . he had no idea what he would do. But at least *he* would choose it.

In desperation he begged his memory to save him, to bring before the eyes of his heart the face of the girl he had once loved, the praying girl. She had not been especially beautiful, but there had been a light in her, a radiant goodness. He had daydreamed for years that one day they would meet again. They would walk side by side under the chestnuts and acacias of Warsaw. They would discuss art. Perhaps they would marry. Then they would give to each other the beautiful mysteries of love. In their embrace there would be no fear, no shame.

But as he stood on the stage, Pawel found to his horror that the more her face came before him, the more dense was the blackness that filled him.

At the lunch break, most of the students went out, and Pawel covered himself with the robe. The assistant brought him a bowl of thin soup and a chunk of bread—this, then, was the meal the master had promised. He drank the soup in a gulp and tore into the bread. As he wolfed it down, he suddenly saw himself in the eyes of the two or three students who had remained to finish their sketches. Something in their glances frightened him. It was pity. But it was not the pity of a human being gazing sympathetically upon the suffering of a fellow human being. It was the pity of free and powerful individuals gazing upon a tormented animal.

At that moment he realized the full extent of his situation. He fled behind the screen and dressed himself. He secured the *fiori* next to his skin, went to find the master of the academy, and asked for payment.

"I pay only for a full day's work", he scoffed.

"Please," Pawel begged, "I am sick and hungry. Do not do this to me!"

"You are doing it to yourself. Now get back to the studio and take off those rags. I need a reliable employee. Perhaps tomorrow you can do some janitorial work if this sort of thing bothers you so much."

But Pawel knew—he did not know how he knew—the man was lying. From the very beginning he had wanted "a corpse", as the assistant called it, merely a body for his students to study.

"Give me my wages", Pawel cried feebly.

"Get out of my academy", the master said with a voice as cold as death. "And do not let me see you here again, or I will call the police."

Pawel was too exhausted to fight. He dragged himself down the stairs and went out to wander in the streets like a survivor in a heap of ruins. It seemed to him that the world had become a blast zone, a vast desolation in which only corpses staggered around looking for their own lost faces.

# 4

Pawel went into a crowded café and found an empty table heaped with dirty dishes. The waiters did not notice him as he drank a half-cup of cold coffee and ate the fragments of bread that customers had left. He stared out a window at the river. He had no place to go. He knew that his life was over.

It was in this condition that he happened to overhear an argument. Several elegant men at a nearby table were discussing the rise of the National Socialists in Germany.

"If Hitler comes to power," one of them said, "you will see that he who begins by burning books ends by burning people."

"He's definitely anticulture", said another. "Have you read *Mein Kampf*?"

"I *struggled* my way through it. Mental rot, strident Teutonic romanticism with a sinister undertone."

Pawel glanced at this last speaker, a distinguished man in his late forties, and recognized a well-known French novelist named Goudron. He caught Pawel's eye and beckoned to him. "You, the younger generation," he said, "what do you have to say about this?"

Pawel looked away and said nothing.

"Come, come", laughed the writer. "You were listening to us. There is intelligence in those sad eyes, young man."

The writer pulled back an empty chair and offered a basket of baguettes. Wearily, Pawel went over and sat down, staring at the bread.

"So," said one of the men at the table, "so, younger generation, tell us what you think about this Hitler."

"He will try to take over everything", Pawel murmured.

The men at the table looked bemused. Some shook their heads. The writer Goudron stared at Pawel with interest.

"Why do you say that?" he prompted.

Pawel shrugged and looked away. He had said too much. He longed for them to go so that he could devour their table scraps.

"Come, tell us", said Goudron.

"No one will be sure of what he is doing", Pawel said. "No one will have the courage to stop him when they realize." He said this, not because he possessed any understanding of history, but because he knew that evil men always seize what they want.

Pawel's reply was met with little enthusiasm among the group.

"Nonsense", said one of the companions. "All the man proposes is some extra *lebensraum*—some space for his people."

"Ah, you do not know the Germans", argued another. "You were too young for the Great War."

The famous novelist said to his companions, "If you read *Mein Kampf*, you will understand. It is all there." Then he turned to Pawel and said, "I think you are correct. Hitler is a Rhine crocodile. And many in today's world have developed the habit of feeding the crocodiles, which in the end only increases their appetite."

He bought Pawel a café au lait and ordered a croissant to go with it. Shortly after, the group broke up and Pawel was left alone with him. He asked Pawel where he was from and what he was doing in Paris. When Pawel murmured a brief description of his predicament, the writer gazed at him with a sympathetic expression, pondering. Arriving at some conclusion, he insisted that Pawel come to his home. A temporary refuge, he said.

Goudron's residence was in the Montmartre district. It was a spacious eighteenth-century mansion called the Château des Brouillards—the castle of the mists. He gave Pawel a small bedroom in the servants' wing, and there on the first night Pawel slept for sixteen hours straight. It was an unspeakable luxury to sleep in a warm, clean bed. Upon waking, he dressed himself in a purple robe and entered the bathroom connected to his room. There he found a deep tub in a chamber of glistening white tiles. The tub had already been filled by an invisible servant. Soaps of various colors, washcloths, and towels had been laid out on a marble shelf as if for a visiting dignitary. Pawel nimbly entered the bath and soaked in it until the water cooled. After toweling himself off, he shaved in front of the mirror, parted his hair with a silver comb, squared his shoulders, and otherwise made himself more presentable than he had looked for many years. He paused a little when he noticed in the expression of his face an odd mixture of bewilderment and relief.

Returning to his room, he found his clothes, laundered and pressed, neatly folded on the end of his bed. Clean though they were, the holes and paint spatters remained. When he opened an oak wardrobe to see what it contained, he discovered new clothing that fit him perfectly. He dressed himself in these and went out to search through the château for his rescuer.

In a spacious kitchen hung with copper pots and pans, Pawel found a maid. She informed him that the master had already left the house for the day and that she had orders to bring the visitor his breakfast in the dining hall. There she served him at a vast rosewood table, so great in length that two dozen people could have found places with ease. Seated on a gilded chair emblazoned with the insignia of a French royal house, he ate copious amounts of food. Forcing himself not to gobble, recalling his best table manners from Zakopane, he marveled over each new detail of his extraordinary good fortune.

Throughout that first day, he roamed through the château, gazing at the paintings and sculptures that filled practically every room, picked up books and read snippets from them, napped, and ate a great deal at two more meals. In the late evening Goudron returned, bringing with him a party of guests, all of whom were men of letters. After a friendly, if cursory, greeting to Pawel, the writer assured him that he should make himself at home, that he could stay as long as he needed. He then retired with his guests to a private meeting. Pawel drifted off to sleep that night feeling in his heart the resurrection of hope, as muscles cramped by exhaustion and chill will slowly unbend in the warmth of shelter.

As the days went by and stretched into weeks, Pawel's gratitude grew until it became limitless. His host was the most considerate person he had ever met, and also the most cultured. During their brief discussions—a few times in the grand entrance foyer, once over supper at the rosewood table—never did the writer assert his learning or social status. There was about him a certain diffidence, which struck Pawel as a charming attribute in one so famous. The man was intellectually stimulating and humorous at precisely the right moments and in just the right quantities—brief, incisive, permitting ample space for response. He asked concerned questions about Pawel's origins and listened carefully to the replies, though he did not presume to make commentary on these, further enhancing Pawel's sense that he had stumbled through a magic doorway into an alternate universe that was lavish with erudition, generosity, and infinite goodwill.

Thus, Pawel entered a new class and a new stage of his life. Many a *salon* did he attend during the year or more he lived there, always silent, always lingering on the edge of crowds. In Goudron's parlor and ballroom, he listened to several of France's most important academics, poets, and novelists hold forth on various topics. He did not like them much, for it seemed to him that they lacked the great writer's largeness of mind. They tended to sarcasm and critical remarks about the professional and private lives of other gifted people. Goudron had many friends in the avant-garde as well, among them Picasso and his consorts, Gertrude Stein and her companion, revolutionary

74

painters from America and Russia, actresses from the burlesque theaters, and circus performers. Pawel absented himself from any party that Picasso attended.

Goudron gave him a studio in the château's disused greenhouse. It was an enchanted place, full of light and space and heated by an enormous ceramic oven that fed on charcoal. The clay tiles were from China, small gold dragons on fields of jade green. Goudron purchased paints and canvas for him and gave him pocket money. He called it a gift, but Pawel was adamant that it should be considered a loan. He told the writer he would one day repay him for his generosity, and indeed, as a token of this, Pawel often worked in his garden, against his host's protests. Pawel insisted that he did not want to be a burden, that he must contribute to his upkeep, even if only a little.

He loved that garden with its sweeping view of Montmartre and the basilica of Sacré-Cœur silhouetted against the gray-blue sky. There an incident occurred that he would often remember. He was raking leaves one day and stopped by the iron fence to gaze at the white dome floating above the "holy hill", as it was called in the neighborhood. He supposed that he was experiencing one of his "spells"—a cessation of time and motion, a hushed silencing of inner turbulence. He felt an indescribable longing to go there, to see if it were possible to return to the lost peace of his earliest childhood. It seemed to him that a great heart dwelled in that place, and that it was calling to him. He did not know if this mysterious feeling promised a human love or a divine one. The latter seemed less likely.

Suddenly, Goudron was standing beside him. He took the rake from Pawel's hand, dropped it to the ground, and handed him a glass of dark red wine. He smiled at Pawel, looking intimately into his eyes. Then, gesturing to Sacré-Cœur, he said in a tone of gentle amusement, "*Sic transit gloria caeli.*"

It was a strange remark, its meaning obscure, so Pawel said nothing in reply.

"Paint it if you wish", Goudron said. "Everyone else does. But do not be seduced by its charm."

Thus, Pawel never went there.

Whenever he painted, he felt the hint of newfound joy. It was like the first, damp, scented breeze at the end of winter, like sunrise pouring into the hollow of a mountain pass. He walked beside the Seine and no longer hated it, though he was still disturbed by the memory of how magnetic it had been at his lowest moment before rescue. He painted many clichés: the parks of Paris, the bistros, the brightly colored barges, the facade of Notre Dame in a snowstorm, the rainwashed streets and the flowering gardens of the holy hill in spring—the typical subject matter of naïve young artists in his position.

Only once did he depart from his notion of what constituted the life of art. Just once, during a low moment when he succumbed to nostalgia, a longing for his homeland, a yearning for the happy years at Zakopane before Papa went away. From this faded realm an image surged up with such authority that he could not *not* paint it. It was an imaginary scene, yet it seemed to Pawel as real as his past had once been: in the foreground, against a wall of dark green conifers, wood smoke rose from the chimney of a hunter's alpine cabin; a cinnamon-colored bear dipped its paw into a black pool in which golden fish thrashed their tails lazily, its mouth open to devour what it could catch; in the sky above the peaks, a cascade of angels descended like snow falling on the hushed and tranquil earth; and upon the heights a knight rode a white horse, engaged in combat with a dragon.

Goudron thought it was not a style Pawel should pursue. It was too much the *pastoral*, he said, too much a symbolist romance with mystical undertones, the sort of thing that had been tried and rejected in the previous century. Pawel was crestfallen.

"I did not know", he said. "I thought it was original."

"No", replied Goudron in a sympathetic voice. "It is not."

It would be a mistake to assume that theirs was a business arrangement, as if Goudron were investing in the future value of an unknown struggling artist, or that it was simply the case of an older man of culture bestowing disinterested philanthropy. No, the relationship grew steadily into one of unexpressed love. Pawel thought he had found the guidance of a true father, one who would unlock the greatness within him. He believed that in return he was giving to Goudron the companionship of a son—a blessing the man sorely missed because he was divorced from his wife, who lived with their children in South America. Little by little, Pawel's confidence grew. He trusted Goudron's judgment absolutely. The writer was exquisitely exact in his assessment of Pawel's paintings. Even Goudron's bluntest comments pleased him, for it proved that his patron was a sincere man, not a flatterer, and that their friendship was built upon mutual respect.

Goudron told Pawel that his work was good technically, that it had "soul", but was unfocused. Above all, it needed more experience. If Pawel were to make a total break with the past, he suggested, and immerse himself in the ethos of the new Europe, great things were sure to come from him. It was not inconceivable, he added, that within a year or two Pawel could be exhibiting at one of Paris' important galleries. It would not be difficult to arrange.

"Is not everything, in its own way, experience?" Pawel mused. "Surely I have experienced much already."

"Yes", Goudron replied. "You have had many trying experiences. You are bitter and yet—strangely—you are also innocent. You have not yet inhaled the fragrance of *les fleurs du mal*."

"What are you suggesting?" Pawel asked.

"Do not look so alarmed, my young friend. I am merely saying that if you wish to be an artist of *this* century, one who will illumine *our* age, you must unlearn what you have been taught. You are angry and bitter because you are very much a child of the Old Europe, and the Old Europe has failed you. Of course, it is natural enough that you would feel a certain dismay over this. However, you must understand that a new world is being forged by men of culture. Hitler and Stalin will make some noise for a time, but they are the death rattle of the old age. They will soon be gone."

Pawel said nothing. He felt that he was not entirely in agreement, though he could not have explained why this was so. In the face of Goudron's great intellect he felt pathetically shallow.

"The very foundations of life are being overthrown", Goudron went on. "He who would be a creator must know how to destroy."

"Destroy?" Pawel replied nervously.

"Yes, destroy. To destroy old values—false notions of good and evil—is to clear away the cultural rubble of millennia that is choking us, so that a new thing might be built. For us—me with my novels, and you with your painting—the destruction of *artistic* norms is the necessary precondition for acts of purest creation."

Pawel shook his head, uncomprehending.

Goudron laughed, clapped him on the shoulder, and said with a fond smile, "We will make a good team, you and I."

Pawel was honored by this, but still, during the weeks following the conversation, he found it increasingly difficult to paint. The pastorals of Old Europe now seemed facile to him, even dangerous. The quaint, the charming, the pretty—were these not contributing to false norms? Were they not, in their own way, delaying the building of the new civilization?

But what of his strange and singular vision? From what hidden reservoir had the image of angels and dragon and knight emerged? What was its role, if any, in the new world? It was neither quaint nor charming; it was, in fact, stark and haunting.

It moved him, though he did not know why. But Goudron had told him it was a false trail, a waste of time.

How, then, to paint in such a way that he would contribute to the new civilization? How? This oft-repeated question produced no answers, regardless of how hard he tried to wring one from himself. His mind seemed unable to supply any themes, nor would his imagination produce visual forms other than the standard imagery churned out in the thousands every day by the artists of this city, each convinced of his originality, each blindly plodding along the old tired paths that led nowhere. How futile it all felt!

\* \* \*

In December of that year, a *Bal de Noël* was held at the château, attended by hundreds of people. Some arrived at the gate in expensive automobiles, others in horse-drawn carriages. The famous and the aspiring were there in abundance: artists, poets, theater producers, actors, university students, journalists. Throughout the evening, a string quartet played romantic pieces from Italian and French operas of the previous century. Countless white candles illumined each room.

Goudron was everywhere among the guests, urging upon them caviar and vintage wines, asking after the health of the famous and familiar, issuing brilliant *bons mots*, charming the large number of jeweled and costumed women, especially the elderly. Pawel observed him with admiration, marveling over his ability to converse with a variety of human types with great ease, displaying no artificiality or condescension. It was obvious that the writer was well liked—even loved—by many.

"Beware of that Hemingway", Goudron declared with a wag of a forefinger as he addressed a group of young writers gathered about him in front of a crackling fireplace in the ballroom.

"But do you not think he is extraordinary?" replied one of the audience disingenuously. "*A Farewell to Arms* is pure genius!"

"It is pure cinema", Goudron replied with an arched brow and a tone that evoked much laughter. "As a manufacturer of cinema script, he has been forced to assassinate all adjectives and adverbs. Thus does lingua franca become literature."

"And yet, Monsieur Goudron, is it not you yourself who are the master of minimalism? Perhaps Monsieur Hemingway has sat as a disciple at your feet."

Goudron laughed good-naturedly and changed the subject.

Pawel wandered away searching for a less-crowded corner of the château. So far no one had spoken to him, though many had noted his presence with curious and lingering glances. His discomfort was aggravated by his attire, lent to him for the occasion by his host: a black tuxedo, black Moroccan shoes, a crenulated white shirt, a crimson bow tie so *minimalist* that it was little more than a ribbon. He left the ballroom just as a Puccini piece ended. Making his way past the grand staircase into the wide entrance foyer, he avoided the lure of the music salon across the hall, from which there now came the sound of a piano playing the sweeter sort of Chopin. He opened a door beside this room and entered a small study where Goudron was accustomed to read alone or write letters. Lined with floor-to-ceiling bookshelves and appointed with Persian carpets, comfortable chairs, and a settee, it was not so small as to be cramped, nor so large a space that a single occupant might feel his solitude slipping into loneliness.

In fact, Pawel found himself not alone.

"*Entrez, entrez*", said a languid male voice. The voice belonged to a hand that held a brandy glass being used as a baton to accompany the arpeggios penetrating the walls faintly from the salon. The person attached to it was as yet invisible, seated on the far side of a high-back easy chair, warming himself, apparently, before a rack of burning logs in the fireplace. Pawel slowly went around and faced its occupant.

"Ah, it's the prince", declared the man.

In appearance he was a unique person. Closer to forty years of age than to thirty, tanned, with golden hair slicked back from the dome of his brow, blue eyes half-hooded by the lids, he was extremely handsome, even unpleasantly so. His lean body slouched in the chair, his long legs crossed at the knees, the uppermost leg bobbing up and down. He too wore a tuxedo, though it was violet in color and shimmered as if made of soft metal. His shoes, strangely, were white and brown saddles, with spikes on the soles.

Smiling ironically, the man said, "Pardon my attire. I arrived late and haven't had time to change."

As Pawel did not reply to this, but continued to stand uneasily by the fire, gazing into it, the man snorted and said in a dry tone, "You are, no doubt, the latest addition."

"I am a guest of Monsieur Goudron", Pawel murmured.

"Aren't we all."

"He is my benefactor."

"You are in residence, then", said the man with a broad smile.

"Temporarily."

"Of course. It is always temporary. Let me guess. You're an acrobat."

"No, I—"

"*Non, non, non,* do not deny it. He adores acrobats, especially the gamins from La Cirque du Paris."

"I am an artist", Pawel said, wondering even as he said it if it was true.

"An artist!" the man laughed. "Formidable!"

The way he pronounced the final word made it evident that he was not French, though until this moment his diction had been perfect.

Pawel was about to leave, when the man sat upright and said, "Tell me your name, prince."

"I am Pawel Tarnowski."

"Pawel Tarnowski. Polish? Yes, Polish. How delightful. So,

he is penetrating deep into Slavic territory now. This is a breakthrough."

Pawel made to leave in earnest, but the man blocked his way with a leg, and without rising offered his hand.

"I'm Audrey."

"Monsieur Audrey", Pawel mumbled, giving the hand a single shake. It was a large hand, but soft, the fingers elongated and elegant like everything else about him.

"Just Audrey. That's the way we do it in Chicago. And forgive my manners, won't you? Too much brandy after too much golf, not enough supper. Speak English?"

Pawel shook his head.

Audrey tossed a look at the door. "I don't blame you for trying to escape. That's what I'm doing, too. The great escape artist, that's me. Writer. Famous. European fling. Bright young Yankee thing. Get back to the old narrow streets and narrow minds, that's what I always recommend. But you, of course, have never known the wide-open plains where the buffalo roam and the hog butchers moan, where never a discouraging word is heard, have you? So, for you there is no need for a great escape, is there? Only small escapes for Old Worlders. From what are you escaping, I wonder?"

"I do not understand what you are referring to, Monsieur."

"Neither do my readers." He uttered a short laugh. "Which, luckily, has not discouraged them from buying my books."

"You are a writer, then?"

"As I have already implied. Or, to put it another way: yes."

"I read a great deal", Pawel offered timorously. "I am very interested in fiction."

"*Very* interested? Good for you." Audrey took a long sip from his glass. "I encourage that in young people. Doubtless you are very interested in serious fiction, not light fiction."

"Yes, I think this is so", Pawel said, half-consciously sitting down in a chair opposite the writer. "Kafka especially—"

82

"Kafkhaaaah!" Audrey burst out, spewing a little brandy from his mouth, laughing and coughing simultaneously. "Kafka, Kafka, Kafka. Now that *is* serious. Poor dear prince. You won't need to read my novels, then, because I am the quintessential purveyor of light fiction. Though of course it is cleverly disguised by my degree from Harvard and my numerous short stories that have appeared in *serious* journals. It's all reputation, you see—Pavel, is it?—it's all inflated image, Pavel, and connections and who wants to impress whom with what and for what reason."

The man took another draft, chuckling. Intrigued, despite himself, Pawel decided to delay his departure.

"Achille Goudron—now, there is a serious fellow. A very serious fellow. Poor man."

"Why do you say *poor man*?" Pawel asked. "He is greatly admired. He is a great writer."

"Achille is a talented writer, to be sure. But so earnest, so unhappy. He is always telling me to get more serious. He loves to quote Flaubert, you know, regardless of the occasion, who said that writing is like a cracked kettle on which we beat out tunes for dancing bears when all the while we long to move the stars to pity. Told me once that my novels have the seed of greatness but that I'm unable to develop because of my attachment to cheap adulation, to golf, and to love affairs, in that order of preference. He's right. Copious quantities of all three are what I like best. May it ever be thus. The world is far too serious, have you noticed?"

As Pawel did not reply, the writer went on.

"Poor, poor Achille with such a nasty bite on his ankle. That wife. The missing children, the election to l'Académie française. Such huge expectations on the shoulders of such a lonely little boy."

This comment made Pawel draw back a little, for it seemed not only bizarre but demeaning of his mentor.

83

"He is a wise person", Pawel offered in defense.

Audrey merely laughed.

"He is not at all wise, dear prince."

"Please do not call me that again."

"But are you not this week's favorite of the Sun King? I warn you, if you remain for any length of time in this faux castle, you, dear prince, will fall into the dungeon of his splendid agony."

"What do you mean?"

"Time will tell, time will tell . . . "

"It seems to me that you insult a great man."

"Time will tell", said the writer again, after another sip of brandy. "Listen, if you want some free advice, here it is: all those who love Achille eventually fall into the maw of his unfillable hunger. As many have done before you, as I once did, so you most assuredly will, if you do not quickly return to the circus."

"I am not in the circus", Pawel corrected.

"Oh, but you are. You most assuredly are."

If Pawel's curiosity had kept his dislike of the man at bay, this was now swept aside. Angrily, he stood to go.

"Ah, so young, so good-looking, so naïve, so cruel."

"It is you who are cruel", Pawel replied vehemently. "And ungrateful, for are you not a guest in this house?"

Leaning forward and assuming a sober, reflective expression, Audrey shook his head. "That is where you are wrong. So very, very wrong. I paid for my admission, you see. I paid for it a long time ago."

"How did you pay?" Pawel demanded, in no way convinced by anything the man had to say.

Audrey smiled sadly. "Let me ask you a question. A serious question. It is this: Why is his hunger insatiable? What, really, is he searching for?"

"I do not know. I do not know if he is searching for anything."

"He is searching—oh, yes, he is searching. He seeks what he can never have. The man he seeks will never be found."

"What man?"

"Precisely."

"I do not know what you are talking about."

At that moment the door opened and Goudron himself burst in, carried forward on a gust of Strauss.

"Oh, there you are, Aubrey. Come with me. There's someone you *must* meet!"

Rising to his feet, the American flickered a smile at Pawel, and turned to their host.

"Not another adoring socialite, Achille, *please*!"

"Nothing of the sort. A very important literary critic. Smokrev."

"Ah, the count."

"You know him?"

"Only by reputation. Is he one of your planets, or simply the moon of a planet?"

"An asteroid."

"More than that, I hear. The man is deliciously dangerous. Rumored to be a fascist, writes a regular column for *Lettres Françaises*, collects outrageously pornographic art. Really, Achille, the company you keep! Worst of all, his essays have destroyed some good writers and made a success of more than one bad one."

"Yes, yes, but he's quite amusing. And rather a pariah. The Polish community in Paris despises him, and for that reason he doesn't move in their circles."

"Better and better. Well, lead the way, my dear, I've been dying to meet him."

The two men went out, leaving Pawel to unravel the mysteries. In the end, he concluded that Audrey or Aubrey was one of those pitiable people who are polluted by ambition and envy.

\*     \*     \*

In January, Pawel attended a performance of *The Suppliants*, a tragedy by Euripides, staged in an auditorium of the University of Paris. He went with Goudron and a group of the writer's young friends. Tickets for all were courtesy of Goudron. There was to be a party afterward. Pawel accompanied them with some reluctance, for he was not greatly interested in live theater and had, as well, developed a dislike for the intensely animated students who perpetually orbited the writer.

Sitting beside Goudron throughout, silent, wrapped in his personal isolation, he remained unmoved as the great war play unfolded its themes: the desolation of those who lose their beloved ones in the conflicts begun by men of power; the blindness of those who launch such wars, reaping a harvest of slaughter and shame that others must bear. As the drama progressed, the mothers and young sons of the slain warriors begged the victorious king Theseus to give them the bodies of the vanquished, that they might be buried with honor. Theseus listened to the pleas of the women and the boys, and with a flourish of largesse granted their request, but only after extracting political concessions.

Pawel did not so much follow the plot of the story as he listened to a profound cry from the depths of the bereaved hearts. He heard it faintly at first, then it grew and grew within him. In the final scene, it swelled and burst as the boys cried out:

> I am wretched, bereft of my poor father,
> I shall be orphaned in a barren home,
> *Not cherished in my father's hands.*

Pawel sobbed, rose abruptly to his feet, and left the auditorium. For hours he walked the streets of the city, nursing the agony of an abscess that had opened without warning in his

86

chest, perplexed by it, hating it. He could make no sense of it whatsoever, for his father was not slain. He, Pawel, was no orphan. While it was true that his father had not cherished him, had constantly disapproved of him, that was an old history that he had completely shaken off, had he not?

Finally, long after midnight, he arrived at the château and entered on silent feet. There he found Goudron in his private study. The writer had fallen asleep in the high-back armchair by the fireplace, a glass of cognac half-empty on a table beside him, an open book on his lap. Pawel sat down on a chair opposite and regarded the man for a while. *Here is my host*, he thought to himself. *Here is my benefactor, the one who has rescued me from a sea of troubles. Why has he done so? Why does he keep on helping me? Here, truly, is my father not slain.*

Now for the first time Pawel understood that the writer cherished him. This mysterious adoption was inexplicable and undeclared, yet it was precisely the implicitness of their friendship that increased its beauty. A wave of gratitude washed through him, easing the pain, sealing the abscess.

Goudron startled awake, coughed, and rubbed his eyes.

"Ah, my young warrior", he murmured. "Stripped of armor, pleading before the gates of Athens. Is it the apotheosis of courage? Or is it desperation?"

Uncomprehending, Pawel shook his head.

"You see these children", Goudron went on, "bearing in their little hands the bodies of their noble fathers which I gained for them: I and my city give them as a gift to you."

Pawel shook his head again. Goudron laughed.

"You left early", he said in a whisper, gazing at the glass of cognac.

"I needed to think", Pawel replied.

"And to feel, I suspect."

Goudron reached for the glass and sipped from it with a studious expression.

"Let the past depart, Pawel, with the ashes of our fathers! The air above us holds them now; melted by fire, they have winged their way to Hades!"

Goudron got to his feet unsteadily. "Theseus gains the bodies for the grieving sons, it's true", he slurred. "Yet there is a double meaning, for he has also taken their lives—a generous man twice over. A generous king."

He swayed on his feet, then took a hesitant step toward Pawel, stumbling.

Pawel gripped Goudron's arms and held him upright.

"Ah, ah", the writer breathed, his eyes swimming, "Hermes, messenger, stay with me on my course, for the past is present and the present is becoming the future again."

"I do not understand what you mean", Pawel said. "You are tired. You must go to bed."

"Again and again and again . . . "

"It is late."

"Yes, it is far too late and I dallied too long, bound by the yoke of a lawful bridal bed."

Suddenly, Goudron's eyes cleared. He laughed ruefully, took a step back, and steadied himself.

"Too much classicism for one night", he said. "Really, you should see Brecht."

"Brecht?"

"Brecht. *Threepenny Opera*. A play."

"I have not heard of it."

"No? It has taken Europe and the Americas by storm. It must have passed Poland completely by."

"I . . . I have not seen much theater", Pawel stammered. "Yet tonight I felt the power of this art for the first time."

"Yes, power. Always there is power. And politics. And race. And culture. But Brecht, ah, Brecht has become a communist, and is losing his creative powers as a result."

"I . . . I would like to write something", Pawel offered,

88

hoping to dispel the growing obscurity of Goudron's remarks. "P-perhaps a play about P-poland."

"A play about Poland", Goudron smiled. "A fine idea, if you wish to attempt it."

"It is just a thought. I am not sure I have the skill."

"It will take Europe and the Americas by storm!" Goudron declared. With that, he turned and moved unevenly to the grand staircase and ascended to the rooms above, chuckling all the while. Pawel went to his room in the servants' wing and fell into an uneasy sleep.

\* \* \*

Soon afterward, Goudron left for Algeria to take the warmer climate. He intended to proceed from there to Tunisia, where he would remain for some months completing a novel. During this period, Pawel lived alone in the château. Every night, after the cleaning woman went home, it became completely empty—a splendid shell. Day after day he wandered aimlessly from room to room. He tried to read one of Goudron's novels and found the style to be as lucid as Kafka's, but the story practically impenetrable. The book was all about human relationships. Complex relationships filled with nuances that Pawel could not grasp. It seemed very French. His mind wandered and he gave up.

On two or three occasions he sat by the fire in the study and tried to visualize a great Polish drama, tried to pour onto paper a distillation of the Slavic genius, passion, folly. It came to no more than a few sheets of scribble. He soon realized that it was pathetic and imitative. He gave it up and returned to painting.

Now loneliness became a constant ache that was not so much a desire to see his patron again, but a general mood of abandonment, as if he were adrift on a sea of limitless horizons with no land in sight, as if he had no past and only an indefinite future. Any human company would have been welcome, but even when he went out to shop for food or wandered through the art galleries, he could barely bring himself to look people in the eye.

Once he thought to himself how wonderful it would be to meet a beautiful woman—lovely in form and heart and mind. But these surges of warmth were merely wistful imaginings, swiftly come and gone.

"Why am I so alone?" he asked the walls of the château. "Why have I not found someone to love? Am I a man? But what *is* a man? Am I a child? And if so, how do I become a man?"

Unwelcome memories came to him, surging up in his imagination, spreading to his thoughts, then to his heart. He recalled those disturbing moments of his youth when, unable to find the courage to reach out to women, his longings had turned to men—the vaguely remembered infatuations, unspoken, never acted upon, instantly regretted. He had pushed them away as temptations, but they now returned with unprecedented force.

"What is happening to me?" he asked himself. "Oh, no, surely not that!"

Frightened, he paced through the château of mists, upstairs and downstairs, and circled the garden a hundred times until he was so exhausted that all desires abated. Occasionally, his eyes would be drawn to the white basilica on the holy hill, but always he crushed this childish nostalgia.

"You must go forward", he admonished himself. "You must not go backward."

Where was the future to be found? What was the meaning of his life? Was there meaning in any human life? If so, what was the truth of life and where would he find it, if it existed? In love? No, love was a social contract for the propagation of the species, and its price was always the destruction of freedom and creativity!

Back and forth. Argument and counterargument.

"All love is either betrayal or imprisonment!" he declared to the twittering sparrows who had found their way into the greenhouse through a broken pane of glass, and to the golden dragons who lived there.

"No, not all. There is one who does not betray or imprison, there is one who seeks the truth—my benefactor, my father in Art. He is a prophet of the future new man, and he is willing to struggle for the destruction of false social values, so that a new thing will be born in civilization."

How grateful Pawel was for his one true friend. Yet he was also aware that he could not allow himself any stronger feelings for the man.

"I am stone", he declared. And having said it, he slipped into that state of numbness in which nothing could harm him.

Even so, he was increasingly frustrated by his lack of inspiration. Unable to concentrate, feeling a growing darkness all around and within, he walked the streets of Paris day after day, week after week, searching into every art gallery, seeking confirmation of what Goudron had told him. The public galleries seemed to be dead memorials to the past, and Pawel now felt nothing but distaste for the paintings he had once loved. Yes, even Renoir, Degas, and Monet, those hero-giants of the recent past, could no longer move him. That they were geniuses he did not doubt. But if Goudron were right, they were too preoccupied with beauty, their vision of a harmonious world the product of prejudiced eyes that had never been humiliated, had never starved. In disgust he strode from the Musée d'Impressionisme, raging within himself against the bourgeoisie and the pampered lapdogs they called artists.

In the commercial galleries it was no better. It was all ambition and posturing and prettiness.

One day, however, as he entered a small gallery in Montmartre, he halted before a painting by Georges Rouault. It was an image of Christ in agony, nailed to the Cross. He did not know why it moved him, for he no longer had any faith. He supposed it evoked images from the pageants of his childhood. Yet it intrigued him, for the artist had achieved a synthesis of traditional subject matter and revolutionary technique. It was semiabstract, but in essence not an abstraction. This was inexplicable. There was a power in the image that made Pawel wonder if he had overlooked something in his annihilation of the past.

He obtained Rouault's address from his dealer and wrote to him—he lived at Versailles. Of course, Pawel was straightforward about his position. He declared that he believed in nothing, but that the painting of the crucifixion had impressed him. He asked if Rouault thought all traditional avenues of art history had now been closed, as so many art theorists maintained. If they were not closed, then what should a young artist pursue? Should he, Pawel, go in the direction of absolute abstraction, or to symbolism, or to a new kind of figurative realism?

Rouault answered with a courteous letter. He discussed the current art scene critically and emphasized that the confusion of modern art had its source in issues deeper than questions of style. He concluded by saying, "A man can create only with the material of what he loves."

Pawel replied with a curt note: "What if he loves nothing?"

Expecting that his bluntness had effectively terminated the correspondence, Pawel was surprised a week later to receive a reply:

> The man who does not love does not yet know himself. Inside every heart is an image of love—however buried it may be. He must seek it, and find for himself his own language, the words that will unlock the hidden icon.

"How will he do this?" Pawel countered on a little postcard of a nude by Matisse.

Rouault replied on a little postcard of the rose window of Chartres cathedral: "By submitting himself to the forces of life. By suffering."

But this was too bleak. Pawel thought he had already suffered far too much.

He wrote a rejoinder on the back of an advertisement for a nude dancing parlor, a poster he had stolen from a billboard for this purpose. "Suffering has not taught me to love", he said. "It has taught me to hate." He folded the poster, enclosed it in a large envelope, and mailed it, thinking, *Goodbye forever, Monsieur Rouault; no doubt this will stretch your tolerance to the breaking point!*

During the following week, Pawel felt some remorse over this act, and also pondered what he had written to Rouault. Did he really hate? Yes, it seemed to him that he did. He hated the smug indifference of the masses. He hated those who caused wars and filled the streets with discarded lives. He hated the successful artists who navigated the world with such unerring talent for self-advancement. He hated people like the concierge, and Henri the painting master, and the gallery owners, for whom there was no greater god than money. And Photosphoros, who would have gladly seen him starve (he was sure of it) to preserve the "purity" of his way of life. He even wondered about Rouault's motives. His hatred, as he nursed it, spread like dark fog. Only Goudron was exempt. Only he had proved himself free of sullied motives.

Rouault did not reply, and Pawel assumed bitterly that he had washed his hands of him, like all the other good religious people.

"Christians!" he sneered.

Then, to his amazement, Pawel received a long letter from him. Rouault apologized for his silence. He had been very ill and was still recovering. He had prayed for Pawel and had offered his sickness to God for him.

93

Do you know, Pawel, that even though we have not met face-to-face, I feel I know you very well. I, too, have felt your anguish. You must come to Versailles and meet my wife and children, and also some friends of ours. Maritain is a Catholic philosopher who was once an atheist. His wife, Raïssa, is also a philosopher, and a mystic. She is Russian, a Jewess who has come to Christ.

Pawel was filled with conflicting emotions. Despite his life-long aversion to social contacts, he suddenly felt a longing to meet these unusual people. Yet he hesitated to leave the city. Was there not a danger that he might be so impressed by the circle at Versailles that he would be seduced into their anti-quated view of things? Should he turn aside from his heroic and solitary search for a new language of his own? He argued with himself, now this way, now that.

Curiously, Goudron telephoned from Algiers at the very moment he was on the brink of tossing everything aside and going out to meet Rouault and the Maritains. The writer listened patiently while Pawel described the exchange of letters. Then, speaking in a rational tone, he countered the artist's ideas with great eloquence, humor, and subtlety. He assured Pawel that the new humanism was superior to Rouault's so-called Christian humanism, dominated as it was by a cruel tyrant god who could never be placated. He said Rouault was a religious fanatic, too much influenced by Léon Bloy and the Maritains. It would be a mistake to go to Versailles, he said.

"Besides, I have excellent news for you, my friend, news that will convince you this is not the time to be distracted from your course. You must persevere in the path you have undertaken. I have just completed negotiations for an exposition of your work at the gallery where Picasso and Braque exhibit."

This news was thrilling, yet mixed with it was a sense of depression alternating with desperation, for Pawel had very little to show for his months of labor, and none of it was original—well, excepting the vision of Zakopane, but of course that was a worthless piece, leading nowhere.

He wrote to Rouault, explaining that for the present he was unable to travel, that he must prepare for a show of his work that would open in the autumn of the following year.

"Perhaps one day we will meet", he concluded. "Perhaps you and your friends would care to attend the opening reception."

It secretly pleased him that he could offer such a grand invitation, that he was now apparently on a level of equality with him, and possibly one of superiority, for was not Rouault a sad remnant of a dying world, and was not Pawel a forerunner of the new?

But, strangely, he seemed well pleased by Pawel's good fortune and replied that he would be delighted to attend. And so their curious correspondence—a dialogue between believer and unbeliever—continued during the following months.

In his next letter, Rouault wrote:

Cher Paul, the image of the rejected Christ is the most difficult of all to paint. The artist must avoid melodramatic effects. He must draw the viewer into the interior agony of Christ, which is similar to the dark night of the soul. Few can look at this subject without prejudice. Many a Christian looks at it and sees an ancient cliché, a religious message to which he gives assent— no more, no less, than that. Yet if his eyes are clear, he can see the majesty of a God who suffers with us and in us. Christ is always with us. He is in agony until the end of the world.

Alas, the atheist looks at my crucified Jesus and sees only the death of God. Do you think that God has died, Paul? Ah, young painter, it is we who are not alive! The hearts of modern men have grown cold. My deepest longing is to one day paint the face of Christ with such authenticity that even the most hardened heart will be converted by it. But as Fra Angelico once said, *To paint the things of Christ one must live with Christ.* And so, the artist must be willing to be crucified if he would paint such an image.

Wounded by his criticism of unbelievers, Pawel replied:

Monsieur, is it not enough to desire, as I desire, to paint an image of Man? If an artist were to create a human face, with all its beauty and nobility radiating through its ugliest wounds, would this not achieve something as great, perhaps greater? Could anyone, upon seeing such an image, ever again hurt another human being?

Goudron returned from Africa and quickly settled into his writing routine and round of parties, from which Pawel almost always absented himself. "I must work!" he solemnly declared.

With agonizing slowness, paintings began to fill the walls of the studio. He set himself a schedule of one per week. He worked in a rage of frustration, rage against his technical limitations and rage against the limitations of creative intuition that he believed had been inflicted upon him by the lies of Old Europe, especially his Catholic upbringing. He painted Notre Dame burning under a hail of bombs. He painted a dress ball at which danced the petite bourgeoisie, who wore war medals on their chests and chains about their ankles, their eyes sly, grasping, lifeless. He depicted with graphic realism Henri the painting master as a portly nude on a stage, surrounded by jeering students, his eyes insane with humiliation. Also the concierge as Medusa. Photosphoros as a Pharisee among the Sanhedrin. And scenes of degradation—not Toulouse Lautrec's ladies of the evening, but the despairing eyes of the syphilitic prostitutes.

"*Formidable!*" Goudron said. "You are breaking through to your own language. This, at last, is original!"

In his letters to Rouault, Pawel described his new work in detail. A tone of sadness entered the replies, not because of the subject matter itself (for Rouault also painted the human condition, complete with prostitutes). No, he was concerned about something else.

When you expose such moral agony to the eyes of the world, you must not forget the dignity of man, even in the most degraded ones. Cher Paul, the artist must always ask himself, am I painting the surface only, or am I revealing the eternal soul of my subjects? Without this, we only add to the agony. We too would be merely using the prostitutes—and worse, for we do not pay them.

Pawel was struck by the depth of compassion in this man, an empathy which seemed to contradict what Goudron had said about the old artist's cold and tyrannical version of religion. He wanted to meet him more than ever. But again he held back.

He suspected that if the people at Versailles were to meet him they would instantly penetrate his darkness, without any ability to relieve it. They would look into his soul the way Rouault looked into the souls of harlots and clowns. He would be a subject, or worse, an object. Their admirable compassion purely abstract, they would regard him as fresh material for their pious reflections. Doubtless they would treat him with a certain correct charity, but they would not ask him to return. If that were the case, Pawel felt, his darkness would increase. He could not risk it. He knew he would never survive it.

Still, the dialogue intrigued him. In a final exchange of notes, Pawel asserted that at this point in history it was necessary to demolish language itself in order to penetrate to the foundations of meaning. By destroying, he proclaimed, one opened the path to a new golden age of creativity.

Rouault replied:

Beware, Paul. Turn aside from that seductive way of thought. Language—and for you and me this means visual language—must be purified, not destroyed. If you lose symbolism, you will lose your way of knowing things. If you destroy symbols, you destroy concepts.

There is another danger. If you corrupt symbols, concepts are corrupted, and then we lose the ability to understand things as they are, rendering us vulnerable to deformation of our perceptions and our actions.

Once more, Rouault urged Pawel to come to Versailles. Hearing about this, Goudron told Pawel that he would be better off to meet the German expressionists. Shortly after, they flew to Berlin. There they attended a private exhibition of the great painters of that school, people like Bechmann, Kirchner, and Dix, who even then were being mocked by the National Socialists. In their paintings they did not seem to destroy or corrupt symbols; rather, they rearranged them in disturbing new ways.

Goudron and Pawel went to Bechmann's studio and watched him working on a mural called *Departure*. It was full of personal mythology and scenes of torture: a naked man with his hands chopped off, bound to a pillar, a shrieking woman wandering the halls of madness, shouting about an old unnamed crime, and warning of another yet to come. It seemed grotesque to Pawel, but sheer genius. In the center panel a king gazed out to the ocean, making ready to depart. It was visual Kafka.

After they left Bechmann's, Goudron took Pawel to a quarter of the city where the night life was avant-garde. Entering an underground club, Pawel was startled to see semi-naked men dancing on the stage. He looked away.

People at the next table greeted Goudron as if they were old friends. One, a slender man of about eighty years, dressed in a pink velvet evening jacket, said to him, "*Ami*, I am struggling with the concept of nakedness in my latest novel."

"Aren't we all, Heinrich?" Goudron replied, causing much laughter among people at nearby tables.

"No, no, I'm serious." The German gestured to the youths cavorting on the stage. "Is it lust or is it symbolic manifestations of the subconscious?"

"Lust, Heinrich. No doubt about it."

"*Ach!* You French! There's too much Proust in your blood.

Well, I say that nakedness is always a subconscious symbol of metaphysical states."

"*Meta*-physical? I say physical."

"No, no, listen to me now! Nakedness is the primal art form, the dramatization of Lost Eden arising from the racial memory."

"Find yourself a nudist spa, Heinrich, and stop your philosophizing."

"It's existential vulnerability, you see, and whenever——"

Goudron turned his back to the velvet gentleman.

Angrily the old man snapped, "To speak with you, Goudron, is to put a finger into tar!" His words were swept away by a new piece that the orchestra began to play full volume. The music was haunting. It came inside the ramparts of the self.

"My friend Kurt wrote that", Goudron shouted to Pawel. "Kurt Weill."

Throughout the room were people in elaborate costumes. There were many couples dancing. At the tables, dignified, well-dressed couples kissed without restraint. They were all men.

"This is a very strange place", Pawel said as the music ended.

Goudron laughed. "Only in the beginning. It's rather like home to me."

"Home?" Pawel murmured, his eyes widening.

"You needn't play the game of naïveté", said Goudron. "It is charming, but far too late for that." He put an arm around Pawel's shoulders as he snapped his fingers for drinks. The waiter brought green absinthe, and Pawel stared into his glass as if the emerald liquid had been scooped from a swamp.

Goudron downed one drink, then another. Pawel sipped his, hating—and loving—the taste.

"Ah, my bitter innocent," Goudron smiled into his eyes, "drink to the dregs. Drink, and we shall crown thee *Prince de Beauté* !"

Then he took Pawel's face in his hands and kissed him on the lips.

Pawel stared at him in shock and jerked his head back.

"Come here", Goudron laughed. "You want another."

"N-no!" Pawel stammered.

Clumsily, he pushed Goudron away and stood. The crowd roared with laughter, enjoying Goudron's humiliation. Pawel stumbled toward the exit and ran from the club.

Shedding tears, he stomped around the streets of Berlin throughout the night. A paroxysm of self-hatred took hold of him, and in that state he found yet another bridge from which to hurl himself, a span over the River Spree. But his anger saved him. He saw in an instant Goudron's whole strategy during the previous year. He had built up Pawel's immense respect and love for him, his dependence upon him, only to reveal it all in the end as a calculated sexual seduction.

Pawel went back to Paris on his return ticket. Goudron was not on the flight, presumably because he wanted to avoid Pawel, or wished to ease his humiliation in the pleasures of Berlin. Upon landing at the Paris airport, he took a taxi to the Château des Brouillards and quickly collected the clothing he had worn a year before. He looked about the studio and felt for his paintings a loathing so intense he did not care what happened to them. They were, after all, Goudron's creation. Let Goudron keep them as repayment for his hospitality. He hesitated over the vision of Zakopane, but decided to leave it, for it was too large to carry. He took only the small painting of flowers he had purchased with his gardener's wages.

While stripping his bedroom of items that were distinctly his own, Pawel came upon Rouault's letters. Pondering them, he considered going to Versailles, but felt certain that in the presence of those Catholic mystics he would feel only shame. His darkness would be starkly revealed. He would be doubly demolished. Summarily, he threw the letters into the parlor fireplace and burned them.

"I will return to my native country", he declared as he

watched the flames devour the useless words. "I do not belong there, but even less do I belong here. In fact, I belong nowhere. At least in Warsaw I can begin again."

Staring with hatred at the cultural splendor of the château, he shouted: "What am I?"

Glancing into a mirror, he saw the contorted face of an enraged man. A rather handsome man, a beautiful shell containing a writhing mass of contradictions and self-deceptions. He hated the face he saw before him, and he watched it become more hateful as he hated it.

"Prince of Beauty", he snarled. "He knew you better than you knew yourself. Well, no more! I am leaving. I will go back to the land of the dead and I will become stone. Yes, I am a stone man. Never again will I permit another person to see inside me or to touch me."

And so he left for the Gare Saint-Lazare with the intention of catching the first train leaving for Poland. The thought of going the direct route through Berlin filled him with nausea, and moreover it meant waiting another day, so he bought a ticket on the Vienna train, which was departing within the hour.

He hoped to make connections for Warsaw in Vienna, but upon arrival there he found that he did not have enough money for the last stage of the journey. He would either have to walk across the Carpathians or quickly find some employment. To his dismay the Paris experience repeated itself. There was little work to be found. He washed dishes in restaurants whenever he could be hired, but there were many others jostling for the few available jobs. The pay was extremely low, the hours never sufficient for the purchase of a ticket. He spent his last money on food. He walked and walked, looking everywhere and anywhere for help. It had come before; perhaps it would come again. He wanted to pray but could not. Eventually, when he became hungry enough, he cried out, "God—if there is a

God—I beg you to help me! But do not let help come at the price of degradation. I cannot bear it any longer."

A few hours later, Pawel wandered into the Kunsthistorisches Museum. There he found eight paintings by Brueghel, including *The Blind Leading the Blind* and *Peasant Wedding*. Standing before the former, he saw his face in each of the souls falling into the abyss. Neither did the jolly wedding scene lift his spirits, for he could not find his face in it; instead he saw what he would never have, never be.

Then he came to a work by an anonymous artist of the late nineteenth century—it was a *Last Judgment*. He could not understand why he had not heard of the painting before, for it was clearly a masterpiece. The image was not so complex or populated with grotesque characters as Bosch's famous painting of the same title. No, its power was magnified through simplicity. The artist had portrayed the second coming of Christ as the return of the Lord to a world devoured by evil. In the upper half a luminous divine order descended into a field of demonic energy and universal abomination. People staggered about the desolate landscape, unable to look up to the light. They could no longer see; they could no longer believe. They thought that ruin was the sum total of reality. He could see it in their faces, their despair, their fear, their terrible loneliness. The loneliness of the apocalypse. And in those faces he saw his own face.

Pawel burst into tears and wept openly in front of the painting. It seemed to him that the artist had captured his experience perfectly. How had he done that? Had he, too, felt what Pawel had felt, had he once been where Pawel now was?

He no longer believed in Christ. But in this fantastic scene, leaping with angels and demons wrestling each other over the souls of men, he saw the drama of his inner life laid bare. Yes, it was a hopeless world, but the despair was relieved mysteriously by the magic of art. To find a painted incarnation of his darkness was to step outside of it for a moment, and in a sense, to transcend it. To be master of the hallucination, after all, was to be above it.

Just then a guard grabbed Pawel's arm and was about to conduct him out, for he was sobbing loudly, uncontrollably. Then a hand took his other arm, and a voice argued with the guard. When Pawel had ceased weeping and cleared his eyes, he looked up to find that the guard was gone and a very old, very bent man was holding his arm and regarding him with a look of sympathy.

He was dressed impeccably in a fine suit, wore a homburg on his head, and held his body upright on a cane. He possessed the most wrinkled face Pawel had ever seen, dark brown, set off by white hair and a mustache.

"Young man, you are troubled by this painting?" he inquired politely.

"Yes. No", Pawel replied.

"An odd answer."

"It unlocked a grief in me."

"Ah, then it has done its work properly."

"Who are you?"

"Me? A nobody. Yet a retired postal clerk is permitted to love art. Do you also love art?"

"Yes, I love art."

The old man nodded toward the *Last Judgment* and said, "Never in my long life have I seen anyone weeping before a painting. There is no greater, nor more sincere, compliment one can pay to an artist."

"If I could meet the man who painted this," Pawel said, "I would thank him. For it seems to me that no one could paint such an image if he had not experienced its subject. He has left a message for all who have been where he once was."

"Yes", said the other thoughtfully. "Yes, I believe that is true."

"I wonder who he was? I wonder if he is still alive and where he lives. Has his life been successful, happy?"

"Tell me, what do you think is his message to you?"

"More than just Christian mythology. He is trying to say that even when everything appears lost, there is help."

"Yes, you have heard him speaking across all these years. Yet you have heard only a part of the message." At this point he patted Pawel's arm and added, "An old man should remind a young man to be cautious about what he calls mythology."

"I think we are foolish if we wait for help to come from the heavens", Pawel replied.

"Ah, so young, so young", sighed the old man. "Would you excuse me, please? I wish to see to some matters, but I will return shortly. Would you consider being my guest at dinner?"

Pawel became suspicious.

"My wife died recently", the old man said. "We were not blessed with children. I would appreciate some company."

When Pawel's benefactor returned, he led him out to a waiting cab. The old man instructed the driver to take them to a restaurant near the train station. There he purchased a sumptuous meal for Pawel. He made no attempt at conversation, and at the end of the meal he stood and offered his hand. Pawel shook it and thanked him for his kindness.

"I must go now", said the old man. "I do not think we will meet again. I know nothing about you other than that you have been through a great suffering. I think you will do much good in the world. Do not lose hope. Find your way home."

When he had gone, Pawel discovered an envelope on the table. It contained enough money to purchase several meals and a ticket to Warsaw. There was also an unsigned note, in which was written:

My friend,
I thank you for weeping over my painting. I have waited more than fifty years for such a compliment. I painted it when I was as young as you, during a period of darkness, a time when I

believed there was no love in the world. From then on I could paint nothing. God speed you on your journey. There is love in the world. You will find it.

## 5

Pawel arrived in Warsaw on a Sunday afternoon, in time to hear the bells of the city pealing in the winter sky. It was a beautiful and pure sound. The air was clear, the atmosphere itself at rest. After Paris, his city seemed small and decent.

He went first to the family apartment on Zielna Street, only to be informed by the landlord that it had been rented to strangers. He next went to the rooms of his eldest brother, Jan, on Swietokrzyska. Just before Pawel's departure for Paris, Jan had been engaged to a woman named Sara Nohler, a Jewess, a medical student. His clockwork shop was successful. His future seemed assured. He was deliriously happy. Pawel now dreaded the reunion, fearing that the total failure of his life would be revealed by the stark contrast between himself and his brother.

As he climbed the staircase to Jan's apartment, Pawel bitterly told himself that life belonged to the strong. Life made no sense whatsoever—the predators in Paris, the old gentleman in Vienna—yes, even the rare moments of human mercy seemed to be the exception, not the rule of life. In that frame of mind he found it practically unbearable to face Jan, but when his brother opened the door and greeted him with jubilation, Pawel knew that Jan cared about him and that his self-pity was a loathsome thing.

"You are home at last!" Jan cried. "Come in, come in! Meet my wife, meet my son! Sara, Itsak, quickly, quickly! A miracle!"

Pawel ate a meal with them, during which he said little, responding to their questions about his travels in so spare and curt a manner that they grew uncomfortable and probed no further. He did not inquire about their life, because its abundance was evident all around him. There was a welcome distraction when the boy, barely able to walk, toddled across the carpet to his father's outstretched arms, falling again and again, squealing with delight at the great game.

Though the conversation was stilted, caused no doubt by Pawel's morose silences and by the unacknowledged, unresolved hurt of his departure years before, Jan tried to keep the reunion light. At one point he proudly displayed a new golden-brown piano in the parlor.

"It's a Bechstein", he declared. "Horribly expensive. But Sara's income from the clinic is growing, and the shop is doing well now. The Swiss cuckoos, you know, and the British pendulums—very popular."

Sweeping Itsak into his arms, he sat down on the piano bench with the child on his lap and began to play. His touch was slow but competent.

"Chopin", Pawel said in a subdued voice.

"The Polonaise in B", Jan nodded.

"When did you take up the piano?"

Jan lifted both hands from the keyboard and raised them as if in surrender. "Before you left for Paris I began lessons. I didn't even tell Mama and Papa." He laughed. "Of course, Madame Zitovski told me I was hopeless, said I have the fingers of a turnip farmer. But I did not give up. Ah, Pawel, Pawel, if God had given me hands like yours, I would now be concert master at—"

He was unable to continue because the boy began to bang the keys. Jan squeezed his son tightly and kissed his cheeks again and again. Clearly, Itsak was a golden child, beaming with the love and security showered upon him. Pawel examined his own hands and wondered what good had ever come from them.

When Sara carried the boy off to bed, Jan's face sobered, his eyes filled with tears, and he put a stubby hand on his brother's arm.

"There is sad news, Pawel. I am sorry to tell you that Papa died last November. It was his heart, so weakened during the prison years. Now he has gone, our beloved Papa."

Pawel felt nothing—numb, blank.

"And Mama?" he asked.

"She is not well. She has been sick all winter and is living with Aunt Irma at Mazowiecki. We will go see her soon. Soon."

Drying his eyes, he went on. "There is more. We have been trying to reach you for months. I am sorry to say that Uncle Tadeusz is also dead, but I am happy to inform you that he has left you his business."

* * *

And so the remainder of his life was decided for him. Uncle Tadeusz had rescued Mama and Papa many times in the past, and now, even from beyond the gates of death, he was rescuing their child. Yet he had been—always, it seemed—a curmudgeon. Decades earlier he and Papa had come to Warsaw from their father's failing estate south of Krakow, Papa to clerk in a law office, Tadeusz to open a bookshop. The family library was the foundation of the latter enterprise, which gained an excellent reputation during the following years. But it had declined as Tadeusz himself declined. He became a "character", one of the thousands of idiosyncratic shopkeepers and self-made democrats who called Warsaw the center of the world. He sat all day in a captain's chair by the front door, and whenever the bell chimed for customers, he would lay his walking stick across their ankles before permitting them entrance. If their hands were unclean, he would invite them to wash in the basin of water he kept by the door. If they refused, they could not enter.

When Jan took Pawel to the bookshop down in Old Town, they found the walking stick still there by the door in the umbrella stand. It was made of cherry wood, its ivory handle the white eagle of Poland. They stared at it, bemused. Tadeusz had hit people with the stick. Not hard—a light rap on the calf or thigh. Some understood him, and faithful customers found the tradition of washing up quite amusing. Tadeusz had always insisted that they were privileged to have the opportunity to read through a nobleman's library. He made many enemies and kept few friends. He was not unkind; there was nothing personal in his petty tyrannies, but he was definitely the ruler of this miniature kingdom.

In his last years, while the outside world was falling into torture and madness, shouting over countless old and looming crimes, Tadeusz shuffled about the shop in carpet slippers, climbed his rolling stepladder for obscure titles, and slept in his chair while the neighborhood urchins stole *zlotys* and mint candies from his desktop. In the end, like a king going into exile, he departed.

*   *   *

Pawel's inheritance turned out to be a collection of a few thousand books that not many people wanted, and a small number of icons. The name of the business was an embarrassment. He winced when he saw its gilded wooden letters above the door of the shop: *Dom Madrosci,* House of Wisdom. He had forgotten how much he disliked those words. So pretentious. So very much the arrogant tone that was typical of the Polish upper classes. If Tadeusz had been even the least bit wise in his dealings with people, the name of the business would not have been so ironic. But then, who was Pawel to judge him for failure in human relationships?

One of his first acts as proprietor was to remove the letters and have them replaced with something more discreet. He used the Greek word *sophia*, for wisdom.

Zofia

KSIEGARNIA ANTYKWARIAT

*Perfect!*, he thought to himself. *Language bridges the gulf between peoples, yet it can also separate them. Let them jump to their conclusions. Obscure and reveal. Reveal and obscure. Only the scholarly will be irritated. Most others will think I have named it for my nonexistent wife.*

The new name did bring in the curious, but there was not much for them to buy. Tadeusz's mind had become distracted during his final months, and he had failed to replenish the shelves as they emptied. The place had been undusted for eons. The financial records were in complete disorder. It took Pawel two years to get the business functioning again. Little by little the number of customers increased. People occasionally came into the shop just to see the walking stick, to smile at it and remember, but few of them purchased books. From time to time, woebegone poets and writers of the obscure Polish kind would linger, spend hours hunting in the stacks, and purchase volumes that even Pawel considered of no worth. Doubtless, they found things in them that his eyes could not see.

He was, on good days, hospitable. He poured tea. He engaged in cautious literary exchanges. Of course, it was necessary to repel the repeated overtures of friendship offered by sincere young intellectuals, male and female. So many of them found him "interesting". But he did not ever again wish to expose his heart to the pain it had suffered in Paris and Berlin. He despised people who were attracted to him. He knew that only his image was "interesting". He knew that if they were to see beneath the shell of his handsome exterior, they would find a man full of holes, riddled with doubts and negations. His only certainty was that no savior—human or otherwise—would be interested in him.

In the years just prior to the German invasion, the business began to show a modest profit. Indeed, Pawel wondered if his sensitivities and failures might have a purpose after all—a kind of rearguard action against all that he had come to loathe in

Paris. In late 1936 he was possessed by a whim to launch *Zofia Press*. He used it to print a collection of Kaszubian folk tales and an anthology of unknown poets (all of whom, he had to confess, were distinguished only by being customers of his shop). He also published a translation of Vladimir Soloviev's tale of the Antichrist from *War, Progress, and the End of History*. Why this little extract so interested him he could not say. He was intrigued, he supposed, by the dialogue between the absolutely powerful and the weak of the earth. Perhaps it recalled, as well, the apocalypse painted by the old man in Vienna. None of the three titles sold more than a few hundred copies, but the remainders helped fill the shelves. Their failure did not trouble him. He no longer aspired to any kind of human success. He had no desires to paint, to be loved, or to be great. He was content to be a mediocre man. His calling, if one could call it that, was to be the world's last archivist of futile tales.

Even so, he was still unhappy. He did not trust his fellow human beings. He could not forgive those who had betrayed him, and as he observed with a cold analytical eye the thunderclouds boiling just across the border to the west, he sensed that a great many more unforgivable events were soon to occur. Despite the high drama of the massing political unrest in Europe, he was haunted by a growing ennui, a sense of futility. Although his life was set in a certain order, his work provided little satisfaction and his leisure hours were empty. He felt no pleasure in anything, and thus during the momentous year of 1938 he began to ponder the attractiveness of death, believing that nothingness was release from the intolerable imprisonment of his self. Seeing his misery, his brothers urged him to return to the sacraments. He replied with a look of wordless contempt.

One night in mid-August he stood on a bridge over the Vistula and leaned toward the water, but lacking the will to hurl himself in, drew back. With trembling legs he returned to Sophia House and sat in the darkened parlor. After some hours of mute anguish, he began to yearn for even a transitory respite from the mood of despair. He considered doing what his brothers had long suggested. More than once they had told him he should make a pilgrimage to the shrine of the Mother of God at Czestochowa. He understood their motives. They were gambling on a miracle of transformation that would relieve them of their chronic worry over their shadow brother. They wanted "God" to fix him. Of course he felt no compulsion to feed this shallow concern of theirs. Yet a change of scene was not unreasonable, after all, even if it were only an escape from their well-intentioned nagging, their frowns, their oft-repeated "poor Pawel"—their cloying anxiety that merely underlined his sense of failure.

His single visit with his mother that summer brought no consolation, for she was suffering from brain fever and did not recognize him. She clung to Jan and called him "Papa". She died a year before the Germans invaded and was buried at Mazowiecki.

For weeks he pondered the journey to Czestochowa—and a shorter one as well. The graveyards were nearby, full of realism. Life was short. Life was absurd. Life was carnivorous—no, omnivorous. Although in the past he had occasionally observed the curious twists and turns of fate, had noted that life did at times cast up surprises on the beaches of a permanently stormy sea—debris from shipwrecks, empty shells, and other marine life of astonishing beauty—still, these were the exceptions that proved the rule. Life was dangerous and always fatal. Yet, he admitted, one must not reject out of hand the possibility that there was some hidden meaning in the surprises. Such a thought was possible, of course, only in a trough between the pounding waves.

Thus, in one such trough, he took the train to Czestochowa, despite his reasonable certainty that God did not exist, despite his conviction that if God did exist he would have no use for the flotsam of humanity such as Pawel Tarnowski. At the Jasna Gora monastery he went through the motions of faith that he recalled from childhood, that is, the physical motions. He knelt and stood at the proper moments. He made the gestures that he now believed to be purely cultural artifacts but that he could not entirely abandon, respecting at least the feelings of those who still believed, the crowd of humble pilgrims around him who gazed with unquestioning fervor at the altar and the icons.

Later, as he knelt before the icon of the Black Madonna, he felt nothing but emptiness. He glanced up at her face and thought that she was cold and somber. He saw the two gashes on one cheek, which for some reason the monks had not repaired—an ancient wound that had taken on historical significance. Then, as if by an optical illusion, her countenance softened and her eyes returned his look with great tenderness.

"I too have received blows", she said. "And a sword pierced my heart."

Startled by the intensity of this imaginary and wholly one-sided conversation, he drew back sharply and stood up. Had these thoughts come from himself? Yes, surely they must have. The subconscious, of course. At that moment, inexplicably, a rush of feeling returned to his inner world. He longed to weep. To cry out. It hurt terribly, like blood beginning to move in a frozen limb, yet there was a harsh exuberance in it that promised the return of life. And in this state, he was struck by the possibility that whatever was happening to him might have come from a source beyond the limits of his enclosed self. He staggered into a confessional.

The confessor was young. He was not one of the Hermits of St. Paul who lived at the shrine, but a priest who had come on pilgrimage. He spoke Polish with a German accent. He was firm but kindly in his manner, and, after giving Pawel absolution, he instructed him to attend Mass immediately and to receive Communion for fortification and healing. He also asked if they might meet face to face. Reluctantly, Pawel agreed.

When the last bell of Mass was rung and the sanctuary deserted, he went out onto the bright mountain and found there the face he had seen through the translucent screen of the confessional.

"I am your penitent", he said to the priest, who wore the brown robe of the Franciscans.

"I am Father Andrei", he replied.

"My name is Pawel. Why did you want to speak with me?"

"I felt that you need to discuss certain things about your life."

"My life?"

"You have done well to confess and to be reunited with the Lord. He is love. He will not abandon you. But we creatures are always free to abandon Him, is it not so?"

"And so you deduced from my sins that I am a betrayer", Pawel said, his eyes and voice guarded.

The priest looked at him gravely. "I cannot discuss a confession with you. I am bound to silence unto death."

"If I ask you to discuss my confession with me, may you then do so?"

"Yes, then. And only then."

"Then I release you to speak."

The priest was silent. He turned toward a path and began to walk, beckoning Pawel to accompany him. Pawel noticed that he limped badly and that there was an ugly scar on the cheek that had been turned away from him in the confessional.

"Will you tell me", said the priest, "why a person such as you would wish to dispose of himself like so much garbage?"

After hesitating, Pawel replied in a low voice, "The logic of self-destruction could not be debated. My life was worthless."

"Worthless? Why did you think your life was worthless?"

Pawel looked down at the ground and remained silent. Three children ran across the leaf-strewn hill in front of them, dragging a reluctant kite, which twisted and bounced along the ground. Their melodious cries faded into abstractions.

Eventually he looked up, though not at the priest, and told the story of his life to the sky.

\* \* \*

Pawel omitted much of his childhood and youth and mainly described his Paris years and all that followed. When he was finished, he glanced toward the children running about the hill and noticed that they now had their kite in the air. They were cheerfully quarreling over who would hold the string.

"Who are you most angry at?" the priest asked.

Pawel frowned, pondering the question a minute before replying. "Strange to say, I am most angry at Photosphoros. Even more than Goudron. Even more than the master of the painting academy. Why? Why that Russian priest?"

"We expect so much from a man of faith, do we not? Especially a priest. He is an icon of the Father. And when he proves himself less than God, as he inevitably must, it is as if an icon has been defaced. That was a hard test for you. A very hard test."

"Was it? I have not thought of it as a test."

"If one is called to an unusual work in the Kingdom of God, it is necessary that the roots of pride be burned out as soon as possible, otherwise pride would destroy him. Pride is the deathbringer. It ruins everything, even the greatest works conceived with the highest ideals."

"I am not called to an unusual work, and certainly not for God."

"Does any man know himself so well that he can make such a statement with certainty?"

"I should know myself by now."

"It is my belief that no one is without value. Even the most wretched—"

"Even one as wretched as myself? Thank you, Father, but my experience belies your words. Man is a predator. Man is a wolf to man."

"Some become wolves because they do not know the value of a soul, nor do they know their own souls."

"Photosphoros seemed to know me very well. With such little effort he read my soul."

"If he read your soul, he read it incorrectly. Still, God used him."

"What do you mean? How did God use him? Does God speak through foul-tempered old men?"

"Usually he speaks through kinder voices. But he uses everything for the good of those who love him. It was an old man's weakness. Do not take it so much to heart."

"I cannot seem to rid myself of the memory."

"The memory must not be disposed of. It must be understood."

"Understood? What good would that do? I hold onto scraps of hope, but really, there is not much inside this penitent worth saving."

He looked directly at the priest to see how he had taken this. The priest returned his gaze steadily. They walked on, beginning for a third time the circuit of the grounds.

"Pawel, do you see the root of the cycle? It is here."

"What do you mean, *cycle*?"

"Unforgiveness locks us into unbelief, and unbelief deepens the unforgiveness. It revolves endlessly unless we make a stop. Unless we forgive."

"Forgiveness?" Pawel murmured coldly. "What is forgiveness?"

"Forgiveness", said the priest, "is a key."

"A key?" Pawel said tonelessly. "A key implies that a door exists."

"Or a narrow gate."

Father Andrei paused. Taking a seat on a park bench, he gestured that Pawel should sit beside him. Pawel sat down stiffly and watched the children, who now had the kite soaring higher in the air, arching toward the dome of the shrine.

"We wish to be *worthy* of being saved", Father Andrei continued. "Which is another way of saying that we, every one of us, whether we know it or not, wish to be our own god, that is, to save ourselves. We want paradise without his Cross, forgetting that the Cross is the only way to reenter the original harmony we lost in the Fall of Man. *This* is the narrow gate."

"I see no gate. I see only the walls of a prison."

"We do not like to be poor, Pawel. Yet it is this very poverty that opens one to the life of God. It is this that cracks open the prison walls."

"Why is it so complicated? Why does God not fix it all?"

"It is not complicated. God has saved us, but he will not force salvation upon us. Love never forces. Love thrives only in freedom. We must choose to accept what he offers."

"I have received no offers."

"Have you not? I think God sent you messengers: Rouault in Paris. The old painter in Vienna."

"Messengers? I did not recognize them as such."

"Why did you not?"

"I don't know", Pawel replied uneasily. "I trust no one. I hate being in need."

"But all human beings are in need."

"I want only to be left alone."

The priest said nothing. He let Pawel listen to the contradiction in this declaration.

"I have always felt that my soul is exposed", Pawel burst out in a harsh whisper. "I have no armor, no clothing. When I was naked before the art students, it was the greatest suffering of my life. Why was that so?"

The priest looked pensively at Pawel.

Pawel swallowed, perplexed by a fear rising in his breast. He recalled the little incident by the fish pond in Zakopane, the night Great-Uncle had undressed him—to dry him. This memory was quickly swept aside by the more recent stripping in Paris.

"Why do you think I am—" he asked in a subdued voice, "—why am I so unusually sensitive on that point?"

"It seems you are unusually sensitive about many points, Pawel. I confess that I am puzzled by the mixture of sensitivity and naïveté in your nature—yes, you have spoken of both during the telling of your story."

Pawel shrugged. "I am no longer naïve. I know enough about human nature."

The priest smiled gently. "It seems to me that you are especially sensitive about your being. Is it because you are unsure about your being? Do you not know that you are loved?"

"Love? When I stood before the eyes of those students, love was beyond my comprehension. Dead. Perhaps it never existed."

"Love did not die. It was eclipsed for a time."

Pawel slowly turned to the priest. Peering at him, he said, "Why did you ask me to speak with you?"

"We are close to the same age. I saw in you how my own life might have gone if circumstances had been different."

"What do you mean?"

"I was a lonely child, no brothers or sisters. My parents were teachers in Dresden. They were intelligent, good people. One uncle was a bishop, another a representative in the Reichstag. My parents fought hard for the development of a Catholic vision in German politics. Though my father was German, my mother was a Polish Jew who eventually converted. This meant some suffering for me as a boy.

"When I was eight years old I was given a singular grace. It occurred one day when I was beaten by classmates on my way home from school and lay bleeding on the steps of the cathedral. I understood that I was a despised thing. I had never been hated before.

"I looked up to the cross suspended over the city and the world, and I saw Jesus nailed to it. Then he spoke into my heart, spoke without words. It was not rational thought, you understand; it was rather a *perception*. He told me that no human love would ever fill the hunger within me. Though every genuine love is from God, it is an incarnation, a reflection. In this world it will always be imperfect. His love is perfection. It contains everything. For the first time in my life I *saw* this love not as a theological abstraction. It was real—*ach,* our poor words!"

"Unfortunately, it is still an abstraction for me", said Pawel. "But you have not yet explained why you wished to speak with me."

"That same voice spoke when you were confessing."

Pawel looked at the other sharply, wondering if he was really a priest.

"The voice said, *Here is my little son whom I love greatly. He has been broken. He will do a unique good in this world, but first he will be tested by fire.*"

"I do not believe this! I do not believe this!" Pawel said vehemently. He stood up abruptly, his hands trembling, and without saying goodbye, strode away through the town of Czestochowa. He did not understand his reaction and brooded in great distress as he returned to Warsaw.

*   *   *

A few months later Pawel noticed, quite by accident, the face of a Franciscan friar gazing at him from a poster on a billboard near the university. The name was Father Andrei. The scar was the same. He was scheduled to speak that night on the subject of National Socialism. At the last moment, Pawel decided to attend, and squeezed into the back row of a concert hall in the music faculty.

It was a stirring lecture. The priest described the camp of Sachsenhausen, where he had been imprisoned for reading from a pulpit the two papal encyclicals against National Socialism.

"The Holy Father is working very hard to preserve the freedom to practice our faith in the areas that will soon come under the domination of this pagan movement. On Palm Sunday of 1937, his apostolic letter *Mit brennender Sorge* was read from every pulpit in Germany. It threw Hitler into fits of rage. The pope's letter made very clear that National Socialism is a pseudoreligious movement, idolatrous, completely unacceptable to civilized men. He pointed out that 'Whoever identifies, by pantheistic confusion, God and the universe is not a believer in God. Whoever substitutes a dark and impersonal destiny for the personal God denies thereby the Wisdom and the Providence of God.' Taking up each point of propaganda in the Party doctrine, the Holy Father refuted it by comparison with authentic doctrine."

The priest did not describe his personal experiences at length, and of his escape he said almost nothing, though the students and professors pummeled him for more details. He kept to the subject of ideological struggle and gradually brought the assembly to where he wanted them.

"Catholicism is a religion of absolute truths", he told them. "No Catholic is permitted to vote for an evil law or an evil ruler, even if they appear to be lesser evils than, say, economic or social disorder. One cannot compromise a part of the truth without the eventual collapse of the whole. I am here tonight to warn you that this is happening in Germany. Great evils are soon to come in the wake of that collapse."

The meeting ended very late, and Pawel was among the last to leave. Father Andrei was packing his briefcase when Pawel approached him.

"My brother", said the priest. "So good to see you again."

"I wish to apologize, Father, for my behavior at Czestochowa. I was rude to you when I ran off."

"Yes, we run at times."

"Do you have a few moments to talk with me?"

"Of course. Let's go for a walk."

They went outside into a night full of stars and strolled toward the friary, where the priest was staying.

"Have you been constant in the practice of your faith since we last met?" he asked in an inoffensive tone.

"Yes", Pawel replied. "Though my heart is not in it."

"Ah, the heart", mused Father Andrei.

"I live my life. I expect nothing from it."

"Ah", he said again. "But what is the heart?"

"I do not know."

"Do you still wrestle with thoughts of self-destruction?"

"No. That's gone."

"Good. Keep praying. Do not drift from the sacraments."

Pawel changed the subject: "Are you living here for a time? Or will you return to Czestochowa?"

"My superior believes that the storm is coming within a year or two. I am wanted in Germany by the Geheime Staatspolizei, and if they come here, I will be captured. He is sending me to Canada."

"You do not sound happy about this."

The priest looked thoughtfully at Pawel.

"It is God's will, so I am happy."

"But what do you feel?"

"As for my feelings, to go is peace, to stay is peace. It is not important for me to know."

"And what does your heart say about this, Father?"

The priest flashed a look at Pawel and smiled.

"What does your *voice* say?" Pawel pressed.

The priest was silent.

"Tell me, Father, why do voices never speak to me?"

"A soul must be well seasoned to discern among voices. There are many voices that come to us from the unknown, and the Evil One is capable of disguises. It is important always to ask which voice speaks the truth with love. That is the voice you should listen to. Even so, it is better to hear no voices."

"Why?"

"Because *faith* is what God desires most from us. Moreover, we poor creatures are easily deceived. That is why he permits us to hear with this sense only in extraordinary circumstances."

"You describe a world of shifting images and illusions, mirages, mazes. How can one trust anything?"

"It is a grace. It is entirely a gift to hear the voice, and another gift to recognize it as genuine."

They paused, and the priest looked around the square. A young cavalry officer rode past on a magnificent bay gelding, its hoofs clopping noisily on the cobblestones. They observed its passage.

"Pawel, it is unlikely that we will meet again on this earth. So perhaps it is not wrong if I reveal something to you. Your path and mine are curiously entwined. You struggle against despair, which is perhaps the greatest temptation of our century. All manner of evil flows from this primeval wound in man, this conviction that he is absolutely alone, this terror that his sufferings are meaningless. Is this not also your fear?"

"Yes."

"Rest assured, my brother, that it is not so. It all has meaning."

"How can you say this with such certainty?"

"If I tell you a story, will you promise that you will never repeat it?"

Pawel nodded.

"In the camp I was tortured. It was the worst. There was degradation as well as physical torment. They wished to break the sense of manhood, you see. This scar, this bad leg are only the surface. At the very lowest moment, when I thought I had lost everything, the will to endure, the ability to pray, when I was only a sack of broken flesh containing a broken mind, God sent a gift. A sign. The Mother appeared in my cell. I saw her with my eyes. More than an interior light, she was visual as well. She was accompanied by two angels. She was weeping. I saw my guardian angel also, and he too was grieving. What light flooded my heart in that darkest hour!

"She held in her hands a crown of thorns, and the tip of each thorn was dripping blood. The crown glowed with powerful light, radiating a color that is inexpressibly beautiful, a color that does not exist in this world. She offered me the crown. *This is the crown of martyrdom*, she said. *Do you accept it?* And I replied with joy, *Oh, yes, my Lady*. For, you see, at that moment death would have been a blessed release from torment.

"Then she withdrew the crown a little and offered me another. It was of purest gold, and it shone with a very bright light, though a different color I had never seen before. *This is the crown of obedience*, she said.

*I do not understand*, I said to her. *Is it not possible for me to choose both?*

*It is*, she said. *These crowns fit one within the other. They are always together. You will suffer much in this place, but your martyrdom is reserved for the time of the end. You have years of life ahead, and your witness is to be for the strengthening of many souls. Do you accept?* And I replied, *Yes*.

"Then she placed the crown of obedience upon my head and placed the crown of martyrdom next to her own heart. With that, the vision ended."

"The subconscious is capable of . . ." Pawel mumbled, gesturing with his hands.

"Yes, I know all the arguments", said the priest, stopping before a gate. "Ah, look! We are already here, and it took no time at all. The future will be like that, my little brother—come and gone before we have time to be masters of it."

"But how will I know . . . ?"

"It is necessary to know only one thing: God is with you. Trust him. Do not be afraid."

# 6

My Kahlia,

Unexpected events have occurred. I have a guest who will not be here for very long. How to find a passage to safety for him? It is practically impossible, but Bronek may know a way.

Over breakfast this morning my guest told me, in a courteous manner, that today is his people's New Year—Rosh ha-Shanah. I asked him to spell it out for me, and he did so, writing it on the border of a journal from Brussels, 1933 (ironically, beside an article reassuring its readers that Hitler would never start a war in Europe). When he licked the tip of my indelible pencil and bent over this scribal task, it struck me full force that never before have I been thrown into such close proximity with the ultraorthodox, though of course I know many Jews. He is so different in culture and temperament from Sara (who is thoroughly modern) and my lawyer Bahlkoyv (who is liberal), and Kohn who used to sell papers at the corner (devout but ordinary). Ordinary—yes, but they are gone, and now this apparition lives with me.

How alien these black-suited Hasidim! Yet the boy's clumsy attempts at communication take the form of universal gestures, the common language of man. Turning the paper around for me to read, he smiled at me shyly, and pronounced the soft Jewish syllables slowly, precisely—teaching me—assuming that I would desire to learn. My tongue bumbled over the pronunciation and made him laugh. Such instantaneous delight from such a somber face. How like the young everywhere: caught in the snare of a vicious war, yet impelled by the enthusiasm and guilelessness of youth.

My position is now made precarious. He must leave, and soon.


The door chimes banged against the glass, and Pawel glanced up to see a woman he recognized from the parish, Mrs. Lewicki, scowling at him, clutching her coat lapels over a hidden burden.

"Pan Tarnowski, I wish to sell you some things of great value." She opened her coat and thrust a bundle of books onto his desk.

He examined them, four titles, every one of them with damaged spines. The first, Dostoevsky's *The Possessed*, translated into Polish, had a trite message scrawled on the frontispiece and badly yellowed paper—obviously cheap newsprint. Printed in 1912 at Saint Petersburg. The second, Cyprian Norwid's *Fate*, published in Warsaw shortly after the turn of the century, with an introduction by the critic Przesmycki. Ink stains and torn pages smelling of mold. The third, Leonov's *Badgers* in Polish, printed in 1924 by Shabashnikov the Soviet publisher. Damn, a communist. But decent typesetting and good binding.

"Where did you find this book?" Pawel asked, without showing emotion.

"It was Janusz's, from the winter he studied in Zurich. A professor gave it to him. You understand why I have to sell my son's books", she pleaded. "I haven't heard from him since the Germans came. My husband has spotted fever. I need medicine, food. There is no work! You will buy these?"

Pain crossed Pawel's face, and he raised his arms helplessly.

"I have no money."

"You have money!" she cried angrily. "You are rich. Your brother has a good clock business. Your uncle left you a fortune!"

"Look around this room and see my fortune. And as for my wealthy brother, he has a wife and child to feed. My sister-in-law is . . ." He was about to say *Jewish*, but refrained.

"Then give me some food, aspirin, anything", she pleaded.

He rummaged through his belongings and returned with a bar of Castile soap, a cabbage riddled with wormholes, and a blue jar containing half a dozen sedatives, which Sara had given him during the worst period of his suicidal crisis. To these he added a few small coins, the only money he had left in the till. He showed her the empty cashbox.

She took the things and left without a word.

He had not looked at the fourth book. It was an older Russian work from the late eighteen hundreds. A fine Cyrillic font on good rag paper, with tinted photographs of icons. MOCKBA 1897. An examination of the icon painter Andrei Rublëv. The name was unknown to him. Rublëv? Painstakingly, he translated a few lines of text:

> Andrei Rublëv was a monk and icon painter, born in Russia in the year 1360. He grew up during the wars against the Tartars, and as a young man placed himself under the spiritual direction of Saint Nikon, successor to Saint Sergius at the monastery of the Holy Trinity near Moscow. Little is known about his artistic training other than that he studied for a time under Theophanes the Greek. Rublëv is universally considered to be the greatest master of Russian icon painting. . . .

The proof was in the images themselves. He fell silent before them. They were like wells. The eyes, especially the eyes, were silently, eloquently full.

Pawel breathed again, and realized he had not inhaled for several seconds. Here was the visual equivalent of what he had felt in front of the icon of the Madonna at Czestochowa, a resurgence of life, a somber and brilliant light. A mystery so deep and so high that you either ran from it or you knelt in reverence.

There was a loud thump from the floor above.

Two browsers were in the shop but they did not look up from their books.

Avoiding notice, Pawel went to the storeroom at the back, climbed the stairs, passed through his bedroom to the curtained closet, and stepped up the last flight to the attic.

He found the fugitive shifting a box.

"You must be absolutely silent", Pawel whispered vehemently. "You could be the death of us both!"

"I am sorry", said the boy. "I dropped a book by accident."

"A book? Where did you get a book?"

He pointed to the stack of crates by the landing. The lid of the topmost was open.

"I was going mad up here. It helps if I read. Please, do you mind?"

"No, no, of course not."

"They are Jewish books, Yiddish, Hebrew. *Talmud, Midrash.* You have a sacred library here. A whole *yeshiva.*"

"I'm sure they can't be a Jewish library, because the man who sold them to me was a Catholic lawyer from Lodz."

The lawyer, Pawel now recalled, was an associate of Bahlkoyv. They had negotiated the purchase in October 1939, just weeks after the invasion.

*Several people have asked me to dispose of their collections in exchange for British pounds or American notes, if this is possible*, the lawyer had said.

Of course by then it was no longer possible to obtain foreign currency. Pawel had none.

*You have a reputation for discernment, Pan Tarnowski. This shipment is being thrown upon your mercy.*

The lawyer asked a fair price in Polish money. Pawel accepted.

*You will find that the contents are more than you might expect. Some of the volumes are not representative of the bulk of the material. Guard this treasure well. If circumstances permit, I will repurchase them, at a reasonable profit for you, when the Germans have been pushed back.*

At the time, they had agreed that the books would remain in

temporary storage at Sophia House, not for sale—for a few months only. The lawyer was certain that the British would swiftly repel Hitler's grandiose plans for Poland. Thus, impelled more by cultural loyalty than by good business sense, Pawel had accepted the twenty wooden crates without examining their contents.

In autumn of 1940, he had unscrewed one of the lids and taken a cursory glance inside, only to find cheap penny novels, badly written biographies of saints, revisionist Soviet history, the Gospels in Chinese (unreadable), some poorly illustrated children's books from Amerika (also unreadable). The most dismal mishmash of incompatible titles he had ever seen. He had dismissed the purchase as his one great error of judgment in the history of Sophia House. *Treasure!* he had grumbled in disgust. Assuming that he had been cheated, as he had so often during his life, he looked no deeper.

Now he completely unpacked the box.

"There were some worthless things on top", the boy said. "But underneath, see, *The Chumash* in Hebrew with the classical Jewish commentaries! A great find, is it not?"

"I do not read Hebrew", Pawel murmured.

Most of the other books were of the same sort. As he proceeded to unpack more boxes, he realized that this must be the library of a Scripture scholar, disguised for transportation from Lodz to Warsaw.

Realizing that he had left the shop untended far too long, he hastened downstairs. His two customers had departed. On his desk was evidence that in his absence a third had come and gone.

Dear Tarnowski,
I found the poet Slowacki while you were invisible. The price was written in pencil on the flyleaf, so I have taken the liberty of purchasing the book without your knowledge. I hope this is not too overbearing of me. Money enclosed.
With regards,
Dr. Haftmann

Haftmann! Oh, no! While he was upstairs opening a mine of Jewish literature, a German major of the Reich Culture Chamber was down in the shop looking for words of enlightenment from a Catholic prophet-poet!

Alarmed by the narrow escape, Pawel stood staring at the note until he had calmed himself. Then, seized by a thought, he pocketed the money, put the "back in ten minutes" sign on the window, and went out onto the street. Haftmann was nowhere to be seen. He locked the door and walked hastily toward the main thoroughfare, turned left, and proceeded to the apartment block of Mrs. Lewicki. He knew her residence because they both regularly attended Mass in the parish and usually returned to their respective homes by the same route. He found her apartment on the second floor. There was a crucifix on the hall-side of the door.

When she opened to his knock, her face instantly writhed in anger.

"It is too late! Our exchange was final!" She would have squeezed the door shut if her strength had been greater than Pawel's.

"One moment, please, Pani Lewicki", he said, pushing the money through the opening. "I did not realize the full value of the books. Here is the balance of what is owed to you."

She looked at it, took it, and closed the door without a word.

\* \* \*

Haftmann. Never was there a more well-bred gentleman. Would that all invaders were this sort! Three years ago he had entered the shop for the first time. He wore his gray Wehrmacht uniform with a regal, though diffident, bearing. Soldiers followed him around, gathering up the titles he pointed out, mostly anti-Nazi literature and anything with Hebrew letters on it. All periodicals were confiscated. He deposited a stack of German propaganda newspapers printed in Polish.

Tall, silver-haired, courtly, he introduced himself as Major Kurt Haftmann, and offered his hand. Pawel turned away and did not take it.

"Of course, I understand your feelings perfectly", said the German in fluent Polish. His voice was deep, refined, hinting at erudition. "In your position I would be furious. If it is any consolation to you, I suffer no little anguish over the performance of my duty."

*Anguish?*

"I was a professor of literature before the Party insisted that I help the Reich in its cultural needs. Actually, I am a *doctor* of literature. I am not a soldier—only a hired consultant, really, just a layman. Do not hate me with such absolute conviction until you hear me out."

Sheer curiosity persuaded Pawel to listen.

Haftmann gestured the soldiers outside.

"You no doubt expect us to behave like the Teutonic barbarians you consider us to be. Many of my compatriots have not failed to meet your expectations. But there are others among us who do not like the extremes to which some in the Party would take us. Personally, I am disgusted by the destruction of any cultural material. Degenerate or not, it is art. This is especially true of writing, which is my first love. The war will not last long. We are winning spectacular victories everywhere. Nothing can stop the will of the Führer. This is a fact of history. It is destiny. But no vision is perfect, and I expect that when the war is over we will view the preservation of various branches of literature with greater tolerance."

Pawel uttered his first words in a subdued voice. He spoke in correct, if laborious, German:

"Hundreds of your own writers have been burned. You have heard of Thomas Mann, Heinrich Mann, Brecht, Zweig, Heine, Werfel?"

"Yes, and I am appalled by the destruction of their books.

Because of this I wish to help you, and I ask you to help me."

"Help you?"

"You understand that this conversation has not occurred. Truth is a luxury we cannot afford at this particular moment in history."

"It is a necessity we cannot afford to do without at any point in history."

The German smiled ironically. "Ah, I see you are a brave man."

Pawel stared at him without replying.

"The extreme elements intend to destroy everything that falls outside the parameters of their concepts. These are tragically limited parameters. My official mandate is to seek out and to destroy libraries and works of art that propagate an anti-Aryan view of existence. I know exactly how I must appear to you— I look the perfect monster. But I have as great a love of literature as you, perhaps more so. Please understand, I wish to *save* the great works of civilization for the future generations."

"Your Goering said that when he hears the word *kultur* he draws his pistol."

"The *kultur-kampf* is a complex problem. I will say only this: Herr Goering and Herr Goebbels will not always be with us. Better minds will one day make the policies. The Führer, of course, is presently occupied with military strategy, and thus certain cultural questions must wait for the post-war *risorgimento*."

"How do you want me to help you?"

"I see by your expression that your question is a formality. You have decided not to help me in any way whatsoever, because you think I am a deceiver. You have the fervid glitter of the outraged idealist in your eyes, and I know it well, having observed it on my own face frequently. I know that you cannot yet trust me, but I ask you to at least listen.

"I repeat, the Reich wishes to destroy everything outside its strictly defined notion of culture. I believe that one day the parameters will return to normal, perhaps within ten or twenty years. One day it will surely come."

"Why are you so sure?"

"Because always there must come the counterthesis. Have you read Hegel?"

"No."

"Surely you have a philosophy section here", said the German, casting his eyes about the shelves. "This bookshop is in a class above the others I have visited in Warsaw. You cater to the cultured, to the philo*sophe*, do you not?"

"Here you will find classical philosophy and Catholic philosophy", Pawel murmured coldly.

"You still don't grasp it, do you?" the German replied, eyeing him carefully. "I am trying to tell you that when you see me you see two men. The official who is bound to destroy what you hold sacred, and the inner man who intends to save it."

"Which are you? You cannot possibly be both."

"Spoken like a true zealot!" Haftmann smiled again. "It is quite possible to be both, but I assure you that the inner man is the authentic one. The official will go through the motions; he will destroy many useless titles and some valuable ones, of which there are numerous copies safely put away."

"Why don't you confiscate everything?"

"Total confiscation would drive all treasure underground. Even if we were to scour every square centimeter of the occupied nations in search of banned books, we could never succeed in finding them all. People would die to preserve them. That is where you play your part.

"Here to this shop, people will come one by one, without drawing any attention, and sell you their treasure. You will remain open for business. All I ask is that you keep your eye open for any work of exceptional quality, books of permanent value to the coming generations, and ensure that I may consider them for purchase—*purchase*, I say. I do not have sufficient funds to offer a subsidy for your business, or to pay you for your help in the form of a stipend. I can tell by the contempt in your very transparent face that this would defeat my case instantly, wouldn't it? You would interpret it as bribery or collaboration."

Pawel looked away.

"I cannot help you", he muttered.

"Before the war you sold books. You will continue to sell books. Nothing changes. Where is the compromise in such an arrangement?"

He was right, of course. Provided he was telling the truth and the procurement of fugitive literature was, indeed, for the purpose of saving it. The entire question turned upon the axis of the personal integrity of this *Doktor* Haftmann. Now here was a paradox. Obviously Haftmann was a Nazi. And he had some kind of power, which was suspicious in itself, a definite argument against him. And by his own admission he was a split man. Could one ever trust such a creature?

"You don't believe me", the German said.

Pawel did not answer.

"You don't have to believe me. Merely wait. You will see that I do nothing to harm your shop."

He handed Pawel a sheet of paper stamped with a purple swastika.

"However, this document informs *Zofia Press* that it is strictly illegal to publish books, pamphlets, or copies of any printed material. This is law throughout Poland and all the governed territories. My apologies. But you may take consolation in the fact that the bookselling branch of your firm is permitted to remain open for business."

Haftmann picked up a copy of Soloviev's book.

"You published this?"

"Yes."

"I haven't heard of him. Who is he?"

"He was a Russian religious thinker who died in nineteen hundred."

"What is it about?"

"The author was convinced that the advent of the Antichrist was upon us in this century."

"Ah, then you must surely believe that *we* are the Antichrist. Or perhaps the Soviets?"

"You are both forerunners", Pawel blurted.

"I see." Haftmann smiled with one side of his mouth.

Unable to stop himself, Pawel tried to explain. "Soloviev depicts the reign of an Antichrist who is so thoroughly convincing, and appears to be so good for humanity, that he will be considered the savior of mankind. The Christians and Jews who oppose him will seem to be the enemies of God. Soloviev wished to warn—"

"I grasp your not-so-subtle point: the Reich does not for an instant seem good for mankind. Am I correct?"

Pawel said nothing.

"And of course, since we are brutality incarnate, it is not possible that we are *the* Beast. Yes, yes, I have read the Apocalypse of Saint John."

"You are a Catholic?"

"No. I was a Lutheran in my youth—a fervent one." He laughed. "You might say I believe in culture now."

With that, he made his departure, saying as he went out the front door, "Trust me."

Pawel's first act of trust was to burn the propaganda newspapers.

A week later Haftmann was back. He entered like an ordinary customer and browsed through the shelves for an hour. Pawel pretended he did not notice him.

"This is marvelous!" said the Major excitedly when he came to the desk, waving a book under Pawel's nose. "An early Hamman!"

Pawel nodded.

"Do you know him, Tarnowski?"

"I have read a page or two."

"He is a solitary figure in German literature. One of the great ones. Hardly anyone knows about him, but he is like Goethe or Schiller!"

Pawel regarded him thoughtfully. This German officer, dressed up in his disguise, was behaving like a little boy at Christmas.

"Listen, listen to this! It's from the *Aesthetica*: 'Speaking is a translation—from the language of angels into the language of men—so that thoughts become words, objects become names, images become signs.' Do you see it?"

The words of the writer were oblique and out of context, but the one thing Pawel did see was that Haftmann might be exactly what he said he was. He was indeed two men, and moreover, the inner one seemed to have the upper hand.

"Yes, I see."

"Please," he said, handing over payment, "I would like to examine anything by this author."

"As you wish", Pawel said reluctantly.

"Thank you. Also, if you would kindly put aside anything by Péguy or Pascal, Dostoevsky, and Bloy—I have not yet been able to find *La Femme pauvre*, you know. It is such a pleasure to read these prophets, so full of real blood. Also, I like that Englishman, Jones, though I must say he is a very difficult poet. I hear even his own countrymen cannot understand him, but I think it is because they do not know how to read properly. Every now and then he strikes a fabulous blaze of illumination in the mind with his images. Do you know *In Parenthesis*? A portrait of war—friends of mine in Britain smuggled it out to me—"

And so forth. It came all in a rush, and Pawel was momentarily overwhelmed. The enthusiasm, the densely packed information, the compulsive outburst of passion for abstractions. It was not unfamiliar—many of his customers were like this. He was still uneasy, but found it difficult not to be disarmed by this very, very odd Nazi.

*   *   *

Pawel closed up shop at four o'clock. It was dark and raining outside. The wind was blowing yellow leaves off the thrashing lime tree in the courtyard. On just such an afternoon, decades ago, he had pressed his face against the glass and watched.

"Uncle Tadeusz, the branches are waving goodbye to their leaves."

But Uncle Tadeusz had merely grunted at the five-year-old and told him not to mess the pane with his runny nose.

The bookseller Pawel Tarnowski went up to his living quarters and made a meal of vegetables, soup, the last of the black bread, and tea. When he brought it to the top of the attic stairs, he saw that David Schäfer was sitting on the floor, legs splayed out with stacks of books around him. The boy raised his hand in greeting.

Pawel grunted an acknowledgment and set the tray on a trunk.

"In the future, whenever you hear footsteps, you must hide", he said sternly. "Also, you must be very still during open hours. While I was downstairs in the shop this afternoon, I heard the water pipes running. It echoed all over the building."

"I am sorry, Pan Tarnowski", said the boy in a subdued voice. "I needed to wash. It has been a long time since I was able to clean myself."

Pawel made no comment, though he did notice that the atmosphere was now less offensive.

"The floors are thin", he murmured, relenting a little. "Many of my customers know that I live alone, and some of them will become suspicious."

They thought about this as they consumed their meal.

Again the boy wolfed his food, and again he looked ashamed.

"There wasn't much to eat during the last months", he breathed.

"You are thin. I see by your shawl and clothing that you are an ultra-orthodox Jew."

"We are the Hasidim."

"Yes, I know", Pawel replied curtly, trying not to resent his guest's presence. "Why is your hair so short? I thought you people wore it long."

"One day the Germans broke into our *yeshiva* and took all of us, teachers and students, into a busy street. They stripped us and mocked us for the passersby to see. They lined us up and hit us with rifles when we tried to cover our bodies for shame. Good people didn't look. Bad people looked. The Germans made a film of our nakedness. Through a loudspeaker they announced that the ghetto is necessary because Jews carry lice. Lice breed in hair, they said, so we must have our hair shaved. They shaved us bald and beat us and chased us away into the streets without clothing. It was a humiliation."

Distant gunshots tapped against the window. Pawel looked in the direction of the sound.

"It's getting bad in there. Do you have any family inside the ghetto?"

"No. They are gone. Thousands of people are taken every day. It depends on the number of trains."

"We must be more careful about avoiding detection. Fortunately the shops on either side are empty. They are boarded up. There is no one to hear you in those directions. You must never forget, however, that beneath your feet is sudden death."

"Where could I hide if an intruder comes by surprise?"

Pawel went to a side wall of the attic and rapped, then crossed the room and rapped on the facing wall.

"I thought we might cut a hole through to the other attics", he said. "But it's not possible; the stone goes all the way to the roof."

"Could we stack the wood crates at the far end, by the window? There are enough of them to make a wall almost as high as the ceiling. We could double or triple them—a fortress! I would leave a spy hole. If someone other than you comes up, I can be out the window and across the rooftops before they know I have been here."

"They would hear the window going up."

"I can be very fast. I can make a little room behind the boxes. I will sleep there. I need only a mattress and reading material. I can work. I am strong."

This was inaccurate.

"What work could you do for me that would not get us both into a labor camp?"

"At night I could sweep the shop below, wash dishes, mend things. Do you have a needle and thread? I see that your suit jacket is frayed badly at the elbows. I could make you a good patch from the fine cloth inside."

Pawel looked at his elbows. It was true, they were in disgraceful condition.

"Also, with your permission, I could go through these boxes carefully and separate the good books from those of little worth. Then you would not need to spend time on this."

Pawel pondered the suggestion. "If I give you paper, would you list the title, author, date of publication, and the condition of each book?"

"Of course!" The boy's eyes lit up with pleasure.

"There are bookseller's symbols for a volume's characteristics. Do you think you could learn them?"

"Then I may stay? It would take some time."

Pawel sighed. His solitude was precious to him, and he would sorely miss it. But what was the alternative? To send the boy out into the city, even under cover of dark, was almost certainly to condemn him to death. He would be caught before he had run ten blocks. Perhaps in a few months this child would be strong enough to attempt the flight from Warsaw. But for now his health must be rebuilt. Pawel faltered over the word *child*, for the visitor was almost as tall as he. He must get a message to Masha, begging her for extra food.

Like an unwelcome guest, the word *beautiful* also shot through his mind. And with it came the full realization that the face of the visitor had been fashioned in so harmonious, so perfect, a form that one wished to stare or to look away. He had studiously ignored the fact until this very moment. It struck Pawel suddenly that to permit the eyes to linger was a temptation to render him into an *objet d'art*. A beautiful thing, but still—a thing.

Averting his eyes, Pawel nodded abruptly. "Yes. You may stay."

The boy took Pawel's hand and squeezed it. He looked at the man with gratitude and affection. Both the look and the gesture were completely childlike.

"You are one of the *hasidei umot haolam*—a righteous Gentile."

"Me? Righteous?" Pawel laughed humorlessly.

"You are a tree of life for me, Pan Tarnowski. The Torah is the tree of life. Thus, the Torah lives in you!"

Pawel stood up, mumbled an excuse, and went downstairs to complete the day's records. His eyes refused to focus on the paperwork. Words tumbled confusedly through his mind: *Torah. Child. Tree of life. Righteous. Beautiful.*

Inexplicable fear wriggled up from a deep cavity. Fighting to retain his concentration, he read his way slowly through the text of the Rublëv book. The images quieted him eventually. The world ceased to reel. After midnight he went wearily to bed.

## 7

There were, of course, levels of fear. Pawel's present predicament jarred him from the chronic angst of his mental outlook
and directed his attention to the larger context of survival.
Habitually he looked inward—into himself, into the warren of
his shop, into the books themselves. Now, however, he was
forced to look out the apartment windows in a way that was
unprecedented for him, that is, analytically. His neighborhood,
which until now he had taken for granted, had become a hostile terrain fraught with dangers.

From the parlor window overlooking the street, he surveyed
a scene of mixed disasters. Half the buildings had been gutted
by bombs or damaged by fire. In this sense it had fared better
than much of Stare Miasto. The apartments directly across from
Sophia House were abandoned. Flanking him on both sides
were empty shops. Yet, a few doors down, people still lived, and
business was conducted as usual. Many eyes observed the
comings and goings of inhabitants and shoppers. For most
people, watching had become the main preoccupation, after the
primary task of self-preservation. At any point along the length
of the street, all activity could be seen by those who cared to
look. It was no more than a single block, though it had been
twice as long before the late eighteen hundreds, when it had
been cut in half by a wall built to enclose the yard of a school
for children of the nobility. The school was now no more than
a heap of rubble, though the wall had not lost a single brick. At
the other end, the west, his cul-de-sac opened into a larger
street, which in turn ran south as far as Jerozolimskie Avenue. A
few blocks to the east was the river.

Walking down the gloomy unlit hallway to the rear of the apartment, Pawel made a mental note to warn the boy against standing near windows. Though the single attic gable was small and overlooked the back courtyard, the situation would be obvious to any neighbor who happened to glance up in that direction. The cap, the shawl, the face—yes, the face, especially.

Entering his bedroom, he glanced out the window and down into the courtyard. Narrower than the street, it was accessible only by a walkway beneath an overhanging apartment. It contained trash cans, rusting bicycles, a number of foraging cats, and the single diseased lime tree that had been planted by Uncle Tadeusz when Pawel was a child, and had appeared sickly even then. Children seldom played there, for it was always in shadow. Here too could be seen extensive damage: facing Pawel was the apartment block on the next street over; a majority of its windows were missing glass, and lights never went on inside. Even so, there were residents, mostly old people scattered at random throughout—more eyes, more observers. Patriots, informers, haters of Jews, humanitarians—who could predict?

And if the worst happened? What then? Hide in the attic until the SS or Gestapo smashed down the doors? Or crawl out the coal chute into the courtyard? But surely an informant would point out to the Germans the building's peculiarities and they would simply surround it. They were no fools, and if the rumors were true, they were experts at ferreting fugitives out of hiding places. If they besieged the house without warning, there would be little chance of escape. Only a flight across the rooftops would remain open, and even then an escapee would be an easy shot. Should the boy flee alone, leaving Pawel at his desk trying to deny everything? Would the Germans believe his lies? Not likely. So then, he would have to go out onto the roof with the boy and scramble along the slate tiles in a desperately unrealistic bid to remain unheard and unseen. One crack from a rifle and he, Pawel, would plunge three stories to shatter on the cobblestones. He hoped it would be a shot through the heart.

*   *   *

The following days were uneventful. Masha, thank God, arrived with sacks of vegetables, the miraculous gift of a pound of tea, a basket of eggs, and another sausage, this one as thick as a goose neck. She had not brought Adam with her because the trips were becoming increasingly perilous. She confessed to hurling more food over the ghetto wall and recounted her horror when she heard the stampeding and squeals of ecstasy on the other side.

"What is happening in Poland?" she cried. "It's insane! Where are they taking all those people?"

"To labor camps", Pawel said uneasily.

He did not mention his guest to Masha. She did not repeat her intimate kiss, nor did either of them refer to it. She gave him a chaste peck on each cheek, which he returned in an identical fashion. She left briskly, after promises of prayers for protection had been exchanged.

That evening he sat at his desk in the bookshop, contemplating the mounting ironies of his life. His life? What was a life? Was his life no more than the archives of experience contained in a small tin box? Or was his life the box itself? Propelled by these unanswerable questions, he took paper and pen in hand, avoiding the mesmerization of subatomic time-and-motion problems that were ever to be found in a droplet of purple ink. Cutting through abstraction toward a semblance of action, he wrote the following:

Archive in a tin box, Warsaw
29 September 1942

This house is a locked box. My life, too, is a locked box. The entire country is a locked box. What, then, is really happening

143

in Poland? Anything can be done within it. Everything depends upon the character of those who control the box.

I must ask my guest for more details of the ghetto. Once or twice I have tried to do so, and each time his face became masked, expressionless, only the eyes revealing a measureless grief connected to the loss of his parents. How many people have died in there, really? Two days before his unexpected arrival, I walked past the ghetto gate at Plac Mirowski. A small crowd of ordinary Warsaw citizens had stopped on our side of the wire and were gazing in. They merely watched, as if observing a tragic entertainment. The sky was heavily overcast, the sense of dread palpable. By the sentry post, a girl about eight years old lay in a pool of blood while German soldiers stood around her, smoking cigarettes, bantering as if nothing significant had happened. They had shot her for trying to smuggle food into the ghetto. She held a shriveled potato in her hands. As she died, the soldiers kicked it out of her fingers, and it rolled away into the gutter, where other children scrambled for it.

I was certain it was an isolated incident—terrible, but no more than an aberration.

I am a monster of the intellect. Only three weeks ago I watched a child be murdered, another potential victim hides in my attic at this very moment, and I sit here writing. O God, who is the madman? Are people like my brothers the sane ones—Bronek with his gun and his conspiracies escapes out of the mental prison into which the enemy locks everything. Jan escapes inward into his clocks, those miniature models of the universe. But where is my escape route?

Later, he prepared a supper tray, casting glances out the window from time to time, seeing in his mind's eye countless starving people little more than a stone's throw from his apartment. They foraged desperately for a potato while he would feast on an entire turnip and slices of boiled cabbage. Weighted with guilt and gratitude, he climbed the stairs to the attic. Pausing on the landing, he observed David Schäfer at the far end of the room, pacing slowly back and forth in front of the gable window, reading and reciting in a low voice. The boy's concentration was total.

Pawel cleared his throat. "If I were not who I am," he said in a warning tone, "you would soon cease to be who you are."

David looked up, startled.

"Did you not hear me on the stairs?"

The boy blushed and shook his head.

"You must, *must* take greater care", Pawel remonstrated, his lips thinned to a line as he placed the tray on a trunk.

"I am sorry, Pan Tarnowski."

"You were parading in front of the window too."

"The light was fading. You understand, it was of utmost urgency that I complete my reading of this tractate—"

"Were you trying to *advertise* your presence? Why not throw open the window and yell? Why not shout for all the world to hear, 'A Jew is hiding here!'?"

"Truly, I am sorry. I won't be so careless again."

Pawel took a light bulb from his pocket. Earlier that day he had bartered a fine little copy of Sienkiewicz's *Bartek the Conquerer* in exchange for three used bulbs. Could this boy understand the sacrifice? Did he think that light cost nothing? Pawel screwed the bulb into a socket hanging from a wire strung along the roof beams. That done, he hung a piece of black cloth over the window.

"At night—this curtain—always. In the daytime—stay away from the window—always."

"Yes, always", came the mumbled reply, accompanied by a chastened nod.

As they ate their meal, Pawel's frustration with the boy declined, replaced by consideration of what such carelessness meant. If anything, it revealed a certain naïveté, a lack of cunning that seemed unaccountable in a survivor of the ghetto.

What kind of personality was this, really? There was something childlike about him, and something ancient too. He was generally serious by temperament, listening, perceptive—like the dilated pupil of a dark eye. Yet his solemn poise was perfectly natural, neither pretentious nor portentous. His dignity radiated equally in his philosophical moods and when he was restored, in rare moments, to the lightheartedness of youth. These qualities, combined with his extraordinary appearance and his melodious voice (pitched somewhere between an adolescent tenor and a man's gentle bass), now evoked in Pawel a profound uneasiness.

The feeling of attraction, he told himself, was the result of loneliness relieved by companionship—a tentative fraternity with someone not unlike himself.

After the meal, which was consumed in less than three minutes, David got up and crossed the room to a teetering maze of books. He knelt down between two stacks.

"Much progress today", he said, his mood subdued but recovering.

There were three main divisions and several lesser ones that represented subcategories. The books on the right were of exceptional value, according to the boy's tastes and convictions. There were many biblical studies here, and much philosophy. He called it "the house of gold". On the left were those he considered useless. For the most part he had judged correctly: silly Polish romances, political fiction from Berlin of the twenties, facile historiography, and other items. He called this stack "the pillar of salt". In between the two was the largest pile: those works about which he was not sure, and in this selection Pawel found much good literature. David called it "the borderlands".

Clearly, such material had not come from a *yeshiva*. Perhaps it

146

had come from Bahlkoyv's Catholic lawyer friend, who in all probability had grabbed books from diverse sources in order to camouflage the top layers of each crate. *Incredibly optimistic*, Pawel thought to himself.

They had refined the procedure until it was now a routine. In the evenings, Pawel would bring food to the attic, and after they ate, the bookseller would go over the day's sorting. From the central pile he now pulled a large volume—an anthology of plays—and began to flip through its pages, pausing over words or phrases that seemed to leap from the cryptic text.

"Do you like this Englishman?" the boy asked.

"I am trying to decipher him."

"He is very interesting."

"You think so? I have tried to read him in Polish translation, because the whole world raves about him. He is unnecessarily complicated, like a painting embellished with too many decorations."

"But one must understand the poetry of his embellishments. One must read him in the original English. If you knew English as I do, you would see that he never uses a word foolishly."

"What possessed you to learn this difficult language?" Pawel asked, putting the book back on the pile.

"Once, long ago, my father and mother wished to live in Amerika with my uncle who is a tailor in Brooklyn. That is a part of the vast city of New York. I have studied this language since 1931 when I was six years old—the year my uncle left. We waited and waited for enough money and for permission to emigrate. We waited too long."

Pawel frowned, remembering 1931, the year he had arrived in Paris filled with grandiose dreams, a fervent acolyte of the goddess Art.

David returned to sorting. It was interesting to catch a glimpse of the boy's mind, for a great deal of it was revealed in his judgments. Observing him make his selections, Pawel commented at one point, "You seem to know literature well. That is unusual."

"Why is it unusual?" David replied.

"Do not your people keep to themselves? I thought you despised everything outside your culture."

The boy mused on this, his expression neutral.

"*Despised* is a strong word."

"Am I wrong in this?"

"It is true of many among the Hasidim."

"But not you?"

David's tone was careful as he made his reply: "I despise no one. Man is incomplete within himself."

"Even the Hasidim?"

"Yes, of course. We are men. . ."

"You hesitate."

"I wish to say that in my private reading of the thoughts of men—men of all kinds—I have found much good." He paused. "And much evil. Usually the evil is woven into the good."

"Where did you study literature? Do you not live a life separate from the world?"

"My father gave me his permission to read in the libraries of the city, especially the university library—though never have I been a student there—so that I might understand the languages of man."

"Language is a gift, as you said the first day we met."

"Yes, language is a gift. But I do not so much mean the lexicons of language. I mean the soul of language—celestial language."

"Celestial language. A beautiful expression. Is that an important idea in Hasidic thought?"

"In a sense, yes. It is implicit in the writings of some of our teachers."

"It is the same in ours. But more than implicitly."

"In your literature it is largely implicit, I think."

Pawel paused at the boy's use of the word *your*, as if the vast and variegated archipelago of Western literature were a single entity.

"You have read novels, then?" he asked.

"Yes. Sometimes in the original languages, which is the better way. I have enjoyed German, French, Italian, English—"

Pointing to the largest pile, Pawel said, "You call it the borderlands. Why that name?"

"It is the territory between the poles of wisdom and foolishness", David said soberly.

He had placed Shakespeare, Thomas Mann, and Sigrid Undset in a subset of this pile called (with a swift smile) "the house of the righteous Gentile". But Sigmund Freud, a Jew, he had put on a heap called "the house of the clever fools". He had labeled a smaller stack "the house of the *sitra ahra*".

Pawel knelt to inspect the books so categorized. About them he knew next to nothing. They were, for the most part, spirituality and theories of psychology.

"Why are you so sure these come from the *other side*?" Pawel asked.

"There are *dybbuks* at work in these writings."

"What is a *dybbuk*?"

"An evil spirit."

"You should be careful about saying an evil spirit is influencing a man merely because you disagree with him. Perhaps there is truth to be found in his ideas."

"Yes, there would have to be. One does not give a deadly gift to an enemy by wrapping it in a package stamped with the words *lies, poison, deception*. One wraps the deadly gift in a pleasing package, upon which is written *love, peace, unity*."

Pawel picked up one of the books and fanned through it. Arrested by a few lines, he stopped and read a page, then another.

"Your eyes are troubled, Pan Tarnowski. What is it?"

"A poem."

Pawel read silently through the entire text.

"Can you recite it to me?" the boy asked.

"I'm not sure you would enjoy this. It's like wading through a swamp. The symbols are confused."

"In what way?"

"The author says there are two primary forces in existence and that both are god-devils—the Trees of Life and Eros—both are a mixture of good and evil. The Tree of Life he calls the Growing One, Eros he calls the Burning One. Eros has the form of fire. It gives light by consuming, by destroying. Good and evil are united in its flame. Good and evil are united in the Tree of Life by the process of growth."

David's face contorted in disgust.

"There is but one Tree of Life", he exclaimed. "The Torah! In it there is no evil!"

"Apparently the author doesn't agree with you. He seems to be saying that we will not find happiness until the tree of life and the tree of knowledge of good and evil are integrated within us."

"Evil integrated within us? That is ridiculous!"

"There is more. It is a hymn to some supernatural being."

When Pawel had finished reading silently, he looked up.

"He believed that the most high god contains within his divinity both Jehovah and Satan as equal partners—"

David covered his ears. "Stop! It is an abomination. I cannot bear it!"

"Yes, of course. You are right, it *is* a horrible idea. But it's just a poem."

The boy exhaled.

"Words have power", he said intensely. "They have a life of their own. They shift the balance of the world."

Pawel pondered this, lost in reverie for some moments.

"You are a very unusual young man", he said at last.

David looked perplexed. Frowning, he gestured to the pile. Speaking slowly, he said, "Do you think so merely because I can smell poison? Of course, I do not know much about the designs of the *dybbuks*, but this man wishes to abolish the distinctions between good and evil. Does he think they are mirror images of the same ultimate divine power?"

"It would seem so."

"Pan Tarnowski, this is an idea that originates in the other side. They would like us to believe it in order to make their work easier."

"Their work?"

"They would destroy in us what remains of the likeness of the All-Holy One, which we lost when our original parents fell. This author wishes to reverse the Fall of Man? He will not succeed." Here David Schäfer pointed to the *sitra ahra* pile with rabbinical authority. "These would lead us to another Fall of Man!"

"When I listen to such thoughts coming from your mouth it is like hearing the soul of an old man speak through the lips of a child."

"My father used to say that to me. Yes, and in those very words." He looked pensive then added politely, firmly, "I am not a child."

"Was your father a professor?"

"He was a tailor. He had wisdom."

"Where is your father now—do you know?"

The eyes turned upon Pawel were so motionless, so grief-stricken, that he was momentarily taken aback.

"My father, I am certain, now rests on the breast of Abraham. He was taken away to the *Umschlagplatz* two months ago. I hid in the sewers."

Pawel parted the window curtains. The night clouds were lit by the moon. Then he realized that the sound of gunshots had become so ordinary they no longer demanded attention.

*　*　*

I do not understand why God does not act, does not tear open the veil of the cosmos and reveal to the Jewish people his new covenant, and to the Gentile people the evil of their wars and persecutions. The pain that I feel regarding this question is out of proportion to my concern for the fugitive in the attic. I must conclude, therefore, that the pain arises from a more personal source. Is it my own feeling of abandonment that I see writ large in their plight?

My mind tells me that God is present, even in the midst of this war—yes, I admit that I do believe everything I have been taught about him. Yet the heart trembles before the abyss of his silence, his inaction in the face of catastrophic events.

I believe with my mind but not with my emotions. Thus I continue to be, as always, a split man. Can one ever trust such a man? I do not trust Haftmann the *Gespaltenmensch-Übermensch*, the Superman split within himself. So why should I trust this box of contradictions, this dossier of futile tales that I presume to call myself?

David Schäfer—now here is a unified soul. There appears to be no interior division, no split between faith and personality, intellect and feeling, or any other aspect of his being. There are moments when I resent his unquestioning self-assurance. There are moments when I envy it. The Jews are adamant about their beliefs. Is this the reason they are so widely disliked? And why has dislike so swiftly grown into an irrational hatred? Irratio-nal—by which one usually means an aberration that is purely psychological, sociopolitical, or cultural. Is it just that?

This boy who has found shelter with me is a fugitive because the enemy wishes to destroy him. It cannot be that God's will intended him to come to me. Surely if the powers of human evil had not set in motion this disastrous war, he would have grown up to be a teacher of wisdom among his own people and never would our paths have crossed. But his family is dead and he is hunted. Has God now moved to a second plan? Is this twisted heart of mine part of a divine plan? How can that be? Surely my condition is an evil accident!

Pawel put down his pen, heaved a great sigh, and straightened his back with audible clickings of vertebrae. The cup of tea beside him had grown cold. He drank it down. He rubbed his eyes and trimmed the lamp. A cold autumn rain pelted the glass of the shop's front windows.

He tossed and turned all night on his bed and kept the red votive light burning before the crucifix and the household icons.

\* \* \*

Early Sunday morning there came a frantic rapping on the coalman's window at the rear of the building. Pawel stumbled blindly downstairs to open the back door.

Bronek crashed in and stood there panting. Short, burly, the platinum hair of his childhood now brown and shaggy—in every aspect of his person he valiantly preserved the peasant strain of the Tarnowski line.

"Pawel. They are killing the people they take away to re-settlement."

"Perhaps a few are dying . . ." Pawel mumbled.

"No, they kill everyone!"

"It cannot be true."

"It is true! It is! There are several death camps. The underground has received word that Majdanek and Treblinka are not the worst, though they are very bad. There is a labor camp south of Krakow, near Oświęcim, where they have killed hundreds of thousands. It is getting worse."

"Hundreds of thousands? That is impossible."

"It *is* possible. There have been a few escapes. Not many—you could count them on your hands. They all say the same thing."

"They are merely repeating rumors. These things have been said since last summer."

The two brothers stared at each other, Pawel defensively, Bronek breathing heavily, his lips thinned to a line of frustration.

"Damn it, Pawel!" Bronek barked. "Must you always hide from the truth!"

"What do you mean—hide?"

Bronek rolled his eyes and threw his hands in the air.

"What do you mean?" Pawel demanded.

"What do I mean? What do I mean? All right, I will tell you what I mean! You infuriate me. Jan too has had enough of your endless miseries. Poor Pawel, so full of sadness! So dark and brooding. My, how he has suffered, our poor Pawel. Why don't you snap out of it? We are tired of holding your hand. You are no longer a child."

"I—"

"Why have you always been so unhappy? I know why. Mama babied you. Papa babied you. Babscia and Ja-Ja babied you. You were the little darling. Always the oohing and aahing over the adorable Pawelek. Well, we are sick of it. Grow up! It's a hard world. People are dying. You cannot go back to the nursery."

Now anger replaced shock. "You don't know what you're saying."

"I know very well what I'm saying. When Papa went away you became an imbecile. When you came back from Paris you were even more an imbecile. When are you—" Bronek stopped himself. He rubbed his face. Pawel saw that his brother's hands were trembling, dirty, the nails split. His eyes were sunken from fatigue and hunger.

"I'm sorry", Bronek mumbled. "I didn't mean it."

Though Pawel felt a great wave of resentment roll through him, he sped it on its way with an effort of the will.

"You are hungry, Bron", he said tonelessly.

His brother nodded.

"Come upstairs. I will make tea. Masha brought some."

Over two cups of scalding black tea, cut with sugar, Bronek sat fidgeting nervously while Pawel remained in silence trying not to take offense. The late autumn sun poured through the window overlooking the square. The lime tree sighed outside the glass, asking for asylum. He opened the window and fresh air came in.

"I need your help", Bronek said in a tone of supplication, embarrassed that he must beg so soon after giving an insult.

"I have no money," Pawel replied, "and if I did, I would not give it to you for guns. The Germans drive an enormous machine. You are talking about getting killed for no purpose. Like a bee stinging the treads of a Panzer tank. Should I give my own brother the weapon with which he will destroy himself?"

"They must be taught that there is a price to pay for violating the borders of another nation. But I did not come for money to buy guns. Here, look at this."

He handed over a sheet of paper on which was typed the following:

ATTENTION ALL LOYAL POLES!

In the Warsaw Ghetto, behind the wall that cuts them off from the world, there exist several hundred thousand condemned who are awaiting execution. The executioners rush through the streets, shooting anyone who dares to leave his house by night or appears suspicious by daylight. Thousands of children have become beggars, their parents dead or taken to the transports. Many little bodies lie about the streets with German bullets in their heads. Women and girls are raped by gangs of soldiers. Unburied fever victims lie everywhere. The prescribed number of daily transportees is from five to ten thousand. The Jewish police are obliged to hand them over to the executioners. If they fail to do so, they themselves perish. Madness and hatred rules every act. The loading of people onto trains is so brutal that many do not reach their destination alive. Children are hurled into boxcars in heaps. The doors are sealed. The crowds within are so tightly packed that the dead cannot fall. There is no food, no water.

The trains take the people to places of execution, which have been built on many sites of our land. What is happening in the Warsaw Ghetto is occurring in numerous small and large Polish cities. Already the total number of Jews murdered exceeds a million. Rich and poor, old and young—all have been condemned to execution by *Generalgouverneur* Frank, obeying the orders of Hitler.

All good Catholic people! We cannot be like Pilate! We must not wash our hands of our Jewish brothers. We cannot actively oppose the German murderers, but we can save many from their hands. Give them sanctuary! This protest is demanded of us by God, who forbade the killing of the innocent. It is demanded by our Christian conscience. The blood of the victims calls to heaven to bring down justice. Those who do not support this protest are not Catholic.

### THE FRONT FOR THE
### RESTORATION OF POLAND

"Is this true?"

"I told you—it's true!"

"How do you know it's true?"

"I know. Believe me, I know."

"It's too fantastic. It can't be true. And what am I supposed to do with this? If I post it in my shop I will become a dead man."

"I am not asking you to do anything so stupid. I am interested in your press. We must make copies."

Pawel shook his head. "No."

"The blood of the innocent is poured out hour by hour, and you say no?"

"We could not possibly escape capture. The press is noisy. Furthermore, it has sat in the cellar for three years. Some of the parts are rusty. I do not know if the ink is still good. Besides, where would I get paper?"

"You do not have paper?" Bronek said with dismay.

"Well, I have a carton of typewriter paper hidden away. But I am saving it."

"Damn!" said Bronek, thumping the table. "For what are you *saving* it?"

"I have thought of writing a few things", Pawel murmured.

His brother merely stared at him.

Pawel relented. "I will keep a hundred sheets and you may have the rest."

Bronek gripped his arm.

"God bless you", he exhaled.

"As for the offset press, it is out of the question." Then, impelled more by shame than by patriotism, he said, "I do have something that may be of use to you. Come."

In a corner of the basement, beneath a rotting canvas, they found an ancient mechanical handpress. Its black enamel carriage was in good condition, but its platen was beginning to rust. Pawel scrubbed it clean with a rag. He spun the wheel, the gears worked, and the platen did its job almost silently.

"It is slow, but safer", he said, as if he did not believe his own words.

"Perfect."

From a wooden crate wrapped in oilcloth Pawel removed a package of paper and put it on a workbench beside the press. He counted off a hundred sheets.

"These I will keep. The rest are yours. It's my hope that what I write on my paper will help as many people as what you write on yours."

"What are you going to write that will *help* people?"

"I don't know."

"You, my dear brother, are a puzzle", said Bronek, shaking his head.

"Now let's lay the type. It's Sunday. Nothing will disturb us."

As they worked side by side, Pawel considered whether or not he should inform Bronek about the fugitive in the attic—desiring to prove that he, no less than the valiant, was capable of providing sanctuary. He decided against it. Bronek's personality and his chosen avocation in the underground were almost certainly fatal. If he were captured, it would be best if he knew as little as possible. On the other hand, if he were captured and confessed that the printing had been done at Sophia House, the end would come with the same finality. Nevertheless, he did not mention David Schäfer.

When the type was correctly set, Pawel installed the tray in the press and left Bronek to the printing. Hours later he returned to the cellar and found his brother exhausted.

"A thousand sheets done!" Bronek groaned. "And only eight thousand nine hundred to go. That big press over there could finish the whole job in two hours."

"Yes, and have us in Gestapo headquarters by sunset."

\* \* \*

Bronek worked night and day. Occasionally he had help from anonymous figures who slipped down the coal chute and left by the same opening.

Pawel warned David that there were people in the house, coming and going at all hours. He must take extra care to remain out of sight and to avoid making noise of any kind.

"Are they dangerous people, Pan Tarnowski?"

"They are not Germans, nor are they collaborators. They work with the underground. But in these times, we must assume that no one—I mean no one—is reliable."

The boy's face remained studious, assessing the remark.

"No one?"

"No one."

"I believe that you are making a general statement without sufficient room for distinctions."

"What?" Pawel half-laughed.

"*You*, Pan Tarnowski, are reliable."

Pawel shrugged. "Don't be so sure."

"I am sure", said the boy in a low voice, with a look that was both profound and unreadable.

\* \* \*

9 October 1942

Kahlia,

Why is it so difficult to write to you this night? The sounds of gunfire have waned into silence. The clock ticks on the wall by the bust of Paderewski. My desk has become an entire landscape. On every floor there are secrets. In the cellar there are heroes scurrying about, furtively planning a revolution of mice. In the attic there lies an extraordinary presence, a live coal resting on a bed of decaying books. I do not understand why this house does not burst into flames. That a human being so young, so vital, should pursue wisdom is a great enigma.

David Schäfer informed me this morning, "We have a saying: the man who has nothing is the man who has everything."

Now here is a difficult saying!

Who is he, this sage? And why has he been dropped into my hands? I of all people—a man afflicted with introversion and an overly sensitive temperament!

I fear him. Yet his presence has mysteriously, and without precedence, brought a small happiness into my prison cell. How absurd! When he goes, the darkness will only be worse. Perhaps that is why I fear him. Yet I also have come to feel some affection for him. It is classic transference, of course. The despised outcast, the solitary sufferer, the dispossessed—I look at him and see (O strangest of delusions) my own face.

I do not dare to use the word *love*. It is a word that disguises our selfish pursuit of relief from loneliness. But why do I feel, Kahlia, the very feelings I once felt—and which I still feel—for you? It is a mute passion. It is not an impulse of the carnal kind, like the furtive desires of my famous writer. Oh, let it not be that!

I must not feel! I cannot! I have guarded my heart for too many years. I am stone!

Language is a gift, he says. Also an affliction, I silently reply. Such a guileless face could not bear the utterance of this truth. A bridge promises traffic, yet can so easily be demolished, increasing the bleakness of isolation.

He tries repeatedly to bridge the void by teaching me Yiddish or Hebrew words.

This evening: "My *tallis* and my *yarmulke* are all I have left." He explains that the former is his prayer shawl, the latter his skullcap.

I reply: "You have nothing. Therefore you have everything."

His face falls and he remains silent. In this I see the perennial human problem laid bare. Even in a person as gifted as this young prodigy, the convictions of a great mind do not necessarily transform the heart.

Bronek was finished by the dawn of Wednesday morning.

"Pawel, you must go see Jan", he said at their parting. "I had word last night that Sara and Itsak have been arrested."

Then he left carrying a package of illegal posters.

After closing up early, Pawel made his way to Swietokrzyska Street. Jan's shop was locked, and the curtains of the upstairs windows were closed—no one was at home in the apartment. Halfway down the block, an old woman, sitting on a crate selling battered metal pots, signaled to him.

"Pan Tarnowski has gone to the main ghetto entrance to look for his wife and child", she said.

He found his older brother standing five meters from the barbed-wire gate, craning his neck, searching back and forth.

A sign over the gatepost read:

WOHNGEBIET DER
JUDEN

BETRETEN
VERBOTEN

A street cleaner sloshed a bucket of water across a pool of blood and began to scrape it toward the gutter with a wire broom.

"Jan, I heard. Can I help?"

"The police will not help. I cannot help. Nothing will help. I wait here. They may have been put into the ghetto, and their angels may guide them past this gate. I have sent in many messages with strangers, also packages of food and money. I pray it reaches them. If they are here . . ."

They stood together watching. Jan did not look at him.

"Do you sell books to the Germans?" he asked in a low voice.

"Yes."

"God, what kind of a man are you?"

"The kind of man who believes truth can change even the most hardened heart."

Even as he said it he knew that the words came out of his mouth choked and feeble, sounding like nothing more than the excuses of a weak man. Jan merely appraised him with a look of contempt, then turned his eyes back to the gate. The silence became unbearable, and Pawel hurried away, forcing himself not to run.

\* \* \*

David Schäfer was engrossed in cataloging when Pawel brought food to him that night. He left the tray beside the boy and went back down to the shop without a word.

He tried to glue the torn spine of a leather-bound dictionary but made a mess of it and eventually pushed it away. Words. Mountains of words, none of which was capable of driving away the voracious dogs of war. Unable to work, he stared into the gloom of the maze of books. Jan's rebuke lodged in his heart like a spear.

He sat without moving for close to an hour, his head in his hands. He tried to turn himself back into stone, but could not. An immense weight of loneliness settled upon him and compressed his thoughts, his feelings, his very flesh into a sewer of pure anguish.

*What kind of man are you? What kind of man are you?* The tone of disdain worsened with every repetition of the unanswerable question.

"What kind of man am I? Listen, I will tell you, Jan. I am a coward. I am a failure at life. I am no good at being a human being, let alone a man. I am nothing. I am less than nothing, for nothingness is clean and simple."

Loneliness, loneliness, endless loneliness. The words of critics had always been able to demolish him, because there had never been a counterword to tell him what he was, to speak his own true name, or to smile upon his hidden face. There was no solid foundation within, no edifice of confirmation built by decades of shared love. No spouse, no beloved, no friends, only a family who had never understood him.

What was he? All the messages he had received regarding this subject were conflicting. They revolved in a cyclic trance, endlessly negating each other. What kind of man was he? An alien, a madman, a hero, a mutant, a pilgrim, a crippled child, an aspiring saint, a depraved sinner? Most of all he was a dwarf, digging in the obscure galleries of literary mines, searching for glittering veins. He was a curator of dreams. Yes, the final archivist of futile tales.

For him there would be no joy. No indestructible bond, no fairest love, no sweetest embrace. No poems, no names of endearment. No purpose.

Now all certainties crumbled. First came the insinuations of rats, gnawing away at the core of reason. The rats transformed themselves into roaring bears with wide-open jaws, red eyes thrusting at him out of the crushing weight of the night. Then they became emboldened monsters strutting through his mind. They sneered. They told him dark, hopeless things—lies, lies, oh yes, he knew well enough that they were lies—but lies were the shadow of truth, were they not?

*There is no love for you*, they said. *You are an aberration, destined for destruction.*

He knew that the thoughts were distorted imaginings caused by hunger and psychic anguish, by too much solitude, and by the abiding fear. But this did not silence them.

He was a perfect biological package, but his mind was deformed. How could such fundamental damage ever be fixed? Could the void of lovelessness within the exact center of his heart ever be alleviated by a glance, a touch, an embrace? Who would be willing to embrace him? Oh, many, many had desired him, had desired most of all to turn him into their malleable *objet d'art*. But none of them had known him, and none of them, if they were to really know him, would embrace him. Who could melt stone?

"It is very difficult", he said aloud. "It is very difficult for a man to believe that God loves him, if he does not know the love of another human being."

Why had he said this? And to whom?

Into his mind there flashed the image of the fugitive high above him in the attic. The face radiated solace—its warmth, its openness, its beauty. *Beauty?* What was he saying! He thrust the thought away. There were no consolations for a man such as himself. No—his daily fare would always be trays of cold lead.

He now saw all of his weakness in stark clarity. One by one he recounted his failures: his father's disappointment, the miserable performance at the university, the monastery that would not accept him. Picasso's eyes like black agates analyzing him and finding him unworthy. The legions of gallery owners who lied to him or told him the truth—either way it hurt. Then the Russian holy man, the *staretz* who would not take him as a disciple. The eyes of the French painting master, the eyes of the students. The writer who wanted only a romance, who would not have looked twice at him if he had been unattractive. And last of all, Kahlia, who had looked at him once, briefly, and left without a backward glance.

For a moment his sense of self was completely shaken and he felt himself to be disembodied, a consciousness adrift in a universe that lacked all orientation—no gravitational force of any kind. Hunching over, his face on his knees, he began to whisper to someone, anyone, not knowing to whom he spoke. Was it to Father Andrei? No, even he had departed.

The ache opened like an abscess and began to leak its contents:

"Why have I never known what I was made for?" he cried.

He jumped to his feet and wandered around the shelves, weaving in and out of the aisles between the central stalls.

"My father, my father! You gave me life but you did not tell me how to live!"

The silence contained no answers.

"Why have I always been so alone?"

He sobbed noiselessly.

"O God, you gave me hunger for love. Then you tell me I may not have love."

He breathed vehemently: "I cannot hear you! Why do you not speak?"

Gunshots.

"Why are there only two choices: this endless solitude, or degradation? I want to die. I want to live. I want to be alone. I want to love."

To love? To love whom?

Did he mean a real woman, a real man? But what were these, the real and the unreal, the symbols all mixed within him, condemning him to eternal isolation under the sheet of darkness, the impress of a bear paw on his flesh?

"Rotting cherries", he babbled.

The lust-maddened bear pulling the child's limbs from their knot under the blind stars, the jaws opening wide on the child's chest, eating into the core, the paws playing, playing in the most private places, the child's mouth clamped, lungs heaving for air.

"Love . . ." he gasped at last, staring at the walls as if he were just released from prison, only to find himself in a larger cell.

He tried to throw off the bear, but it was locked within him. Wrestling, wrestling with it—a bad dream, an old dream—he knew it well, every hair of its sweat-matted chest, its crushing weight, its frantic panting, tying together pain and unwanted pleasure as a child's screams were forced deeper and deeper under the waters of silence.

Leaning against a bookshelf, eyes blinking rapidly, Pawel tried to catch his breath and suppress the scream rising in his throat.

Then, because only a more powerful dream could dispel the bear, the face of David Schäfer arose in his mind again. The boy's eyes were open and dark, potent, his presence the dilated pupil of the universe reaching toward Pawel with an open hand, whispering, *You are a tree of life to me.*

"A tree of life!" Pawel cried. "Me? It would be wise for you to stay away from me, for I was not always so nice, and might be like that again."

But this was a horror too deep, this was to become the bear itself.

"A lie, a lie!" he breathed. But a lie this strong could be countered only by two warm hands reaching for his own, the earnest gratitude in the eyes, the love shining through them—

Instantly all sound and movement ceased.

Love? Had there been a hint of love in the boy's eyes?

Pawel sat down and hung his head.

Love for him? Love from a wholly alien soul, who did not, could not, know him?

Seized now with a greater anguish, and enraged by the impossibility of such a consolation, he began to mutter to the walls of the cell.

"O God, how can I love with the pure love you demand when this weight is in me, pulling me daily toward disaster? I am becoming drawn to him, I tell you, and I cannot break the hold it has on me."

Tires screeching. Voices shouting.

"What should I do? To detach him by force, to send him out my door, would be to kill him. They would destroy him instantly."

More gunfire.

"Why have you done this to me?"

He jumped to his feet and began to pace again. Rubbing his face, throwing up his hands and dropping them, pacing back and forth across the shop, faster and faster, he felt shadows whispering indictments against him, forces pressing down upon the thin shell of his mind.

He hit his chest with his fist. It hurt. He hit it again, harder.

"I hate my heart! I hate it!" he shouted.

Wind blasted at the window.

"Kill it! Take it out of me!"

But his heart persisted in its place, insulted by his own hand.

Klaxon horns. The muffled roar of an explosion on the other

side of the city. Men shouting down the street. Vile German curses. Rifle butts hammering on a door. A woman's wail. A child's scream.

He was powerless to stop it, helpless, alone, without weapons of any kind.

His face writhed as he glared at the maze of books. Literature! Literature—the Olympics of garden gnomes! The chatter of the demented! He strode forward and swept a shelf of volumes onto the floor. Then he smashed another shelf, and another. Rampaging through the shop, he tossed books left and right, pushing over stands, kicking the heaps of words left and right. Millions upon millions of useless words, words that massed into whole ranges of delusion, words that promised everything and delivered nothing.

Breathing heavily, his fists clenching and unclenching, he surveyed the wreckage, laughed, sobbed, and muttered imprecations. Then he dragged his body upstairs to the bedroom. He looked once at the icon corner. Then looked away from it.

He lay down on the bed, pulled a cover over his body, and curled into a knot. For the first time since the years of his unbelief he did not pray. He lay for hours, staring into the cesspool of existence, listening to the violated city, measuring every unanswered cry, every whine of a bullet, certain that each marked the death of a soul. The bear feasted, gore dripping from its open jaws. Still, Pawel clung to the last scrap of his will and fought. If it would eat him, it would pay dearly. In the meantime, he would close his eyes, for a moment only . . .

## 8

In the morning he awoke feeling both drugged and sore, as if he had been savagely beaten. His chest ached. His mind was black. He shuffled into the toilet chamber, glanced at his face in the mirror, and shuddered.

"Pawel the Beautiful!" he snarled. "Sweet Pawelek!"

*You have become the bear,* said a voice in his mind.

Startled, he took a step backward.

*You desire the abomination.*

No! No, he did not want the images of degradation that now began to flash before his mind's eye. Nor did he want the emotions they prompted. But with every effort to banish them they returned with greater force, pounding against his resistance until it began to dissolve like a château of mists dispersed by a storm wind.

He could not at first believe it. He who had suffered under the attentions of Goudron, was turning into Goudron! It could not be true. Yet it was true!

Was it true?

If he was not the bear, it could not be denied that he was another kind of predator. In a spasm of self-loathing he grabbed his straight razor from the sink and exposed his left wrist. He stared at it. No, it would take too much time that way, the pain would be intense and prolonged as consciousness dribbled away. Then he stared at his throat in the accusing mirror. The vulnerability of the pulsing vein cast him suddenly into one of his "spells"—he stared in anticipation at the drop of blood that would roll toward the point of a nib, and hang suspended for a micro-instant before falling on the final page of his life. *Do it,* he thought, *do it!* Now the summation of his botched existence was concentrated into one throb, relievable by a single swift strike against the tyranny of his flesh. One act, and the locked box would open, releasing him into . . .

He could go no farther than that. Into what? Nothingness? Hell?

A lesser protest was possible. He jerked his arm upward, intending to slash his face diagonally from cheek to cheek, for it was infinitely reasonable to disfigure what was already disfigured within. One slash? No, make it two!

Without warning, the two slashes on the face of the Woman of Czestochowa erupted in his consciousness, as her eyes gazed into him with an intimacy that contained neither accusation nor freighted motive.

He hurled the razor across the room and it clattered against the far wall. Then he stomped down to the shop, intending to throw open the front door, to go out into the street. He would march up to the first German he could find and strike him in the face. They would shoot him on the spot and that would be that!

He was unprepared for the sight that greeted him on the ground floor. He stopped short and stared. No books littered the floor. Several torn volumes were stacked neatly on the mending table. Scattered papers had been arranged in a pile on his desk.

He stomped back upstairs to find David. The boy was sitting at the kitchen table, his glance riveted to the floor. He slowly looked up.

"I must go", he said.

Scowling, Pawel answered, "There is no place to go. They would kill you."

"If they kill me, they kill me."

"Why do you want to go?"

"Because I am killing *you*."

"You are not."

"I do not want you to die because of me."

"My life is not so precious."

"You think so? That is sad."

"Sad? Who gives a damn about sad? You are staying."

"Why?"

"I do not want you to die because of *me*." Then, in a caustic tone that was directed only at himself, he said, "Should I add murder to the list of my many achievements?"

The boy stood up without looking at Pawel. Confusion, fear, and withdrawal wrestled for mastery on his face. He turned abruptly and went to the attic.

Pawel remained without movement for many minutes. Then he went into the bedroom and sat down on the bed, facing the icon corner.

"I do not believe in you", he said aloud.

The icons did not reply.

He snorted. "I want us to speak together about this, but you do not answer me."

Silence.

"But how can you speak if you are not there? And if you *are* there, why would you speak to one such as me?"

He laughed coldly.

"You will not talk to me. Then I will talk to you. I will talk to you as if you are real, though you are just a story. Yes, a folktale about God. I will say my part and I will make up yours."

The dialogue flowed effortlessly from some source of creativity within himself. Even as he gave it full release he was puzzled by the inventiveness of his imagination. The supernatural character he created seemed unpredictable, but this only reinforced his argument: the untapped resources of the mind contained a universe so big that it was mistaken for a metauniverse. If God, then, was no more than an image projected on the screen of consciousness, he could not take offense.

The stone in Pawel's heart was simply there. Who or what had put it there? It would not go away. It was real. But was anything else real? Was he, Pawel, no more than a rat in a maze? Or a character in some demented playwright's imagination? If that were so, he would submit to it no longer. No, he would not! He would stop running through the little sewer or the little script. He would unmask it, strip it of its disguise. He would demand an explanation!

"I am alone", he seethed. "Why am I alone?"

*You feel alone, my son.*

"Am I a son? I do not feel like a son."

*You are a son.*

The bitterness swelled into vehemence. "I have no father!" he cried angrily.

*You have a father.*

"Where is my father? The place where he should be is empty."

*Emptiness is a place of waiting.*

"I have waited all my life."

*A little longer and you will be full.*

"I will wait and no one will come."

*All is coming to you.*

"I do not believe it. Happiness is for others. Not for me."

*Those who think they are full cannot receive. You can receive.*

"I am filling, filling, filling—with pain. That is all, just pain."

*After a long emptiness, the filling is felt as pain.*

"If you are the voice of heaven, explain divine providence to me. Can you justify the ways of God to me?"

*Is God on trial? Or is man?*

"I do not know. I merely asked a question."

*The question is full of assumptions. It is full of pride.*

"Why is this boy here?"

*You and the boy were born in a battleground.*

"Why? Why are children born in a battleground?"

*It was not God's intention from the beginning. In the beginning man and woman were created to walk with him in the Garden, to live in perfect peace, to give themselves to each other, and to him, as a gift.*

"Yes. I studied my catechism. I know everything you will say."

*That which men think they know best, they often know least. Fear rules you.*

"Are my fears groundless? The world is being destroyed all around us."

*The universe is damaged, but not destroyed.*

"The world is swarming with soldiers who wear belt buckles that say *Gott mit uns*—God with us."

*The season of the liar is brief. The truth will win.*

"Truth? Tell me the truth about this boy. Why is the very thing that I fled thrust upon me at the moment when I am weakest?"

*Grace is best revealed in weakness.*

"I see no grace."

*You do not know yourself.*

"I know what I am."

*You are man. You are caught up in a storm of great intensity. Soon it will be over.*

"Yet even if I survive, a war will rage within me until the end of my days."

*When all is accomplished you will wear this humiliation like glory.*

"Glory?" he spat out.

*You will thank God for each and every suffering.*

"Is this the argument? I am not convinced."

Into his mind there came the image of a garden. A man and a woman walked together in it, hand in hand among the creatures of the air and field. A being of light walked with them and within them, for he was the source of their union. Light filled everything. Then a serpent entered the garden. The serpent hated the light and knew he had no power to hurt it, except through its creatures. The serpent coiled about the two and whispered false pictures into their minds. They turned away from each other into the shadows spun by the serpent.

Then the two fled and hid themselves and were finally cast out from the garden. An angel with a flaming sword guarded the gate lest they bring death and falsehood into it again.

The two knew shame. They were no longer one. They no longer trusted each other, for they both had believed a lie. Then the races of mankind poured from them. All manner of good and evil poured from them, each child with a wound in its heart. A boy was born of the Jews. The wound within him lay dormant. He did not know that it existed.

When this boy saw deer in a park he would lift his hands and gasp at their beauty. "Oh Papa," he would cry, "I have seen the most beautiful thing. He wears a coat of red velvet and golden trees grow from his head." He would touch their damp, black noses, and they would not leap away. When blue pigeons plunged like bolts of grace from steepletops, he laughed and imitated their trajectory with his flashing eyes until they landed at his feet, coo-cooing. He spun dreidels in patches of sunlight. He weighed ideas as if they were measurable on brass scales. He rolled words around in his mouth as if they were hot cubes of chocolate or the sugared icicles that dripped from the limbs of bushes, licked in the melt of March. *Mama* was warm cream. *Gun* was thunder. God, *Adonai*, was wine pouring from a rock cracked by a prophet's staff. *Fayer*, Fire, was ember and incense on October nights when the chestnut leaves were burned in heaps in the city parks. His name was a king's name, and a king's wisdom dwelt in him, though it was a portion only.

Then, in his mind's eye, Pawel saw an old man staggering around the rubble heaps of bombed ruins. Naked, save for a *tallis*, which he wrapped about his loins, he groaned in agony for the destruction of all that was true and beautiful and good in the world. "Everything is lost," he cried, "everything." He passed men and women who laughed at his nakedness.

"Repent!" he shouted at them.

"Repent of what?" they mocked.

"The fire is coming", he said.

"Look around", they answered. "There is no fire. We have defeated the fire."

"All is normal", said another.

"All is not normal", said the old man.

"Peace," they shouted, "peace!"

"There is no peace!" said the old man.

They threw rocks at him and he ran away. He fell and got up, fell again and crawled, cutting his flesh on broken glass. Through the ruins he went on hands and knees until he came to the edge of a bomb crater. In the bottom of the crater was a priest, saying Mass on a box illuminated by the stubs of candles. His chalice was a tin cup, and his paten was a broken plate. The priest was a pope, assisted by three bishops. Thirty or forty people knelt around the altar, dressed in rags. They were worshipping the Host that the pope was lifting up. Its light was dazzling, and it pushed back the darkness for a time. The people worshipped, but they were frightened. The pope prayed, but his face streamed with tears.

*Look up*, said a voice.

The naked old man in the *tallis* looked up, and there in the sky above the pope was a woman clothed with the sun, and upon her head was a crown of twelve stars. She looked down with great love upon the huddled group in the crater. She glanced at the old man in the *tallis*, and smiled.

"Elijah", she said.

Then Pawel saw that the old man bore many wounds in his soul, though he was the boy who once had touched the velvet antlers of deer, and lived to tell of it, and danced for the joy of it.

Pawel felt dizzy. His imagination was sliding out of control.

"Who is Elijah?" he said.

But the folktale did not answer.

"This has no meaning for me."

*You are part of it. It is real. And yet it will not come to pass if you turn toward the shadows.*

"You have not answered my question."

*What seems an accident to you is wholly within the plans of God. A great blessing has come to you.*

"A blessing? That is absurd."

*You cannot see the whole. You see only a part. The greater part of the battle is waged in realms above you.*

"Then mankind is no more than vermin, and I am the most verminous of all. Better to be stone. I *am* stone. No prophet's staff will crack this heart."

*You are not stone, though you desire to be stone. The liar plays upon your fear, telling you that there is nothing beyond your pain.*

"Is there anything beyond this room, this hunger, this desolation?"

*He wants you to believe there is nothing beyond the pictures he has spun in your mind. Resist him and he will flee.*

"And what of love? Whether he comes or goes, the problem remains: there is no love for me."

*The man you seek is within you. The image of the son, and the image of the father.*

A loud creak on the floorboards above his head snapped Pawel out of this reverie.

The dialogue was entirely a creation of his mind, he knew. And yet it had offered a counter argument to his condemnation of reality. Perhaps, after all, his anguish was so persuasive that it could eclipse the most real things and make them appear as shadows, and at the same time make shadows into an appearance of the real. *Mistaking the part for the whole*, the voice had called it. Only moments before, he had doubted life itself. Now, strangely, he doubted the doubt.

Wondering if he had misunderstood everything, he stared at the icons. Try as he might, he could not will himself entirely into stone. He now remained without movement, without imaginary dialogue, without prayer. The longer he remained in this state the more did the agony decline, and in its place there came an inexplicable quiet. He did not want it, but he had to admit that it was better than torment.

When at last he stirred, he went up to the attic landing and saw that David Schäfer was bent over a book, rocking back and forth, the *tallis* covering his head. Pawel did not disturb him.

He went down to the shop and worked for several hours repairing the damaged tomes. His rage and despair were gone, though a confused grief still gripped his heart. When daylight passed from the windows, he returned to the kitchen. There was little to eat, but he managed to put together a meal of vegetables and bread crusts smeared with a dab of rancid lard (an extravagance he felt they deserved after the ordeal of the day). He called up the stairwell to the attic, but David did not respond. He went to the top of the stairs and called from the landing. The boy did not at first answer him. Eventually he tore his eyes away from his prayer book and said in an expressionless voice, "I am not hungry. Soon I will sleep."

Pawel went back to the ground floor and sat at his desk. The electricity was off. He lit a paraffin lamp and took up his pen. Though he felt a desire to write to Kahlia, he found nothing to say to her, nothing at least that would be comprehensible to a sane human being.

Before him the book on the Russian icon painter lay open at the face of Christ. The eyes reached out of the page and invited Pawel to meet his glance. The curious stillness he had experienced in front of the household icons was now redoubled.

*The man you seek is within you*, the voice had said. What did

that mean? How could it refute the indictment of his lovelessness? How could it fill the abyss of his abandonment?

"Within me?" he asked of the eyes of Christ. "Where within
me?"

If the imagination was a crack in the solid wall of his prison,
and if he could go through it, what then? What would he find
on the other side? Would he stumble into another battlefield,
where mad dogs tore at the carrion knights who had fallen in a
valiant but meaningless clash of arms? Would the dogs eat the
flesh of man, and man eat the flesh of dogs, slaves to an endless
cycle of murder and illusion and transmutation into more carnage in a descending spiral of negation?

*Within*, the voice had said. Was it a deceiver's voice—or a
father's? Could he risk seeing the pit within his soul? What if he
should discover that he too was a devourer?

The eyes of Christ did not answer. They merely told him
that he must go within and see.

Gradually it became clear what he must do. He took the
stack of white bond paper and set it before him.

"A hundred pieces", he whispered. "That is all. Everything
must be contained within its borders."

Then, bowing over the first sheet, he inscribed in fine italic
script:

### *Andrei Rublëv*

Those were the only words he was able to write that day, but in
the ensuing weeks he added many to them as the crack in the
solid wall of his prison widened, and continued to widen until
it became an open window.

# ANDREI RUBLËV

## A PLAY

BY

PAWEL TARNOWSKI

# ACT ONE

## Scene One

*The front door of a cabin on stage left. In front of the cabin is a small garden. Beyond it is forest. Above is a blue-black sky. A man stands in a field, stage right, gazing at the dawn. Gradually a streak of golden light appears above the trees. Sounds: a chorus of birds. The man is* ANDREI RUBLËV *in peasant clothing.*

ANDREI

Fire rising! Good father, sun, lie upon our mother the
    earth.
Cover her with the heat of your body.

*The sun glints on a distant dome of a Byzantine church. Far away, bells ring slowly.*

Ah, there the monks are gone to prayer, and I am about my
    own.
The prayer of the sweating brow and the hoe is a good
    partner for ecstasy.
Sing for me, little fathers; it is my wedding day!

ANDREI *hoes in the garden.*

Now the high white sun shall bud us forth a Savior,
for all the duke's men are sleeping off their wine,
and love overcomes her enemy, Time.

*He stops hoeing, then looks to stage right.*

When will Masha come? And how shall I tell her that I am
    torn,
first one way and then another?

*Faint Byzantine chanting in the distance.* ANDREI *speaks to the soil as if preaching.*

Listen, now, listen—they are singing—if you are wise little
    seeds,
you will burst forth and push, push toward the light.

*A woman enters from stage right, wearing a dark green cloak over a bright peasant dress.*

MASHA [*scolding*]
    Andrei! Who are you talking to?
ANDREI
    Masha, look, the soil itself is drinking in the music.
MASHA [*exasperated*]
    Might just as well pour a jug of *kvass* on them! And look at
        you!

ANDREI *inspects his hands, clapping off dirt.*

MASHA [*affectionately*]
    Only hours until our wedding and you dig in the garden!
    I can see well enough that I am to marry a fool!

ANDREI *tries to amuse her, grinning, dancing around her, playing the fool.*

ANDREI
    Ah, sweet Masha, tonight you will rule this place.
    Until then, I am Prince of the Turnips!
MASHA [*glancing around*]
    Mad boy!
    Yes, I shall rule [*sighs*], though it feels absurd.
    My father's house has ten goats and a milking maid.
    The logs are thick.
    There are sheepskins heaped upon the beds,
    and a fire that never ceases bakes a glut of bread.
    Still, I shall try to tame this little palace.

ANDREI's *face grows grave and he wishes to tell her something. Then he shakes off the mood, smiles tenderly, and cups her face in his hands as if for a kiss*

ANDREI

This is the night, this is the night when you shall come to
my cold cave.

Together we shall fill it with sweet fire.

MASHA [*pushing off his hand*]

There will be time enough for embraces!

ANDREI *laughs, then grows quiet. He looks up at the sky.*

ANDREI

I have questioned movements in the heavens

as armies move upon the earth.

Is it right that in these times you and I propose to make a
oneness?

Masha, have you guessed the why of things?

MASHA

It is the way of things we must consider, not the why.

MASHA *wanders over to the porch of the cabin, then starts in excitement. She bends and picks up an object and examines it with fascination.* ANDREI *does not notice.*

ANDREI

There is a voice within me that says I shall not be what I
propose to be . . .

[*slowly, cautiously*] . . . and that we shall not marry. Masha,
do you hear me?

MASHA

Andrei, this is a *wonder*! Oh, but you are magic!

*She turns to him and smiles ecstatically.*

Is this for me? Is it your gift on our wedding day?

ANDREI

> I painted it last evening as the sun burned down in
> > the west
> and was held for a moment in the fingers of the birches.
> There was a silence then, a tender break in the flow of
> > things.
> All beings caught their breath, and the tree ignited into
> > fire,
> burning, unconsumed.

MASHA [*intensely*]

> This image burns!

ANDREI

> It is the tree of Moses. There is a cross hidden in it.

MASHA

> I do not understand. I see no cross.

ANDREI

> A voice spoke to me from the heart of that glory.

MASHA *throws up her hands and laughs a contrived laugh.*

MASHA [*to herself*]

> They told me he would make a spouse both virtuous and
> > strong.
> A fine match, they said!
> But I am cursed, for he is also a man of dreams and follows
> > after *voices.*
> No fear. If he listens to his wife and God, he will come to
> > no harm.

ANDREI *looks at her intensely.*

ANDREI

> There is a thing I must tell you, but it is hard.

MASHA

Well, speak now. We do not want ghosts rambling through

when we are years wedded and there is no escape for a

woman.

ANDREI

I saw our Savior standing in the burning bush.

He gazed at me and beckoned;

from the tree he said most gently, "Come."

MASHA

What madness is this, Andrei? Voices and visions!

*She grabs his hand and pulls it against her breast.*

Do you feel this drum of heart? I breathe. I laugh.

[*She laughs.*]

And I shall be the Queen of Turnips who rules beneath

your eaves.

ANDREI *removes his hand.*

ANDREI

To a labor he called me, a holy work still hidden from my

eyes.

MASHA *recoils as if stung.*

MASHA

And is our love not holy? A man and woman pour their

very selves

into a bowl of flesh. And very soon we two shall take and

drink,

give and eat.

It is each other we shall consume.

*There is a long pause while ANDREI looks at the soil and then at the sky. MASHA continues, pleading.*

We will mix our heat, ignite a fire

to raise up over all this northern void. [*She gestures.*]

We will push back darkness, rebuke the winter night.

That is true gold, burning from the icon of our lives.

Is it not God speaking through our eyes?

ANDREI

Only partly so. Though we are flashes of fire,

We are but reflections of a hidden light.

We are not the light itself.

The way of man and woman,

The way of soul and soul, is a sacred path;

but there are others,

and to another I must go.

MASHA [*anguished*]

And only moments since you begged me for a kiss!

ANDREI

For a brief moment I forgot. I fell into the waking sleep,

in which we move from one unseeing to the next.

You must understand me—that dream is more awake to me
    now

than what we here enact.

MASHA [*shaking him by the shoulders*]

Awake! Awake, Andrei!

Tell me this is a false dream; this is your last foolishness;

this is not God; this is *kvass*!

ANDREI

This is the wine of God.

This is the trumpet blast that calls and calls but none
    attend.

None can see, none can hear.

The heavens are pulled back and one enormous Word
    comes up

over the rim of the world.

And a kingdom bursts forth to those trumpet blasts
as we sleep within our walled cities.

MASHA [*crying loudly*]

Andrei Rublëv!

*She turns to flee, but he catches her by the arm.*

ANDREI

Masha, dearest one, do you not know the man who stands
before you now?

This torn heart holds back a river of hot seed yearning to
spill into your field.

I would stroke the wheat of your flesh and gently break
together

the bread of our labor. The children who would come to
us are real to me.

MASHA [*bitterly, disbelieving*]

The fertile talk of lovers! The poetry of God!

False lover! False man! You leave me so alone.

ANDREI

There is nothing I can give you, then.

MASHA

Nothing, nothing. Give me nothing of yourself, or all.

I will not keep an amulet of you to obsess myself.

Far better to be plainly cruel.

Cut. Break. End this lovers' duel.

ANDREI

Take at least my painted miracle. It is my self, my own true
seed.

MASHA

You wound me with this giving, disown me with this gift.

*MASHA takes the painting, embraces it, and leaves with downcast
eyes.*

ANDREI
I . . .

*He gazes after her. Light fades. Bells ring slowly in the distance.*

## Scene Two

ANDREI *is seated by a stream, head in hands. Behind him is a birch copse, with no underbrush. There is the sound of birds calling, and the burble of a flowing brook. The sky is deep blue, one or two stars appearing. He looks up to a passing bird.*

ANDREI
Sing, you winged glory. Sing of the infamous Andrei
    Rublëv,
who spurns a bride to follow after voices.

*The warble of a lark. Andrei sings in the same notes:*

Andrei Rublëv is cruel; Andrei Rublëv is heartless.

*He looks up at the darkening sky as more stars appear. The lip of the moon is now slowly rising above the trees and crosses the sky throughout this scene.*

Speak, silence!
Must you now depart when I have need of you?
Voice, word, bursting into form.
[*raised voice*] Come to me.
[*shouting*] Return!
[*quietly, passionately*] Be reborn!

*He pauses, listening to the silence.*

The night is still. Hear the silence of God.

*He looks around himself.*

The forest awakes soon, and the cities sleep.

What did you call me forth to see?
I am helpless before all that is about to be.
There is a knowing, though, like secret knowledge,
like birch smoke on the wind. In this moment all juggling
    of doubts
and hopes, and questions, all costumes of the self.
To be a painting peasant or a pilgrim of the unseen, to
    father generations
or be a father of the soul . . . all possibilities lie within me.
A thousand thousand people lie unborn within my loins.
Am I a nation that shall not come to be?
In this moment of choice I see the forms that are our
    attempt to give shape
to the unknown. They are before me now.
With my eyes I see only darkness; now and then a spill of
    stars
illuminates a deeper darkness. It is night.

*The trees begin to rustle. The gentle sound of a breeze.*

But I gaze through spaces you have parted in the trees.
It is the wind which, knowing, courses through with sighs
    from pungent fields
and happy village streets, bearing home the long exhalation
    of angels.

ANDREI *embraces himself and looks up.*

I feel them round me, these presences. They are tall and
    fierce upon the hills,
their crystal eyes are poised to stand and wait, yearning for
    our silence.
Are they jubilant when we notice, at last, the stars?

*A branch cracks in the forest.* ANDREI *looks up with a start.*

What beast hunts me now?

*He hides behind the trees. A beautiful woman dressed in white and gold and rose, ribboned with silver streamers, dances onstage from stage left. Haunting music begins, deeply mysterious but very beautiful. The woman sings the notes of the lark song.*

WOMAN [*singing*]
Andrei Rublëv, where are you? [*She looks to right.*]
Andrei Rublëv, where are you? [*She looks to left.*]

ANDREI *emerges slowly from darkness.*

ANDREI
Who are you?
WOMAN
My name is Kahlia.

ANDREI *turns away fiercely.*

ANDREI
Go, myth, do not deceive my eyes! You are too lovely to
bear.
KAHLIA
Do not fear me. I am but a servant of the mystery.
ANDREI
Now I know that you deceive, for mystery is merely
ignorance
that shall disperse when we have found the facts.
Beauty—beauty is a well that shall never be plumbed.
KAHLIA
Dearest little brother, you speak as if you've mastered
what you barely know.

*She begins to dance. Her dance is pure and noble. It is classically beautiful but free-form, and all the while the mysterious music increases in intensity and harmonious movements. The music is in minor keys with Russian undercurrents, using balalaika and wind instruments.*

ANDREI

Cease this intoxication. Tell me who you are.

KAHLIA

I am one who is sent to tell you this:
I am your little sister of the arid bliss.
You are a prince without a kingdom,
you are a child without a home.
Come dwell in me, and find my love
more delightful than wine.
Fragrant my perfume.
Come kiss me with the kisses of your mouth;
come know my name, like oil poured out.

ANDREI

I know these words. They are old Solomon's song, his
    hymn to love.
Draw me then, and in your footsteps let us run.

ANDREI *follows her in the dance, but she continues to elude him
gracefully.*

ANDREI [*pleading*]

I charge you, do not stir my heart,
nor rouse it before it should awake.

KAHLIA

Your heart is yet untempered.
You love, yes, you love.
But you would throw away your life generously for any
    cause
that strikes you at the moment
as noble and beautiful and true.
You love this, now that, then another,
following whatever impulse courses through.

ANDREI *stops and looks dismayed.*

ANDREI

This may have once been so, but now I know what I am for;
I was made to give myself to you.
Whoever assembled you did exceed all art and skill.
I will plunge into your eyes forever, my soul companion,
happily drowned in an ocean of joy.

*The woman looks at him compassionately. They stand facing each other, a few steps apart.*

KAHLIA

Littlest brother, you do not know your own heart.

ANDREI

Then teach me about my heart.

KAHLIA

I come not to arouse the fires of Eros outside a holy bond.
It is the love between being and being I sing.
Within the beauty of this manly form and this woman's
grace,
there is a dialogue of souls. You have not learned its
language yet.
You are asleep.

ANDREI [*pinching himself*]

Ouch! I am awake enough! These eyes are open.
This tongue wags. This heart leaps from peak to peak.

KAHLIA

You sleep, you sleep, and your heart sleeps too.
One day I will awaken you under the tree, my little one,
my brother.
There where your mother conceived you,
there where she who gave birth to you conceived you,
I will awaken you, for love is stronger than death,
love relentless as Sheol.
The flash of it is a flash of fire,
a flame of the Lord himself.

*She crosses the stage, and* ANDREI *follows her at a distance, taking one or two uncertain steps. She turns and speaks to him.*

You who came unto my gardens
and listened for my voice,
now hasten away, my beloved.
Be like a young stag on the mountains of spices.
Listen well and follow,
for you shall see me like this no more.

*She dances off to stage left.*

ANDREI [*stunned, calling out longingly*]
Come back, my love,
come show me your face,
for your voice is sweet
and your face is beautiful.

*The haunting song of the lark.* ANDREI *seats himself by the brook. The wind rises, and a dog barks faintly in the distance.*

"Listen well and follow", she said.
"You shall see me like this no more", she said.
Oh, I do not like the taste of contradiction!

*He stands and paces around the stage.*

Where shall I find her?
She whom my heart loves.
Gone now, leaving a trace of indigo feathers in my hands,
and I, a blind man, feeling the night with my fingers [*he gropes blindly*],
for messages she has left on the wind.
I fall back now into my dream.
I cry, as soaring children dreaming of flight will cry in sleep,
and I, like fathers plowing sterile earth,
am left with nothing but to weep.

*The lark song repeats.* ANDREI *turns and listens carefully.*

Kahlia, how is it that I shall see you no more,
yet you will awaken me under a tree, you say?
Must I embrace a long and dreadful loneliness until that
    day?

*Once more the lark sings.*

And if I am to follow, how shall I know the way?

ANDREI, *center stage, faces the audience and stares blindly up.*

Shall it always be that I am blind—
shall be a kissing pilgrim who wanders alone,
and not alone?

# ACT TWO

## Scene One

*Winter, midday. Snow covers the ground. The sky is white, the sun pale. A stack of split firewood sits beside a log cabin. Behind is a forest of pine trees. There is an icon over the door of the building, and from its roof there rises a brilliant red Byzantine cross.*

*The sounds of axes splitting wood and wind blowing are heard. Two monks are stacking firewood. One is old with a long white beard. The other is young and beardless. They stop and stare at a man in rags who enters from stage left. The stranger is* ANDREI RUBLËV.

ANDREI

Good fathers, have you bread to spare and a bowl of water
    for a beggar?

*The old monk runs forward and embraces* ANDREI *tenderly.*

NIKON

Welcome, Christ!

*The young monk,* DANIIL, *puts his hands on his hips.*

DANIIL [*loudly, sarcastically*]

Father Nikon, can't you see: that parasite is no Christ?
He's a wandering leech searching for a vein.
Unhold him before he bleeds you dry.

NIKON

Ah, surely he is Christ twice over now. Not only hungry
    but insulted.

DANIIL [*disgusted*]

We want no strangers here.

NIKON

You are right, Daniil, this is no stranger. Enter in, brother.

DANIIL

Brother?! There is not enough bread for your real brothers.

NIKON

Have you not heard it said that every stranger is the Savior
in disguise?

[*turning to* ANDREI] Enter in, brother.

DANIIL

These are bad times. Tartars raiding in the fields have
burned the harvests,

torched the towns.

NIKON

Come.

ANDREI

I thank you, holy father. My name is Andrei Rublëv.

I beg your patience more than bread. I have lost my way in
this forest.

If you could spare me rest for one night, I will depart more
swiftly than I came.

NIKON

Stay a lifetime, if you please. This is God's house, not mine.

ANDREI [*distressed, with weak voice*]

No, I cannot stay.

Three years I have wandered across this world and shall not
cease.

I am searching for one who flees me down the labyrinthine
ways.

I do not know who or what she is. Only that her name is
Kahlia.

NIKON

Kahlia?

ANDREI

She is a bird who carves spiral wakes into the air.

She is the lark ascending or the swift descent of hawks.

I see her in a child's face, a gesture in a dance,

a storm of cottonseed on wind.

NIKON [*nodding*]

Yes, I know her, too.

ANDREI

You know her! Tell me where she is, she whom my heart
seeks.

NIKON [*gently*]

She is here.

DANIIL

Father Nikon! What cosmic buffoonery! This beggar raves;

he is sick with talk of birds, and you encourage it.

Let us be content with facts. There is no bread and he is ill.

What will the brothers say? Unhold him or you'll catch a
vile disease.

NIKON [*gestures to Daniil*]

Silence, Daniil.

*The young monk obeys grudgingly. Then* NIKON *kisses* ANDREI *on both cheeks and leads him across the stage toward the door of the building.*

ANDREI

I am the cause of trouble, Father. Let me offer payment of
a kind.

I was a painter once and could decorate your cabins well.

I might paint a skylark that's a wonder to behold.

DANIIL

Humble, too.

ANDREI

I can discern the rainbow, if you provide the paint.

In winter you would have upon your walls a vision of trees
with reds and golds to cheer your hearts.

NIKON

You paint, you say?

ANDREI

Once, long ago.

NIKON

But not the holy icons.

ANDREI

No. I am not a saint.

NIKON

You answer well, though time will tell.

I have much to teach you.

DANIIL

What! Teach this fool? You cannot mean it, throwing pearls
to swine.

This sort will steal the bread and gulp the sacrificial wine.

NIKON

You misjudge him.

DANIIL

I am your apprentice. I'll not share space with some cagey
peasant.

NIKON

We are all cagey peasants before God.

You are my most gifted student, Daniil.

But I warn you, pride has rotted greater gifts than yours.

This man seeks no glory.

He has learned the essential lesson. Study him well.

DANIIL *tosses his head and rolls his eyes.*

CHORUS OF MONKS [ *chanting in background* ]

There is an icon in the world,

outcrying being's fall from light;

it is a fire within our dark, our inner space,

that speaks a word of love, of grace.

198

What womb will bring this word full forth?
In all the world is there one soul who'll waste
his life for God, who'll speak of Light?
The Light who's born not once but over and over
in every soul that waits.

Other makers on the wall of caves
will blink the sightless eye,
pictures formed by Lucifer himself,
appearances of light, a bending of essential form.
A mimicry of life,
his temple is a mass of graves, a billion icons left unborn.

But he who follows inner eye,
accepts the search, the grief, the sigh,
will follow deeper channels of the heart,
and advocates will take his part,
while man condemns what yet abides.

Strip this beggar of his filthy garments,
drive him up the hill of skulls,
grind the pigments of his will,
render all things down to wine and bread,
an empty gut, a pilgrim's hut.

Show him private fathers weeping under trees,
uncaved prophets crying for the beat of a single raven's
      wing,
for bread in the mouth and honey on the tongue,
or one sweet song by children sung.
Show him, show him, a broken hive,
and it may be that he shall be
very, yes, very alive.

Show him Truth, show him fire,
help him read aright the devices of the Liar.

And on the day he bleeds beside a road,
his beauty failed, his body nailed
to someone's ornamental tree,
tell him that he wakes that morning to be free.

NIKON

Daniil, take this man and wash his feet, then show him to a
bed.
The cell of the dead Saint Sergius will do.

*DANIIL looks disgusted but obeys. The two men enter the cabin.
NIKON, center stage, piles two blocks of wood, then holds a third
block, staring at it. The light begins to fade.*

Is this a final gift before the end?
A noble heart within a tent of rags?
But still a heart that is untrained to stability.
It is impatient and young.

*NIKON looks down at the wood in his hands.*

Tree,
good servant, wood,
what shall be done on you,
an icon or a man crucified?
It is murder what we do to others
in our confused flight.
Pride and fear breed hatred,
at best dishonest truce with night.
Empty and afraid he comes,
bearing old lamentations,
seeking honest labor
or a trade of beauty for some bread,
to purchase peaceful weariness and rest,
and maybe graceful death.

*Stars begin to appear.*

White are my whiskers, old my boots,
now and then I see the roots of growing things.
Every night above the trees
I watch the universe appear.
Perhaps it is coming soon,
before the ending of the year.
Come it may on hooves of Tartar bands
or in a sleep.
I wonder what it is to be dead.
I'll stoke the fire and go to bed.

NIKON *moves across the stage toward the cabin. He stops, turns, and addresses the audience.*

Innocence comes visiting,
in huddle-camps of fear.
Fragile genius walks through winter,
across the long abyss of our dark age.
Is it right for me to make my quick escape,
making apologies, pleading age?
I think not.

*He pauses.*

Can this sore old heart take hope again?
[*raised voice, looks up to right*] I thank you!
[*raised voice, looks up to left*] I thank you!
for sending this child to me.
I will do what I can.
I cannot die yet.

*A bell rings slowly as* NIKON *walks toward the cabin.*

## Scene Two

*Interior of a log room. In the center of the wall is a window, covered with a white screen for projecting images, as in a motion picture. When projection begins, there should be a fading in and fading out of each consecutive image, with a few seconds' overlap so that visually the effect is subtle and does not give the impression of a distracting play within a play.*

*In a corner of the room is an icon of Christ with a red votive light burning before it. On either side of the window, toward the front of the stage, there are two low tables and benches facing the center. ANDREI is on stage left, DANIIL on stage right. NIKON walks slowly between the two. Both students are painting on small panels that lie flat on their tables. ANDREI is now in monk's robes.*

NIKON [*in a firm instructor's voice*]

The icon is a window.

ANDREI and DANIIL [*in unison*]

The icon is a window.

NIKON

And to whom shall it open?

ANDREI and DANIIL

To those who wait before it.

NIKON

Who will wait before it?

ANDREI and DANIIL

Those who are poor.

NIKON

And who are the poor?

ANDREI and DANIIL

Those who are empty.

NIKON

Who are the empty?

ANDREI and DANIIL

Those who desire nothing.

Those who desire to be nothing.

NIKON

Good. Very good, my sons.

It must be added, though, that this "nothing" is not the
evil darkness

of negation. It is the nothingness of Christ before Pilate.

The scandal of God violated on a Cross.

DANIIL *yawns and stretches, puts down his brush, and appears to be
very bored.* ANDREI *leans forward.*

ANDREI

Father, tell us how it is that one may desire to be nothing.

NIKON *pauses, thinking of his answer. At this point, images of icons
gradually begin to project on the screen and are changed every five to
ten seconds, continuously until the end of the scene.*

NIKON

When one ceases to desire anything, even to desire to be a
successful *staretz*,[1]

ceasing even to desire to desire nothing.

When one is content to simply be,

to walk humbly, to love God.

DANIIL [*laughing*]

Well, riddles within riddles. That is the fox who swallowed
his tail.

NIKON

A monk is one who gives up everything.

Leaving the world of things and souls turned into things,

he arrives at a secret place of the heart where he is given
everything.

[1] *staretz*: a Russian holy man.

ANDREI

Even beauty?

NIKON

Especially beauty.

But not the forms of beauty that can be possessed.

For to possess her would be to kill her. And Lady Wisdom would not

permit the death of her little sister.

ANDREI

I have often wondered why we speak of this or that as he and she.

It is plain, of course, that Beauty is a mother,

for all have drunk from her breast.

I have seen the long lines of convinced sinners turned around by her caress.

Oh, I too have felt her sacred smile.

It poured, poured into my own abyss

when just a small apocalypse ago

she mercifully entered in.

DANIIL *raises his eyes in disgust and grimaces at* ANDREI.

NIKON

Wisdom too is a woman—but old and plain.

At first glance she is a maiden aunt.

Few desire her.

Few have discovered her great secret, the sweetness of her glance.

DANIIL

Give me Beauty every time;

Lady Wisdom can fend for herself.

NIKON

In the ancient days to desire her was called *philosophia*— love of wisdom.

And *philokalia* was the love of her little sister, Beauty by
name.
You know not one if you know not both, Daniil.
DANIIL
Ha! Introduce me to the younger first!
NIKON
It is the elder you should court.
In time of locusts and brittle twigs,
when bushes of holy fire refuse to ignite,
and your heart is a bowl emptied by cold wind,
all your grain scattered and your soul become sterility,
she will sit by the void where you have been planted,
where no word, no voice, is heard.
Where only an absurd wind contradicts the bad news,
she will be your companion,
for she is the patroness of all inhospitable soil.
Brief is her theophany,
but longer than the thorn that pierces and protects.
Far out, out into the vastness
shoot the yellow dusted bees, going with purpose
about their vocation.
But you have made your home in deprivation,
your only purpose to have no purpose;
your only wealth is emptiness.
While others push, push forth from fertile flesh
the sweet Jordan almond, orange bloom,
the herb, the berry,
you are trodden underfoot,
broken,
thrown upon the garbage heap, the fire.

*Both students gaze stricken at their master.* DANIIL *cups his hand to
his mouth and addresses himself to* ANDREI:

DANIIL

I think he is a bit extreme!

NIKON [*gesturing to the screen on which icons are being projected*]

I see them before me, brothers,

as if they still exist,

the children of my soul,

blown by gales of war,

plucked by thieves,

eyes gouged out by madmen and devils,

erupting by the score into roses of flame,

a garden of cruel glory grown by Tartars.

ANDREI

Some say there is no hope, holy father.

Some say the end of the world draws near.

NIKON

The end of the world draws very near.

It has drawn near since the beginning.

DANIIL

That is an old specter striding across the stage of history.

Four hundred years ago deluded souls thought the world
was ending.

All Europe was in panic.

NIKON

In the year nine ninety-nine, as the millennium
approached, the world was very ill.

It was like a man who came close to death and then
recovered at the last moment.

Because he recovered—and believe me, my sons, he only
barely recovered—

should we now say that he never was dying?

And when the time comes that he will truly die, should we
then say,

"Oh no, he will not die, for once long ago he nearly died
    and didn't"?
DANIIL
    But how can a world end, I ask you?!
NIKON
    If a world can begin, it can end.
    It is far more difficult to create a world than to destroy it.
    Look around you! Do we not live and move and have our
        being
    upon the face of a miracle?
    We have ceased to notice what a marvel it is.
ANDREI
    Father, what use, then, to pour out a life to make an icon?
NIKON
    Truth must be spoken, even if none see, none hear.
DANIIL
    Such morose thoughts! Father, give us a word of truth—
        about women.
    Real women.
NIKON
    If you wish to know about women, read the Book of the
        Apocalypse.
DANIIL
    I read it once.
    A normal man cannot make heads or tails of it.
    It's a bore!
NIKON
    It is a written icon, full of terror and woe,
    beauty and wisdom—a chronicle of our own demise.
ANDREI
    I opened it once and wept. It seemed to be a mirror in
        which I saw
    my own heart.
    I could look no more.

NIKON [*gently*]

All comes to pass,

but be assured that those who do not take up the sword

will inherit the earth.

DANIIL

Women! Tell us about women!

NIKON

In the Apocalypse there is a bifold image of humanity

at the end of the ages.

One is of the Bride: pure, radiant, wise,

made holy and waiting for the Groom.

The other is the whore of Babylon, proud and lustful,

deceiver and persecutor of the Church.

DANIIL

The holy book looks much unkindly upon the other half

of our race.

NIKON

Not so.

Think on this, my sons:

the evangelist was party to a deeper truth:

harlot and bride are within us all.

Childless, childless goes the whore

to a death before the body's death.

Yet if we choose a higher spouse

we shall be fertile by his word,

gestate it in the silence of our souls.

And bear it forth to bring salvation to this world.

DANIIL *laughs.*

DANIIL

Come, come, good father, you exaggerate.

Have we brought salvation to this world?

Look at these vile times.

Fourteen hundred years have passed, and the world is more
   lost than ever.

[*spreading his arms wide*] Where are the harvests?

[*frowning at* ANDREI] Where are the long lines of
   convinced sinners turning round?

The light of Jerusalem's extinguished!

NIKON

This is Nazareth.

A simple place,

where bread is baked and wood is chopped,

where the prayer of nobodies goes up like cook-smoke.

The boy Christ grows in our midst

waiting for his day.

DANIIL

This lesson grows foxier by the minute. Let's get back to
   facts.

Christianity has failed.

NIKON [*sadly*]

If you find it so, why do you stay?

DANIIL [*defensively*]

It is good enough soil for a young man to grow a talent.

NIKON [*sighing*]

Be seated. I will tell you of women.

Once I went to my master, Saint Sergius,

the founder of this monastery.

I was young then, and believed perfection was the product
   of my will.

I thought holiness was only for the strong. A secret pride
   was in my soul.

It was a worm boring toward its core.

"Father, a word!" I begged Saint Sergius one day,

"Father, tell me what I must do to be perfect. I pray eight
   hours a day;

I eat only one meal; I wear a hair shirt;
I have given all that I own to the poor.
Yet I am still troubled that I am not perfect."
Sergius said all I had done was good
but that I had not yet understood perfection.
"Go," he said, "go and dream the deep dreams of God.
He will teach you."
So I went away and slept.

In a dream our Savior came to me and knelt beside my
    bed,
writing with his fingers in the dust.
"Nikon," he said, "you do well, but you have not yet
    attained
the perfection of two married women who live in the
    village."

When I awoke I went down to the village, a half-day's
    journey by foot.
And there I found two women who spoke no rash words,
who lived in humility, patience, and charity,
sanctified their actions with prayer,
and put up with the ill humors of their husbands.
It was there I learned humility.

*The students look at each other for a few seconds.* NIKON *then claps
his hands as if to break a spell and continues.*

However, let us cease to talk of women,
those most glorious creatures of God, lest we lose our
    balance
and totter dizzily off through the forest in search of villages.
DANIIL
Is there still a wrestling at your age?
Surely a weight of years brings relief from that battle!

NIKON

You shall have to ask someone older than I.
I know one thing.
I am a sinner, though one more beguiled by God.
Until my final day I hope and pray for grace enough
to pour all love into the offspring of my soul [*points to
    icons*].

*Bells, liturgical music—Byzantine, polyphonic.*

## Scene Three

*Night.* ANDREI RUBLËV's *sleep is troubled. He lies on a cot beneath
the icon of Christ, below which burns a red candle. The room is in
semidarkness. A child's voice, sweet and clear, is reading the Gospel of
Matthew 17:1–8, the account of the Transfiguration. The voice begins
close to inaudible, then within seconds increases to slightly above
normal speaking level.*

CHILD'S VOICE

Six days later, Jesus took with him Peter and James and his
brother John. He led them up a high mountain where they
could be by themselves. There in their presence he was
transfigured. His face shone like the sun and his clothes
became as dazzling white as the light. Moses and Elijah
suddenly appeared to them. They were talking with Jesus.
Then Peter spoke to Jesus. "Lord," he said, "it is wonderful
for us to be here. If you wish, I will make three tents here,
one for you, one for Moses, and one for Elijah." He was still
speaking when suddenly a bright cloud covered them with
shadow, and from the cloud there came a voice that said,
"This is my Son, the Beloved on whom my favor rests. Listen
to him." When they heard this, the disciples fell on their
faces, overcome with fear. But Jesus came toward them and

touched them. "Stand up", he said. "Do not be afraid." And when they raised their eyes they saw no one but Jesus.

*Toward the end, the child's voice fades. Then there is silence.* ANDREI *wakes with a start and half-rises from his cot.*

ANDREI

I thought I heard a child speaking to me from the depth of dream.

Was it an angel, or a son who will never be?

*He puts his feet on the floor, rubs his arms, and looks around. Then, tentatively, with foreboding:*

I am afraid.

DANIIL *enters hastily through door on left. Wind and snow blow in with him.*

DANIIL

Rublëv, awake!

ANDREI

I am awake.

DANIIL

Haste, we must flee.

ANDREI

From what must we flee? All that we fear is within ourselves, is it not?

DANIIL *looks exasperated and slaps his legs.*

DANIIL

No time for wisdom, dear brother saint.

This is the hour of good sense.

A time to run full speed into the forest.

Tartars!

ANDREI

All is quiet.

DANIIL

There is fire on the horizon.

And distant cries borne upon the wind,

carried on the cold night air.

I heard them while out walking by the river.

ANDREI

Why out so late in the night and the wind?

DANIIL

I was restless, lured by something.

A voice I thought I heard.

ANDREI

Ah, this night is full of voices.

Holy angels, or the spirits of the air?

DANIIL

I fear this night.

Is it to be a feast of darkness,

a dance of violation,

a cauldron of despair?

ANDREI

Or the moment of absolute faith?

DANIIL

If only it were the spirits of the air,

the inhabitants of Pandemonium!

No, real Death gallops on swift hooves,

and I do not wish to be in his path.

Let us delay that meeting for another day.

ANDREI

The time must come in every life when that old monster,
     Death, appears.

All must wrestle at close quarters with him. Why not now?

DANIIL

Are you crazed? No one wins in that debate.

No words yet invented can save you from his argument.

Run, evade, is my advice.

Delay as long as possible the coming of that fate.
It will give us time to paint a little,
and leave a small memento on the earth.

ANDREI

I left a girl who would have been my mate,
an inheritance of children to enrich the world.
What took me from her?
A voice that is fading now, faded, faded.

*ANDREI suddenly looks up at DANIIL's face.*

Why is it I am still torn between love and—Love?

DANIIL [*yelling*]

No talk of women. Let's go, Andrei!

*Bells begin to ring in alarm. Faint voices in the background swell to shouts and shrieks amid the sound of galloping horses.*

*DANIIL grabs ANDREI and makes for the door. At that moment NIKON enters without a word and gathers them with outstretched arms. He herds them toward the icon, and they kneel before it. NIKON is in the center, with the younger men on either side. NIKON's arms are raised in supplication.*

NIKON

Pray, brothers, not to be spared,
but that our hearts will keep courage and the truth.

*Shouts and shrieks increase in volume. The monks bow slightly toward the icon.*

DANIIL

Can we no longer flee?

NIKON

There is little hope of that. But should a miracle occur, and
    you be spared,
go to Moscow. Seek out Theophanes the Greek.
He will teach you all I have failed to impart.

*The door bursts open. A* TARTAR *warrior strides in, sword in hand. He has a fierce Oriental face and is taller than the other figures. All three monks rise,* NIKON *first.* NIKON *steps forward.*

NIKON

Peace!

*The* TARTAR *strikes him down with the sword.* DANIIL *takes a staff and swings it at the Tartar. The* TARTAR *lifts his foot to* DANIIL's *chest and pushes him across the room, where his head strikes the wall and he collapses, unconscious. The* TARTAR *approaches* ANDREI, *who stands calmly.* ANDREI *extends his arms in a cross.*

ANDREI

Welcome, Brother Death.

*The* TARTAR *raises his sword, then laughs. He brandishes it around* ANDREI's *head, but the monk remains motionless.*

TARTAR

"Welcome, Brother Death!" [*laughing*] Ai, this Russia
is a land full of strangeness.
Fools abound here thicker than teats on pigs.
Well, you are fat enough for the butcher.

*The* TARTAR *raises his sword high but cannot bring it down. He looks at* ANDREI, *puzzled.*

You, young sorcerer, what spell is this that holds my killing
     arm?

ANDREI

No spell. My only power is to have no power.
Nothing I know of holds your arm
save what's in your heart.

TARTAR

I have no heart. There is only the sword and rule.
There is only the terrible knowledge of the victor.

A muscled arm and thigh, my falcon's eye;
these are my negotiations with life.

ANDREI

It may well be that life intends to dull your point.
God himself has said your time of rule is brief,
and peace shall eternally succeed unto peace.

TARTAR

Peace! Only fools and weaklings talk of peace,
that ancient dream of simple men.
Those who hold the sword know the sovereignty of death.
None of us escapes alive.
Death is peace, and he who holds this blade is death's
agent.
But speak on, speak on.
I am bored with slaughter.
A little entertainment suits me well.

ANDREI

You speak of courage, but tell me this—who is stronger:
one who is ruled by fear and must hold a weapon
to prove his false invincibility?
Or one who stands powerless
with peace reigning in his soul?

TARTAR [*blustering*]

The one with the sword, of course.
He knows the structure of the world,
he knows that strong men inherit the earth
and win what they aspire.
Do you take me for a child?

ANDREI

Yes. You are a small child engulfed by impressive
armament.
You are deceived to think it your true shape.

TARTAR [*beating his breastplate*]

It is molded to my flesh.

I am a glorious animal.

I am my god's beast.

I am terror.

I defeat all hearts,

I break all enemies upon the battlefield.

ANDREI

But not the ones within yourself.

What small enemies you vanquish here!

TARTAR

But larger than I'd thought.

You intrigue me with your monk's prattle.

ANDREI

The armor molds you, Brother Death.

One day you'll take it off, and then this world will be
washed.

And children will play without terror

in the wind.

TARTAR

Until that day it is men like me who rule the world.

We play with blood.

ANDREI

I know of One who is coming,

One who conquers with a Word.

He puts forth his foot not to crack a neck,

but to break a tomb,

and crushes with his foot the Lie.

Will you not pray with me to him

and hasten the coming of his day?

TARTAR

I'll do more than that, little fool.

I'll turn you loose to labor for that day.

217

I'll watch to see if this great planetary argument
proves you right and me the fool.
It interests me to see if your one enormous Word
shall radiate throughout all the burnt world.
Or if my blade will have the final say.
Until then I think that I shall keep to burning [*brandishes sword*].
Go! Go! Before I change my mind.

# ACT THREE

## Scene One

*Interior of a cathedral. Three whitewashed apses face the audience. Scaffolding covers these from stage left to stage right, to a height halfway to the top of the mural space. The center apse contains an uncompleted painting of Christ. A bent old man, with a blanket over his shoulders, sits on top of the scaffold, dangling his legs. Beside him are pots of paint and heavy brushes. With gasps and groans he lifts his legs and shifts his body to face the audience. He dangles his legs again. He is* THEOPHANES THE GREEK.

THEOPHANES

You grow old, you grow weary,
poor beast of burden.
In this wild country even a genius must go shivering
to his grave.
[*yelling*] Servants, where are my wine and bread?!
[*murmuring*] Oh, my flesh aches for the sun of Athens,
my soul for the golden courts of Byzantium.

VOICE OFFSTAGE

No, it is not permitted. The master is at work.

DANIIL [*from offstage*]

But we have a message for your master.

*DANIIL enters, followed by* ANDREI. *DANIIL wears a white bandage around his head.*

DANIIL

Greetings, sir, from your old friend, the monk Nikon,
unfortunately now deceased. He sends us to you.

THEOPHANES

How so, dead?

Old age or arrow?

Fever or sword?

DANIIL

Sword.

THEOPHANES [*matter-of-factly*]

Ah, the sword. Tartars, no doubt.

I have heard they raid and ruin to the north and the east.

Vladimir burned, and Holy Trinity.

But they would never dare assault upon Moscow.

DANIIL

They are beyond all daring, sir.

They do what they will do, and none can hold them back.

THEOPHANES

And Nikon gone, you say. Why does he send you to me?

I have no cells for two boy monks. I am a ward of the
    duke.

DANIIL

Honorable Theophanes, I am Daniil Chernyi, apprenticed
    in the holy art under Nikon.

He promised me that I would find in you the skill that was
    incomplete in me.

THEOPHANES

Can you paint?

DANIIL

Excellently, Master. I was considered the most gifted of his
    students.

I can—

THEOPHANES [*tonelessly, distracted*]

Yes, yes, yes.

And who is that gaunt bird behind you?

ANDREI

My name is Andrei Rublëv, Master.

THEOPHANES

Can you paint?

ANDREI

    I know next to nothing.

THEOPHANES

    A good answer. If you had said yes, I would call the guards
        and have you thrown into the river.

    He who thinks himself God's painter knows neither God
        nor icons.

DANIIL

    You say this, the greatest painter of all the Russ!

THEOPHANES

    And beyond, as far as Constantinople.

DANIIL [ *to Andrei* ]

    A curious mixture of humility and pride!

THEOPHANES

    You must discern the office from the man, young dolt.

THEOPHANES *then gazes up to heaven. Then, long-sufferingly:*

    Nikon, old companion, what joke is this you send me in
        the end,

    a buffoon swollen like a bladder with his pride?

DANIIL [ *indignantly* ]

    Buffoon! Unlike a court painter I could name,

    I do not prance for princes to generate some fame.

    I am my own man.

    I am considered in some quarters to be a person of genius.

THEOPHANES [ *guffawing* ]

    Well, well!

    Young genius, meet old genius.

    We are both bags of hot gas, dear boy.

    The difference between you and me is that sixty years of
        life

    have punctured mine.

    A pointed truth accomplishes this as finely as a blade.

DANIIL *fumes. While the above exchange was occurring,* ANDREI, *not listening, wandered over to the central apse and now stands gazing in rapt attention at the painting of Christ's face.* THEOPHANES *looks at* ANDREI *silently for some moments, then gestures toward him.*

I feel it in my bones,

there stands fragile genius; there the future dwells.

[*loudly*] You! Rublëv! Do you wish to paint?

ANDREI

If it is your wish, Master.

THEOPHANES

Then you shall. You are my apprentice.

ANDREI *bows to the old man.* THEOPHANES *climbs painfully down the scaffolding.*

DANIIL [*outraged*]

And what of me?

THEOPHANES

Your arrogance is so naïve it is almost innocence!

Tell me, can one little cathedral contain three geniuses?

DANIIL

There is nowhere else for me to go.

The world has become a dangerous place.

If I cannot nest beneath the duke's wing,

then I am a dead genius.

*A faint bell rings once, then twice.*

THEOPHANES

At last, a note is sounded on the sweet bell of humility.

Agreed, you stay too.

But of course it is demeaning to inflict apprenticeship on
    so great a talent.

I offer you a more singular role. You will be unique,
    essential to our cause.
DANIIL
    Splendid! When do I begin?
THEOPHANES
    Immediately:
    you'll grind the pigments, and then, when done,
    you'll clean the brushes,
    and after that, you'll scrub the floor.
    I know that you shall accomplish all with genius.

    THEOPHANES *shuffles out slowly to right, bent over his cane.*
    DANIIL *is infuriated. He huffs and folds his arms melodramatically.*
    ANDREI *approaches and touches his shoulder.*

ANDREI
    Daniil, I am sorry.

    DANIIL *shakes off* ANDREI'S *hand and exits, stomping. This is
    followed shortly by a few seconds of haunting music, very faint.*
    ANDREI *is left alone on the stage. He turns to left and right.*

    Music that is soundless.
    Fire in the bones.

    *He turns and faces the painting of Christ on the apse wall.*

    Gold is glory, red is pain,
    blue is wisdom, white is pure.
    All move together in the dance that is sure.
    All breathe in beauty [*inhales*].
    All breathe forth wisdom [*exhales*].

    *A few notes of a lark's song.*

    A night bird!

    *He turns this way and that.*

223

Kahlia!

*Silence.*

The path comes forth from dreams,
passing away into a dream.
What's left is now.
A moment when the soul chooses to cry beyond its place
    and time.
From every human soul a word is born, or torn.
It lives awhile and goes with it unto the grave.
[*He gestures to mural*] But here a word is born that speaks in
    all the thronging tongues of man.

*The haunting music begins again, barely audible; then it increases
gradually.*

Singing down through ages and ages,
to all the children of the earth.
"Listen, little ones, listen", it sings.
"Listen. The great mystery is not just a marvel on a wall.
It is within. It is within us all."
[*looks down at his hands*] Oh, I am uncertain. I think it
    better to be
an artist of the hoe.
This flesh is suited for the yoke.
I am unworthy.
I am too poor.

*Music. Lights fade, leaving an image of Christ's face burning in the
darkness.*

## Scene Two

*Three apses. Many smaller icons are on the side walls. The central face of Christ is completed. The apse mural at stage left is also completed (Saint John the Baptist). THEOPHANES and ANDREI are on the scaffold in front of the apse, stage right. They are working on the uncompleted mural of the Mother of God. Below, DANIIL is sweeping with a large twig broom. From time to time he casts a look above.*

THEOPHANES

What day is this, Andrei Rublëv?

ANDREI

The Feast of the Transfiguration, Master.

THEOPHANES

How long since God sent you to me?

ANDREI

I do not know.

Time swells, fades, meanders.

It is a golden river in the autumn sun.

All things pass away;

only this remains [*points to mural*].

THEOPHANES

Yes, yes, but how long?

DANIIL [*shouting up to them*]

Twice three years, add four months,

and twenty-seven days.

[*quietly to himself, in resignation*] Time's no river.

Time's long, steady-paced,

and remorseless as a mule.

THEOPHANES

The duke has given me seven years to make the invisible
     visible.

Well, we are nearly through, soon done in good time.

[*sighs*] My old fingers creak.
Daniil, Daniil, fetch my cane.

THEOPHANES *begins to descend the scaffold slowly, with great effort.*

DANIIL

Yes, good Master.

*Face-to-face at the bottom,* THEOPHANES *looks at* DANIIL.

THEOPHANES

Tell me, do you still wish to paint?

DANIIL

Do not be cruel.

THEOPHANES

Were I to say that for seven more years it is your lot to
sweep and scrape,

to retrieve the fallen brushes of your aerial brother [*points
to* ANDREI],

would you decline to accompany us further through time?

DANIIL

No. The circling of the seasons is adequate reminder of
our aims.

Spring gives way to winter. Birth to death.

We circle a gully-hole into a pit.

All men go down into it.

Ambitions shrink before this fact.

THEOPHANES

Perhaps this serving has burned the dross from you.

DANIIL

I do not know.

I eat. I breathe. I pray.

I lay my body down to earnest sleep.

THEOPHANES

And measure time like a miser, it seems.

DANIIL

　　To answer your question:

　　It is good if I paint;

　　it is good if I do not, but—candidly—a little less so.

THEOPHANES

　　Aha! A bitter note is hiding here?

DANIIL

　　I know of none.

　　I am an emptiness waiting to be filled.

THEOPHANES [*yawning rudely*]

　　I must be off to take my nap.

　　Kindly bear these brushes up above

　　and if you're moved to do so,

　　add a stroke or two.

　　That robe is wanting deeper blue.

DANIIL [*shocked, moved*]

　　Master, do you mean . . . ?

THEOPHANES

　　Yes, yes.

THEOPHANES *exits stage right.* DANIIL *climbs up the scaffold and sits a foot or two apart from* ANDREI.

　　*A pot of heavy brushes is between them. Both sit perfectly still, facing the mural, their backs to the audience. Twenty to thirty seconds pass. Slowly,* ANDREI *reaches across and places an arm around* DANIIL*'s shoulders, inclines his head toward* DANIIL.

　　DANIIL *bends toward* ANDREI *until their heads touch for an instant, then part. They continue to sit perfectly still, then* DANIIL *bends suddenly, overcome with emotion.*

ANDREI

　　A stroke of gold is needed here,

　　some glory woven into pain.

　　Christ's face is shining now;

　　you are his icon.

From your own encounter with the Cross
you will extract the colors of the Resurrection.

DANIIL

Andrei, I think that I no longer can.

There is nothing in me.

ANDREI

Nor in me. Just begin.

[*gestures*] Look. See to that stroke of blue.

There will be another after it to beckon you.

DANIIL *begins to paint slowly, tentatively.*

DANIIL

The window must be cleansed to permit the passage of
light.

ANDREI

And to whom will it open?

DANIIL and ANDREI [*in unison*]

To those who wait before her.

ANDREI

And who will wait before her?

ANDREI and DANIIL

Those who are poor.

ANDREI

And who are the poor?

ANDREI and DANIIL

Those who are empty.

ANDREI

We are almost empty, Daniil.

When we are completely so, we shall be made full.

DANIIL

You are always full, Andrei.

You are a ruble, I am a kopek.

This glory pours from you.

ANDREI

> You are gazing at a window from the outside.
>
> There is a thing within that worries me.

DANIIL

> I've fought the worm that rots the fruit in me;
>
> don't say there's one in you!
>
> You, the subject of my past envies.

ANDREI [*slapping the scaffold*]

> You envied a man upon his cross.
>
> I fear this thing in me that hunts for beauty.
>
> Not a yearning of the flesh but a passion for the visible.

*He gestures reverently toward the icon of Christ.*

> I love this face,
>
> I love him, but I wonder, could I love him burdened
>
> with the agony of the world, torn and ridiculed,
>
> underneath his Cross,
>
> the malice of the human heart hurled upon him,
>
> no looks to attract our eyes,
>
> broken, ugly, covered with vile abuse?
>
> [*passionately*] Is it the ubiquitous goddess Beauty I worship?
>
> What errors might I do in her name,
>
> if given half a chance?
>
> I dare not think of it.

*Faint chanting in background—male chorus.*

> Nor do I trust humanity, yet I am embedded in it.
>
> We are children roving about the world,
>
> possessing all, naming all, knowing all,
>
> except ourselves.

DANIIL [*gesturing to the icon of the Mother of God*]

> Perhaps Lady Wisdom could speak a word or two
>
> of her small sister.
>
> A goddess, Andrei, or a friend?

These two might, hand in hand, guide us through a brutal
    age.
ANDREI
    You speak well. Your own gold's been tested in fire
    and found to be true.
    It is my turn, brother, to learn from you.

    Forgive me, I was caught on the hook of a bitter doubt.
    I saw us gathered round this transfigured face upon a
        height,
    like Peter, James, and John,
    except that from the distance of a millennium and a half,
    the light had grown thin.
    I wondered if it would always be,
    that we who dream these dreams enhance the image of our
        hope,
    hold it high to calm our terrors
    and to ease the wound of our mortality.
DANIIL
    Grievous is this mortality,
    but also glorious.
    There is a puzzle here.
    Do we need to know its solving?
ANDREI
    It is the artist's danger,
    being master of the form,
    to forget that he is poor,
    to think he is the master of the invisible reality,
    which this reflection represents.

    *He glances toward the icon of Christ.*

    I asked him once if I would ever see
    his hidden face so veiled by imagery.
    But he was silent.

DANIIL

The icon of the silent God.

ANDREI [*his voice rising passionately until it is a sustained cry*]

O Three-in-One,

O lavish blue fire,

flashed from silver foil,

O holy green, and pure vermilion,

you are a wine poured into creatures made of mud.

It is a grief, it is a grief!

My hand and my eye and my heart

fall, fall, fall so far from the face that this little scribble
represents.

DANIIL

I think an artist is a man hung upon a tree.

ANDREI [*nodding*]

He is you. He is me.

DANIIL [*laughs, attempting to break the mood*]

He is an idiot babbling through town,

subject to his neighbors' curses,

stoned by children when he stumbles down

from mountain visions, crying,

"Dreams, dreams for sale!

Two for a kopek, two for a song;

if you won't buy them, just take them for free!"

ANDREI

He is God's fool.

And though he wanders through the trees, the fields, and
the cities,

he has seen a light upon a mountain.

It is this light we strive to paint.

This burst of glory is our seed.

DANIIL

Yes, but bursts of glory go up in smoke without a
moment's notice.

ANDREI

No different than the sower in his field
whose harvest is put to the torch.

DANIIL

Precisely, dear *staretz*!
Tell me why over all this carnage there broods a silent God.

ANDREI

I am not certain, brother.
But was it not ordained that the transfigured Christ must
    go down
silently into the valley where all light is extinguished,
all glory violated on a cross?
His submission to this death has shattered Sheol's gate,
freeing us from despair and hate.

[*singing*] "Christ is risen from the dead,
trampling on Death by death,
And on those in the tombs,
lavishing light!"

DANIIL

Is death defeated?
Then tell me why so difficult to make,
why so easy to destroy?

ANDREI

I do not understand why death is still at work.
I think its time is short, and it will fiercely fight
to the last gasp. It is this gasp we now endure.
Until it is finished, evil will go on
casting insults into the secret face of God
and use us too!

He knows the human heart cannot resist a cry of "Why"
when innocence is ruined;
and hearing only silence, the heart must erupt in agony:

"Where is God? Where is God?"
And as the years of silence spread,
while the ravager despoils at will,
would you or I see the corruption of a child and not take
    arms?
Or watch our lifetime's work erupt in flame at the whims
    of blind men,
and not be tempted to reach for a sword?

DANIIL *is silent, looking down.*

ANDREI

How much can a soul be taxed?
How much this soul endure?
I am a man of peace, but there is a killer sleeping in my
    soul,
one who in a moment of madness might grab the tools of
    evil
in an attempt to defeat evil.
Thus I would find myself doubly defeated!

*He turns to face mural of Christ.*

I do aspire to see that hidden face,
whose image is both beyond me,
and buried in me, too.
But first I must pass this inner dark,
the inheritance within me of my fallen race.

I will rise [*stands upright on scaffold*]
and part the night,
will be the old wrestler, guardian,
defeater of my own private fear.

DANIIL

You wrestle for both of us.
You are a saint.

233

ANDREI [*amazed*]

    Me, a saint!

    I do not know what such a thing is.

    Come, let us leave this labor for another day.

    The night is near.

*The two painters slowly climb down opposite sides of the scaffold. As they do so, the chanting that has been barely audible increases; the male chorus chants.*

MALE CHORUS

    He who mysteriously spoke to Moses on Mount Sinai
    and said "I Am Who Am",

    today manifests himself to the disciples on Mount Tabor,
    and reveals through his person

    that human nature is reestablished in its original splendor.

    As witnesses to this grace and partakers of this joy,
    he raised up Moses and Elijah, the forerunners of the
        glorious

    and saving Resurrection

    made possible by the Cross of Christ.

*As the chant continues, the painters exit to opposite sides of the stage.*

    When David the forefather of the Lord foresaw in spirit
    your coming in flesh, he invited the whole creation
    to rejoice, crying out, "O Savior, Tabor and Hermon shall
    rejoice in your name", for indeed you ascended this
        mountain

    with your disciples.

    Through your Transfiguration you returned Adam's nature
    to its original splendor, wherefore we cry out to you,
    the Creator of all,

    "Glory to you!"

*The chant continues as the light fades, leaving only the face of Christ radiant, with accents on reds and golds.*

O Lord, today on the mountain of Transfiguration,
you have manifested the glory of your divinity.
The disciples saw your clothing as radiant as light,
your face more brilliant than the sun. Unable to bear your
overwhelming radiance, they fell upon their faces,
and heard a voice bearing witness from heaven:
"This is my Beloved Son, who came to the world
to save mankind."

*Darkness.*


## Scene Three

*Night.* ANDREI *is asleep on a mattress at the foot of the scaffold.* THEOPHANES *paints on top of the scaffold, with an oil lamp and candles for illumination. He works bent over, his back to the audience, for thirty seconds. He hums the notes of the preceding Transfiguration chant.*

   ANDREI *cries out in alarm, wakes, and half-rises.* THEOPHANES *looks down at him and pauses in painting.*

THEOPHANES
   What? Poor fellow, did a red horse gallop through your
      mind?

ANDREI *is groggy. He rubs his head, sits up, and faces the audience.*

ANDREI [*with much feeling*]
A dream.
I saw a tree,
the burning bush abright with God's fire.
All manner of human beings converged on it to see,
to touch and capture mystery.

They wished to possess God.
They wished to hold him
in order that they would not be possessed
by him.

They tore the leaves from it,
they chopped and split,
until it lay stripped and broken on the ground,
with sap oozing into the shadows of the earth.
I wept fiercely, for I loved the tree.

ANDREI *looks up to* THEOPHANES.

Then our friend Nikon appeared, and he was robed in
    light.
He knelt by me and consoled me with his eyes.
Then he spoke.
NIKON's Voice
    These are the children of man in the time to come.
    These are the generations who will be at the end of the
        age.
ANDREI
    "Does the end draw near?" I asked.
NIKON's Voice.
    It draws very near,
    then withdraws, then draws near again.
    The time is short.

    Toward the end, the people of that time will become
        unrecognizable.
    When the advent of the Antichrist approaches,
    people's minds will be clouded by their passions.
    Dishonor and lawlessness will wax strong, and the world
    will be in agony, though few will see its cause.
    People's appearances will change, and it will be impossible
    to distinguish men from women. These people will be cruel.

236

Love will disappear and fear will reign.
Deceit and greed will infest all but a few.
Lusts of every kind will flourish, and murder of the
    innocent
will spread across the world; their blood
will be like a second Deluge.

True shepherds will be rare, and woe to those who
    remain
on earth in those days, for they will completely lose faith.
And were they to wander east and west, they would scarce
    find
anyone at all to speak a word of holy wisdom.
Even were they to hear one, they would not believe it,
and even if they were to believe it, it would not matter to
    them.

Prophets will be murdered at street corners
while the last children observe,
and false prophets will be exalted
while merchants proceed about their business, uncompre-
    hending.
Old men and women will hide, knowing,
having seen it all before.
And many, disturbed by this commotion,
will turn higher the soundings of their muse,
a magic screen full of moving pictures and lies.

These unhappy people will live out their lives in comfort,
without guessing the deceit of the great Liar.
They will be drunk on power, drugged with knowledge.
They will fly through the air like birds
and descend to the bottom of the sea like fish.
They will attempt to change nature.
They will tear matter apart,

and finding not God,
they will say he never existed.

THEOPHANES

Was there more?

ANDREI

More? Yes, more.
He said the work we had accomplished would soon be
ashes.
A darkness approaches, one so deep it will appear that
Light
itself has been extinguished.
He said my soul would turn upon itself;
it would despair of words, of images, of all exchange.
Sinking inward, I would wrestle there at close quarters
with the enemy and his lie.

Nikon said I would have to choose between poverty and
despair,
and were I to choose power as remedy to despair,
I would be a slave forever.

Yet if I choose to rejoice in my own powerlessness,
the time will come when I will be filled.
And my work, these dreams painted in the twilight of our
times,
will be like stars pricked in the black heavens,
holes through which paradise pours.

Greater than a dream, greater than a reflection,
will be the words born from me, if I hold firm.
Words born in silence and failure, tested by fire.
Words that give life, luminous as the sun.
It will come, he promised, if I choose aright,
a word born from my poor gut, my tired eyes,
a word to shatter chains and shout gladly down the ages
unto the last engagement with the foe.

ANDREI *puts his head in his hands.* THEOPHANES *stares down at him.*

THEOPHANES
Hmmm! This is a burdened mind.

*He climbs down the scaffold and pulls* ANDREI *to his feet, then leads him over to a window, stage left.*

Look, look at the cosmos. See the divine order!
How deep and inexhaustible it is,
how glorious, never to be extinguished.
Curious, is it not, the motion of those fires cutting arcs
    across
the black dome of night.
An artist is painting there with light.
See how he makes the sun and moon and stars revolve
    around the earth
so intricately.
ANDREI
It may be so, but I am troubled by a thought.
Perhaps it is we who turn and turn again,
a giant's spinning top,
and these, the fixtures of the sky, are just the appearances
    of flight.
THEOPHANES
God alone knows.
The children of the future may plumb the depth of that
    great mystery.
ANDREI
In my dream those children had eaten from the tree
of knowledge of good and evil.
They understood many things.
But when they gathered around the tree of wisdom and
    beauty,

they understood it not.
A gnarled and ancient form, they thought,
a structure in need of dismantling,
rotten wood to fuel a revolution.
They tore it apart in search of the secrets of its life,
and found none,
having killed it.
THEOPHANES
An earthly tree, a heavenly fruit.
A fearful dream, my boy, but dreams are not reality.
ANDREI
They are a shape of the future if we do not consider well.
Those people to come are real.
The future breeds a special kind of man.
He will know if we are ignorant about the sky.
He will know the code of all the universe. He will fly in it,
and maybe find that we are just a spark among the
     conflagration,
that all the cosmos is afire.
Then, judging by the surface only,
he will think that we circle endlessly in it, without aim.
Knowing all, he will think that existence whirls about his
     very self.
He will be a black hole sucking everything into its mouth.
THEOPHANES
But what if we are ignorant, and he correct?
ANDREI
Which would be the more dangerous form of ignorance?

*They stand looking out the window. Suddenly, there are alarm bells
and shouts.* DANIIL *bursts in with arrows protruding from his back.
He collapses into* ANDREI's *arms. There are shouts of "Fire! Fire!"
Lights simulate fire outside the windows and the opened door. There
are hoofbeats, screams, cacophonous bells.*

*The* TARTAR *enters.* THEOPHANES *hobbles forward and points long brushes at him like a sword. With one blow the* TARTAR *strikes him down. Then he moves toward* ANDREI.

ANDREI *grabs the old man's cane and is about to swing it at the* TARTAR, *when he stops himself, looks at the cane, and throws it to the floor. Then with great difficulty he opens wide his arms.*

TARTAR

What? Again? This little man who sticks in my throat?

And silent too.

No more "Welcome, Brother Death" from you?

ANDREI *bows his head, still with raised arms. The* TARTAR *lifts his sword and is about to strike. But he cannot, and is exasperated.*

Once more this harmless fool defeats my aim.

I'll tear you apart in search of answers when I come again.

Until that day it is enough to destroy this straw [*points to icons*].

[*loudly*] Speak!

ANDREI

Leave the images, I beg you.

For the children of the future.

*The* TARTAR *gestures violently toward the audience, but remains facing* ANDREI.

TARTAR

What! For them?

They value nothing save their appetites and toys.

[*loudly*] Torch this place!

Demythologize this race!

ANDREI [*crying out loudly in despair*]

All is futility and madness!

All that is beautiful is killed before birth;

only darkness unto deeper darkness is born on this earth!

TARTAR [*roaring*]

Go! This is your last reprieve.

ANDREI, *head bowed, exits slowly stage left. The* TARTAR *gazes up at the murals, then turns to face the audience. One hand is on his hip, the other on his sword. He glares ferociously, addressing the audience:*

Now for a burning.
But when I come again, you will not know me.
I'll be the new barbarian, dressed in fine suits
and wearing falsehood like a crown.
I'll not ask for much;
I'll ask only for your worship;
and you will be seduced by peace,
calling down upon your heads
the judgment of a bitter fire.
(*roars again*). Go! The play is ended. Go!

*He brandishes his sword. Images of flames. Sounds of burning, crackling wood, and screams fading into silence. Total darkness.*


## Scene Four

*Darkened stage. Dawn is approaching beyond a line of trees. As the light increases, an old bent* WOMAN *crosses from stage right to stage left, carrying an enormous bundle of long dry sticks on her back. There is a field between her and the forest, and in it there appears to be a black pillar. She reaches center stage and stops beneath a skeletal, dead tree. She stoops to pick up branches from the ground, adds them to the bundle, then straightens and faces the audience.*

WOMAN

What? Still here? [*She goes on a few steps.*]
Do you think our play will end by fire?
Should fire, the first word, also be the last?
It is certainly not the fire you think—

the torture rendering all down into black, over which
   whirls
a voice crying, "Nothingness!"

No. It is a different fire I praise.

*The light increases and the black pillar is revealed as a man with his back turned to the audience. The shape turns slightly, and the audience now sees that it is an old* MONK *with a hoe. He begins to scrape the soil with it. The* WOMAN *observes him, then continues.*

You see that one. He is a shell that keeps its shape from
   habit.
[*calling*] Old man!

*The* MONK *stops and looks at the* WOMAN.

WOMAN
   Shall fire have the final word?

*She laughs, a little madly. He does not answer.*

So, has life made you silent, while I am now a hurricane of
   noise?
MONK
   Death has made it so, not life.
   [*bitterly*] Life is death, and death is release into
      nothingness.
WOMAN
   What voice is this? What monkly complaint have you?

*The* WOMAN *throws her pile of sticks onto the ground between herself and the* MONK.

MONK
   None. None.
   I have cried all cries; I have raged all rage.
   I am empty now.

WOMAN

And is this "emptiness" your tomb?

Does this kind of silence nurture love,

or only breed a deeper silence until you freeze into eternal
stone?

What lie is this?

MONK

You ask questions as if there were answers.

The voices that drew me once are mute.

The music of creation is full of screams,

the cries of women mad with grief,

their babes dismembered, their men slain,

their daughters taken into captivity,

their houses rubble, their hearts burned.

WOMAN

Fire cleanses, little father.

MONK

Fire destroys.

WOMAN

It purifies our common wound,

cauterizes festering pride.

MONK

It turns the face of beauty into skulls.

WOMAN

And does it not raise up again?

Feel the warm fondling of spring,

see the cottonseed on the wind.

The voices fallen into death are roused again

to indestructible rites.

MONK

Time will litigate who is right in this, old woman.

But I think nature is no mother, killing as she breeds,

for saplings suck their life from blood-fed soil.

She is a queen who leaves a heap of corpses in her train.

And man, her selfish child, thinks of nothing
other than his gain. Armies of them erect their forts and
    barns.

WOMAN

Do you fault us? It is a frigid land.

MONK

More frigid to the soul.
The universe is cold
and merciless.

WOMAN

The universe is damaged and full of grief,
but it is warm.

MONK

This Eden is illusion, a brainless dance,
where clever talking beasts express their pain.
All men admit the universal wound,
regardless of their dress, be it silken robes or armor . . .

WOMAN

Or humble monastic cloth. Are you not also man?

MONK

Yes, but not by choice.

WOMAN

Tell me, then, what you would rather be.

MONK

A little less than an angel; greater than this mud.
No longer will I tear my very flesh in search of immortal-
    ity.
But I am caught between an *either* and an *or*.
The glory of the universe was made for us,
but we are also dust.
Explain that riddle.

WOMAN

You philosophers and your riddles!
There's too much solving in your soul.

MONK

    I seek to understand my pain,

    and thus unloose its grip on me;

    I wish to turn my loss to gain.

WOMAN

    So, you too wish to gain.

    Not gold, of course, not kingcraft over men,

    guarded turrets on a height,

    or swift ships upon the lake of fire.

    Ah no, you desire the humblest coin,

    and stamped upon it the word *Beauty*.

MONK

    Long past are the days when once I thought

    this coin would ransom the heart of a dark age.

WOMAN

    How goes the ransoming?

*The* MONK *stares at her but says nothing. She bends to pick up her bundle of sticks, groans with the effort, turns, and prepares to depart.*

    This applewood is hard, but makes good heat.

*She pauses in thought, then turns back to the monk and drops the bundle onto the ground.*

    Once I knew a boy who could paint a dream.

    In the midst of winter he made a tree burst

    into green flame;

    with a stroke of brush,

    saplings sprang to life upon his board.

MONK

    A tree died to make his board.

    Dreams, dreams, you say.

    We are pushed from dreaming wombs into the fires of

        experience

    and there consumed in agony to feed another's nightmare.

WOMAN

There is fire and there is fire. Which fire do you mean?

MONK

The fire that destroys.

WOMAN

Ah, it is of the other fire I sing.

That boy had such fire within his bones.

He became a monk.

You might know his name, for he was famous

among the princes and the tribes.

That name was nearly mine.

MONK

I know his name, for it was mine.

WOMAN

So, Andrei, you did not fade within your dream.

ANDREI

I followed after voices,

but they are silent now.

The boy you knew no longer exists.

WOMAN

Has he become a proud void, refusing to be filled?

ANDREI

A hollow trunk.

In the end they will throw me on the pyre.

*He points to the bundle of sticks.*

My burnt skull shall be a nesting place for swallows,

a metaphor for pious monks.

WOMAN

Could it be that emptiness is just a hollowing of vessels?

Were you not once a bowl full of colors?

You dipped into your very self and painted miracles.

ANDREI

Paint! I will never paint again.

247

All my work is up in smoke,

my wasted years a great mistake.

I know it now—we never do awake.

WOMAN

And I have laid six children in the soil,

my life consumed in ceaseless toil.

Is your suffering of greater value than mine?

My womb is dry; my eyes are empty riverbeds.

[*raising her voice*] If I speak now it is not to wound,

but to lance a festering sore.

I tell you this: you sicken on your own aborted glory.

ANDREI [*anguished*]

Stop!

WOMAN

We are enclosed within a mystery,

the sacred flux in which we laugh and weep

and bear the generation of our souls.

Did you create the dancing of the spheres,

inscribe the loveliness in children's eyes?

And did you give yourself the power to paint a universe

upon a little square of wood?

What daring that you now condemn

the very life you fail to comprehend!

ANDREI

Not life condemned, but beauty.

For Beauty is a false goddess.

She is come full circle now—

she makes her point with large flakes of ash

falling through the burnt roofs of abandoned cathedrals,

or with elegant ribbons of blood unfurling

in blue waters.

Beauty is without conscience.

You ask me to court her, she whom once I loved.

But I did not know her.

She no longer exists. She died in a fire.

WOMAN

Once she was a dream of saints and kings,

a song released on the wind.

You danced with her.

ANDREI

That Kahlia, that beauty,

was a hymn sung into the void.

An invention of my mind.

*The WOMAN stares at him. She lifts the bundle of wood onto her back and groans loudly. From beneath her rags, she flings one, then another, gold-and-red ribbon over her shoulder. She makes steps to leave.*

ANDREI

Masha, I know it is you.

*The WOMAN dances clumsily with her load, and the haunting music begins.*

WOMAN

No. It is I, Kahlia.

ANDREI [*in a loud prolonged cry*]

Kahlia!

*He falls unconscious at the foot of the tree. KAHLIA goes and stands beside him. She gazes lovingly down upon him.*

KAHLIA

My little brother whom I love.

You shall be a man of prayer again.

Hope shall be in you like bread in the mouths of children.

You will again take up your brushes

while all the world forges the sword.

Beneath the Tree of Life, O dreamer,

you shall awake;

I shall call you forth from these brief dreams.
And when you rise, you'll make for us

*In an emphatic voice, with a second's pause between each of the three
final words, she continues:*

a sweet,
holy
fire!

*Boom of bass drums. Total darkness falls suddenly. Then bass drum
booms three times. Then three strong trumpet blasts. Icons of* ANDREI
RUBLËV's *greatest works are projected upon the sky. Music and bells
and a mixed chorus singing the Song of Songs in Byzantine mode.*

CHORUS
I hear my Beloved,
see how he comes
leaping on the mountains,
bounding over the hills.
My beloved is like a gazelle,
like a young stag.

My Beloved lifts up his voice,
he says to me,
Come then, my love,
my lovely one, come.
For see, winter is past,
the rains are over and gone.
The flowers appear on the earth.

The season of glad songs has come,
the cooing of the turtledove is heard in our land.
The fig tree is forming its first figs,
and the blossoming vines give out their fragrance.
Come then, my love, my lovely one, come.
My dove, hiding in the clefts of the rock,

in the coverts of the cliff,
show me your face,
let me hear your voice;
for your voice is sweet
and your face is beautiful.

I sleep but my heart is awake.
I hear my Beloved knocking.
[*softly*] I sleep but my heart is awake,
[*more softly*] I sleep, but my heart is awake.

*Music fading into silence.*

## [END]

# REFINER'S FIRE

# 9

Archive, 2 November 1942

This little tale is saving my life. To write of Kahlia and Sophia has engaged the latent powers of my mind and distracted me from the obsessions of my heart.

How great is the mystery of the human soul! Each contains its measure of folly and glory. We choose to increase the one or the other. Life and death are set before us. Hope and despair. Love and devouring. Thus we shape the form through which heaven or hell may act.

I have asked God for detachment—indeed, I ask for it daily—and it is given. I feel considerable relief for the moment but wonder how long it can be sustained. I reassure myself that time is finite. The war proceeds toward its unknown resolution; regardless of its outcome it must end one day. Then I will be free. In the meantime I feed my guest, I respect his dignity, and I guard his autonomy as well as his life. This is the form my damaged love is permitted to take.

Moreover, I can make a little world on paper. This is my sole potency, my offspring, my legacy. It does not matter to me that it may be nothing more than an anodyne against the pain of reality. If, on the other hand, the act of creation is a plunge through the barriers of unreality that encompass our times, then I am a man with an escape route. I do not know which of these is true. For the moment, at least, it is an alternative to madness.

\* \* \*

Throughout November, the play poured from him unabated, unpremeditated, replete with religious thoughts that he had not suspected were within him. This was especially disturbing because of his recent wrestling match with God. He was stricken with remorse whenever he recalled that angry dialogue-monologue, and especially so after he stumbled across a passage in Scripture stating that those who were angry with God courted destruction. Thus, fear was added to his shame.

During his reading of the Old Testament, he halted before an idea expressed by several prophets: "The beginning of wisdom is fear of the Lord." He felt that surely this was an unsolvable conundrum. Should one fear a "God of Love"? And if so, what kind of fear had the prophets intended? Terror? Craven groveling? If that were so, man's whole understanding was a delusion, the splendor of the universe was a beautiful face cleft by a sword. And the most horrible aspect of it would be the inescapable conclusion that both face and sword were the slaves of a cosmic barbarian. Pawel weighed the matter this way and that, and the view from each angle seemed to offer arguments against the other. If God was a tyrant, as Goudron had accused, then love was simply not possible—only obedience from fear of punishment was possible. If, on the other hand, he was pure Love, as people like Rouault and Father Andrei believed, why did so many of God's servants speak of his wrath, his justice?

Intricate and difficult problems multiplied. Each question precipitated more dilemmas.

In the first few days after he had taken up his pen to compose *Andrei Rublëv*, he had wept often, primarily from anguish over the contradictions of his character: the longing for divine order, his utter inability to open his heart to it. Early on, he had taken himself to confession at the local parish, confessed his anger at God, and been absolved by a priest, yet he had returned home only to find his dread and shame waiting for him.

A week later, after Mass, he tripped absentmindedly down the icy steps of the church and fell, banging the back of his head and bruising an elbow and shin. He lay stunned on the sidewalk for a few seconds, until a young nun knelt beside him and helped him to his feet. She gazed into his eyes with sympathy.

"Trust Jesus in all that is to happen", she said. He dismissed her words as the sort of pious bromide that only nuns are permitted to say to strangers. He busied himself brushing sand and ice chips from his clothing and did not reply.

"Fear is our great enemy", she went on in a quiet voice. "Fear locks us within ourselves."

"The war cannot last", he murmured.

"The war will last until the end of time. But if you live in fear, you cannot hear the voice of God."

Pawel looked more closely at her.

"Abandon yourself to our Lord with full confidence", she concluded. "Then the devils cannot touch you."

*Devils?* wondered Pawel. He thanked her for her assistance and hurried away down the street.

\* \* \*

In the ensuing weeks, as he continued to work on the play, his anguish steadily diminished and he was able to focus on the questions posed by the characters and the central theme. The problem of fear and love was unresolved, yet it cycled in his mind less obsessively. He could see that it was working itself into the play almost of its own volition. It came to him gradually that a God who permitted himself to be humiliated and brutally executed was demonstrating something about the nature of his love in a way so radical it could not be misconstrued. Pawel saw the immensity of the universe and his own insignificance within it. Yet God had suffered for *him*—Pawel—a small man, a mote of dust. Why did he do that? What, precisely, was going on in this very strange universe?

Rouault's painting of Christ in agony surfaced in his imagination. He appropriated the memory and adapted it, so that in the play it became Rublëv's iconographic Christ, which was at one and the same time an image of the revealed face of God and a window that opened to the unseen face of God. Why this convergence of hiddenness and revelation? Was it intended that man love the revealed but tremble before the hidden?

Perhaps fear of God was entirely different from the paralyzing terrors that were the demons' playground. Was there a holy fear, one compatible with confidence in God? If God were indeed pure love, then the Old Testament meaning of the word *fear* did not mean the dread that people felt when threatened by natural calamities and attacks by enemies. Fear of the Gestapo must be entirely different from the supernatural fear that Moses felt when he saw the burning bush. And surely it was not the same as the reverent awe that the apostles felt on the mountain of the Transfiguration. Nor was it the fearsome attraction—containing both longing and unworthiness and dread of loss—that he had felt for Kahlia when she played Bach at Warsaw University. That had been a rapture in the presence of inaccessible glory. Glory in a human form, revealing, yet withholding. She had been for him an icon of the radiance of perfect *being*. Glory as . . . love.

Love?

What was love? Every question led inexorably back to that.

Archive, 28 November 1942

Love. The Greeks called it *exousia*, a breathing forth of being. Is exousia a kind of soul-bridge, the bridge of celestial language? The mind says yes. The heart also longs to say yes, but cannot.

Kahlia, Kahlia, you are fading from my mind, dissolving upon the night wind. I would search for you in the streets, running and running until this ache has spent itself utterly, if it were not certain that a German bullet would put an end to my pathetic little romance in short order. Would I be running toward or from—I know not which. But what am I fleeing, what am I desiring? Attraction or repulsion; speech or silence;

union or alienation. It seems I want them all—I am a divided heart.

I read and reread my play as it materializes before my eyes and am amazed that all of this should come from me. It seems that a work of art is also exousia—a mysterious revelation of being. Is it, then, a form of love? If so, where does it come from?

And who is it for? It does not matter if no one sees, no one hears. The artist's only concern is to bring it into existence. He must speak without listeners. He must do so without thought of reward. This is the path that lies before me. If I were to turn from it, I would surely die. I cling to this with a ferocity that is shocking.


As he continued to write, all else faded into the background—the cold outside the frosted shop windows, the chill in his blue fingers, the sporadic firing of guns, the presence of his guest. During this period the pain of excessive attachment did not disappear altogether, but he made an uneasy truce with what remained. He reminded himself that, given the wrong pressures, he could easily be drawn into it again. He warned himself that he should not mistake for love the impulse to escape loneliness. An icon in the heart could degenerate into an idol.

\* \* \*

"Excuse me, Pan Tarnowski", said David Schäfer one evening, placing a bowl of steaming soup before Pawel as the latter read quietly to himself at the kitchen table.

"Yes?" he murmured, glancing up distractedly.

"I did not wish to interrupt. But you have not eaten today."

Pawel set aside the book on Russian spirituality that he had been devouring and stared into the bowl, which resembled nothing other than a vessel full of spilled blood.

"You should eat", the boy urged, sitting down before his own bowl, the contents of which he began to consume with a certain haste. "There is strength in these beets", he added. "Minerals and sweetness." Then, abandoning etiquette altogether, he lifted the bowl in both hands and simply drank it down in three great gulps registered by the larynx bobbing in his thin neck.

Pawel spooned a little soup into his own mouth and took up the book once more.

"We have not spoken", David interrupted again, blinking rapidly, his voice timorous.

"We have not spoken? What do you mean?"

"Since the day of your anger, we have not truly spoken with each other."

"We have spoken—often. I'm sure of it."

David shook his head.

"Well, I have been preoccupied", Pawel said indifferently.

"Ah, you are involved in serious study of a field that interests you?"

"Yes, of course." Pawel resumed reading.

"We should speak about the day of anger."

Exhaling through his nostrils, Pawel closed the book definitively and stared at the table.

"Why should we discuss it?" he asked in a low voice.

"It remains like a great crevasse between us."

"Why should it? It was a bad day, that's all."

"Pan Tarnowski, as I said on that day, it seems to me that my presence is a burden to you, indeed a burden so great that it is killing you."

Pawel's face become more masklike than ever.

"And as I said on that day, you are not killing me."

The boy nodded but would not meet Pawel's eyes. At last he looked up and asked tentatively, "What was it, then, that troubled you? Why were you so angry? You created a little disorder in the shop. Some books were broken. I heard shouting and—"

"It had nothing to do with you."

David cleared his throat. "I find this difficult to believe."

"Believe it."

"But what caused it?"

"The absurdity of my life."

After a pause of some moments, David risked a final question.

"Am I not part of your life?"

This hung in the air, generating so many trains of thought in Pawel that he found it impossible to reply. To distract himself, he finished his soup and let the boy clear the table. Immediately afterward, they both found separate rooms in which to muse privately.

It was true that Pawel had hardly spoken to his guest for weeks, other than to give perfunctory directions for the cleaning chores or to discuss the cataloging. David was perhaps two-thirds of the way through this Herculean labor. He had also fallen into the habit of preparing meals, for Pawel had missed so many that the boy had taken matters into his own hands.

*   *   *

"What are you writing, Pan Tarnowski?" David asked one night not long after. The shop door was double-locked and all the blinds closed. David had finished sweeping between the aisles and was now approaching the desk, emanating naked curiosity. Pawel covered the manuscript with his arm.

"A story."

"I like stories very much. Would you let me read it?"

"It is unfinished."

"When you are finished?"

"I don't think it would interest you."

"It would interest me. I know."

261

"Why do you think so?"

"Because you wrote it."

"It's not well written. What could possibly interest you in it?"

"Because you are my friend", he said tentatively, turning away, embarrassed. Both man and boy resumed their work without further comment.

*Friend?* Volumes of irony, vistas of disproportion opened within Pawel's mind. He sighed, gathered the sheets of manuscript, and went upstairs to his bedroom, where he could write in peace.

*       *       *

That week, feeling stifled by the shrunken world of shop and apartment, he went walking in the streets. The first day, he strolled along the river on Gdanskie, where he observed laborers repairing a bomb-damaged bridge. Revived by the fresh air, he resolved to take more exercise in the future. His attitude was so much improved the next morning that he ventured farther afield, crossing the Vistula into Praga, where he wandered through Praski Park. At its north end he followed a path into the zoological gardens.

Coming upon a cluster of people huddled behind a blood-spattered snowbank, he thoughtlessly stopped for a moment to see what had happened. He knew that in these times it was dangerous to look too closely at anything that was not his personal business. Yet the blood held him. They were butchering an animal, which he supposed was a horse until he noticed the antlers. A woman was chopping the rack into small pieces and stuffing them into a burlap sack. Three men cut away at the body with knives, saws, and hatchets while two children scurried about scooping up blood-saturated snow in tin pails, cramming gobbets of it into their mouths. The adults stared at Pawel for a moment, swore at him, and waved him away. He reversed his steps and returned directly to Sophia House, remembering all the way home those times during his childhood when he had gazed in awe at the herd of red deer in that park. He was appalled, as well, by the desire that had leapt in him to scavenge some of the meat.

The following day he felt the need to go in the opposite direction, as if to remove himself as far as possible from the scene of carnage that still haunted him from the day before. He walked westward on Wawelska with no goal in mind other than to clear his head. At some point along the route, he came upon a small church, in front of which two elderly nuns were standing side by side, looking at the steps. One was sobbing.

"I was here the day they put it up—when I was a little girl", she said through her tears. "My mother brought me to see it. Such singing that day! And the archbishop offered the blessing Mass."

"It will be repaired", said the other. "One day it will be as it was."

"It can never be as it was! Look at this! Look!"

The steps were covered with shards of colored glass. A window above the main entrance to the church was defaced by several gaping holes. Pawel climbed the steps and inquired if he could help.

The nuns looked at him distractedly and shook their heads.

"The Germans did this?" he asked.

"No, not the Germans. It was wild bad boys."

"They threw bricks and stones", said the other. "We were at prayers when we heard the first crash. Sister and I came out as fast as we could, but by then they had done more damage."

"We couldn't stop them. We pleaded with them, but they just laughed and kept on."

"Such bad language too!"

"Our own Polish boys! Why would they do such a thing?"

Pawel gazed at the debris littered around their feet. The eye of Christ, part of a hand, a piece of heart surrounded by thorns.

One of the nuns bent to pick up the heart, the other went inside to find brooms and shovels, and Pawel walked on.

\* \* \*

As the winter weather worsened, Pawel and David spent more and more of their evenings at the kitchen table. It was warmer there because the hot plate added a little to whatever meager heat the radiators could produce. Coal was in short supply. On one such evening Pawel buried himself in a book while David mended a torn piece of cloth with needle and thread.

"Excuse me, Pan Tarnowski."

Pawel looked up with some irritation.

"I'm sorry. You were reading", the boy murmured with a dip of the head.

"Obviously."

"I apologize. An interesting idea struck me, and in my enthusiasm I did not consider that you might prefer to read than to . . ."

"Than to what?"

"Than to discuss it with me."

"What is the interesting idea?" Pawel asked with a sigh.

"It was nothing. Please return to your book."

Pawel resumed reading.

"Is it an interesting book?"

Pawel closed the book.

"It would be better for you to tell me your idea."

"It is not important."

Pawel leveled a stare at him.

"Actually, in a sense it *is* important", David hastened to correct himself. "It is about language."

"Language?"

"Yes, our favorite subject."

"And what do you think about language today?"

"I am thinking about the language between you and me."

"What do you mean?"

"There is so little language between us."

"I do not understand."

"I mean that we seldom speak together. Why is this so?"

"We speak", Pawel shrugged.

"Yes. But our silences are not speaking."

"Our silences are not speaking?"

"In my family there was much speaking and much silence. The speaking of words flowed from the speaking of our silences."

"What are you saying?"

"I mean that I do not understand your silences, for even silence should be a word."

"What, then, is silence?"

"It is being."

"Being? Are you referring to philosophy?"

"Yes, and more than that. Spoken language and silence are keys."

"Keys to what?"

"To communion."

"What do you mean by communion?"

"At-oneness."

"Please do not tell me you are a Buddhist, David Schäfer", said Pawel, hoping that this curt remark would end the interruption.

"I am not", the boy replied in an affronted tone. "I am a man. This is common to all men."

"In what way?"

"When a man hands you a key, this has a certain meaning. A word is a key. A word is an action. Subtract the action, and the meaning has not been expressed. Moreover, each man *is* a word. As you are a word to me."

"In what way am I a word to you?"

"This I do not understand entirely. But in its most common sense, you speak a word of protection. You hide me. You feed me. This is your side of a dialogue."

"It is not really a dialogue. I do it because it is the right thing to do."

"But to do the right thing is to speak a word, and to shift, a little, the balance of the world."

"You perhaps invest too much significance in what are really ordinary actions."

"Is our life here ordinary?"

Pawel mused on this before answering. "I suppose it isn't. But the whole world is in turmoil. Nothing in these times is ordinary."

"Nothing in any time is ordinary, I believe."

Pawel shook his head. The boy's points were becoming obscure.

"Let us say, Pan Tarnowski, that you and I live on opposite sides of a street and that this street divides two different worlds that are incomprehensible to each other. Let us say that I hand you the key to my door, and you hand me the key to your door. We open our doors and there we are—we are gazing into the interior of each other's homes. Is it not a blessing?"

"There is nothing within my interior that you would find of interest."

"This I do not believe."

"Why would you want to see?"

"Because man is not made to be alone."

"We are not alone."

David dropped his eyes. In a low voice, he said, "One can be alone, even in a household full of people who speak incessantly."

"You have reinforced my point. Speaking is not necessary."

"Ah, but speaking *is* necessary. I do not mean the noise of the mouth, but the speaking that flows from silence."

"Now you have completely lost me. What, really, are you trying to say?"

"True speech is seeing as one. The union of silence and the

union of true words that flow from such silence. This union is an expansion of vision."

Intrigued, Pawel gestured, "Continue."

"A thing is not truly said unless the speaker is willing to offer his own blood as surety for the words that come from his mouth or pen. The blood need not flow literally, but the willingness to let it flow is essential for authenticity. In the uncertainties of life, the spilling of our blood may be demanded of us, or it may not. That is not our decision. Our act of choice is to be willing."

"So you believe that what a man says must be backed up with his life."

"Yes, if it is to have authority. This is why we must take care with our words. A word changes existence. We must protect the purity of language, for it carries the sacred from one to another."

Pawel frowned and laid his book on the table. "An old painter once told me something similar. He said that if symbols are corrupted, concepts are corrupted, and then we lose the ability to understand things as they are. Then we become more vulnerable to the deformation of our perceptions."

"And thus our actions", David added emphatically.

Pawel was suddenly startled by the fact that these words were coming from a seventeen-year-old boy, one who hardly had had time to live, let alone to study the great ideas of civilization.

"The degradation of language is a symptom", Pawel said as if in summation, wondering if anything more could be added to the discussion.

But David Schäfer seemed inexhaustible.

"Language can give us prayer and poetry and song and words of love to offer to another. Yet language can fall to the lowest level, like a noble servant put to degraded uses to increase the master's profit. By reducing him to the lowest level of service, the master in fact degrades himself more than his servant."

"Like a philosopher forced to shovel manure in a barn."

"Not exactly. Shoveling manure can be a noble act, if it is genuine service. I mean, rather, that a philosopher might be forced to sell evil things for his master. Lies, for example."

"Or a man might be forced to strip himself naked, so that eyes can devour him as an object of interest or desire."

David shuddered. "Yes, like that. Or stripped naked as an object to be viewed in a propaganda film."

Pawel and David fell silent. The boy was the first to shake off the mood.

"Language can give us prayer and poetry, shouts and cursing", he continued in a subdued voice. "But it is not the source of prayer, poetry, shouts, or cursing. There is the voice of the soul that comes before spoken words. I think we can experience this pure tongue of the soul without words."

"Once again, you reinforce my argument that speaking together is not necessary."

"Yet even now we are speaking of it."

Pawel smiled. "Yes, it is so."

"A state of pure being is speaking and listening simultaneously."

"Always? You make such adamant statements."

"Yes, that is a fault of mine, I admit. At least you will agree, Pan Tarnowski, that there can be such moments."

"It is possible . . ."

"You do not seem certain, as I am certain."

"I have not experienced it."

"Are you sure? Sometimes in the middle of a busy street, yes, even in the ghetto, I would feel the great union, the great peace when speaking and listening were attuned to the voice of the Most High."

"I have felt this rarely in my life, mostly when I was a very young child", returned Pawel. "Time slowed then, a sense of wonder expanded. Angels sent messages, poured out over the world. One had only to look up to see it, to hear it, to receive the messages. But childhood ends. Reality conquers all."

"Childhood should not *end*", David said with a certain earnestness. "It should take a more mature form, but its innocence should not cease."

"I agree. It should not. But it does."

"Can you not find it again? It is everywhere—all around us. It can be sparked by the flow through the air of wheeling pigeons; or the colors flowing across the ever-changing sky; or the flow of ideas from one's lips to the ear of another when you know that your word is spoken in the central current and heard in the central current and returned in the central current."

"The current of what? That is the question—of what? Water? Traffic? Noise?"

"Fire. The current of holy fire."

Again they fell silent, as each considered what the word *fire* might mean to the other.

David went on. "If a person does not have another with whom he can speak in this manner, then he is condemned to stare at his own reflection."

"So, is this wrong? Should we not know ourselves?"

"Can you know yourself, really, in a reflection? A reflection is an inverted image, and flat. May I put it another way, Pan Tarnowski? We tend to experience the self as the center of all existence. Thus, I risk turning everything and everyone around me—oh, you see, I said *around me*, as if all that is not me merely revolves about me."

"A figure of speech."

"Yes, but a figure of speech that arises from a fundamental attitude."

Pawel smiled quizzically, once again startled and amused. "Continue", he said.

"As I was saying, I run the risk of turning everything around me into the less real. And if I do that, then I too become less real—no, I should say that I experience less of my *genuine* reality, though I might *feel* more real by this obsession with the self."

"I do not follow you."

"In reality, other people are as real as me, yet I do not experience them this way."

"But that is life, is it not?"

"That is damaged life."

"If what you say is true, then all human existence is damaged."

"Would you not agree that it is?"

Pawel nodded abruptly. "Yes, I agree."

"So, how are we to move beyond the prison of mirrors in which we see only our distorted reflections? How are we to move beyond the solar system of the self and join in the great dance of the universe?"

"How? I do not know for certain. But a first step may be . . ."

David waited for Pawel to complete the thought. The latter lowered his gaze and stared at the floor for a time, grasping for an elusive answer to the boy's question.

"I suppose one practices putting the other ahead of the self", he murmured, without looking up.

"Yes, I believe so", David nodded. "Small choices at first, growing into greater movements. But we must *choose* to do so." Suddenly, he smiled for no obvious reason. "In this way— by conscious choice—one breaks the hypnotic trance of the mirror."

"Do not be so harsh about mirrors. We can learn much from them."

"Or be trapped in them."

"Yes, but in our reflection we see either how large we are, like Narcissus, or how small we are, like Saint Francis."

"Who is Saint Francis?" David asked curiously.

"A spiritual teacher of my Faith."

"Ah. Now I must admit, Pan Tarnowski, that you have a point. I think you are saying that a mirror is not all bad or all good. It is a place of choosing. Is it not true that when we look into a mirror, a question is formed and an answer beckons?"

"Does it?"

"A window is a kind of mirror. One can see only the reflection, or one can look through the reflection to what lies beyond the enclosure of the self."

As before, Pawel was reminded of David's youth, so unreal did the conversation seem to him. Summarily he brought it to a close:

"What came to you as idea has become a maze of metaphors", he said. "What for me began as a maze of metaphors has become idea."

"Yes", the boy nodded. "This is interesting."

\* \* \*

"I like to hear stories", David said a few days later, as he was serving bowls of mashed turnips. "I like to tell them, and I like to have them told to me."

"You do?"

"I have already mentioned this."

"Ah, yes, you told me."

"What is your story about?"

"It's a play. Not a very good one. Just something to pass the time."

"May I read it?"

"It is only a rough draft."

"That does not matter. It is the soul of the story that matters to me."

"What about style?"

"What is *style*?" David asked.

"The way the author tells it. What he leaves out or puts in.

The sound of his voice, the rhythm and the freshness of the words . . . everything about it."

"Oh yes, I can see this is important. But what if you have all those and the story is untrue, a beautiful shell with nothing inside, a statue with no heart—like a pagan idol?"

"That is not good either. You may be surprised to know that many artists of my acquaintance believe that style is everything. When I was a young man living in Paris, most of the people I met sincerely believed that if a work of art looked beautiful it simply did not matter what was being communicated. If it was beautiful it was true."

"It must be that much falsehood is spread this way."

"I think so. But what if a writer has both a good story and a good style? Ah, then you have—"

"Glory! A holy glory!"

"I was about to say magic, but that is a bad word for you, is it not?"

"Magic is from the *sitra ahra*."

"What about your *Kabbala*?" Pawel asked, picking up a volume from a little stack that he had brought down from the attic for further investigation. David's eyes darkened.

"Isn't it about magic and Jewish philosophy?" Pawel went on. "I rescued it from the discard pile the other day. Why did you reject a famous text like this?"

"Have you read it?"

"No."

"I have read it. There are two main books, the *Book of Creation* and the *Zohar*. There is much in it that is purest wisdom, and yet it is mixed with the doctrines of the pagan East and the concepts of him who is the angel of poison and of death. There are many angels in it who are not mentioned in the sacred Scriptures. Their messages are questionable. I think some of them may be fallen angels in disguise. This opens the doors of the soul to dangerous intruders. It is a book composed of many pieces that do not fit together, and one must step carefully to avoid a fall into the regions of the damned. My father said so, and I believe he was right."

"Your father, he was an educated man?"

"Not greatly. *Yeshiva* only. He did not go to the university. I have already mentioned to you that he was wise. My mother too was wise, but my father had unique wisdom. People said he was a *zaddik*, a holy one. He was very troubled when he heard of it. He was a scholar of the Torah and the *Kabbala*. As a young man he was fascinated by hidden mysteries, as young men often are, and was drawn into many years of study in that field. When he was older he departed from it, because he had come to believe it was not healthy for the soul."

"What did he think was wrong with it?"

"The problems I have already mentioned. But more than this, he thought that practical *Kabbala* encouraged a fascination with secrets, supernatural things, and this prepared the inner life for pride and spiritual deception. He said that one should not read this book until after the age of forty, and then only if one were blessed with exceeding wisdom and devotion to the Most High, the Master of the Universe. Even so, my father, who was wise and devoted, ceased reading it altogether."

"You are fortunate to have had such a father."

"Yes."

"Not everyone has such a father."

"Tell me, Pan Tarnowski, did your father not teach you to discern good from evil?"

Pawel glanced over to the window.

"My father? I hardly knew him. He hardly knew me. He was arrested by the Russians when I was very young. He was returned to us when the Russians were driven out."

"How happy you must have been!"

"He had been gone for three years. He was like a stranger when he returned, a broken man. He had seen terrible things in

273

prison. He looked at me and did not see me. Gradually he recovered, but even so, I felt that he could not really see me. I was his son, and he did his duty, but his mind was always elsewhere. He spoke to me only of inconsequential things. He did not listen. He did not inquire."

"But surely he cared about you."

"When I was a youth, he began to take a little interest. He wanted me to become an engineer so that I would have prosperity and be spared the kind of suffering he had experienced. That was the substance and the frontier of his love."

Even as he said this, Pawel's thoughts faltered. There was something not entirely accurate about this summation. Into his mind there flashed a childhood memory of his father beseeching him with outstretched arms, his eyes full of pain, yearning that Pawel would come to him, whispering, *dziecko*, my child, *mój synu*, my little son. But Pawel had turned away.

David's gaze—sober, reflective, compassionate—was fixed on Pawel's eyes.

Pawel inhaled suddenly and straightened himself. Clearing his throat, he tapped the *Kabbala* with his forefinger.

"You say you have read it?"

"Yes", David nodded. "It is a sin of which I am much ashamed. My father forbade me to read it, but I read it secretly, for I was enticed by fascination of it. It was an act of disobedience. I should simply have believed my father, for I found that he was right, and now I have certain words and images in my mind that I do not like. It is necessary for me to struggle against them, especially when I am extremely fatigued. At such times I am vulnerable to fear."

"Yet you say it has wisdom in it."

"It has good in it, but also the enticements of the enemy. It contains a poison wrapped in the pleasing packages of mysticism."

"So, you think there is good mysticism and bad mysticism?"

"Yes, of course."

"And what if bad mysticism is wrapped in good style?"

"The answer is obvious", he shrugged. "It would be the most dangerous poison of all."

"How can we know which is which?"

"I do not think it is entirely a case of *knowing*. There are certain signs in a text. This is the realm of knowledge. More important, we must pray to have wisdom, which is the realm of the spirit."

"You never cease to astound me", said Pawel, shaking his head.

"And I too, Pan Tarnowski, am always surprised by you." David paused. "I do not understand you. Forgive me for saying this."

"Am I *sitra ahra*?"

David looked confused.

"Of course you are not. Why would you ask such a question?"

"I'm not sure why I asked it."

"Does not one of your commentators write that 'all men have sinned and fallen short of the glory of the Most High'? This is a true saying. I too have sinned by disobedience, though, thanks be to the All-Holy One, I have been preserved from the other acts into which mankind so often falls."

It was said candidly, without smugness.

"Yet I am like every other man", he added. "I could do those things."

They pondered this without further comment. Later they went upstairs and David showed him the day's sorting.

"What shall we do with the bad mysticism?" Pawel asked.

"You ask me? They are your books."

"I thought perhaps you might have some suggestions."

"I think we should burn it with the other ones on this pile."

"Are we to become like the Nazis?"

"They burn books because they hate the truth. We would destroy a book because we love the truth. But only after judicious thought, only if it was clear that the book contained a deadly poison."

"I am not sure you have convinced me", Pawel said.

"A book is a word spoken into creation. Its message goes out into the world. It cannot be taken back."

"Yet every book does a kind of work, does it not? Some do a great work and others do a lesser work, and some do it badly and some do it well, and so on. They all do a work, and that is how civilizations grow."

"But if a book is a false word, it is a seed of destruction within the civilization. Is it wrong to end its work?"

"Tell me, David Schäfer, do you think we should burn Hitler's autobiography?"

"That is a difficult question. I think perhaps it should be kept, because in the future it will be necessary to understand why our times are like this."

"What of the *Kabbala*? Doesn't it have something to tell us about Jewish life? If we begin to burn all the books that contain some untruths, we will never stop burning."

"What you say is not untrue. And perhaps in a world where people desired truth, it would be possible to read these things and not be pulled into the darkness by them. But we are living in a time that has lost its senses. Should we give them poison in their condition?"

"Then let us pack these books away for a better period of history", Pawel said.

"Some of them I would still destroy. They can sicken the soul in any era."

It was an especially cold night, wind blowing hard from the northeast. They took an armload of material down to the boiler in the basement and threw a few volumes onto the smoldering coals.

"I am a bookseller", Pawel muttered uneasily. "It is my business to save books."

"May I make a correction, Pan Tarnowski?" the boy said humbly.

"All right, make your correction."

"If I may say so, your business is to save truth. If ever you had been tormented by the *dybbuks*, you would not hesitate to burn these. I have met people with broken minds and infested souls who thought they could play with such matters and remain unharmed. Can we not think of these flames as a way of bringing good out of evil? These books serve the enemy. They lure souls into darkness. We have put them to better use. For a short while they are providing heat for those who would search on your shelves for wisdom."

Pawel flashed a look at the boy. "You have a point", he murmured.

*   *   *

Late the following afternoon, an unusual customer arrived at the shop. Pawel did not like the look of him from the moment the doorbell chimed. The man closed the door behind him soundlessly and remained without moving at the entrance, his body unnaturally still, surveying the interior with eyes that lingered over anything on which they alighted—the cane in the umbrella stand, the height of the ceiling, a candlestick—as if he was engaged in the elaborate creation of an impression. The eyes flickered with the subtlest currents of amusement. He was in his late thirties, with a pencil mustache and graying hair slicked back with pomade, and was elegantly dressed in a black lamb's-wool coat to his ankles. He removed his leather gloves and began tapping them lightly on his palm.

After a long look at Pawel, he wandered into the alcove containing art books, and there he remained for some time, emanating his presence. Pawel ignored him.

At last the man approached the desk with his selections.

As Pawel counted up the total he could feel the other's eyes upon him.

"I know you from somewhere", he said at last in an affected voice, aristocratic, high-pitched.

"I don't believe we have met", said Pawel.

"I am Count Smokrev."

*Smokrev?* A note sounded in Pawel's memory—elusive and, for some unknown reason, disturbing. There had been a nobleman named Smokrev in Paris, he recalled vaguely. A literary type? A writer perhaps?

"But I am sure I know you", the count said.

"I do not think so. My face is not uncommon."

"*Au contraire*, your face is unique."

Disgusted, Pawel was about to wrap his purchases in paper when the count pulled a volume from the stack. It was a book on Greek art.

"One question", he said with an arched brow. "I think there is an error in this, which should, in all fairness, lower the price."

He cocked the other eyebrow inquiringly. Pawel waited.

"You see here, on page three hundred and eighty-six," the count went on, inserting a manicured fingernail into the book and flipping it open, "the author has wrongly attributed this sculpture to Praxiteles. Admittedly, the subject matter is a naked man fondling a young male. Now, if you turn to the next page you will see the *Hermes* of Praxiteles, one of the greatest works of art of all time. Here too we find the most superb specimen of male beauty one could imagine, and he too is fondling a naked boy . . . excuse me, I have made you blush."

"I am not blushing", Pawel said, though he knew that his face was hot with embarrassment.

"How perfectly charming", the count smiled.

Controlling his irritation, Pawel said in an even voice, "I

believe you are correct that this piece is not by Praxiteles. It is probably by Milo. However, your interpretation of the *Hermes* cannot be what the sculptor intended. It could be a portrait of a father carrying his son out of the river where they have bathed together. They are about to clothe themselves, but the father momentarily pauses and is reaching up for grapes to feed his child."

"Charming", the count whispered.

"I will take ten percent off the price", Pawel said tonelessly.

"That will not be necessary", said Smokrev, laying a stack of money on the table.

As Pawel wrapped his purchases, the count suddenly drew a sharp breath.

"I know you. I know you."

He tapped his lips with his gloves.

"Yes, I saw you at a salon in Paris. You were the companion of the novelist, Goudron. How simply incredible! To meet you here after all these years!"

"Incredible", Pawel mumbled.

"You devastated him, you know. It took months for him to recover." He laughed meanly. "Why, it was the longest lapse between *companions* he ever endured."

"Whatever you may suspect is in your own mind. Monsieur Goudron was a benefactor. He took me in when I was without any means of survival."

"Yes, yes, yes. Such a *generous* man he was. Always so compassionate to the attractive."

"You misunderstand. It was an act of charity on his part."

"Ah, my fine young friend, Goudron was never wrong in his *selections*. He was unerring in his tastes, and unerring in his ability to spot—how shall we put it—the *responsive*."

"In my case he was mistaken", Pawel answered shortly.

The count drew back, smiling archly, yet troubled by a doubt. Himself the veteran of many groundless hopes and failed campaigns, he entertained the possibility that the bookseller might be telling the truth.

"I must now ask you to leave my shop. I am closing for the night", Pawel said coldly.

"One might interpret such a tone as a rebuff. But I am not offended. You are the Pawel Tarnowski of the brass plate on the door, no doubt? And is there a Pani Tarnowski? Your mother, perhaps? Her name is Sophia?"

"I live alone. I will ask you to leave now."

The count put a calling card on the desk.

"This little shop is quite a discovery for me. There are some unusually fine things here. However, you simply must dispose of that tasteless bust of Paderewski. Do you have any Russian icons for sale?"

"I have no Russian icons for sale."

"But someone told me that Tarnowski in Old Town had icons."

"That was my uncle. He is deceased. There are none for sale."

"Ah, *c'est dommage*. Myself, I prefer the passion, the *heat*, in the Serbian and Cypriot schools, but I am trying to enlarge my collection. Some cool northern mysticism would be good for my soul. Not that I am a believer, you understand—I worship at the altar of Art. But you would be *sympathique* to that. You are a painter, are you not?"

"No, I am not an artist."

"But my dear fellow, I distinctly remember Goudron telling me that you were a painter—a rather ungifted one, he said, but *sincere*. He found you most amusing."

Pawel stood abruptly and was about to conduct Smokrev to the door when the count glided away.

"Read my card", he tossed over his shoulder. "You would be most imprudent to make difficulties where it is unnecessary."

Pawel slammed the door shut behind the man, making the

bells ring and the glass rattle. He locked up, pulled the blinds closed, and sat down fuming at his desk.

When he could bear to look at the card, he learned the identity of his customer:

Count Boleslaw Smokrev
Reich Culture Chamber
*Polish Liaison Office, Warsaw*

The following day Haftmann arrived.

"Good morning, Tarnowski", he said pleasantly. Pawel gave him a curt nod. As usual, Haftmann went through the shelves systematically, waiting for other customers to leave. When the shop was empty, he turned on his heels and said, "Can you suggest any titles for me to consider today?"

"*Nie!*" Pawel answered sharply in Polish.

Haftmann came over to the desk and asked thoughtfully, "Is there a problem?"

"Your associate Count Smokrev. He is a problem. Why did you send him here?"

"Smokrev!" Haftmann said, his face souring. "I did not send that parasite here. My guess is he stumbled upon you by accident. He works for us sometimes. He is a collector. Did he buy anything?"

"A few art books."

"There, you see. That is typical of him. His visit meant nothing. But he is a venomous man, so I suggest you not make an enemy of him."

"Why do you think I may have made an enemy of him?"

"That face of yours—that dangerously transparent face which reveals everything at all times. I can tell that you despise him, and you can be sure he knows it, too. Aren't you capable of subtlety?"

Pawel looked down at the count's card lying on his desk, and on an impulse tore it up.

Haftmann raised his eyes to the ceiling.

"Very dramatic, Herr Tarnowski. I congratulate you on your impressive gestures."

Pawel sat breathing heavily, his eyes snapping, his fingers flipping nervously through the papers on the desk before him.

"What is that?" said Haftmann.

Pawel saw opened before him the third act of *Andrei Rublëv*. His face went white, and Haftmann noticed it.

The German turned the stack of pages. Pawel muttered that it was a worthless manuscript written by an unknown Polish playwright.

"And who is he, this Andrei Rublëv? That is not a Polish name."

"He is the subject of the play."

Haftmann shuffled through the stack and came to the title page.

"You wrote it."

Pawel groaned. "It is useless stuff. A daydream. Give it here."

Haftmann took a step back and his expression became more formal.

"I would like to read this."

"No, it's not ready. It's only a first draft."

"I will read this", said Haftmann firmly, clamping his fingers on the bundle.

"*Nie!*"

"*Tak!*"

"*Nein!!*"

"*Ja!!*"

Haftmann's eyes were suddenly ice, and his grip iron.

"Tell me, my benefactor from a distant land," Pawel said in a ferocious tone, "tell me why you are so insistent on reading my *play!*"

The last word was shouted.

Haftmann burst out laughing and released the papers.

"Oh really, Tarnowski, you are an owl! So ponderous! So intense! You are an overdose of a serious drug! Ten thousand playwrights in this world are forever trying to get someone to read their silly plays. And you do everything in your power to prevent anyone from reading yours."

"It was not written for everyone. It was written for my own meditation."

The German removed his cap. Suddenly full of manners, he asked permission to sit at the rickety chair by the book-binding table, a few feet from the desk.

"Forgive me, Pawel Tarnowski", he said, half-smiling. "You must understand that it was a moment of professional schizophrenia. Major Haftmann surfaced for a moment. He will not do so again."

"I am reassured."

"Please believe me. Truly, I am most interested. You may recall that I am first and foremost a professor of literature. I could be of help to you. Some stylistic advice perhaps. It is not inconceivable that one day I could translate it into German for you. There are other possibilities, but I must read it if I am to be of any assistance."

"But I did not ask for your assistance."

"Correct. However, you never refuse the help I offer you in other matters, do you?" These pointed words were said in a tone of exquisite courtesy.

Pawel's lips tightened and he dropped his eyes.

"Well, then, I accept that you do not wish to lend me your manuscript. Is there only one copy?"

"Yes. I could not obtain any carbon, and I am short of paper."

"I can help you with that. Tomorrow I will have paper delivered to *Zofia*. Do with it whatever you wish."

"An overwhelming gift, Doktor Haftmann."

"And be reassured that you do not have to lend me your

manuscript, although the offer still stands, should you ever wish to have it duplicated. My secretary can have it typed out in a few days. She is most efficient."

"That is generous of you, but for the time being—"

"Of course. I do understand. By the way, is the play of a political nature, perhaps?"

"The play is spiritual in approach and deals with some questions of aesthetics. It is set in medieval Russia."

"Far from the land of the Prussians?"

"Yes."

"An allegory about a barbarian invasion?"

"It is not an allegory."

"Very good. Well, I must be going. And I do regret my lapse into an *alter animus*. Please do not think unkindly of me. It will not happen again."

"We have both been under a great deal of strain", Pawel murmured.

He saw Haftmann to the door.

"Doktor, may I ask you a question, a very blunt one?"

"Our relationship is based on a mutual candidness for which we would both pay a high price if it were to be discovered. I hope that someday you will come to trust me. I am not what I seem. Please, feel free to ask me anything."

"Is it true that the SS transport people to the resettlement camps only to kill them? The rumors say that you are gassing and burning large numbers of nonmilitary people."

Haftmann frowned. "What a fantastic thought! I am not especially fond of my compatriots in the SS and the Gestapo. Some of them have been brutal. There have been some deaths, some injustice. But on the whole it is simply untrue. We have established a system of labor communities throughout Poland, Germany, and Belorussia. I will admit to you that it is a form of exploitation, but this is the usual behavior of conquering nations for a short while after an occupation. The situation will normalize soon. Large numbers of people murdered! That is the product of inflamed imaginations. It must be paranoia. Or propaganda from the Resistance. Good night, Tarnowski."

"Good night, Doktor."

Pawel locked up after him, then sat down at his desk. Fear, gratitude, and resentment circled within. He exhaled loudly.

"An overwhelming gift, my dear Doktor", he muttered. "I am really most grateful. Yes, how gratifying that you will normalize the situation soon! Thank you for relieving us of our paranoia."

His mouth twisted bitterly. He gathered up the sheaf of his play and hid it beneath the tin box in the bottom drawer.

"That was stupid, Pawel", he said to himself. "You went too far with him. You must be very careful with this."

The next day a delivery man dropped a package inside the door. Bound in green paper and red string, stamped with a purple swastika, it contained five hundred sheets of fine bond paper. With it was a bag containing a flask of schnapps, three pounds of China tea, and a note.

Pan Tarnowski,
I have agonized all night over my lapse. I consider it extremely gracious of you to have forgiven my fault so quickly. Please accept these small tokens of my respect and my gratitude for your efforts. In our own quiet way, you and I are both attempting to restore the world to order. I know it is impossible that you would come to trust me completely. After all, I am dressed in the sinister battle gear of the conqueror. But I do look forward to a time when you will no longer see me as a mortal danger.
                                        Sincerely,
                                        Dr. Kurt Haftmann


Haftmann was back a week later, and Pawel thanked him for the gifts. Would it be possible to have a copy of *Andrei Rublëv* made? Cordially, Haftmann agreed. Would it be a burden to ask the professor for his critical commentary, anything, really, that would suggest artistic improvements? And to this also, Haftmann agreed.

## 10

Pawel did not see Haftmann for several weeks. Smokrev, however, came into the shop frequently, bestowing smiles with his sculpted lips and saurian eyes. He would spend an hour or two mining in the stacks and always bought something, usually in the field of the visual arts or light modern literature—one day a folio of engravings of Viennese architecture, the next a biography of Italian opera composers, and so on.

"My dear young fellow", the count declared in a voice so loud and dramatic that other customers lifted their heads and directed their attention to the sales desk, hoping to overhear something of interest. "My dear, *dear* young man, if you were ever to hear the cries of anguish in Rossini's love songs, you would never doubt that passion is the divine madness that the gods bestow upon their most favored children."

Pawel endured it for the sake of Smokrev's cash, with which he was able to obtain fuel for the furnace. Winter had set in with a vengeance, and the heap of coal in the cellar was dwindling far too quickly. He also parted with two of the landscapes from the apartment, selling them for a fraction of what he believed they were worth. The money from this enabled him to buy the odds and ends that desperate people brought in for evaluation.

New acquisitions were delivered by a strange little woman who arrived unannounced one day, opening the shop's front door so violently that when it struck the umbrella stand, the glass rattled and the bells lashed dangerously. She poked her head inside, scowled at Pawel, and went out again, returning a moment later pushing a handcart before her. As she struggled to get the wheels over the stoop, cursing to herself all the while,

Pawel examined the apparition. She was about fifty years of age, dressed in rags, her feet wrapped in felt cloth secured by twine. Her short gray hair was covered by a black kerchief decorated with a pattern of red poppies.

Though Pawel certainly had never met her before, she seemed uncannily familiar to him.

*Baba Yaga!* he thought with alarm. Then he permitted himself a wan smile.

Memories of the childhood stories Ludmilla the maid had told him at Zakopane returned with startling clarity. "Always be good, Pawelek, or Baba Yaga the witch will get you. Night and day, she flies through the stormy air seeking little children to snatch, but only the bad ones can she see. Riding in her mortar and pestle she travels far and wide, her wicked eyes sweeping the world in search of such a child. Woe to him when she finds him, for she takes him home to her terrible cottage, which stands upon four giant chicken legs and is thatched by the human hair of her victims. Then she boils him into soup, and eats him."

This, while Babscia embroidered with needle and thread a flowered doily for the sofa in the parlor, smiling to herself, casting a glance at little Pawel. And Sweet Pawel, Pawel the Beautiful, tiptoed back to the pantry, where he replaced the single stolen ginger candy in its crockery jar.

Baba Yaga pushed the cart across the shop floor and stopped beside his desk. Her eyes were an enigma of obscure and cynical threats.

"You buy books", she rasped. It was a statement, not a question.

He nodded. "It depends on what kind of books."

Peering at him suspiciously, she threw back a sheet of dirty canvas covering the top of her load and revealed a heap of volumes. As he looked through the individual titles, she stood by, wheezing and dripping snow onto his paperwork.

Most of the books were of poor quality. But there were a few items of interest among them: a history of Poland under Russian rule, a cookbook, a complete set of Goethe. He made an offer. She accepted. Taking the money without thanks, she wheeled her way back out of the shop and banged the door behind her.

He knew that it was a mistake to purchase items that were not in demand. He had hoped to buy some extra black-market coal but foolishly succumbed to the allure of his interest in all things Russian. Not many people were wasting time perusing cookbooks these days, and as for Goethe, few were interested in German literature at this point, although there was a chance that Haftmann would be.

He flipped open a volume of Goethe and alighted on the following:

> Who rides so late in the night and the wind?
> It is the father with his child,
> It is the writer with his grief. . . .

*   *   *

Still no sign of Haftmann. Smokrev, though, was very much in evidence. In mid-December he purchased a complete set of Shakespeare.

"I do not like the English mind", said the count. "It is uncannily similar to the German. Not at all like ours. We Slavs . . ."

He trailed off when he saw that the bookseller was not paying the strictest attention.

"Do you know what you are?" he wagged his finger at Pawel. "You are like a beautiful big Greek sculpture. A Hermes. Gorgeous—but cold as stone."

Smokrev smiled and observed the reaction.

"That is correct", said Pawel without a trace of emotion. "I am stone. Stone on the outside. Stone on the inside. Do not waste your time."

Smokrev's smirk vanished.

"You always make me feel that I am an unpleasant intruder", he whispered heatedly. "Really, not the best policy for a merchant."

Christmas was dragged in upon the heels of a dismal Advent. David Schäfer observed without comment the humble effects Pawel achieved in the apartment to make the day festive. The extra lamps before the icons, the lace cloth on the kitchen table, the tarnished silver candelabra. Though he did not join in the Christian prayers, he bowed his head when they were uttered. And he eagerly shared the scrawny goose that appeared like a miracle on December 24, dropped off by Masha all in a rush. There was no time to talk, but she gave Pawel a maternal buss on the cheek and forced the little corpse upon him. He and David ate it with turnips, a wizened onion, sage, and a cake Pawel made with barley flour, nutmeg, eggs, and raisins. They agreed it was the finest banquet they had ever tasted. The question of whether or not the food had been prepared in a kosher fashion was unasked. David left for the attic early, and when Pawel went up later to say good-night, he saw the boy standing, swaying, facing the wall at the end of the room, the prayer shawl drawn over his head and rhythmic groans emerging from his throat. He did not know he was being observed. Without a word, Pawel turned and left.

By New Year he was becoming frantic over Haftmann's absence. Had he been killed or transferred? Had he forgotten Sophia House? Perhaps the play was so bad that Haftmann was simply disgusted and his good manners made it difficult for him to face the playwright.

Smokrev had also disappeared over the holidays, and this worried Pawel, because the count had become the primary source of income. He was soon out of money and was forced repeatedly to turn away some excellent books. Worse, he would be out of fuel again before long.

Smokrev came at the end of January.

Pawel spoke first. "Excuse me, count, do you know where Doktor Haftmann is?"

"Haftmann!" He rolled his eyes. "That fool! You know him?"

"Yes", Pawel said cautiously. "He is a customer, though not a frequent one."

He felt instant regret, wondering if he had divulged a dangerous morsel of information.

"Oh? What kind of books does our dear Doktor buy?"

"Old German books, usually. Heavy fiction, *Bildungsroman*."

"Ah."

Smokrev looked bored and waited.

"Y-yes", Pawel stammered. "He is a professor of literature."

"*Was* a professor of literature."

Smokrev blew a cloud of breath before him.

"It is appallingly cold in here. Is the heat off?"

"We are short of fuel at present."

"We?"

"A figure of speech. I keep the furnace burning at the minimum. It is bearable."

"Unbearable! I had hoped to make some purchases this morning. However, I find that your shelves, though they are full, are becoming somewhat exhausted in terms of quality."

"It is difficult to find replacements."

"Perhaps you have some *objets d'art* that you have not yet shown me."

"I have none for sale."

"Surely you have a private collection." He glanced toward the back room, then raised his eyes to the ceiling. "You live in the apartment above, I believe?"

"Yes."

"I would like to see your collection. You may remember that I told you I am a collector of icons."

"I have a Bonelli."

"A rather obscure painter of flowers, if I recall", said Smokrev without enthusiasm.

"It is of good quality. I once went without meals for three weeks in Paris in order to buy it. The dealer said it was a bargain; he said Bonelli was not a major impressionist, but significant in art history."

"Well, let me see it."

Pawel went upstairs and returned shortly, carrying the painting as if it were a priceless object.

Smokrev inspected it with displeasure.

"You fasted precisely two weeks and six days longer than you should have. This *fiori* is unspeakably ugly. I do not believe it could accurately be called *impressioniste*. I am not interested in such things."

"But the gallery owner said—"

"Gallery owners will say anything. Come, do you have icons? I would be prepared to give you an excellent price."

"You could have the Bonelli for a few . . ."

Smokrev threw up his hands and made motions to depart. He tugged his gloves over his fingers, on which there were many glittering rings.

Pawel felt the cold digging into his ribs and knew that his nose was red. According to tradition, blessed icons should only be passed down, generation to generation, or given away. On the other hand, did not the higher law of charity provide for such situations?

"I do have some icons."

"Well, hurry. I am a very busy man."

"If you will wait for a moment, I will bring my collection."

"I would much rather go up. It is, how shall we say, less formal." He laughed nervously.

"Unfortunately, my apartment is in bad condition. It is squalid. It is infested with fleas." *Metaphysical fleas*, he added silently. "I would be ashamed to offer hospitality to a gentleman in its present state."

The fastidious Smokrev wrinkled his nose.

"Then may I sit?"

Pawel pulled the ring-backed captain's chair to the side of his desk and asked the count to wait there until he returned with the icons.

Upstairs in his bedroom, he wrapped the images carefully in felt cloth. It was painful. It was not unlike parting with one's children, or more accurately, like selling one's mother. It might even be, in this case, like selling a relic to the devil. But the cold, the hunger! In the end charity won, and he decided to show the entire collection. Smokrev could choose one according to his tastes.

The count gasped when he saw them.

"Eight! You have eight and most of them exceptional! This is indeed a find."

As he examined the icons, the coy note dropped out of Smokrev's voice, and for a moment he became a reverent man.

"Beautiful", he breathed. "The little Russian Saint Seraphim is extraordinary. The Mother of God *Hodighitria*—'guide on the way'—seventeenth century, certainly Greek, not Russian. Very fine! An Old Testament Elijah, also Greek. I will be honest, this one is quite rare. Saint Joseph with two doves. Mmmm. Not bad, but Polish and too much influenced by the Renaissance. An angel. Lovely, lovely. Gabriel? No, it's Raphael! Fabulous, I *adore* Raphael!"

And so forth.

When he came to the ancient icon of Saint Michael of the Apocalypse, he drew back a little.

"As an art form it is perhaps the finest piece here. My, how it bristles with the symbolism of that nightmare vision. I detest

John. He is too ephemeral. Too much divine retribution. Ugh, he's scowling at me. And look at that poor serpent writhing like an eel on the spear." He laughed dryly. "Certainly a selective exercise of the virtue of Christian love. I have always felt that the angel Lucifer has been unjustly maligned."

Pawel stared at him.

"Oh yes, Tarnowski, the ancient enemy of mankind, and all that. According to *who* tells the story, of course. But he is an angel of light, and I think he may be the very one to lead us to the Being of Light who is the Christ for our age, the One who will heal all divisions and reconcile the opposites that have tormented us during our long and tragic history. Don't you agree?"

Pawel regarded him with knitted brow and said nothing.

"No, I suppose you don't. You are a nice enough young fellow, but you have been completely molded by a limited social environment, dominated by the Church and its criminally stunted propaganda. It is that worldview which causes wars."

Pawel attempted to stammer an argument, but the other went on: "It would be useless to discuss this any further until you have read Swedenborg and the theosophists, especially Madame Blavatsky. Also Doctor Jung—a brilliant man. He has a certain mystical temperament and Gnostic roots, sympathetic to our cause."

"Your cause?"

"The regeneration of the West through a return to primitive instincts and powers."

Pawel was startled by the messianic glint in the other's eyes. The fop, the international *roué*, was merely pathetic, but this was a new thing. He suddenly wished to withdraw the offer of his icons.

Smokrev took out a large wallet and pulled some bills from it. The sum was enough to live on for months. Pawel thought of the fuel and the food it could obtain, and also the power to buy books to replenish the shelves. More than that, it would direct a flow of money into the hands of the hungry. His agony of indecision was resolved by the memory of children he had seen begging in the street.

"Which one do you choose, count?"

"Which one? Oh, I think you misunderstand me. This sum"—and here he placed the bills on the desk—"is sufficient to cover the entire collection. I don't think it an unreasonable offer. It may even be generous, considering the times and the situation in which we find ourselves."

Pawel's face turned red. He was about to refuse when Smokrev said:

"It's all or nothing."

Pawel desired to give vent to helpless rage, but the faces of the street children, of David Schäfer, Pani Lewicki, Baba Yaga, and many others swarmed before his eyes. In the end he said only, "Take them."

Smokrev was delighted.

"Wonderful, wonderful! My dear Black Prince!"

"What did you call me?" Pawel said in a low voice.

Smokrev laughed.

"Didn't Goudron tell you your name?"

"My name?"

"I never met you directly, but I saw you once or twice across crowded rooms. Goudron had so many salons and parties, hundred of ridiculous people of all sorts. He collected them, you know. And he had names for each. That communist courtesan Madame Kortovsky was 'The Red Balloon', and Francoeur the Catholic editor was called 'The Praying Mantis'. Picasso was 'The Minotaur', and you were 'The Black Prince'."

Heat flashed over Pawel's face, and his stomach churned.

"I must work", he muttered.

Thus, Smokrev departed with bundled treasure, dripping his trail of smirks.

*     *     *

In the days that followed, Pawel struggled continuously against feelings of hatred for Smokrev, convinced that he had been robbed and violated. To distract himself, he wrote a few new pages for his play; these dealt with Andrei Rublëv's first encounter with the monk Nikon and later with Theophanes the Greek. It seemed that he had not fully plumbed the depth of the mystery of *kenosis*, Christ's emptying of himself to become man; or at least, because his writing skills were limited, he had not properly expressed it in the dialogue. He determined to give the revisions to Haftmann for insertion in the manuscript.

Strangely, the memory of Father Photosphoros kept returning unbidden to his mind. Photosphoros, he now suspected, had not intended to wound the young Polish gardener, had not in fact despised him. His outburst, in all probability, had been entirely impersonal. The old priest was discouraged by the disasters that had come upon Russia, and he knew that few people outside her borders really understood her soul. Pawel recalled that the priest's monastery had been burned, his fellow monks murdered by the Bolsheviks. His health was poor, he had arthritis, he was in a great deal of physical pain. A heartbroken angry man, he had struggled to maintain the purity of his tradition. He did not want anyone coming along on a whim and deciding, as Pawel had, that he was going to be an iconographer. It was holy ground, and Pawel had naïvely stepped onto it without removing his shoes.

"I was so desperate, so in need of encouragement", Pawel said to himself. "But what was God saying to me through that old man? Did he want me to learn something about myself, to show me that I preferred approval and consolation to salvation?"

It was a hard thought. He did not dwell on it overmuch.

The following week, Haftmann returned.

"How can you possibly forgive me? Not a word since before December, and here I arrive with no excuses."

"None whatsoever?"

"Only that my duties have kept me traveling constantly. Things are not going well. I was forced to squirm while some of my brainless compatriots burned five hundred degenerate paintings in the Tuileries in Paris. I managed to prevent some Matisses and van Goghs from being immolated—those idiots in the Culture Chamber cannot distinguish between genius and frivolity." Haftmann sighed. "You are about to ask for your manuscript."

"Yes, I am."

"The manuscript is in safe hands."

Pawel offered him the sheets of new dialogue. "I have made some changes. Can you please add these to the text? I hope it is not too late."

Haftmann pursed his lips and took them. "No, it is not too late", he said, his face distracted, or uneasy. He put the papers into his briefcase.

"Doktor, have you read my play?"

"I am almost finished. Please be patient a while longer. You have no idea how busy I have been. I read the first act in Paris, the second in Amsterdam, and so on. My secretary is at work copying Act One."

"I see." Pawel's face could not hide a plunge into gloom. "Can you tell me what you think of it?"

"I found it rich in insights", said Haftmann, pausing. "There were some charming passages . . ."

"You hesitate."

"It lacks clarity, coherence. The thematic structure is con-fused. The architectonics are a problem. You are primarily a poet, not a literary intellectual."

"Then you do not like it."

"I did not say that. I like it well enough. However, I am not fond of the simplistic rhyming, which would suffer if translated. I also regret to say that you do not really understand the Russian soul."

"What do you mean?"

Haftmann laughed, shaking his head. He strode to a shelf, pulled a volume from it, and returned to Pawel's desk. Putting on his wire-rim reading glasses, the professor-major flipped pages until he stopped at a passage. He smiled conspiratorially to himself.

"This is Dostoevsky's *The Idiot*. Have you read it?"

"Not yet. I have been intending—"

"But you must read it. Here you will find the soul of Russia. In *The Idiot*, a holy fool by the name of Prince Myshkin moves in the circles of the bourgeoisie and lower nobility of the tsarist era. He proclaims that beauty shall save the world, and in the end demonstrates that beauty alone can save no one, not even the Christlike Myshkin himself."

"I fail to see your point."

"I have not yet arrived at my point." Haftmann's smile broadened as he turned more pages. "Curiously, here at the close of the novel, this wise innocent, this Christ-figure, bursts forth with the most vitriolic speech attacking Roman Catholicism—which is *your* spiritual home. Dostoevsky does the same in *The Brothers Karamazov*. Have you read the Grand Inquisitor section? No? You must. You will find that it expands your horizons immensely. It is so perceptive and so deliciously full of malice against your beloved papacy. This is the real Russia."

"Perhaps you have misinterpreted Dostoevsky's intention—"

"Read it and see."

"Even if what you say is true, it proves only that no man entirely escapes his origins."

Haftmann pursed his lips. "Yes, a good point. But one that cuts both ways."

"And what of Soloviev? He is as great as Dostoevsky, yet he loves the universal Church, despite her flaws. He too is Russian. Is he not also the real Russia?"

Haftmann shrugged pensively. "*Touché*. You must read Dostoevsky, and I must read Soloviev."

Pawel leaned forward, pressing his point. "Doktor, is the soul of a people defined only by its failures?"

"What do you mean?"

"A man may cross frontiers, but he carries his homeland within him. Should we apply this principle to your own homeland?"

Haftmann stared at Pawel for a few seconds, then waved away the question.

"Ah, the Russians, the Russians! There are none like them. Full of passionate contradictions. You should realize that beneath every Russian, even the most serene and lettered one, there is a barbarian who longs to strip, paint himself lurid colors, and shriek as he hurls himself at the enemy—perceived or otherwise."

"That is true of many races."

"Why do you like them so much? Why did you make such an effort to publish Soloviev? Why did you set this play in Russia?"

Pawel, strange to say, had never given these questions much thought. He had merely succumbed to an attraction and thrown himself into it with a passion.

"I'm not sure", he said at last.

"You aren't sure? Weren't the Russians every bit as nasty to Poland as we have been? Why this idealization of your conqueror?"

"It is not idealization."

"Romanticization, then."

Pawel had no immediate answer for this.

"You have not answered my question", Haftmann prompted.

"I'm intrigued by them", Pawel said, gazing into space. "Their experience is long and bitter."

"Why would that be intriguing?"

But to answer this question would be to reveal too much.

*Because, dear Major-Doktor, my own experience is bitter.*

When Haftmann realized that no spoken response was forthcoming, he shook his head and said, "You do not know them. Yours is a play written by a young Pole who has never seen Russia."

"They are Slavs. I am a Slav."

"Yes, you are a Slav, in a manner of speaking. But poor Poland suffers from a divided heart. You belong to the mysterious East *and* to the West; thus, you belong to neither."

Pawel frowned, weighing the validity of the German's point.

"It is true, Doktor, that I have never seen Russia, though I have met some of her exiles. May I ask a question?"

Haftmann nodded judiciously, "*Ja!*"

"Could it be that the Polish position is unique? Is it possible that we, belonging to both East and West, yet imprisoned in neither, are able to transcend the boundaries of nations and cultures, and thus see farther? Perhaps we are better able to see the architecture of the soul, which is common to all mankind."

Haftmann pursed his lips. "The architecture of the soul? Possibly. However, I see little evidence of that in your play. It does not address politics, nor does it really come to terms with the sexual enlightenment. Its greatest weakness is the lack of substance. Not that there aren't many substantial thoughts in it. But the *feel* of flesh and blood is missing. This Kahlia, for example, she is your concept of a Russian firebird, or an ethereal fairy princess . . . too self-conscious . . . too obviously a symbol."

"But she is my central—"

"Oh yes, I understand perfectly. She is your central *idea*, but you force your poor audience to sit through a heavy dose of abstractions that you want to tell us through her. That is not the role of art."

"I did not intend to make a work of art, Doktor. Nor to find an audience. It was perhaps only to make visible some interior questions that I think about constantly. By giving them a form, I was able to examine them with senses other than the intellect."

"Agreed. That is legitimate. But is it a work of genuine literature?"

"I do not know."

"And perhaps do not care", Haftmann smiled paternally.

"Perhaps."

"Also, Tarnowski," he scolded, wagging a finger, "you tricked me!"

"I tricked you?"

"The invasion element. You said there was none of that sort of thing. And here it is full force. It could be misinterpreted. Substitute Teuton for Tartar and you have an attack upon the Reich's pacification program."

"I did not intend that. I simply—"

"Yes, yes. But to return to the question of art: I believe you have a primitive work here, but it lacks *lust*. You need to make Kahlia a real woman. Rublëv should make love to her."

Pawel recoiled. "You moderns!" he said angrily. "Is that all you can understand? You think a man is real only if he betrays a vow, leaves a monastery, or cheats on his wife. Then he is a real flesh-and-blood fellow!"

"No", Haftmann chuckled. "That is not what I meant. I merely wish to suggest that your Rublëv is a dreamer, and thus you will lose the interest of most of the people you want to reach. The flesh-and-blood people. Correct?"

"Why is that? I do not understand."

"For a long time the world has been full of romantic young idealists who think their flashes of creative intuition are direct utterances from some divine muse. But their dreams are whims, moods, unnamed and misdirected passions, and when the romance wanes and the dreams grow pale, they must be fired up again by ever stronger doses of powerful stimuli."

"Are you suggesting that I am one of them?"

"Not exactly. I wish only to warn you that romanticism in any form is a distortion of reality."

Pawel could not help seeing an enormous irony in such a comment, coming from the mouth of a man who, to him, looked as though he was dressed in Wagnerian stage costume.

"What I want to impress upon you is this: Though I have only read a portion of your play, so far I detect a very strong whiff of the romantic idealist. You have idealized the Russians, and perhaps you have idealized life itself. This worries me."

Genuinely puzzled, Pawel wondered why a Nazi major would be concerned about such a trait in a conquered subject, a powerless man such as himself.

"Why does it worry you?"

The question seemed to trouble Haftmann. He did not at first answer. Then he frowned and said, "Beware of the energetic young idealists, I tell you. Most of them end—and I say this from experience, for Germany has generated legions of them for a century—most of them end by turning either to drugs or to irrational powers. They begin with abstractions and end with heaps of dead bodies." Haftmann averted his eyes. "There are terrible things happening. I . . ." He looked at the floor and tightened his lips. "Let us not discuss that. Sufficient to say, war is brutal. Let us return to art."

"Doktor, I still need your explanation. How can I make my Kahlia more flesh and blood, as you call it?"

"Make her more like Masha, and if you have to, make Masha more like Kahlia. By the way, I like your earth-woman Masha. She is real. Kahlia is an abstraction. You need passion, Pawel. I say it again: You worry me. Your passions are all in your head."

Pawel felt confused, alternately flattered by the attention and affronted by the bluntness of the major's analysis.

"Are abstractions not real, Doktor? And the great abstractions that are Truth—are they not in some way more real than many of our flesh-and-blood acts?"

Haftmann shrugged.

"I tried to show that Andrei is a real man. He loves Masha. He yearns to be a father in the flesh."

"Ah yes," Haftmann admitted, "there was some of that in the first act, wasn't there? If only the play had been nine-tenths heat and one-tenth abstractions, instead of the other way around."

He suddenly burst out laughing. "Wait, I forgot your *rivers of hot seed!*"

Pawel blushed.

Haftmann guffawed again and again, and because Pawel had never before seen such behavior in the ever dignified major, he now felt himself to be a complete fool—moreover, a fool stripped in public. When Haftmann had calmed himself, he said with a grin, "Yes, yes, those rivers of yours. A good touch— earthy, seminal. I take back what I said about your passions. There is a carnal man inside of you after all. Within this bookworm there is a wild animal!"

"The play is not about *me*", Pawel replied with indignation.

"Oh, but it *is* about you."

"No, no. Andrei is very much a man of flesh, but also of the spirit. Why can't you see that? His search for Kahlia has greater significance because of it."

"Never underestimate the power of repression", said Haftmann to himself, amused.

"And at the end of the play he cannot distinguish Masha from Kahlia, isn't it so? Masha *is* Kahlia. And thus my point was made, that spirit and matter are interpenetrating! The transfiguration of the cosmos. Creation is holy and full of light.

Marriage can be holy, and celibacy can be holy. Each can be a way of love. Each a passion."

"I have not yet reached the end of the play. I shall hurry home to do so."

He was about to rise, but Pawel was launched on an uncharacteristic tangent of self-revelation. "So, you see, Doktor," he said emphatically, "it's not about the physical passions. It's about the longings of the soul."

"Yes, but do we realize these longings in *spite* of the passions or *through* the passions?"

"I do not know what you mean by this question. All I wished to say in my play is that because creation is holy, we must love. We must love all mankind."

"An admirable sentiment. May I ask, do you love *us*, do you love the Germans?"

Pawel fell silent and averted his eyes.

"Mankind is easy to love in the abstract", Haftmann said, eyeing him curiously. "To love an individual is another matter altogether."

"Abstract or individual, they are all human."

"Human, yes, so they are. But abstracted humans are kept at a safe distance."

"Distance offers objectivity. When I see men carrying unbearable loads out on the street, I look at their faces and I say, *there is my father.*"

Pawel paused, surprised by the words that had come from his own mouth. *How strange*, he thought to himself, *how strange that we realize we know certain things only when we speak them.*

Haftmann looked doubtful. "You call it objectivity? It sounds like subjectivity to me."

Pawel went on. "And the hungry women who come in here, it's as if they were my mother. And in their old faces I see my little daughters whom I do not yet have. In the past is written the future, and in the future I see the past. And I see my wife—"

"Whom you also do not have. That is what I mean, Andrei—excuse me, *Pawel*—you will not be free of these painful sensitivities until you love a real woman, body and soul."

"But love is love. It is a power of the soul, not only the carnal act. Any dog can father offspring. One can be a father of the soul without—"

"That question is beyond me", said Haftmann, clearly tiring of this line of thought. "One thing for certain—there is no pleasure in life as powerful as the moment of ecstasy that you and I and our friend the lowly canine have in common and that we all, man and beast, hold in such great esteem."

Lapsing into a private enjoyment of his own wit, Haftmann chuckled to himself while Pawel, reduced to silence, stared at the desktop.

Shaking his head, Haftmann said wistfully, "You know, as I read your play it struck me more than once that the sensibility in your work, which may be your greatest strength—though underdeveloped—is visual. Have you ever given a thought to painting?"

Pawel mumbled, "Yes, I—"

"Then again," Haftmann interrupted, "Poland has never been a land to produce great visual artists."

"What of Canaletto's paintings of Warsaw?" Pawel offered lamely.

"He was a Venetian, the quintessential eighteenth-century Italian tourist. No, Poland will never produce great painters. Great music, yes. But here there will be no Louvre, no Alte Pinakothek, no Palazzo Pitti, no repository of native genius."

Haftmann nodded sagely while Pawel struggled unsuccessfully to think of a single famous name that would contradict this assertion.

Haftmann continued. "At the bonfire in the Tuileries I saw only one Polish painting. A charming work, primitive, powerful."

"Who was the artist?"

Haftmann shrugged. "It was unsigned. The title, *Zakopane*, and the ethos of Galician folk culture permeating the work, confirmed its Polish identity." He sighed. "Unfortunately, it was lost. Up in smoke. I could save only a few, and of course the French works took precedence."

"The Polish painting—" Pawel stammered. "What was it about?"

"Its subject matter? A mountain cabin, a bear gazing into a pool of fish, a knight fighting a dragon, angels dropping from the sky." He clicked his tongue. "A pity."

Haftmann left. Pawel, when he was finally able to move, went up heavily to the apartment. Stunned, disbelieving, turbulent with questions, he wondered if his painting had hung for a brief period in a museum. The Louvre? The Petit Palais? Perhaps even the Musée Nationale at Versailles? If the latter, then it was possible that Monsieur Rouault had seen it. Memories of their old dialogue and the destroyed painting merged into a wave of blackest agony.

*Must everything be taken from me!* he cried.

\* \* \*

Late that night, after David Schäfer had gone to the attic, the anguish Pawel had sealed within himself for several hours broke from its bonds. Seated on the edge of his bed, face in hands, he wept as he had not done since childhood.

"Everything I do is worthless", he sobbed. "Even my play! My stupid, stupid play!"

Its scenes ran through his mind again and again, revealing themselves as shallow ruminations dressed in the costumes of art. Scene after scene, boring, turgid.

"Art, art", he groaned, seeing the flames consume his one good painting, seeing as well the expanding frontiers of his blindness.

"Waste", he whispered to himself at last. "All that I touch becomes waste."

Disconsolate over the lost painting, in fact over the lost life he might have had, Pawel could do nothing for days. He closed the shop and wandered through the streets, observing as he went the many dramas they contained, collecting more material for his growing archive of futile tales—an enormous indictment against fate or providence or whatever organizing principle dominated all lives. He crossed countless streams of human exchange, without influence, without suffering any interference. Poles and Germans alike failed to notice his presence; they walked past him as if he were immaterial—walked through him, it seemed. He went everywhere without dread, because the possibility of sudden violent death was no longer threatening to him.

He was not so enticed by thoughts of death, however, that he willingly provoked any German interest. He obeyed the occupation laws, returned to the shop each afternoon before curfew, and spoke to no one. He merely moved throughout the city as he had done during the aimless rambles of his youth, waiting for something that had no name, perhaps a message from above, like snow, like a sign falling from the hands of angels.

On the third day of his sojourn, as he passed the main rail-yards while walking east along Chmielna, his eye was caught by a street sign. It was Zielna. He turned onto it and went as far as the block on which he had lived as a child. On the left side of Zielna, all cross streets were closed by gates or high barricades, and every window in the tenements was bricked over. Realizing that he had come to the border of the Jewish ghetto, and that his childhood home was just across the street from it, he stopped for several minutes to ponder this additional stroke of fate. What force had determined that he would be born on the right side of the wall? A German soldier standing by a ghetto gate gestured with his rifle that Pawel should move on.

Taking only a cursory glance at the windows of the apartment where he had once lived, he reached the end of Zielna and turned right onto Krolewska. The street was still marred by the bombardment of three years ago. Several buildings were missing. There were piles of rubble on the sidewalk, and Polish laborers guarded by armed soldiers were loading the debris, mostly bricks and chunks of mortar, into trucks. A boy of about ten years scurried past Pawel carrying a slab of splintered lumber, his eyes frantic. When the soldiers spotted him, they began barking and leveling their guns. The child ran into an alley, but it seemed the Germans had no interest in pursuing him.

Pawel crossed the street into the Saski Gardens. Here too the damage had been extensive. The walkways were cracked, the cobblestones entirely missing in many places. Shell craters pitted the grounds. Some of the giant old chestnuts were shattered, and a few had toppled. These had been stripped of all their smaller branches.

Reaching a corner of the park that was hidden from open view, he chanced upon a group of people trying to pull down a dead tree. It was perched on the edge of a crater, with half its roots exposed, tilted at an angle that allowed eight men a handhold on the trunk. Silently, with determined eyes, they yanked it up and down again and again, the arc of the tree lowering little by little. At last, with a sound like tearing fabric, the tree's roots lost their grip in the earth, and the trunk fell with a thud. Instantly, the men began to hack at the larger branches with hatchets and carpenter saws. Women rushed forward with kitchen knives and began to slice off twigs, which they tied into bundles and hid under their children's coats. Within ten minutes, the tree was nothing more than a stump, the people scattered in all directions, and Pawel found himself alone.

Hands deep in his coat pockets, scowling, he stared at it for some time.

"They tore it apart in search of the secrets of life," he whispered, "and found none, having killed it."

Sighing, he shook himself and glanced all about, becoming fully conscious of his surroundings.

"Do you fault us? It is a frigid land", he said. "There is no secret of life here. Only survival."

He squatted on his haunches to inspect the roots. How strange, he thought, that the tree was almost as old as he, that he might have run past the little sapling as a child, touched its soft buds, rubbed its velvet bark, plucked an autumn leaf from it. He recalled the days when he had come with Mama and Jan and Bronek to stroll on the walkways of the gardens, to lie on the grass by the flower beds, poring over picture books, inhaling the perfume of the rosebushes while Mama talked quietly with other mothers on a nearby bench, passing Jan or Bronek or Pawel a plum or a slice of sausage.

Now a shaft of sunlight broke though the heavy overcast over the city, washed swiftly through the park, and passed on. For a moment, a glint had appeared in the soil beneath the newly exposed roots. A coin perhaps. Pawel reached inside the web of claws and tried to extract the bit of metal. It would not move. The soil was frozen. With a splinter of stone, he chipped at the earth until the metal was fully uncovered.

When he pulled it loose he did not at first know what it was. A small sculpture of some kind. He turned it upright and saw a tiny knight battling with a dragon.

\*　\*　\*

Returning to Sophia House, he went blindly up the stairs to his apartment, holding the sculpture in his hand as if it were a burning coal that had dropped from space. So radiant with memories was it, so inexplicable its rediscovery, that Pawel felt the total shock of a profound mystery. He could not think, could not speak. Upon entering the kitchen he found a bowl of soup cooling on the table. His socks had been darned, washed, and left to dry on the radiator. On a hanger, his mended suit coat. In the breast pocket, he found a note written in Yiddish with a Polish translation:

Dear My Host,
The alien and the sojourner have found a dwelling place within your shelter. The orphan rejoices. The angels cry out for gladness.

With respect,
D. Schäfer

\* \* \*

On February 2, he went for the first time in many years to the convent of the Visitation sisters. There were only a few people scattered in the pews. An old priest prayed the Mass in a weak voice. At the time of the homily he had difficulty clearing his throat.

"My dear Sisters, my brothers and sisters in Christ, the night falls deeper on our beloved land. The large-scale deportations have been suspended, but people continue to disappear. Not only the Jews—a third of our priests and seminarians are missing, thousands of them, and unless God intervenes, most will not survive this war . . ."

He broke off and could not continue. He completed the Mass in a shaken voice, the nuns sang beautifully, and the congregation departed in haste after Communion, hoping that no informers had heard the priest's words.

Of the lay people, only Pawel and a woman remained to pray. The sacred Host burned in his breast. Time lengthened out and ceased altogether, until finally the portress rang a little hand-bell and escorted the last two visitors outside.

He was plodding along Krakowski when the woman caught up with him. It was Mrs. Lewicki.

"Pan Tarnowski, I must speak with you. I prayed for you in thanksgiving at Mass this morning."

She took his hand.

"My husband has recovered. It is a miracle. The medicine was a help. It relieved his suffering, and his body rallied. Man does his part, and God does his!"

She rummaged in a large cloth bag and withdrew a lump wrapped in newspaper.

"I intended to give two loaves of bread to the sisters by way of thanks for their prayers. But when I saw you at Communion, I kept one for you."

"That is very kind. It is not necessary", he murmured.

"You did not have to return that day with the extra payment for the books. When you came to give me the money it was like a dream. Only a minute before, I had been at my wit's end, on my knees, praying for a miracle. I was in despair. I kept praying because it was the only thing I knew how to do. 'Heaven is silent', I thought. 'Heaven is silent, and evil is increasing in the world. It is going to win.' Then you knocked. I was able to buy medicine. Now my husband lives and he works. We can eat again. I thank you."

"Do not thank me. My part was small, a nothing. Do you really think evil is increasing?"

"How can you ask such a thing? Look around us."

"It is very bad, yes. But I sometimes wonder if it is more a question of trials. Yes, the trials are increasing. Evil cannot grow. Now and then it is permitted to break out. We suffer and die, then life returns. Evil goes back into the shadows."

The woman burst into tears.

"My son has not returned. Where is he? Where is he?"

Pawel touched her arm.

"Do not lose hope, Pani."

"I know, I know. We must be brave. Everything is possible with God."

"Yes, everything. Many things that are lost will be found again."

"Things, yes. And people", she sighed. "Especially the people."

"Signs too", he murmured. "And symbols, so that language will not be lost. Messages dropping like snow."

She glanced at him without comprehension, wiped her eyes, and took both of his hands in hers.

"You are such a good young man. You need a wife to take care of you. I know a lovely girl, my sister-in-law's niece—"

"Thank you, Pani Lewicki," said Pawel as if awakening, "but it would be impossible now to feed a wife and children. After the war, perhaps . . ."

She patted his hands.

"Such a fine young man", she sighed. "Of course my sister-in-law's niece is only a farm girl. You are a gentleman. You should marry a girl of quality, of education. There were so many young ladies at the university who would have made a good wife for you. I used to clean rooms in the music wing. I remember one—so kind, so bright, so talented. She was the piano professor's daughter. She sometimes taught there and played often at recitals. Her name was Elzbieta. Did you ever see her? You might remember a young woman in a dark green velvet gown, with a white lace collar—mmmm, so pretty."

Pawel nodded.

Mrs. Lewicki's eyes grew suddenly dark with peasant animosity.

"When they arrested the professors, oh, I will never forget that evil day! They pulled her by her long golden braid and threw her, I mean *threw* her, into the truck along with all the others, as if she were garbage. I couldn't sleep for a week."

Because she had resumed her tears, she did not see Pawel Tarnowski hurrying away down the street.

"Kahlia," he whispered, "Kahlia!"

## 11

The money Smokrev had paid for the icons dwindled too quickly. Unable to resist the sight of the destitute, Pawel gave many *zlotys* to women with hungry children passing in the street. He noticed a thin girl and her little brother walking barefoot through the snow beneath the statue of Copernicus and bought secondhand shoes for them. He gave Masha some, and more to Mrs. Lewicki, whose husband was well but out of work again. He also gave to the nuns and arranged for medicine to be sent to their chaplain, who was, they said, recovering from pneumonia. Once, he saw Baba Yaga selling ersatz tea from a steaming kettle in front of the Staszic palace and bought a glass from her. She did not recognize him as the man who had purchased a set of Goethe. She appeared dazed, her cheeks hollow. Into her paw he dropped twice as many coins as were necessary.

The coal bin was emptying again and soon would need refilling. The apartment was still moderately warm, but its atmosphere seemed as desolate as ever. This was caused by the blank spaces on the wall where the icons had once hung. He had hoped in the beginning that the apartment would gradually recover from its loss, would resume its sense of normality—less decorative, but still home. This did not occur. The sense of barrenness prevailed, like the hollowness of a church stripped bare for Holy Saturday. Pawel now realized that the missing icons had been more than windows; they had been presences, like photographs of family members—the mothers, the fathers, the friends in paradise, the guardians, the resisters of the ancient foe. He missed the image of the Mother most of all. He prayed before the crucifix, of course, and there was some consolation in this. When he kissed it, a wounded hand seemed to come from it, calming him, yet inviting him into a terrible mystery before which he could only bow incomprehensibly. The Cross, he knew, was a sign of victory rising above the world; still, that world was a devastated battleground.

On his bedside table he kept the brass carving that Papa had given him so many years ago. Cleaned and polished, it sat there like a returned prodigal reduced to silence, radiating a world of meaning that he had thought was lost forever. Moreover, it offered in its humble way a contradiction to his recent doubts about providence. Or fate. For if the principle that governed all lives had brought this lost word back into his life, surely it had done so for a purpose.

During the previous months, he had sold all of the nineteenth-century landscapes that had hung in the apartment. The only remaining painting was the Italian *fiori* he had purchased in Paris, and for which he suddenly felt great dislike. Smokrev had called it unspeakable ugly. Ugly it was not, yet the contempt dulled the radiance that had once transformed his squalid room in Paris with light from a sun-filled land. It now seemed to him merely pretty, a decoration. Its splashes of color adequately represented flowers but did not convey their mystery or elicit wonder. This painting was no window; it was a mirror reflecting his shallowness. Yes, he was like a child easily distracted by baubles. It seemed to him now that his whole life had been spent in seeking no further than surface appearances. And though he also realized that this was not entirely true, he removed the *fiori* from the wall and went down to the shop with it. There, he made out a tag for a ridiculously low price and put it in the front window.

A week later Haftmann scooped it up with several other purchases.

"Where do you find these things?" he asked incredulously.

"My sources are inexhaustible, Herr Doktor", he said. "When people are desperate they will sell anything."

Haftmann's money enabled Pawel to buy a few good titles. It helped him avoid the temptation to dip into the treasure trove in the attic (the more presentable non-Jewish books). He felt that in some obscure way he had made a promise to be the guardian of the collection. After the war he would resell it to the lawyer from Lodz, and the lawyer would restore the books to their rightful owners, if they were still alive.

As for those useless titles that had camouflaged the boxes—the shallow and the *sitra ahra*—he did not wish to be the instrument of their promotion. They would provide emergency fuel or merely sit waiting for the end of night.

\* \* \*

A Sunday afternoon. Snow was blowing sideways against the windows of the parlor, where Pawel sat quietly reading. On the edge of his attention, he sensed more than saw that David had entered the room and was seated opposite him. Minutes passed, but Pawel did not look up.

"Excuse me, Pan Tarnowski."

*I know that tone*, Pawel thought to himself.

"You wish to say something?"

"Yes."

Pawel groaned inwardly, looking up at last.

"Words are not enough", David declared into the echoing silence.

"Words are not enough?"

"Often have I found myself trying to find a way of expressing a totality—a reality experienced within—but am frustrated in my attempt to find sufficient . . ."

"Sufficient words?"

"Not precisely. I mean carriers of words."

"What are carriers of words, if not words?"

"The central current of language, celestial language."

"Ah, celestial language", said Pawel, vaguely recalling one of their earlier conversations.

"That is why language must end outside of itself, in action."

Pawel put down his book.

"Action", he said dryly. "What actions are at our disposal in this prison cell?"

This seemed to take the boy aback. He remained silent for a time. Then, as if stumbling upon a mislaid insight, he said, "A story is a creative action, both the final work and the series of smaller acts that are part of its creation. We can tell stories."

"People in mental asylums tell stories too. They are often to be seen speaking to the walls or into vacant space."

"They are speaking without action."

"In this we are in agreement—their language is the pacing of a prisoner in solitary confinement, the cell of the enclosed self, speaking to phantoms in the mind."

"True, but if there is a speaker and a listener, there is genuine action."

"What is genuine action?"

"Action, surely, is a level of language, the physical signs of invisible thoughts."

"How is that genuine? In a world regulated by the actions of selfish men, thoughts are always converted into distorted expressions."

"So we believe. So do we limit ourselves. That is why we cannot see farther and deeper."

"How, then, do you propose to see farther and deeper?"

"We spoke of this before, Pan Tarnowski. Do you remember?"

"Not really."

"The man who looks at a window may see only his reflection, or he may see through his reflection to what is outside of himself—to the greatness of the world beyond himself."

"Ah, yes, I remember."

"So, you see, it is possible to learn to speak and to hear the nonlinear, eternal language."

Warming to the subject a little, Pawel replied in a musing tone: "I suppose you're right. Yes, it's possible to see beyond one's self. Narcissus does not suspect there are other forms of beauty than his own face."

"Or his own pity."

"Pity?"

"Pity for himself. The prisoner who will only weep and despair over his situation."

"All right, David Schäfer, I will grant your point. Why else would you and I search relentlessly in books for hints of other universes?"

The boy's eyes lit up with excitement. "So you see it!"

"I see that a man may use books as a reflection in a mirror, or as a window."

"But you prefer the window, don't you?" he prompted.

"At my best, I sometimes believe there is life beyond the glass."

"But you tell stories for others. Your play, for example."

"I wrote the play for myself alone."

David's face fell.

"It is not a good play", Pawel added.

"What is a good play?"

"The heart of drama in a play is the unmistakable message that man must live with the consequences of his actions."

"And of the actions done to him by others?"

A nameless fear flickered in Pawel.

"Yes, also that."

"Where thought stumbles, music and poetry and stories come to our rescue, so that we might understand the world."

"You do not mention painting?"

"I do not wish to include painting. Images are forbidden", David replied.

317

"Ah, yes, your laws. But you are forgetting that stories and poetry and even music can enthrall by deception."

"I think you mean deceive by enthralling."

"At least we are agreed that in certain arts it is possible to hear the celestial language. One can taste paradise for an instant."

David nodded emphatically. "For our people, when we dance—dancing as prayer—we approach paradise."

"For me it is literature. Especially the poetic element in literature. The truly poetic—I mean the fruit of creative intuition combined with the poet's mastery of the tool of language as contractual sign—this can approach mystic vision and other forms of soul-prayer."

"You are saying that whenever two people speak with each other, there is an agreement—a contract, you call it—that a word has a particular meaning for both of them?"

"Yes."

"But even such a contract is flawed by interpretation, is it not?"

"Yes, that also."

"Between two people there is always an assessment of context and personality, correct?"

"Yes, absolutely. It is a factor we must always guard against in ourselves."

"Guard against?" David asked, tilting his head inquisitively.

"Interpretation twists the meaning of the word that is spoken and the word that is heard. In fact, it is not truly heard."

"Still, it is a word. I would not say we must *guard*, for this implies fear. I would say we should be *aware*, and be willing to enlarge our understanding of the other."

"A beautiful idealism. Is that what you do?"

"I try to do this always. I think you do it too, Pan Tarnowski, for you have opened your home to me at great cost, and this, surely, is evidence of much understanding in you."

"I understand very little about human nature. Once I thought I knew everything about it, but no longer. It is simply that I do not believe the Germans should have their way in Poland. All human lives are valuable—beyond price."

"If you believe this, then you are a man of large understanding."

Pawel shook his head. "No, I just hate storm troopers."

"We have wandered from our subject. We were discussing interpretation."

"Ah, yes. Well, I will be loyal to my term *guard*, because I do not have your optimistic view of human nature. All too easily man evaluates other lives according to what they are worth in a utilitarian society—their productivity."

"You mean false values."

"Correct. For me, when a little child speaks soul-thought, in simple forms, I am moved much more deeply than when a doctor of literature speaks the same insight in sophisticated terms."

"Why?"

"Because the phenomenon coming from a child points to the existence of something beyond the limitations of his brain. Its beauty transcends the person's artificial 'worth'—which is based on knowledge as a collation of fact instead of wisdom as a reservoir of truth."

David smiled suddenly. "How do you know such things!"

"I don't know how I know. Do I know it?"

"You speak of it as blood pumping through your veins."

"My fingers are cold with the chill; I cannot feel my own heart. For all I know there's no more than a stone there, and purple ink in my veins."

Now David laughed in earnest.

"You like to joke, Pan Tarnowski. I enjoy this quality in you."

"I am a very humorous man", Pawel replied, rolling his eyes a little.

"But returning to our subject", David continued with a smile. "For me, the way to reduce misinterpretation when speaking with another person is to keep before the eyes of my heart a reverence for the mystery within him, his unknown mission, his identity hidden in the mind of the Most High."

"Do all the Hasidim think as you do?"

The boy grew silent for a while before responding.

"I have been in scholarly correspondence with the great Dabrova Rebbe since I was thirteen years of age. I believe that he sees as I do, but in another field of thought."

"Believe or sense?"

"A good distinction. You are correct: I sense it."

Suddenly, the strangeness of their dialogue struck both man and boy at the same time. David sat for a few moments staring at the window, as if trying to penetrate the barrier that had been placed between his present situation and his past. He stood abruptly and went to the kitchen. Pawel supposed that he wanted to be alone and had gone up to the attic. This was not so, for soon after, he returned with two glasses of tea.

As they sipped it, David resumed speaking.

"Pan Tarnowski, when we speak with another person, are we not always placing him in a category? Even below the level of rational thought, we ask, what mental equipment does this person have, how much time is there, how much trust is there for me to share this little bit of myself? Do we not make this assessment before we begin to speak? It seems to me that engaging in language is always based on such an assessment of person, place, and degree of trust."

"Yes, it is always active in us."

"And then, when I have made my assessment, if I think of what I am going to say, I find that the word already exists in my heart. And if I want to speak to you about it, I must make present to your heart what is already present in mine."

Pawel nodded.

"Then, seeking a way to let the word that exists in me reach you and dwell with you, I use my voice. Its sound communicates my word and its meaning to you. When it is finished it evaporates in the air, for this sound is nothing but air. But my word is now in you, and yet it still remains in me."

"This is true for good words *and* evil words", Pawel replied.

"A degraded word is a blow to the mind. A true, illuminating word is a seed. The fruitfulness of the seed depends on the soil in which it is planted."

"Yet between the evil word and the true word lies a vast territory. You called it the *borderlands*. What is really happening in that country, and what is the significance of all the words spoken in it?"

"I think most human words are to be found there."

"I agree."

"That is why most books are futile, and most conversations, empty."

"The narcissist again."

"Yes", the boy nodded. "Sterilized language ceases to be thought."

"Yet thought needs language in order to be . . . thought."

"Oh, no", David said, drawing back. "That is not correct. Thought may remain unspoken and still be thought."

"It seems we have just bumped into a barrier. We cannot see it, but what is it? How do we get around it?"

David pondered this for a few moments, then replied slowly, as if choosing every word with greatest care.

"The solitary prisoner has little of his own except the power of thought. If he discovers that there is another prisoner in the prison, they may communicate by tapping code on the walls that separate them. If there is even the smallest breach in the wall, they might share a dented spoon or a crust of stale bread. The gifts are important to the prisoners, but not as important to them as the act of sharing."

"So, you're saying that sharing language is a form of action."

"Yes. And developing the scope of language expands the potential for action. If the prisoners are released, they have been prepared for more than would have been possible for them if they had remained at liberty in a world of mundane freedoms."

"I would not call freedom, in any form, mundane."

"Thank you for the correction, Pan Tarnowski. Let me say, then, that upon their release the prisoners will be better able to expand the realm of action from implicit action to explicit action."

"But what if a prisoner is condemned to a lifetime sentence?"

"This kind of prisoner keeps freedom before the eyes of his heart, and thus he remains in his innermost being a free man."

Now both fell silent. By mutual wordless agreement, the conversation ended. Both returned to their previous activities—Pawel to his book, and David to sewing up a rip in his coat.

*   *   *

From early February onward, Pawel began regularly to attend Mass at the convent of the Visitation, for his parish had been closed and the priest arrested. Many city parishes remained open, but the sisters' chapel was nearby, and it was full of memories of his childhood. He also wondered if he would chance to meet the nun who had spoken to him after his fall on the icy steps of the parish church. But among the few sisters who appeared from behind the enclosure, there were no faces he recognized, and he recalled that she had worn a different habit. Still, her words returned to him often.

*Fear is our great enemy* would echo through his mind at the most incongruous moments, during the preparation of meals or the washing of linen. Alternately, he might be gluing the spine of a book and hear, *Abandon yourself to the Lord with full confidence, then the devils cannot touch you. If you are in fear, you cannot hear the voice of God.*

That was all very pious, he thought, very contemplative, very advanced spirituality—perfectly appropriate for the holy people who were protected within their orderly convents and monasteries. But how preposterous for men such as himself, who daily breathed an atmosphere that was almost entirely composed of fearful realities. Impossible!

Then Andrei Rublëv would reply to him, *Pawel, do not say the way is impossible; say, rather, that it is the impossible to which we are called.*

Yes, all arguments, exhortations, imaginings, and doubts found a home in him. Knowing everything solved nothing. Sweet, holy fire was so easily blasted aside by the gusts of bitter, black fire. All the wisdom of his play, which he felt was nothing more than a collection of ideas absorbed during his many years of reading, could not be translated into the least alteration of his own character.

*O lavish blue fire, flashing from silver foil, O holy green, O pure vermilion, you are a wine poured into creatures made of mud*, cried Andrei Rublëv. *Hear me, Pawel! It is a grief! It is a grief when we are enclosed within our fear.*

"Andrei Rublëv, you are right", Pawel would reply, addressing the choir of books in his abandoned shop. "It is indeed a grief! My whole life falls, falls, falls from the face that my poor scribble represents. But what am I to do? I am far from God."

*Surely, you know the meaning of the icon of the silent God*, Theophanes the Greek rebuked him.

*He is near, he is near!* chanted the monk Daniil.

Then the chorus of angels singing, *Your face is more brilliant than the sun, O Lord most glorious. Unable to bear your overwhelming radiance, your disciples fall upon their faces . . .*

"But all men fall on their faces, do they not, for all have fallen short of the glory of God?"

The debates swirled within him, never quite leading him out of the maze of himself, never showing him the ascending path taken by the wise, the exalted, the contemplatives, the saints. Still, he could pray the prayers of the fools, the idiots, the dreamers, and the burnt men. And these he did pray.

One Sunday morning Pawel saw Mrs. Lewicki at the convent chapel. After Mass she approached him while he was still kneeling, and she put a package into his hands.

"This was Janusz's", she whispered. "It's for you. A gift. Pray for my son."

"When did you last see him, Pani?"

"In early September of 'thirty-nine."

"More than three years."

"He was in the cavalry. He rode so beautifully, and so proud of his uniform! But I knew it was a mistake for a smart boy like that who had done well in Switzerland and also had a degree from the Polytechnic. To enter the army at a time when there was so much trouble in Europe! Think of it—communists to the east and the Hitler movement to the west, and we thought we could face them with a few thousand boys on horseback! We weren't prepared!"

"The whole country was unprepared."

"He wouldn't listen to me! He wouldn't listen!"

"Do not lose hope. There is always hope."

"Yes. You taught me that. Please accept this small thing. Keep it for my Januszek."

She left, and the sisters behind the chapel grille began to chant a litany to the Mother of God.

"*Mother of our Creator*," they sang, "*pray for us.*"
*Mother of our Savior,*
*Virgin most merciful,*
*Virgin most faithful,*
*Mirror of Justice,*
*Mystical Rose,*
*Ark of the Covenant,*
*Tower of David,*

*Tower of Ivory,*
*Gate of Heaven,*
*House of Wisdom*, they sang.
"Pray for us", Pawel replied.

\*   \*   \*

Back at the apartment, he unwrapped the gift and found a small, well-painted icon of the Mother of God of Czestochowa. He put it in the empty icon corner beside his bed, above the knight and dragon, and lit a red vigil candle. The room was immediately suffused with presence. He walked through the apartment and found that the whole dwelling was again irradiated by the invisible. He returned to the bedroom and bowed before the icon.

David Schäfer, passing the doorway on the way to the kitchen, paused and observed him.

"Excuse me, Pan Tarnowski", he said with a worried look. "Why do you bow before an image? In the *Chumash* it is written . . . in Deuteronomy it is written that—"

"You refer to the biblical injunction against worshipping graven images?"

"Yes. Is this not a graven image?"

"It is a painted image. But we never worship it."

"Forgive me, but I could not help notice you bowing before it. I have also seen you kiss the other images before they were sold."

"People sometimes kiss the photographs of their parents. It is like that."

"But they are real people."

"Our friends in paradise are also real."

David thought intensely.

"But where does the Most High say that man may now make images?"

"With the coming of Christ the Old Law was replaced by

325

the New. A new order had begun in creation. Before his time the world was infested with idols. Many of the ancient civilizations practiced human sacrifice. Some went so far as to burn children alive on their altars. Even a descendant of King David returned to it. Christian civilization ended all that."

"People are still being burned, Pan Tarnowski. But not by us."

"When men lose faith, they forget. Again and again they forget."

"It seems to me that this war is a vast panorama of forgetting. Many children are dying—"

"Countless human lives are being destroyed, most of them without any real understanding of why it is happening", said Pawel.

"Can we ever understand it? The Most High is infinitely greater than our poor minds can grasp. We must not question his will, even in the face of such evils."

"I think we are permitted to ponder his will. Could it be that whenever great evils strike at the core of our understanding, we are asked to see farther than we ordinarily do?"

David nodded tentatively, though he appeared to be troubled by Pawel's last remark.

"You don't agree?" Pawel prompted.

"In the ghetto, I saw many abandoned children on the streets, begging for food. I gave what I could, but it was not enough. The little bodies, like litter, like trash, on the sidewalk. A dead child shakes everything. You say that evil confronts us with a question—one that is at the root of existence in this world. The Most High permits it, you infer, in order to ask us a question?"

Now it was Pawel's turn to nod without speaking.

"This question", said David, staring at the floor, "has a terrible cost."

"Yet it is not God's primary will."

326

"He has permitted it, has he not?"

"Clearly, he has."

"Why?"

Pawel paused, suddenly aware of a previously unexposed dimension in the boy's thinking. Was it possible that David the unshakable, the adamant, the wholly devoted advocate of the rights of the Most High, was capable of doubt? Only a moment before, the boy had maintained that God's will should not be questioned. Was he now questioning? Or was he weighing the problem of evil for the purpose of expanding his understanding?

"You ask why God permits evil", Pawel said. "I do not know the answer to this. There are arguments one could make to explain it, but they always lack something—something elusive that may be far beyond our ability to comprehend. Would we misinterpret it, even if we could see? All attempts to understand evil fail in the end."

"Perhaps that is why the forces of the *sitra ahra* do what they do, for the angels of darkness know how it shakes our confidence in the Most High."

"Does it shake your confidence?"

David lowered his eyes. "It tests it."

"In my faith we believe there is only one answer to the blows that evil inflicts on us. The answer is not a rational argument. The answer is a man. This man is God himself suffering with us, dying with us, so that he might draw us up to the Most High, confounding all the devices of the enemy."

"The messiah, when he comes, will be a man—not the Most High."

"Now we speak to each other across a gap. This is what divides our understanding, your people and mine. May I tell you what we see on this side of the gap?"

Looking up, David nodded uneasily.

"If the messiah were to come as a man only, it would surely

be an argument against evil, but an incomplete one. If he were to come as God only, in the flesh yet not in reality a man, that too would be incomplete."

"I have read of your theology, but I admit that here I am confused. How does this explain a murdered child?"

"When he came among us, it was to teach us that we are greater than we conceive ourselves to be. Each person is his icon. To burn even one, to hurt even the least of human beings, is to assault God. He shows us his face, and to our shock it is a human face."

"If that is so, why has so much evil been done by his followers?"

"Because such men are not in fact his followers. They do not look beyond the icon to the one it represents."

"Then, surely it is unwise to have such images."

"Should we break all windows because some men see only their own reflections in them?"

David digested this with a frown.

"Still, I do not understand your conception of the Most High. It cannot be correct. Too easily would our regard of him fall to the lowest level. We would no longer worship him."

"God has taken this great risk with us. He extends his hands as a gateway to eternal life. On one palm is written *Truth* and on the other is written *Love*. These two principles are united in his heart. He permits himself to be seized and bound and to have nails driven through those two words—words of the celestial language."

"You are saying that we, the Jews, cannot see what—"

"All mankind is damaged in this way."

David stood and paused for a moment in silent reflection.

"I have much to think about", he said. Then, meeting Pawel's eyes: "So many words you speak to me today. Today, you give me a key to your house."

When the boy had returned to the attic, Pawel sat down on

the edge of his bed and pondered anew the seemingly endless complexity of himself. A key? His house? This household was a maze, was it not? Within the space of a few hours he had prayed the prayers of the burnt men, worshipped and communicated at Mass like an ordinary Polish Catholic, counseled a woman like a sage, bowed like a Byzantine, instructed a non-Christian like a scholastic, and was now swiftly relapsing into the convoluted self-absorption that was his habitual and very modern self!

He shook his head free, got to his feet, and went to make a glass of tea.

\* \* \*

That night he was almost asleep when David's shouts came bounding ahead of him down the attic staircase. Pawel flicked on the bedside light as the boy entered with his prayer shawl flying and skullcap askew, a book under his arm. He threw himself onto the end of the bed and folded his legs in the style of an Indian from *Amerika*.

"Who is this Milton?" he said.

"I do not know."

"He is a British poet. What I mean to ask is *who* is he in the works of the Most High? He wrote this thing," said the boy, waving the book, "and it is *all* about the Fall of Man. It is very interesting."

"David, I am very tired. Tomorrow would be a better time."

"Listen to this, Pan Tarnowski. He is a Christian poet, and thus there are elements with which I have difficulty. But in the foundation of his vision he is rooted in the Torah. The horror of Pandemonium and Chaos. The beauty of Heaven and Eden. It's the subject we discussed earlier today! Listen:

> *"What in me is dark, illumine,*
> *What is low, raise and support;*
> *That to the height of this great Argument*

> *I may assert Eternal Providence,*
> *And justify the ways of God to men."*

"I'm sorry, I don't know English. I did hear the word *Gott* in there someplace, so I suspect it's our favorite subject. True?"

"True", the boy mumbled, ruffling through a small English-Polish dictionary.

"Are you having trouble?"

"Yes, the fine shading of some words is difficult. But one feels a rush of wind. One senses a vast court and Satan accusing man before the Most High. And the poet is not only trying to defend man before the Most High, he is trying to defend the Most High to man! An amazing thing!"

A doubt crossed the boy's face. He looked up. "Is it right to defend the Most High to man? Does he need a defense? Think of his reply to Job!"

Without waiting for a response, David plunged back into the book, his brow furrowed, his index finger moving across lines of print. Slowly, with patient effort, he translated certain passages into Polish and recited them aloud. The ideas were transmitted intact, but Pawel found them dry. Interesting but ponderous.

Without warning David threw himself sideways on the bed with his arms flung wide, staring at the ceiling, his mouth open, his bare feet dangling over the edge.

"It is amazing", he murmured.

"What is amazing?"

"The unspeakable immensity of the drama in which we are involved. Think of it, think of the size of the cosmos!"

The boy's belly was exposed—a slash of white landscape surrounding a navel. Pawel looked away.

"David, go up to bed."

"Oh, yes, yes, Pan Tarnowski. Good night, then."

"Good night."

When the boy was gone, Pawel threw back the blankets and put his feet solidly onto the floor. He shivered and rested his head on his hands. The skin of his arms rose up in goose bumps, but his face was hot, his heart beating hard.

"Enough!" he said aloud. Then angrily to himself: "My life is absurdity itself—in one and the same moment I hunger for the 'drama of the cosmos' and am drawn to the drama of the carnal!"

But *drawn* soon ceased to be the right word. Snared, hypnotized, riveted by an image that would not depart. A scene like a motion picture film began to project itself upon the screen of his imagination, a carnival show in which flames of fire consumed its victim. He shook his mind clear. The images returned, insinuating themselves back into his imagination, until to his horror the incubus was about to ignite him.

He purged his mind again, jumped up, and left the bedroom. At the other end of the hallway, a small window overlooked the street. Moonlight poured in through the frosty glass. He opened it and let the cold air blast him.

He remained in this position for several minutes, until his heart ceased to hammer and the blood drained from his face. But he did not wish to return to the bed. The embers glowed and it would take only a little surge of the bellows to inflame them.

"It has come back", he said.

Green-eyed dogs tore the velvet hide from the flanks of a red deer and crunched its golden antlers while it still lived, its eyes wild with terror, a gash in its throat spurting heliotrope violet, mulberry, chromium red, pump, pump, pump, while its mouth opened in a cry that was beyond sound. Cats clamped their jaws around the limp bodies of blue pigeons that had plunged from steeples like bolts of grace.

*I will give him to you*, said a voice calling from the fires that swept across the fields of snow.

331

"Who is speaking?" Pawel stammered.

*I will make him choose it*, said the voice.

"Love is given, not taken", he whispered.

*He will desire to give it.*

"It is wrong."

*I give where I give and take where I take. You have my permission.*

Then fear gave way to suspicion, to an unease of soul that was a deeper listening, a doubt debating with the part of Pawel that desired to believe the voice.

"Would God violate the will of another?" he asked. "Would God make such a gift without the other willing it?"

*I will place him into your hands and he will desire to stay there. All passion is a reflection of my divine passions.*

The light of the moon seemed to grow dim, and his dread of the voice eased. The arguments went on for some time. He began to think according to the pattern of its thoughts, and wondered if it was really such an evil thing to make an end to loneliness. In a time when men were destroying each other in the millions, why could he not burn with a desire rooted in the very sources of creation? What harm in this? Two beings, each alone, each without a family, surrounded by death?

"Love is love", he said to the moon. "Does it matter which form it takes?"

He stood immobilized, waiting for further dialogue. A moment earlier, while talking with the voice, he had felt surrounded by something powerful and sweet—and rotten—like fermenting cherries. He now felt suddenly nauseous and cold. He had not agreed to the proposal—not yet—but he was weighing it, and the voice waited while he considered.

There was a flash of brief lights, as if by an optical illusion of the mind, and within it Pawel saw an old man in a bomb crater, a weeping prophet, stars revolving in a circular crown, and a raven. The raven flew through his thoughts for an instant, leaving a near audible hallucination of its caws echoing in the silence of the apartment.

"He is a child", said Pawel.

Thus, the fight broke once more into the open.

*He is a man*, said the voice, pressing down hard.

"He is half-grown, in the true nature of a man", Pawel argued. "It would be a grave sin to deform him."

*It is a small sin. Harmless.*

"There is no such thing as a small sin."

*You love him. He is yours.*

"He is not mine! I have feelings of love. Not the substance of love."

*What is the substance of love?*

Pawel shook his head, confused, unable to formulate a defense. With an effort of the will he turned away from the hypnotic dialogue and went back to the bedroom.

*You will obey me*, the voice said.

"This is my mind, this is my mind!" Pawel proclaimed, but a split consciousness suddenly seemed to him more frightening than the attack of an external monster. The monster was within, was himself. Arguing with it, he cried, "One so young cannot choose freely. It would be theft. The answer is *no*."

With trembling fingers he struck a match and lit the vigil light before Janusz Lewicki's icon. Slowly, slowly, the fire, the white landscape, and the voice faded.

"Savior of the world," he cried, "help me!"

*Be at peace, my little one*, said a voice without compulsion. *It was necessary for you to experience this. Recognize that voice and do not again listen to it. Do not converse with it. The deceiver wishes to shake you in his teeth. Come to me, come always to me and trust.*

He gazed into the image of the compassionate face, and there he saw truth and mercy perfectly mingled.

"The man I seek is within me", he said aloud.

Exhausted, he prayed, then slept.

*   *   *

In the morning, he surfaced to the cracking of small-arms fire that sounded near enough to be only a few streets away. He lay in bed for a while, listening to it with eyes closed. When it ceased altogether he fell back a little into the dream from which he had been roused, trying to catch its details as they faded.

A landscape of twilight, foreboding, terror. He stood by a raging fire that was consuming countless little white birds that sought to fly beyond the reach of the flames. Smoke and heat confused them, and none could escape. He thrust his hands into the conflagration, shielding the birds from the worst of the flames, and opened a path for them. His flesh burning in agony, he directed them upward, out of the dark world toward a distant horizon, where the tilt of the planet was silhouetted by the approaching dawn.

Disturbed by the dream, and moved by it for no apparent reason, he got up wearily, worrying anew over his disordered psyche. He stumbled into the kitchen to make the morning tea. David came down from the attic shortly after.

"Ah, Pan Tarnowski, I had such a dream", he announced.

"What did you dream?" Pawel asked distractedly.

"I dreamed that the Germans stormed this building. I was hidden in the attic and you saved me from them."

"Oh, good", Pawel yawned.

"They set fire to the building. You had escaped. But you came back and you ran through the fire and pulled me from it."

"Fire", said Pawel, coming fully awake.

"You were *goel* for me."

"What is *goel*?"

"Ransomer. This is the Hebrew word for one who pays a ransom or debt for another."

"And then what happened?"

"Then together we went to the mountains, where they

couldn't find us. And when we came to the greatest mountain, two angels came out to greet us. They were angels of the Most High. Light came from their eyes, which were like glass. One angel led you into a palace over which there was a sword and a crown. And the other angel led me into a palace over which there was a loaf of bread, a raven, and also a crown. What can this mean?"

"A raven, you say?"

"A raven."

"Do you dream such dreams often?"

"Rarely. Only when the Most High wishes to help me see a hidden thing."

"Was that the end of your dream?"

"No. My angel pointed to you and said, *Because this man has denied himself, he shall go higher. This palace is allotted for him and this one is for you. These two dwelling places are connected and shall have much honor in the heavenly Jerusalem.*"

Pawel looked out the window.

"You dislike my dream", said David anxiously. "Do you think it blasphemous to find a Jew in paradise?"

"No. I believe that all who truly love God, who obey him, and who believe according to their conscience cannot fail to go there. Tell me, do you think it blasphemous to find a Christian in paradise?"

"I am uncertain. Perhaps, after all, it is merely a meaningless imagining of sleep."

"Meaningless?"

"It is a puzzle. I need time to think. But I hope for the two palaces."

"I too hope for this."

"Your eyes contain a unique look this day, Pan Tarnowski. I see both grief and joy."

"Yes, it is so. I am afraid of fire. But I am glad of a promise that we might survive it. Thank you for telling me your dream."

The boy nodded.

"I am glad you are here", Pawel said. "And I think it would be better if you no longer called me Pan Tarnowski."

"What shall I call you?" the boy asked.

"Please call me Pawel."

"Thank you", he said quietly. "Pawel."

He turned and went up to the attic without another word.

\* \* \*

11 February 1943

Kahlia,

"Goel", he calls me. A ransomer. Yes, I suppose this is how he must see my role—halted as he is before my superficial resemblance to a sacrificial hero. He does not know what lies beneath this layer, cannot hear my oft-repeated question, "But who will ransom me?"

It is night. My guest sleeps beneath the eaves, hidden from our enemies. He must not fall into their hands. I could not bear another loss.

Why did I not find sufficient boldness to introduce myself to you that night after your piano recital? The way you played told me more about you than a year of courtship would have. When I was first struck by the sight of you I understood, in a way that I had not until then, that love yearns toward completion in the being of another. I do not mean simply the meeting of the flesh, but more urgently, the union of soul and soul. In all cases, love can exist only as a gift freely given. You did not know me, and so it was impossible for this question to be raised between us. The opportunity to give your love to me was but one of countless doorways open to a person such as you. In the end the enemy decided for us.

If this correspondence were real, no doubt you would think me a fool. But I am consoled by imaginings. I will post this now in the usual place. Perhaps there will come a time when an angel will deliver the box in the bottom of my desk drawer.

Pawel

## 12

The fever hit Pawel as he was shelving new purchases and feeling perfectly well. The next moment his head began to ache, and he felt overwhelmed with dizziness. His legs barely supporting him, he managed to get the "Closed" sign onto the window, pull the blinds, and lock up before collapsing into the chair at his desk. He called the boy's name, and a minute later David peered his head cautiously around the passageway at the back.

"It's safe. The door is locked. I'm sick. Can you help me upstairs?"

He half-crawled, half-pulled himself up the stairwell, with the boy pushing and hauling beside him. His eyes blurring, he stumbled to his room and fell across the bed. David lifted Pawel's legs onto the mattress and ran to the kitchen sink. Returning with a cold, wet cloth, he put it on the fevered forehead. He repeated this for several hours as the sweat poured from the man, soaking his clothing. At some point David helped him to struggle out of his suit jacket, undid his tie, and opened his collar.

"Water, please", Pawel groaned.

David put an arm under under his shoulders and raised him a little, putting a glass to his lips. As the water slipped down Pawel's throat, he gulped it and spattered, and was ashamed of his ugliness. Pistols fired inside his skull, followed by cannonades of pain. Pawel closed his eyes, and the sensation coursing through him was like death. Though it seemed an eternity, within seconds the boy laid him back onto the pillow.

"You are very ill, Pawel. I must go out for medicine."

"Let the fever run its course", Pawel groaned, each word purchased as if by the firing of a gun.

"You need help!"

"You will die if you go out."

The boy said nothing.

"What are you doing?"

"Lighting your candles."

"Leave it be."

"I do it for light."

He was too exhausted to argue.

"Now what are you doing?"

"I am washing your feet."

Before Pawel could protest further, he dropped into oblivion.

\* \* \*

He was in bed for more than a week. Each morning David refilled the vigil lamps and lit them. Following this, he helped Pawel to the toilet, then assisted him back to bed. After that he brought him tea.

Fevers alternated with chills that afflicted him off and on for the first three days; his legs shook violently and his teeth chattered. On the evening of the fourth day, he suffered an extremely high fever and threw the covers off, tossing and turning in his sweat-soaked pajamas, muttering deliriously.

"He should be in a hospital!" the boy said to no one. He sat by the bed throughout that night, watching helplessly, applying a cloth from time to time. Before dawn he fell asleep against his will, slumped in the chair, breathing open-mouthed through cracked lips.

Hours later, Pawel awoke. David startled, opened his eyes, and stared at him.

"You are better!"

"The fever has broken."

"Thanks be to the Most High!"

"Yes, thanks be to God!"

David dashed away and returned carrying a bowl of thin, salty soup that tasted like potatoes. Pawel drank a liter of it. All day long the boy poured liquids into him, and by nightfall Pawel was able to walk by himself to the bathroom.

"I'm recovering", he said. "You can go up to the attic and get some sleep."

"No, I will stay until I am certain."

"Where have you slept the last few days?"

"One night in the chair, three nights across the foot of the bed. That way I could hear if you stirred."

"Tonight you must go back to the fortress. You need sleep."

"For one more night I am the master here", David smiled. "You are too weak to force me upstairs. I will bring my mattress down."

Pawel gestured helplessly.

He lay for another three days, utterly exhausted, his restoration measurable in centimeters. Several times there were faint rappings on the shop door below, but they always ceased.

Throughout this time David sat on the chair at the foot of the bed, his legs up, feet propped on the blankets. He was buried in a thick German volume of philosophy that appeared to be, judging by its cover, completely unreadable. It was nearly impossible to jar him out of it. Every few hours he would jump up and go downstairs, and by this Pawel realized that David had taught himself how to stoke the furnace.

On the evening of the eighth day, when the dark had fallen and only the bedside lamp and the vigil candle shed light, David scraped his chair up toward the head of the bed and continued to read as if obsessed. Pawel thought it a good imitation of the way most boys devoured a cheap adventure novel.

"It is absolutely incredible!" David said, looking up with an astonished expression.

"What?"

"Pawel, the human mind is the most amazing creation. This man has just 'proved' that the universe does not exist. He insists quite reasonably that we—you and I and everything else—are projections of his mind. *His* mind, you see, not yours or mine."

"Who wrote it?"

David told him.

"Yes. This is one of the troughs at which the forerunners of Hitler fed. The man you are reading helped create the social climate that spawned the Nazis."

"Then ideas are more than mere abstractions."

"As the events of our century have proven."

David made a face and tossed the book onto the floor. "This is *sitra ahra*!"

"Yes, I think you are right. It is very bad when brilliant men use thought to destroy thought."

"Perhaps it is better not to think. In life perhaps we should only pray."

"Not to think? Such a notion from *you*?"

"Forgive me, but there are times when I begin to doubt the mind."

"Why did the Creator of the Universe give us this power if he didn't want us to use it?" Pawel asked.

"But the mind is like a dog chained to a post. When he runs he thinks he is going faster than the wind, though he only goes in circles and does not know it."

"A curious metaphor. Did you invent it?"

"Yes. I apologize for its limitations."

"Would it not be more accurate to say that our mad philosopher is like a man with one eye?"

"What is the missing eye?"

"Beauty", said Pawel. "The universe is beautiful. It does not have to be that way. *Why* is it that way? I do not believe this philosopher ever looked at creation. He only thought he looked."

"He never loved it."

"He may have loved parts of it, but not the whole of it."

David nodded in agreement.

"Can I tell you a story, Pawel?"

"If you wish."

Pawel settled back against the pillows and flicked out the bedside lamp. Only the red vigil light illumined them now, bathing everything in its soft glow. Between man and youth the Mother of God gazed serenely from the plane of her image.

David sat up straight and began. Speaking slowly in a quiet voice, he said:

"Once, there was a little country boy who was orphaned at an early age. He never learned to read. His parents had left him a heavy prayer book as his inheritance. On the Day of Atonement he brought it to the synagogue, laid it on the reading table, and burst into tears, crying out, 'O Lord of All Creation! I do not know how to pray, nor even what to say—Here! I give thee the entire prayer book!'"

David looked up and smiled at Pawel with raised eyebrows.

"That's it?" Pawel asked.

"Yes. It's very strong, isn't it? Stronger than it seems."

"Like a bomb that bursts after a short delay."

"You do understand! But more like a flower that turns into seed that falls into the ground of the mind, and sprouts and bears its fruit in time."

"Do you think the little boy was closer to God than the great scholars are?"

"If his heart was open."

"Do you think an intellectual can have an open heart?"

"Of course. But it's rare."

"Rare, you say! Aren't you a people who specialize in study?"

David nodded. "Yes, we are. Yet we know that books alone are not enough. That is why we also dance and sing and seek what is above the mind. The scholar is rich in his mind, and the rich carry so much wealth on their backs toward the gate of paradise. A very great weight this is. Many fail to arrive."

"I see", said Pawel uncertainly.

"If the scholar can lay down his wealth and play like a child, then all will be well with him. Can I tell you another story?"

"If you wish, tell me stories all through the night and all through the day."

"Ah, you are playing, Pawel!"

"Begin, please."

"This is a different kind of story. It is from my life. It is a memory. Do you know what *Hanukkah* is?"

"A festival of lights, is it not?"

"Yes, it is the commemoration of a miracle for our people, the triumph over oppression. In the second century before the Christian era, a band of Jewish rebels formed an army to overthrow the pagan invaders. They succeeded in freeing and purifying the Temple, which had been defiled.

"According to the Talmud, when the rebels searched for holy oil to burn in the Temple candelabra, they found only enough for a single day. Yet miraculously the oil burned for eight days. That is why we have the menorah with its eight branches. On Hanukkah we light it in remembrance that the Most High can save his people even beyond the moment when all hope seems lost.

"The menorah of my family has an extra branch—some do and some don't. The ninth is a thin brass arm extending from the middle, and it carries a solitary candle smaller than the others. It is called the *shammash*, the servant. This light is used to kindle the others.

"On the eighth day of the last Hanukkah I celebrated with my family . . ."

David did not finish. The silence grew until he cleared his throat and continued:

"On the eighth day I had a dream. In this dream an ancestor

of mine, a learned rabbi who is well known among our people, appeared to me and said, *Dovid, a time of suffering is coming upon the world unlike any before. It will appear for a time that light has been extinguished, and most will fall away from worship of the Most High.*"

"Well, your ancestor was correct", Pawel said.

"In my sleep . . ." David hesitated. "In my sleep I cried out to my ancestor and I lifted both my hands to him, but he drew away from me into the sky. *Dovid, my Dovid,* he said, *when you are a man, you will become a light in this world. You must learn the difference between the light eternal and the darkness disguised as light.*"

He looked down.

"Is that all? Is that the end of the dream?"

"No."

"Can you tell me the rest?"

"It's not important."

"Why don't you tell me, and I can decide if it is or isn't?"

"I would rather not."

"You cannot leave me in such suspense. No decent story-teller would do that to his audience."

The boy sighed. "My ancestor said that many would wish to elevate me to a place of greatness, because they would think I am brilliant and would exalt my appearance. Exalt my appearance? What can this mean? Those were his words—such a thing to say!"

"Did he mean your physical appearance?"

"He did not explain. He had come to give me a warning. He told me that I must not take the path of human greatness."

"Must not? A strange thing for a great rabbi to tell a promising fellow."

"Do not joke, Pawel. This is embarrassing."

"Why does it embarrass you?"

"Because it praises me, and I do not deserve this praise. I am not attractive, and I am not exceptionally intelligent."

The boy meant it. Pawel stared at him. He repressed a desire to blurt out that David's ancestor knew David far better than David knew himself.

"Was there more to your dream?"

"My ancestor came to me again, this time carrying a *shammash*. He reached down and placed it in my hands, and he kissed my hands, which surprised me greatly. *With these hands you will do much good in the world,* he said, *but first you will be tested by fire. Always, my Dove, always you must be a little shammash.*"

Pawel sat upright in bed.

"I have disturbed you, Pawel."

"This is a meaningful story. I thank you for telling it."

"But you are troubled. What is it?"

"Several years ago a priest said practically those same words to me. He said that a voice from heaven had told him I would do a unique good in the world, but first I would be tested by fire."

"This is truly remarkable—exactly the same message. What can it mean?"

"I do not know. Yet it was not exactly the same. The voice said, *Here is my poor little son who has been broken.*"

"I do not understand. You are not broken, Pawel. You are a very strong man, one of the strongest I have ever met. You seem unafraid of anything."

Pawel looked back at him in amazement, marveling over that curious faculty, human perception.

"And you are brilliant too", David laughed.

"I am old and sick and wearing down fast", he corrected. "Listen, David Schäfer, let us leave aside the compliments for a moment. I think the important thing here is that you and I have a scrap of evidence that we are not living in a prison-universe. We live in a cosmos that has open doors and windows. Messages from the infinite enter here from time to time."

"Perhaps all the time, and we are blind to them."

"You may be right."

345

David reached over and slapped the blanket beside Pawel. "Such dreams—this is news of the highest magnitude!"

"Highest magnitude? I share your excitement, but you may be exaggerating the significance."

"Ah, unfortunately that is a character trait of my family. Even my famous ancestor had this fault."

*　*　*

When David had fallen asleep on the floor, Pawel turned on the bedside lamp. The boy did not stir. He was no longer gaunt, merely lean, and his hair was growing in with thick black curls. Pawel took up pen and paper and began to write:

Archive, 22 February 1943

Brilliant and beautiful he is. There can be no doubt that if he survives the intentions of those who now seek to destroy him, others will follow who will seek to exalt him. And desire him, too.

Desire. What is this force that is neither wholly love nor entirely sexual drive?

What was it that Rouault once wrote to me? When you corrupt the symbol, you corrupt the concept, and thus follows the corruption of perception and action.

When the corrupted symbol is entwined with powerful physical and emotional desires, it is difficult for man to learn a new vocabulary, especially one that is at odds with his first (and, he thinks, his only) tongue. Despite the fact that it cannot transmit authentic love to him, he clings to it, for it is the only dialect he has learned. His hunger unsatisfied, he craves more and more the very thing that deprives him of what he needs.

Pawel, search for the source of this pain. Try to understand it.

The man I seek is within me. Who is this man? Is it the icon of my lost father?

Is this, then, the source of the primal wound—the sense of

fatherlessness? The wound makes one vulnerable to a lie: you have no father, there is no fatherhood, the universe is abandoned.

The wound begets loneliness.

Loneliness seeks relief in the theater of the imagination.

The imagination ferments a romance.

Then romance, impelled by the generative powers of the body, gradually degenerates into erotic fantasy.

This in turn leaves the soul more frustrated and lonely than ever.

Thus the primal lie begets destruction—worst of all, it does so in the name of love.

Pawel lay back and closed his eyes. He turned out the light. The red glow of the vigil candle suffused the room. All was quiet. Stillness. Harmony. Pigeons ruffled their feathers and bolted for the sky. Herds of deer galloped away into the forest.

He glanced at the floor. There the boy slept without movement. For a long time Pawel held him in his mind as a father would hold a two-year-old on his lap. Then he turned over and slept.

\*　\*　\*

He improved slowly. One evening he lay in bed unable to read, drifting toward the borders of sleep. David had taken up his post on the chair at the end of the bed, legs stretched out on the blankets. He read for a while in the half-light, but his concentration was not on the book. He put it down and looked directly at Pawel.

"Can you tell me a story?"

"A story? What kind of story?"

"Anything."

"You offer me considerable liberty."

David smiled and waited. Pawel thought for a few moments.

347

"I will tell you a story that has been told for centuries. It is not original. There are many versions of it."

"Ah, good. Sometimes a traditional tale is better."

"Sometimes it is the other way around."

"Please, begin."

"In the Middle Ages, a famous young painter was hired to create a mural above the high altar of a great church in Paris. The subject was the life of Christ. The artist labored with persistence for many years, and the mural became known as the marvel of its time. Yet it remained incomplete. The artist, try as he might, could not complete two of the faces: the Christ Child and Judas Iscariot. Whenever he attempted to fill in these empty spaces the results were out of harmony with the rest of the work.

"The artist was greatly dissatisfied with this situation and could not understand why, despite his talents, he was unable to bring the mural to completion. He prayed for inspiration daily, and not long afterward, while walking on the streets of the city, he happened upon a group of children playing. Among them was a boy who had the face of an angel and who radiated goodness. The artist invited him to sit as a model for the Christ Child. With his parents' permission the child did, and the finished image was considered a masterpiece. Yet the painter could still find no model for the face of Iscariot.

"The story of the artist's quandary spread far and wide throughout the country, and many people, considering themselves the possessors of wicked, deformed, or corrupt faces, offered to pose as the betrayer. But to the artist none of them seemed quite right for the part. He wanted a face so twisted and ruined by its surrender to depravity that all who gazed upon it would see sin incarnate. Years passed, and the artist would often go to the church to pray for inspiration. He longed to complete the mural, yet in his heart he hoped that the face of Judas would forever elude him, that no human soul would ever be so deeply sunk in sin that it would provide the perfect model.

"Then one afternoon as he sat in the church, a beggar staggered down the aisle and knelt at the steps of the altar. He reeked and his clothing hung in rags from his haggard figure. He was not an old man, but he was hunched over as if weighted by an immense burden of dark memories. His face was exactly what the artist had been looking for. He took the broken man home with him, fed him, washed his diseased flesh, clothed him, and spoke to him warmly, as if with a friend. He instructed his children to treat the visitor with the greatest respect. His wife, a kind and devout woman, prepared fine meals for him. But the poor man dwelt in their midst as if he were made of stone. He was completely unable to speak.

"He was, however, willing to sit as the artist's model. Weeks went by, and as the work progressed, the beggar would look from time to time at the image of himself materializing on the canvas. A curious grief and horror would fill his eyes. One day, seeing the model's distress, the artist paused in his labor, laying down his brush.

"'My friend,' he said, 'your heart is troubled. What is it?'

"The man buried his face in his hands and burst into tears. After a long moment he lifted his eyes to the old painter.

"'Do you not remember me?' he said, 'Years ago I was your model for the Christ Child.'"

\* \* \*

David sat without speaking, his lips parted slightly, staring at the floor, his eyes troubled. Pawel was surprised by this, for he had anticipated that the boy would be delighted by the cleverness of the tale.

"This story could be interpreted several ways," David murmured.

"You think so?"

"It is a warning. Innocence can be corrupted. It could also be about a loathsome character who finds refuge under the protection of a good man. It is about the artist's greatness of heart. The character is not lovable. The artist merely has pity on him."

"Perhaps. But it could just as easily refer to the humility of the model. Does not his humility teach the artist many things?"

David flicked a glance at Pawel. "Yes, possibly."

For a time they said no more. At last, David raised his eyes and smiled to himself. With the quick recovery of youth, he seemed to have lost his temporary melancholy. "Tell me another", he said, as if the creation of a story were nothing more complicated than taking a breath. His look of expectancy wrung a hoarse laugh from the sick man.

"I have run out of stories."

"Please, Pawel."

"No. Another night."

## 13

The following night, Pawel was in bed, knees drawn up, writing on the blank endpiece of a useless book.

"Excuse me, Pawel."

"You wish to say something?"

"Yes, I wonder if you would care to tell more stories."

Pawel smiled at the boy's persistence. Feeling disinclined to the proposal, yet lacking any reason to refuse, he closed his eyes and searched his mind for story lines, symbols, metaphors. Nothing would come.

He opened his eyes and stared at David. Time slowed, the room faded. It seemed in this moment of suspension that their souls reached out across a void, seeking to know each other. Pawel now saw how very great that gulf was. That they did not understand each other was, of course, obvious to both. But there was something more to it, a condition that could not be alleviated by discussion or information. This grieved him, and he noted that the grief had increased in proportion to the growing familiarity between them.

"Have I burdened you, Pawel?"

"No."

"In your eyes there is something."

"Just weariness."

"I see sadness. First you smile and then you are sad. Why?"

"If I am sad it is merely because my exhausted brain cannot produce an entertainment for you."

"No, it is more. It is a puzzle to me, this thing."

"Ah, now the child departs, the philosopher returns."

"I am sorry. You do not like me when I question you." David

rubbed his forehead distractedly, his eyes suddenly black and haunted.

"I am a *betler*", he whispered.

"What is a *betler*?"

"A beggar."

"You are not a beggar. You are a guest."

"I am a burden to you. I should go away. Please, admit it. I am a burden to you."

"I will not admit such a thing."

"You will not admit it, you say. Such an answer could mean that it is true or untrue."

"You must learn to live with mystery, David."

"My life is nothing but mysteries."

"Then permit me a rabbinical answer. There are burdens, even heavy burdens, that ease the weight of a man's life. And there are burdens that, when they are lifted from a man's life, will crush him."

David's brows furrowed, his eyes probing Pawel's with sober fascination.

"That is very interesting." He paused. "I will think about what you have said all my life."

"All your life? I am honored. Now, if you promise to be silent and avoid all questions for just a few minutes of your very young life, I will try to think of a story. Agreed?"

"Agreed."

"I will compose it on the spot. It will be an original story."

"Ah, excellent!"

"If it is a tale you cannot understand, do you promise not to question me about it?"

"That is difficult. What if—"

"Do you promise, my guest?"

"I promise, my host."

"A tale is a seed sown in the heart. The wind and the rain and the sun come, and if the soil is good, the seed will bring

352

forth its harvest. Does the seed need to know all of this?"

"No."

"Does the soil?"

"No", David laughed.

"First you are sad and then you laugh. Why?"

"I am laughing at you, Pawel."

"I see. Tell me why you are doing that?"

"Because you sound exactly like a *zaddik*."

"A what?"

"A wise man, a holy man, when he tells a tale."

"I am not wise, nor am I holy."

"Yes, yes", said David, grinning. "The *zaddik*, he always says that too!"

"You made a promise. Do not break it before we begin."

"I am sorry. I will now be completely silent."

David closed his eyes. The icon lights cast a red glow over his face, softening the hollows carved by hunger beneath his cheekbones and brows.

Pawel too closed his eyes. What had been impossible only moments before seemed now to flow effortlessly from a reservoir of creation.

This is the tale he told:

Once there was a boy who was prince of a kingdom in the mountains of the East. His father the king went away when the child was very young, barely able to walk, for the queen had died and the man could not bear to enter the house of his first and only love. The king intended to be away briefly, for he loved his son dearly but wished to hide his grief from the people. In the forest, wandering alone and in distress, he happened upon that beast which is called the serpent, the ancient deceiver of mankind, and it overcame him and ate him there. No word of it ever reached the palace.

The boy cried for his father, but the morning mists and the

night skies did not reply. Day after day he cried. Week after week he cried. Months of this were followed by years, until the grief in the child became a pain he could no longer bear.

"Oh, take away this heart of mine and never again let me feel!" he cried to the stars above.

And one evening as he lay upon his bed and slept, a bird flew through the window and plucked out his heart. It left a small stone in its place and flew away. In the morning, when the prince awoke, he felt nothing. Neither happiness nor sadness.

The boy grew and became a young man. He was tall and swift upon the mountains. The greatest scholars schooled him. The bravest knights taught him sword-skill and the code of valor. He hunted bears with his bow and arrow. He slew the smaller serpents that prowled the woods. He was most devout and gave generously to the poor. In all virtues he acted with perfect decorum, though not a thing did he feel. He never cried, he never smiled. Yet he was beloved of the people, for in all things he was most excellent. Thus did many of them wish to make a match for him, to wed him to one or another of the beautiful maidens of the land.

"Too long has the king been absent and the throne empty", they said. "The prince has come into his manhood and is most gifted in all graces and worthy of the throne. He is a regal lad, noble and restrained in bearing, good and fearless."

"He is of an age to marry", said the people to the elders of the court. "Find him a comely and virtuous wife, that we might once again have a queen."

But the prince had eyes for no human loves. When word of the people's desire reached him, his face grew solemn, and he climbed to the topmost mountain of the realm and sat there in solitude for a great while. Night and day came and went. And then night came again under a moon as round and yellow as a bowl of butter melting in the summer heat.

A lark came up the wind and landed on his knee.

"Why do you sit and stare at the valleys and the heights, prince?" piped the lark. "Is your heart in sorrow?"

"No, it is not in sorrow. I feel nothing."

"This is a very sad thing", sang the lark. "My heart is weeping for you."

"What is this thing you call a heart?" asked the prince.

"The heart? Ah, that is too long a tale to tell you here on the peak of a mountain."

"It cannot be very important then. The mountain is the highest place in the whole world. From here you can see everything. Here it is possible to understand the hidden things."

"It is possible to understand *some* things," replied the lark, "yes, even great things. But not all things. Indeed, not the greatest."

"Where, then, can I learn the greatest thing? Will you tell me the tale of it?"

"I cannot", piped the lark. Then it cocked its head and added, "But I do know a way..."

"What way?"

"You must make yourself very small, and then you may climb upon my back and I will fly you to the place of telling, where the hidden things are told, the greatest things in the annals of the heart."

To his surprise the prince felt a flicker of longing within his breast, an ache from the hollow place where once his heart had dwelt and where a small stone rolled around in the cavity. The more he longed, the smaller he became. He shrank down to the size of a hummingbird and climbed upon the back of the lark.

"I command you to take me to the place of the heart", he cried.

"Agreed", sang the lark and went up into the night and the wind.

They flew a great way across kingdoms and seas until they reached a desolate land of gray deserts and dead forests. Upon a high hill they came to a castle. A dragon slept at its gate. The door and windows of the castle were sealed against the light, all except one small window in a high battlement. Beside the window stood the skeleton of a once-great oak. The lark landed on the topmost branch. The prince scrambled off its back and clung to a twig.

"Now sing me the tale", he commanded.

The lark's beak opened and its throat pulsed; its eyes danced as if it were singing, but no sound came forth.

"Sing!" cried the prince.

"I am singing", said the lark.

"That is not singing! That is silence!"

"I am singing in a key you cannot hear. Look!" and the bird gestured with its beak toward the open window.

How surprised the prince was to see a beautiful woman within. She was bending over a bed. Her back was turned away from the two unseen visitors in the branches, but they could hear the sound of her weeping.

"My beloved," she said through her tears, "why has it done such evil to you? Why does it hate us?"

The prince could not see the one to whom she was speaking, for the room was only partly visible, and much of the bed was hidden by the woman's form.

"Listen and be silent", whispered the lark to the prince.

The woman wept a thousand tears and spoke many words in the direction of the bed, but never once was there reply. For a day and a night and another day they sat and watched her as she patiently tended the figure on the bed. The face of the figure lay just beyond view. She fed it, sang to it, covered it with a large blue comforter upon which she had stitched a heart and a cross and the name of the one who lay there.

Another day and a night and a day came and went, and the prince grew weary of watching.

"This is an unfortunate place, and I regret this woman's

pain", said the prince to the lark. "But here is no great tale. I wish to return to my mountain."

"How slow you are to understand, prince, and how little patience you have."

"Quickly, let this be finished! Is she speaking to her child, or to her husband, or to an aging parent?"

"To none of those."

"Then to a friend?"

"No."

"To her betrothed?"

But the lark would not answer. The prince was now greatly irritated.

"Take me away from here!" he demanded.

"That is no longer possible," said the lark, "for you have become too heavy."

With this, the bird flew off, and the prince, to his dismay, found that he had grown large again. The dead branches began to creak and snap beneath his weight. The dragon awoke at the sound, and smelling the intruder, it coiled about the base of the tree, gazing up with malice.

"Come down, O most handsome of the sons of men," said the dragon, "and I will make you master of this palace and king of this realm."

"I will not," said the prince, "for this palace is a prison, and this realm is a desolation."

"Then I will give you better palaces and thriving realms for your playthings. There are many powers and principalities. I need only eat a king or two and all is mine. I will give it to you."

"Why would you give it to me?"

"It is no pleasure to rule the world alone. I would share it with a companion."

"You lie! If you are so generous, why do you entrap this lady who weeps within?"

"She is a madwoman who speaks to mere nothings. I keep her here to while away my idle hours. Her prattle amuses me."

"Go away, you foul thing!" cried the prince. "You are accursed. Begone!"

The dragon uncoiled and stepped back a pace or two, but its malice emanated a hundredfold, and the prince clung to the trunk of the tree for fear that its hatred would drag him down.

"Come down", said the dragon.

"I will not", said the prince.

"By the power of all darkness, I command thee to fall!" roared the dragon.

In the place where the prince's heart had once dwelt there was a dreadful weight pulling him toward the mouth of the dragon. The prince's fingers grew weak around the branches; his head was dizzy from the height, and his will faltered. The dragon saw this and was convinced of victory.

"A diet of kings is my delight", it laughed. "I ate the father of her who is within, and I ate your father too. You also will I devour."

When the prince heard this he cried out, "By the power of the true heart, I command you to be gone!" He drew his sword and, pointing it at the dragon, hurled himself toward the monster. The dragon, taken completely by surprise, could not evade quickly enough, and the sword hewed off its head as the prince crashed to the earth.

For a very long time he lay in the darkness. He felt nothing. It seemed that not only his heart but his body and his mind had been taken from him, and he wondered if he had been devoured by the serpent. Then he heard a woman's voice:

"My beloved," she said through her tears, "why has it done such evil to you? Why does it hate us?"

The prince awoke and found himself on a bed beneath a

blue coverlet upon which was embroidered a heart and a cross and his name. His body suffered from head to foot, and in the center where once a heart had dwelt there was a terrible agony. It hurt so grievously that the prince gasped and opened his eyes. He knew now that he was alive and that a fire burned in his breast, and the pain of it was harsher than death itself. The woman saw his eyes and knew that he was alive. She reached forth her hand and touched the place of his heart, and the fire burned brighter, though it was now a fire that gave light. It grew warm and exceedingly sweet. And with that the pain dissolved to nothing.

"You have awakened at last," she said, "just as he told me you would."

"Who? Who told you this thing?" he asked.

She turned with a smile to the window.

"He did", she replied.

Together they watched the lark fly away on the wind. As it went up over the sea, it dropped a small stone from its beak and nevermore was it seen.

\* \* \*

If Pawel supposed that David's reaction to this tale was certain, he was again proven wrong, as he had been before. The boy remained with his eyes closed for several minutes, displaying neither pleasure nor displeasure, offering no commentary. Indeed, Pawel wondered if he had put him to sleep. But this was not so, for just as Pawel was about to wake him, David opened his eyes.

"The prince", he said in a quiet voice. "The prince found his heart." He glanced swiftly at Pawel. "A whole heart."

Saying no more, he lay down on the mattress and drifted off to sleep. By the light of the candle, Pawel observed him for a time, then switched on the bedside lamp. Taking pen and paper in hand he wrote the following:

To you, O my soul, and to you alone, do I write these meditations. Will I reread them one day when I am old—if I be granted the luxury of growing old?

There he sleeps in a man's body, with a swift-maturing mind that retains a child's innocent heart. Who could have designed this mystery? Yet he too will grow old—if it is granted. And if so, what dramas will his life contain? What will his mission be?

How to strengthen him for his unguessable future? How to love without seizing? All too easily the manipulations of dependence, of familiarity and possession, creep into a relationship. One wishes to draw the beloved close with many harmless and tender strings. How subtly it grows.

One must maintain a vigilance of the heart that is essential to the total gift of the self. No such gift is possible without prayer, for man is not by himself able to master the drive for union and completion. Indeed, I suspect that we are not designed to be our own master. If in marriage it is three who make a union— the bride, the groom, and the Creator—then it must be so for friendship also.

Friend or lover, by the gates of your heart there must stand a watchman, and that watchman is Truth. If you ignore his warnings you must surely know that you are choosing. You alone are responsible for what must come to pass: the death of Love.

\*   \*   \*

The next morning, Pawel felt himself sufficiently recovered to hobble downstairs to open up the shop for the first time in two weeks. He sat on a chair by the door in a patch of sunlight. He wore his brown suit and black tie, with a wool blanket over his shoulders. That he was beginning to resemble Uncle Tadeusz was a cause of no little concern to him, but he picked up the walking stick with the ivory eagle and placed it across his lap. The shop was empty, so he was free to make faces and to grumble in the manner of the old curmudgeon. He spoke his mind to an invisible Haftmann. He struck an imaginary Smokrev with the cane. He liked the feeling and smiled feebly. He sipped a glass of tea and felt contented.

His first customer entered shortly before noon.

Just as before, Baba Yaga wheeled her foul-smelling cart right through the doorway.

"I have books for you."

"Yes? Show me."

A badly tattered collection of the Crimean sonnets of Mickiewicz—as literature, priceless; as history, an artifact; as a book, valueless. A few novels. A collection of children's tales, the Brothers Grimm, leather cover, tooled in art nouveau designs, in excellent condition—probably quite valuable. Finally, an enormous, 722-page piece of Aryan nonsense titled *Glazial-kosmogonie*, a racial theory book published in 1913 by some crackpot pseudoscientist.

"That's popular with the visitors", said Baba Yaga.

He looked at her.

"The visitors?"

"Our uninvited guests from the west."

"You mean the Germans?"

"*Tak!*"

"I'm not interested in this one."

"Then I give it to you."

"I don't want it."

"Use it in the toilet", she squealed, quaking with mirth.

Reconsidering, he said, "I accept with thanks."

She was mentally unbalanced, of course, but then, many decent people who had been quite sane before the war were now behaving strangely.

"Bronek sends you this message", she said, handing him a crumpled note wrapped inside a soiled handkerchief.

> If possible, give me paper for an urgent matter.
> Send it with this tiny patriot.
>
>                                          B.

"You are a friend of Bronek?"

"An associate. I do more than sell tea at the Staszic Palace, where it's helpful to observe the comings and goings of many persons."

"What else do you do?"

"Oh . . . *things*. I cart garbage and buy rags, and I carry messages from one part of the city to the other, whenever it would be difficult for certain persons to do so."

"That is a dangerous trade."

"We must defy the storms."

He held out his hand to her and for the first time told her his name.

She inspected his hand dubiously, then shook it with a wizened squirrel paw.

"Yes, yes, I know who you are. Listen, Pawel Tarnowski, you shouldn't be so stupid as to drop too many coins into my cup. People might think you're rich. They would ask how such a Pole comes by this abundance. Better you should buy shoes for the barefoot ones."

"So, Pani, you are not as dazed as you sometimes appear."

"It's useful to be crazy."

"I suspect you are far from crazy."

"Maybe. Listen, do you have food?"

"Are you hungry?"

"When haven't I been hungry?"

Deliberating for only a moment, Pawel said abruptly, "Come with me."

They limped upstairs, Pawel clumping noisily a few steps ahead of her. "Let's have a glass of tea and a bite to eat", he said loudly. There were sounds on the edge of hearing, which, thankfully, only he could recognize. By the time they arrived at the apartment, David had disappeared into the attic.

"You live alone?" she asked, peering all about with sharp eyes.

"I am alone."

"A large place for a bachelor."

She sat down with a groan on a kitchen chair. He cut bread and sausage—the very last. He made the tea extra strong and put in two lumps of sugar.

She consumed it all quickly, shooting resentful glances at him as if she would have preferred a meal of boiled child—the child Pawelek.

"Your brother has disappeared", she said in a tone of indifference.

"Bronek?"

"The other one. The one who was married to a Jew."

"How do you know this?"

She shrugged. "After they took his wife and child, he worked with Bronek for a while. One day the cellar was raided. Everyone scattered. Bronek has returned, but the other one—"

"Jan."

"Yes, him. He never came back."

Reduced to silence, Pawel watched her pour herself another glass and drop four lumps of sugar into it.

"This is real tea", she said in a suspicious tone. "Where did you get it?"

"A friend. What is your name?"

"You don't need to know my name. Where's the paper?"

"How do you know I have paper?"

"Bronek told me."

"He knows I have run out of paper. I gave him my last."

"He knows your supply has been replenished."

"How does he know?"

"I told him", she grinned toothlessly, indulging in her riddles—her minor powers—and gloating over them.

"You told him?"

She gave him a look and said in a factual tone, "Bronek works for me."

"Bronek works for you?"

"Yes, Bronek works for me", she said irritably. "Things aren't always as they appear. People don't have to be pretty boys like you to do something great in the world."

He drew back, offended.

She laughed. "Listen, there's a war on. It's the devil's harvest. Don't you have eyes?"

"I know, it's bad."

"You don't know the half of it", she said in disgust. "Well, are you going to let us have that paper?"

They went downstairs together, and Pawel asked her to wait by his desk on the main floor. In the cellar he retrieved from its hiding place the package of bond paper Haftmann had given him and carried it back up to the shop. There he found Baba Yaga waiting for him, leaning on her cart, which she had pushed behind the curtain in his absence. With a grunt, she took the paper from him and stuffed it under the heap of rags.

"Does Bronek no longer wish to use my press?" he asked.

"There are too many *guests* who come here. We've found another press."

With that, she wheeled her way out through the door. When she had gone, he looked more carefully through the books she had left on his desk. Among them there was one in French—a novel by Léon Bloy.

\* \* \*

"You have been closed", Haftmann said.

"I was ill."

"Ah, I am sorry to hear it!"

"Doktor, is my manuscript near completion?"

"Manuscript? Oh, yes, quite near. I despair over that shallow woman, my secretary. She moons about the office all day long and types a page or two. She is engaged to a young soldier in the Wehrmacht."

"Is there perhaps another secretary?"

"I'm allotted only one. Be patient. It will take just a few more weeks."

Haftmann went off hunting through the shelves. He was back at the desk ten minutes later, speaking animatedly and waving a book before Pawel's eyes.

"A Bloy!" he cried. "A Bloy! This is a jewel. Why didn't you tell me?"

"I have been distracted. The sickness—"

"It's not *La Femme pauvre*, of course, but it's another I have desired for many years, *Le Désespéré*."

Haftmann stood by the desk, unable to resist an instant leap into the text.

"Listen to this. Listen: *Our freedom and the world's equilibrium are mutually dependent, and that is what we must understand if we are not to be astounded . . .*"

Haftmann looked up. "A cogent writer, is he not?"

"He is very good."

Pawel wondered if the professor truly understood the meaning of the excerpt, for if he did he must recognize it as a threat to his cause. Perhaps the dangerous idea was safely encapsulated in someone else's history. He would try to think about this when Haftmann was gone. His mind drifted. The gnawing in his belly distracted.

"Tarnowski, you are not listening."

"I am. Please continue, Doktor."

"Really, you should read more of the books you sell. This one is an extraordinary blend of French mysticism and the poetic muse: "Every man who begets a free act projects his personality into the infinite. If he gives a poor man a penny grudgingly, that penny pierces the poor man's hand, falls, pierces the earth, bores holes in suns, crosses the firmament and compromises the universe. If he begets an impure act, he perhaps darkens thousands of hearts whom he does not know."

Haftmann looked up with a solemn face. He glanced briskly at his watch.

"It is late", he said in a low voice.

"Doktor, would you say that culture can be created or sustained where there is no freedom?"

Without replying, Haftmann gave him an unreadable look, paid for the book, and left.

## 14

David was back in the attic every night. *Festung Dovid*, he called it, Fortress David. Pawel slept more easily without the presence on the floor. The other presence—the Mother—swelled or faded according to the state of his consciousness and his prayer.

One evening, after they ate a modest supper, David went upstairs early, leaving Pawel to read quietly in bed. At nine o'clock the electricity went off, and Pawel, still recovering from his illness, quickly fell asleep.

In a dream he walked through a forest of birch trees. It must have been a copse among the rolling Carpathian uplands, for in the distance he saw mountain peaks to the south, and to the north the farms of the plains. He was a child again, perhaps eight or nine years old. The sun shone brightly. He was happy.

A voice from the air said to him, "It is coming."

"What is coming?" he piped.

"The seducer of the whole world", said the voice from the air.

"I am afraid", he stammered.

"Do not be afraid."

"I am afraid", he cried loudly.

With that, he fell into a deep pit. He fell and fell, and he fell so far that his screams were lost in fading echoes as the light shrank above him. Plunging with gathering speed, he stretched out his arms and legs to slow the descent, but his fingers were stung by stones and roots whipping past. He landed with a thump in darkness. To his amazement he was not broken.

The bottom of the pit was dry sand. It was covered with little bones.

On hands and knees he groped around, looking for any means by which he could climb back toward the pinhole of light far above him. His fingers touched a body lying beside the wall.

He jumped away when the body groaned, then he realized it was another child, like himself, who had fallen into the darkness.

This child was younger. He picked him up and leaned him against the wall.

"Wake up, wake up, we have fallen into peril."

"Where am I?" said the younger boy. "I do not like the smell of this place."

"What is your name?"

"*Firstborn*. What is your name?"

"I do not have a name."

"*I-do-not-have-a-name*! That is an odd name."

"I once was Pawelek, but I have lost my name."

"Then what shall I call you?"

"I do not know."

"Though you have lost your name, will you help me to climb?"

"Yes."

They had climbed no farther than a few feet when something brushed them off the wall and they fell again to where they had been before.

"It was only a bat", the elder said to the younger.

They climbed to the same height again, and this time a cuff threw them back to earth.

"It might have been the wind", said the younger.

The third time, a sterner blow tossed them to the ground and they rubbed their sore heads.

"You are mine. I own you", said a hideous voice from the darkness, like soft thunder, like black storm clouds containing wrath.

"I am going to eat you. First, I will play with you."

The two little boys jumped up in fright and ran screaming around and around in circles.

Their eyes had now grown accustomed to the darkness, and they could make out the shape of a giant reptile that lay curled comfortably on one side of the chamber. Its tail coiled upward around the walls of the pit, disappearing toward the light.

It opened its jaws and yawned, and the boys, now too frightened to move, looked into its cavernous mouth and saw millions of jewels and millions of human skulls the size of coins. From its mouth there came a belch of fire, and their clothing burst into flames. It sneered at them and sprayed foul water over them, extinguishing the flames. Then from its mouth there emerged a jet of cloud as black as ink, blotting out everything, even the tiny point of light above them.

Its slitted eyes glowed with such malice that the boys threw themselves on the ground and hoped to die instantly. They waited and waited. Finally, Pawelek peeked through his fingers and saw the frightful beast draw back against the wall of the chamber. Its eyes were brimming with hatred and, astonishingly, with fear. The boys looked up and saw that a third child was standing beside them. He was smaller than them both. Motionless, the dragon watched him.

The Child was dressed in white and girded with a golden belt. He opened his arms wide, and the two boys huddled beneath, one on each side. The Child opened his mouth and a little sword came out of it.

He gave the sword to Firstborn. But the boy could not see it, though he sensed its presence. He tried to take hold of it, first one way, then another, but each time it slipped from his hands. He held up his empty palms toward the Child and cried. The sword hung by itself in the air.

The Child opened his mouth once more and another sword came out of it.

He offered this one to Pawelek, who took it in his trembling hands.

"These humans are mine. I will have them", rumbled the dragon.

"They are not yours. You shall not have them", said the Child.

The dragon and the Child stared at each other without further conversation.

The Child touched Pawelek's heart with his finger.

"Stand."

Slowly he got up, fearing at every moment that the dragon would strike him to the ground.

Out of the mouth of the Child came a long scroll of paper like a ribbon. The paper was dazzling white and written on it in gold lettering was a word.

"This is your true name. Eat it", said the Child.

Pawelek ate it.

Strength entered him.

"Why don't you carry a sword?" he asked the Child.

In answer, the Child showed him his hands and his feet, which were punctured through. Light streamed from the holes.

"That one made wounds in my body and now he is afraid of them. With these I will conquer him. Be still."

"Can't I help you?" asked Pawelek, remembering the sword in his hand.

"If you would help me, do not give in to fear. Know that I have already overcome him."

With that, the dragon hurled itself in a rage upon the three children. The Child fended it off by opening his hands and raising them, palms outward, so that the beast recoiled. Yet it rose above their heads, lashing and snarling and spewing darkness over everything. It uttered blasphemies and curses. It vomited lies at Pawelek, who cried out once in terror, but the Child

370

looked at him and strengthened him again. Then he realized that light was now glowing from his own weapon. He brought his heart under control and went down on one knee and raised the point of his sword toward the belly of the monster. The Child's hands too were raised in the air, and the dragon roared, but it was like a heat-crazed lizard trying to devour the blazing sun at noonday.

Without warning, the dragon shrank steadily until he was no more than the size of a wasp—a tiny flying dragon buzzing about their heads.

"Do not be deceived", said the Child. "He is not yet defeated."

Then the beast disappeared altogether.

"This is when he is most dangerous", said the Child.

As these words were completed a tremendous roar filled the pit, and suddenly all about them were fire and darkness and the snapping of fangs.

Firstborn threw himself beneath the shelter of Pawelek and curled into a ball at his feet.

"My little brother," Pawelek cried, "do not be afraid!" And he lifted his sword as the dragon fell upon him.

Pawel bolted upright in bed, his heart crashing, his breath wheezing in and out.

"My God! My God!" he whispered.

He flung his legs over the edge of the bed and sat, face in hands, trying to remember the name that had been the Child's gift to him. But it was gone. Try as he might, it would not return, though it lingered just beyond reach, like a hint of gold.

\* \* \*

He was eight or nine years old that summer. During the month of August he lived with his grandfather and grandmother. The sun shone brightly in blue skies, the hay was thick in the fields, the air sweet with hot pines, the grasshoppers leaping, the white clouds sweeping endlessly across the plains and up over the mountains.

Babscia sewed lace by hand and fussed over his clothing. She made him ice cream in a bucket. She sang mountain songs.

She smelled of lavender and sage. Babscia loved sage and she loved lavender, and had concluded they would be doubly powerful together. Everyone teased her about it, but she did not mind. Pawel thought the scent was rather nice. It simply smelled like Babscia. Each evening she put him to bed beneath a blue comforter, too hot for the August nights, but he liked it because she had stitched his name on top with a heart and a cross. By candlelight she would tell him stories about *Kolibri* the little hummingbird and *Zabawa* the lark. Then she would sway back and forth on the chair beside his cot and finger her rosary while he drifted off. Because he was often afraid of the dark at Zakopane, it was the only way he could go to sleep. He would ask her drowsy questions and she would answer in a quiet voice until his eyelids grew so heavy he floated on the soft feathers and sighed.

"Are there bears near the house, Babscia?"

"None, my Pawelek. If any come close, Ja-Ja will kill them."

"Oh. Is Great-Uncle Nicholas near the house?"

"He is in his cabin. He is sleeping."

"Will he wake up?"

"No, he will not wake up."

"Will he come inside the house at night?"

"What silly questions you ask, Pawelek. Now hush, hush, and listen to Zabawa singing."

And yes, he could hear Zabawa's song, the music that is only sometimes soundless. He could see the stars too, through the window, if he forced his eyes to stay open.

Whenever his grandmother prayed she closed her eyes. Not always, but often, tears like silver threads would seep from the edges.

"Why are you crying, Babscia?"

"I am not crying, my Pawel."

"But I *see* you crying."

"You see me praying."

"I see water coming from your eyes."

"Yes, that is so."

"Are you sad?"

"No, I am happy."

"You don't look happy."

"It is not the happiness of a dance or a joke. It is peace."

"Peace."

"Yes. It comes when you pray. It is like a well that overflows."

"Always?"

"Not always. Sometimes the well is dry."

"How does it fill again?"

"I am not certain. Usually a person must ask. Then he waits. Then it returns."

"When?"

"Whenever it desires."

"Is it cold? Does it hurt?"

"It is warm. It feels wonderful."

"Is it like when Grandfather kisses you?"

"Oh yes, like that. But more."

How lovely the eyes of Babscia. She was very old. She was very soft. However much he tried to stay awake, he was always asleep by the time she left the room.

Grandfather was strong. He had big muscles even though he was gentry. His thick arms were exposed in the sun when he stacked hay. His many religious medallions jingled against his chest like bells in a forest. Eventually they all fell out of his shirt, dangling on their strings. The biggest was a silver disk on a red-and-white ribbon.

Great-Uncle would follow Grandfather around the field,

tripping over the stubble, lecturing Grandfather on the futility of doing his own labor.

"We're rich enough to hire a man."

"That was forty years ago, Nicholas. Nicholas, you must stop drinking! We're as poor as peasants now. In fact, we *are* peasants. Think about it: we rent our house from the neighbor. We own a few trunks full of mementos, some sticks of fine furniture, and our past. That's all. I am an honest man. I have paid our debts. There is only a little money—enough to purchase peaceful weariness and a gracious death."

"Always the poet!" said Grandfather's brother with the one eye.

"Don't forget *Pooderneechka,* Grandfather!" Pawel suggested timidly.

The two old men laughed heartily, suddenly remembering that the boy was there too, sitting atop the heap of hay on the wagon.

"Of course, that's right, boy. We still have *Pud*!"

*Puderniczka* was their big swayback draft-horse. Grandfather had named him that—a lady's powderbox. What a funny thing to call a horse that had once ridden to war! It was because dust and dandruff and oat chaff flew up in a cloud when they slapped his great white rump.

*Pud!* That was not his real name, for he had been a cavalry horse before the turn of the century. Uniforms and horses were very important in Grandfather's house. The other horses had gone with the estate. Grandfather kept Pud only because no one would buy him, a useless, retired gentleman-horse. But he was harnessed for haying every August. There was little need to make hay, just enough for lining the hens' nests and to provide Pud's winter feed.

Pawel was afraid of the old war-horse. Long ago, at age six, around the time his other fears began, he had ambled across the barnyard and walked beneath Pud's dribbling green lips. Pud

374

had nibbled his ears and rolled the long rasp of a tongue across his face, an act that convinced Pawel he would be eaten by the giant horse. Ever since, he had avoided it with determination.

It went on for years, until Pud became a large white terror in his mind. This irrational fear irritated Papa greatly. Mama always defended Pawel, and Babscia also took his part.

"He is a sensitive child", she said. "Just like his father was as a boy."

"I was not *that* sensitive", said Papa. "Women always remember what should be forgotten and forget what should be remembered."

They poked and teased Papa until he laughed, and Pawel was glad to see it, but he did not go any nearer the horse. He knew that Pud wished to humiliate him. Whenever he came into range, he knew that Pud was thinking of him and watching him out of the corner of his great eyes. Pawel *saw* hooves crushing his bare toes, and yellow teeth tearing chunks out of his arm, and kicks knocking him reeling, senseless, across the yard. No, Pud could stay on his side of the fence and Pawel would stay on his.

He did not understand why grownups worried over him so. He overheard their hushed conversations, their words biting into his heart like the large yellow teeth.

"My youngest grandson", said Grandfather, "is the only one of all my grandchildren who doesn't call me Ja-Ja. Why is this? He calls his grandmother Babscia. Do I frighten him?"

"He respects you", said Papa.

"That little boy is like an orphan. Do you put him on your back sometimes up there in Warsaw? Do you walk with him and hold his fingers and let him talk about everything he sees?"

"Life is different now. I do not have time. If I work twelve hours a day, six days a week, it is because I wish to give him a good life. I love him."

"He does not know it. Love is a word. It must have flesh. He will suffer."

"Life is suffering", said Papa.

"Yes, life is trouble. But we should not make more than is our due."

"You do not understand."

"I understand very well. It is because we have become poor", Grandfather said to Papa. "You do not like to be poor, and who can blame you. But it is not so bad to be poor if there is food and love. Better to be poor than a rich orphan. Listen to me, my son."

On haying day, Mama and Papa, Babscia, and the older children went to Zakopane for coffee and sweets. Grandfather wished to teach Pawel a farm skill or two before going to his peaceful weariness and gracious death. Thus, the boy was perched atop the ricks, scurrying around the swaying heap, arranging the bundles of hay in neat rows to ensure a better use of space within the staves.

The sun was straight overhead when they stopped for lunch. Great-Uncle Nicholas came shuffling across the field with a basket and a bottle, and Grandfather waved to him. He waved back. Pawel was not happy to see him and did not greet him.

Great-Uncle Nicholas had consumed a considerable part of the bottle before his arrival. It made him talkative. He lectured about hay, about weather, about the mistakes of history.

"Take old Pud, there", he said. "We should have had him on the battlefield when we kicked the Russians out of Poland!"

He staggered over to the beast and whacked him on the back. Clouds of "powder" rose in the air. Pud continued patiently chewing oats from a bucket.

"Pilsudski managed to give us a free Poland without the help of the old fellow", said Grandfather. "Let him rest. He has won his retirement. In his time he made the damn Prussians think twice."

"Prussians and Russians—they're all bastards", said Great-Uncle Nicholas.

The two old men wrapped their arms around Pud, who tossed his head and neighed until they finally released him and he could get back to his oats.

Great-Uncle Nicholas and Grandfather eased themselves down onto the stubble beneath a tree and finished lunch.

Nicholas offered Pawel a pull on the bottle.

"Drink, boy-chick!"

"No, thank you."

"Are you afraid of it?"

"I do not like it."

"Your grandson is always afraid!" said Great-Uncle with a grunt. "He is always imagining things."

"He is not afraid", said Grandfather lamely, and then Pawel knew for the first time that his grandfather was ashamed of him.

"This boy is afraid of his own shadow."

"Do not say that", soothed Grandfather. "You are not afraid, are you, Pawel?"

By this time both men had been sucking regularly on the quart of kirsch.

"No, Grandfather, I am not afraid."

"He is afraid of Pud!" laughed Great-Uncle.

"Now, Nicholas, Pawel is not afraid of *PooPooPooderneechka*!"

Grandfather lifted the boy and carried him toward Pud. The horse whipped his head toward them, and Pawel saw in its expression an intense threat. That horse intended to bite him.

He wiggled and kicked and tumbled out of Grandfather's arms and sprawled on the ground, with hot tears spurting from his eyes.

"You see, he's a frightened hare", said Great-Uncle with disdain.

"I see only what comes of living in cities", said Grandfather. "In the old days a boy was with his father from morning to night. He learned skills. He grew confident. He learned to be brave. He knew what he was for. What is a little boy to learn in a fancy apartment in Warsaw?"

"I am sorry, Grandfather."

"Don't be sorry, don't be sorry", said the old man, patting his head and dusting him off. "It's all right. It's all right." But Pawel could see that he was sad.

They went back and sat down. Beside the tree was a well. It was no longer in use. It had never been a good well, and the neighbor had dug at a better site. The new well up by the house was always full.

"Do you know, Pawel, that when I was as young as you I learned not to be afraid of anything", Grandfather said.

"Before that were you afraid?"

"Oh yes, I was. Of some things. Bears came out of the mountains in the spring. I was especially afraid of wolves, though later I was less so. But always I was afraid of Wrog."

"What is Wrog?"

"Say rather, *who* is Wrog!"

"Who is Wrog?"

"The dragon that lived in a cave under the city of Krakow."

"Is Krakow far away from here?"

"Yes, but that made no difference, because, you see, there was a tunnel that ran from Krakow...", Grandfather pointed northwest toward the horizon and traced a line across the heave of the land straight to their own hills. "It ran from there, and across there, closer, and closer, to here!"

Grandfather's finger stopped at the well. His eyes opened wide. His face was grave.

"I knew that Wrog could fly like an arrow from his cave under the city and emerge here at night to steal sheep and to capture children and maidens foolish enough to be out after dark."

"Is this a fairy story, Grandfather?"

"It is a *true* story, Pawel", said Grandfather, nodding his head once emphatically.

Great-Uncle snorted.

Grandfather led Pawel to the well and together they leaned over. A draft of cold air hit Pawel's face. It smelled of earth.

"Is he dead? Was it long ago?"

"It was long ago."

"But tell me, is he dead?"

"That is for you to know at the end of the story."

"We must get away from here", the boy cried in alarm.

Grandfather raised a finger sharply.

"*Nie!*" he said.

Pawel stared at him, and his heart thumped terribly.

"Nicholas, where is that rope?" Grandfather called to his brother.

"Coiled on the wagon staves."

Grandfather tied one end of the rope to the tree and trailed it over to the mouth of the hole. He dropped the other end into the blackness. He slid his bent frame over the edge and slowly let himself down into the abyss.

"Grandfather," Pawel yelled, "Babscia would be too sad if you did not come back. She would cry!"

"Let her cry, Pawel", came a thin voice from below. "We must do what we must do."

"Come back, come back. Get out of there!" he screamed.

"It's dry", called the voice from the bottom of the shaft.

A few minutes later Grandfather came up into the light, grunting, breathing heavily, squinting his eyes, and smiling with extreme satisfaction.

"Yes, yes, it's just as I remember it."

"Why did you say, *just as you remember?*" Pawel asked nervously.

"Oh, when I was about nine years old I went down in there to kill Wrog."

"Kill Wrog!" the boy gasped.

"Yes", said Grandfather in a tone that implied it was not really a significant thing.

"Did you kill him?"

"No. Unfortunately, he ran away."

"Why did he run away?"

"Because I was not afraid of him any more. That is the worst insult you can give to a dragon."

"But how did you become not afraid of him?"

"It was difficult."

"But *tell* me", Pawel pleaded.

Grandfather removed a candle and a wooden match from his pocket.

"I took with me a candle and a match, just like these, and I forced myself to descend into the black hole of this well. First I dropped a stone to make sure there was no water in it. Sure enough, it was empty. I borrowed my father's longest rope and lashed it to that tree over there—of course, it was just a sapling then."

Great-Uncle, dozing against the trunk, looked small beside its girth.

"Slowly, slowly I made my descent. I heard rustling below. I heard *snoring*. I smelled sulfur and charcoal, and the rotting bodies of his victims."

Pawel peered over the edge.

"I wanted to run away and hide forever. But instead, I forced myself down, down, down. At the bottom I found . . ."

"What did you find?"

"I found many bones. It stank. Then I found a tunnel opening on the northwest wall, and I knew that Wrog was somewhere inside, brooding, waiting for me to enter. I lit my candle. I heard a hiss from inside the tunnel. I had no weapon with me."

"Grandfather!" he wailed. "Why did you go down there without a weapon?!"

The old man cleared his throat and looked nonplussed.

"It escapes me now just why I had no weapon. I must have forgotten to bring one. Had I been wiser I might have worn a sword like this one." Grandfather went to the hay cart and withdrew a chipped cavalry sword from the toolbox.

"What did you do next?"

"I went into the tunnel."

Pawel held his breath, his fists clenched.

"I shouted to the monster, *Wrog!*"

Grandfather bellowed "*Wrog!*" as he slashed the sword in an arc around his head.

"You were very brave", Pawel's voice trembled.

"Ah, no, my Pawel, I was not feeling brave. But I knew that if I let that evil thing know it, he would be upon me in an instant and eat me for lunch."

"You were afraid?"

"Of course I was afraid! Everyone is afraid. Nicholas over there, he too is afraid."

"He does not look afraid."

"He is afraid. He drinks his courage from a bottle. We drink ours from here." And with his white brows bristling, the old man touched his finger to his heart.

"And here." He poked Pawel's heart.

"You see?"

Pawel let out a long stream of breath.

"What did you do then?"

"When the dragon did not come out, I stepped farther and farther into the tunnel. He withdrew farther and farther into it. I ran after him and he began to beat his horrible wings. He flew from me and went all the way back to his cave under Krakow. There, a few years later, a knight killed him with a sword."

"This is true?"

"It is true."

Grandfather made the sign of the cross upon his breast.

"Who was the knight?"

"His name was *He Who Is Faithful and True*. And do you know what that knight rode upon? It was a white horse."

"This is true?"

"It is true. And do you know who the horse was?"

"Who?"

"Pud. But he was young then. His name was *Fearless*. He too hated the dragon."

"That is a good story, Grandfather."

"Do you like it? I can prove to you it's true."

"How would you?"

"Come."

He picked up the boy and carried him to the stone lip of the well.

"Do you trust me, Pawelek?"

"I don't know."

"I will show you the lair of the dead dragon."

"I would be afraid."

He touched the boy's heart with his finger.

"I know that you wouldn't."

So Pawel wrapped himself around Grandfather's back, and the old man walked down the stone walls inside the earth, letting the rope slide through his hands bit by bit. The sword hung on his belt, clanking against the stones. Where the stone footholds ended, a ladder began and they descended farther.

"Twelve meters deep at least. Think of the men who dug this."

Exactly as Grandfather promised, the bottom was dry and felt like sand. There were no rotten odors. It smelled like the turnips Pawel dug for Babscia from the kitchen garden.

"It's dark", Pawel said nervously.

"Yes. But look up."

Far above them there shone a circle of silver light, like a medallion.

Then Grandfather lit the candle.

The cave was empty. There were no bones.

But there on the northwest wall was a wide crack that yawned into darkness.

"Look here."

Above the crack was a cut in the earthen wall. It was a cruciform shape. A carved stone cross was embedded in it.

"The knight rode back after he slew Wrog, and he put this cross here as a memorial of his deed."

"And your deed."

"And my deed also. Are you afraid, Pawel?"

"A little bit. Did Wrog have any children?"

"If you had seen Pani Wrog you would not ask such a question."

He laughed and Pawel laughed, though he did not understand the joke.

"Do not worry! If there are dragons left on the earth, they dare not enter here. It is the place of their defeat."

Many more stories did Grandfather tell him that day as they sat together and watched the candle burn down until the darkness suddenly covered the cave like a deep blue blanket. When they came up blinking into the light, dusk was near. The sun was a red ball suspended above the horizon. Great-Uncle Nicholas was no longer under the tree, and Pud was sleeping standing up. They snapped his reins and he whinnied and pulled the creaking wagon home. Mama, Papa, Babscia, Bronek, and Jan came out in a crowd to welcome the lost.

Mama cried, "We've not had a word of sense from Nicholas. He's as drunk as a goose in the hayloft. He said all sorts of nonsense."

"What sort of nonsense?" asked Grandfather.

"He said you had gone down into the old well to fight a dragon."

"We did", Grandfather grinned.

"We were worried sick", Mama exclaimed, clutching Pawel to her breast. "Were you frightened, my Pawelek?"

"He was very brave", said Grandfather in a voice that told everyone he was not ashamed.

Before going up to bed, Pawel went into the horse shed and walked beneath Pud's nose. The great brown eyes blinked at him.

He patted the nose and the soft lips and liked the feel of it. He kissed the horse's neck and said, "Good night, Fearless."

Before sleep, Grandfather came to Pawel's room and sat down by his bed. He took the big medallion from his neck and showed it to the boy. It was suspended on a red-and-white ribbon.

"What is this thing, Ja-Ja?"

"When you are a grown man I will give it to you. It is the Mother of God of Czestochowa."

"Was she brave?"

"Oh, yes, very brave."

The boy rubbed the medallion with his finger. He felt the raised letters like a blind man.

"What is this word beneath her?"

"Wisdom", said Grandfather.

It was difficult to keep his eyes open, though he wanted to watch the stars. Grandmother prayed a rosary with him. That night her well was full and brimming over.

Pawel laid a finger on his heart and drifted off, wondering why Ja-Ja had taken a sword and a candle to haying.

## 15

Archive, 4 March 1943

When will this winter end? The gray half-light that shrouds the city continuously seems a little longer each day, yet the sun almost never penetrates it.

I have been reading the poems of Cyprian Norwid, my first encounter with him. He died of poverty and hunger in Paris—of course, where else! Also a rereading of Mickiewicz's Crimean Sonnets. From both I copy out small luminous fragments as if saving them for an incomprehensible assembly. But what would the sum total portray, really? Are these fragments merely shards of a broken mirror, or are they components of a glass mural in a cathedral window, comprehensible only when light pours through it? I do not know which of these I am. I remain incomprehensible to myself. Are all men thus?

If we are God's work of art, and if one is not to succumb to the lure of the anti-icon (the false self), it is essential to seek—regardless of how impossible it may seem—the artist's intention in this work. The beauty in man and nature hints at a mysterious unity in existence. The temptation to grasp at a fragment (both true and false fragments) and to disregard the whole is continuous. Yet if one stops there and goes no further, so ends the possibility of seeing the hidden face—which is Beauty itself. So too ends the possibility of love.

\*   \*   \*

Hostile winds beat against the windows throughout that week. On Friday the last scraps of coal had gone up in smoke, and there was no money to buy more. Pawel and David were forced to resume the burning of books. Rummaging in a dark corner of the cellar that day, Pawel came upon a woodburner and stove pipes. The size of a boot box, it was the portable camp stove that had once belonged to his grandfather. The embossed stags leaping and tossing around the sides were now rusted, but otherwise it was the same. Grandfather had taken it on hunting trips into the mountains and said it kept a tent warm all night once you shut the fire door and tightly closed the vent. There were always embers in the morning, he had bragged.

The entire afternoon of Sunday was spent setting it up in the bedroom, which was the smallest room and easiest to enclose for the preservation of heat. Pawel removed the upper pane of glass from the window overlooking the back alley and replaced it with a sheet of tin, into which he had banged a hole at the cost of an alarming amount of noise and a cut thumb. The piping went up the outside brick wall, though not all the way to the roof. He worried about setting fire to the eaves, but argued that it would be just as fatal if they froze to death.

They closed the attic door and the doors to the kitchen and parlor in order to contain what heat the stove produced. They lit the fire and it raged for a while, feeding upon splinters of the crates they had broken up. But a kindling fire did not last more than an hour. A book thrown onto the little inferno needed a continuous source of substantial fuel in order to be consumed.

Pawel spent Monday downstairs in the shop, dressed in his winter coat and gloves with rabbit fur lining. There were only three customers that day, none of whom bought a thing. David spent his time reading upstairs beside the fitful warmth of the stove and was able to stay comfortable if he wore his felt coat at all times. After closing time, and a miserable supper that amounted to little more than a token, they retired to the bedroom. David brought his mattress down from the attic and unrolled it on the floor. He sat on it, wrapped himself in a wool blanket, and stared into space, engrossed in his own thoughts. From time to time he fed the fire. Pawel lay on the bed reading.

"It has been a long time since we spoke together", said the boy.

"We spoke this morning."

"I do not mean the cataloging. I mean the language of the prisoners."

"Tapping code on the walls of our cells? Have we not already done this? Is more needed?"

"Yes", David nodded. "More is needed. If we fail to speak with true voices, our language dies. In the great fabric of existence, a dead language is one that is no longer lived and acted upon."

"What, then, is a living language?"

"The prisoners desire to speak as a flowing. Back and forth it flows, like the waters of life. It should not cease."

"Why should it not cease? Sometimes rivers become floods, drowning people."

"That is not so with you and me. With us, a drought is the greater danger."

Pawel sighed, put down his book, and said, "Words form only the blueprint of life. Actions the mortar. No action is possible for us."

"We have spoken of this before, Pawel. Have you forgotten?"

Pawel shrugged. Clearly, David was determined to go on.

"As the stonemason strengthens his arms and calibrates his hands through trial and error by practice with the material of his art, so those who speak together broaden and refine the scope of their language."

"Mortar without stones begins as a thick soup and ends as a concrete block."

"Stones without mortar begin as a dream and end as rubble."

Pawel gave a grudging laugh. "That mind of yours, David Schäfer. So fast."

The boy smiled. "Then you will agree that both mortar and stone are needed."

"All right, I agree! What do you want to *talk* about?"

But the tone of Pawel's reply had been pitched a little too sharply. David's eager expression faded.

"I'm sorry. I didn't mean to sound harsh", Pawel apologized.

"I understand, Pawel. As I have done so often, I have invaded your private thoughts. I have been speaking without listening."

He got up and left the room. Pawel returned to his book. He read for another hour, burying himself in an outline of Russian spirituality.

> . . . the spiritual movement known as *hesychasm*. The believer enters ever more deeply into awareness of his condition as a sinner and a poor man before God. It is the stripping away of pride, powers, and all passions save the love of God and man-kind.

Pawel thought to himself, *I must incorporate this into the play. When will Haftmann come?*

At one point he looked up to see that David had returned to the room. He was now seated on the floor, knees under his chin, peering at him with a somber, dilated expression.

"What are you doing?" Pawel asked.

"I am listening to your soul-speech. It is my hope that I am *hearing* it."

"What do you hear?" Pawel said, half-amused.

"I hear pain."

To this there was no possible reply. He opened his mouth to attempt a few deflecting comments, but they died in his mouth. Eventually he cleared his throat and asked, "Do *you* feel pain?"

A single nod. But the boy did not elaborate. Neither did he abandon his listening post.

"So, what is your assessment? Why is there pain?" Pawel asked.

"A life is a word spoken", David replied obliquely.

"And . . ."

"There are two kinds of pain that penetrate to the interior of a life. If a life that is spoken is left unheard, that is one pain. If a life that is spoken is bent into a false word, that is another kind of pain."

"Do not all men feel pain?"

Another rabbinical nod.

For a time they regarded each other in silence.

"The pain a person feels", David said at last, "is a sign of awakeness. This is the price of consciousness."

"Is the pain worth it?" he asked.

"Yes, a thousand times over, yes."

"As long as it is genuine consciousness, and not self-delusion."

Another nod.

Before blowing out the candle, Pawel offered one of his blankets to David.

"No."

"No?"

"We have five covers, Pawel. This is an uneven number. Now you wish to give me one of yours, making it a total of three for me and two for you. This is not wise. You need to be warm. You need to sleep to become completely well again."

"Take the blanket. I insist."

"I refuse." His tone was final.

Pawel could find no immediate argument.

He returned to the bed, lay down, and stared into the darkness above, listening to David's breathing. After a time, he supposed the body on the floor was asleep, and he sighed.

"Pawel," came a small voice, "can I come up there with you?"

"No."

"Would it not be better for us to use the heat wisely? The bed is wide. We should not waste the heat of our bodies. And we would have *five* covers upon us."

"No, it is better this way."

"But why? My brothers and I used to sleep in one bed. We slept well always."

"I have always slept alone. It would be impossible for me to sleep with another person in the bed. Besides, I usually toss and turn. Without intending to, I would push you onto the floor with a crash and you would break your nose."

David laughed.

"Are you very cold?"

"Yes, Pawel. I am sorry. It is not possible to sleep."

"I will sleep on the floor. You come up here."

"I absolutely refuse to let you sleep on the floor, Pawel."

"All right, then, a compromise."

The man got out of bed and covered the boy with a wool blanket, ignoring his protests. Within minutes David was asleep and Pawel spent another night watching the brittle stars fade into a gray dawn.

\* \* \*

"Did you sleep well, Pawel?"

"Not very."

"You were cold?"

Pawel shrugged.

"You see, you did not listen to me", David admonished.

"True."

"I do not understand", he said, burying his nose in a book.

"That must be your favorite expression."

"Does it irritate you?"

"No, but it makes me feel that I must have an answer ready for every difficult question in the universe."

This remark, which was not meant unkindly, was interpreted by David as a rebuke.

"I am a burden", he said in a faint voice.

"I did not mean that."

"It is true. I have made your life a big trouble. You could die because of me. You are cold because of me. You are thin because of me. I eat your food. I annoy you night and day with my prattle."

The boy's eyes filled with tears.

"Forgive me, Pawel. I did not wish to bring this trouble upon you."

"I know that", he said. "But it is not a big trouble. You bring much interest into this house. I led a rather dull existence before you came. Besides, who cared for me when I was ill? Who was that person?"

"It was myself", David said modestly. "A small thing compared to what you are doing for me."

"Even if you brought nothing, and even if you were a complete burden, I would continue to hide you. Never worry about that."

"Why are you so good?"

"I am not good. It is merely what any human being would do for another."

The boy shook his head.

"You are good", he said emphatically.

\*　　\*　　\*

But man at war is good only from moment to moment. The battle resumed within Pawel's heart. His exhaustion depleted the reserves of willpower, which until then he had tapped for resistance to blind impulse, and distracted him from the more important matter of beseeching grace.

Now David Schäfer lay curled each night by his feet like a trusting puppy.

Night and day, ugly thoughts came unbidden to his mind.

*He is completely in your power*, the thoughts said. *You can do as you wish.*

391

He shook them off.

"These thoughts are false", he said angrily to himself. "They are lies. They are death!"

"Do you have an earache, Pawel?"

"Why do you ask?"

"You were shaking your head."

"It was nothing. A fly."

"There are no flies. It is winter."

"Oh, yes, you are right. My imagination."

But the nothings crept back in again and again, and when the boy reached for a new book, and his coat fell open revealing the trousers pulled tight against his flanks, Pawel was forced to look away. When he stretched back on tiptoes like a taut bow, with his arms raised to heaven and his eyes shut, lips opening around large adolescent yawns, it was difficult not to fall headlong into the grip of desire.

Distressed, horrified by himself, Pawel would go walking downstairs in the freezing shop, pacing back and forth, round and round the aisles, exhaling clouds of icy breath. A hundred times, two hundred times, the ranks upon ranks of books reminding him that man is a rational creature.

"I am not a slave!" he would declare with a finality that was not final.

"My God, help me!" he would cry.

Then he would go upstairs to make a final cup of tea before bed.

Prayer helped a great deal. More and more the rosary turned on a mysterious inner faucet. The springs of his childhood flowed again—not always, but sometimes—though he could never predict just when the well would fill.

At other times, after Communion, with the heat of the Presence within him, he saw himself leaning against the breast of the Lord at the Last Supper. Who could explain this? Who describe it? For Christ lay within *him* while he lay within

Christ, buried in his heart. A mystery within a mystery. For a few moments each Sunday he was at peace, and desired nothing other than this invisible union. He wished to remain there forever, but it was eventually necessary to get out of the pew and leave. Even so, he went home enfolded in the sense that he was a child resting in Christ's lap—a poor child, the poorest. "*Dziecko*", whispered the silence. "*Mój synu*, my little son."

Upon his return he would sometimes find David rocking beneath the shawl, murmuring and sighing prayers. Two different kinds of peace would greet each other and tacitly agree to forgo any exchange of words. The need to understand would disappear. They would eat in silence. Time itself would melt into a long winding river that flowed from the mountains to the sea.

At those moments it was enough simply to be. He would sit for hours listening to the silence (if there were no gunshots that day), observing the passage of light across the parlor floorboards, praying, reading the sacred Scriptures, and going finally to bed untroubled by *thoughts*.

\* \* \*

There were other moments when the war took a sinister turn, when thoughts returned in forms that could not be immediately discerned.

He was praying before the icon one morning, before going down to open the shop. For a long time there had been no inner voices of consolation. He did not know why they had ceased, and he wondered if it was because he was not spending enough time in prayer, despite the fact that he was praying more than he had since childhood.

Without warning, a voice said, *You will betray me.*

His heart froze and instantly he recoiled from the spirit of prayer.

He remained kneeling, trembling, while his mind raced around in circles.

In an agony he saw himself as Judas at the Last Supper.

"One of you will betray me", the Lord said.

He was not John, nor was he Peter, nor any of the others. He was filled with darkness—no, he was darkness itself.

He choked back his terror and went downstairs arguing, trying to reassure himself.

"Perhaps it means that this will be a day of unusual temptation; it was merely a warning."

But no, the voice had not said, *Be careful, you are in danger of betraying me.* It had not said, *Be vigilant, my son, the Evil One will tempt you to betrayal.* Nor had it said any similar thing. It had said simply that he, Pawel Tarnowski, would betray the Savior of the world.

"Perhaps a German will come in today, and I will foolishly say something that will cause harm to our Church."

But it was not like that.

Only two customers came in, both of them Poles trying to sell their pitiful armloads of battered, useless volumes. He explained to them that he had no money, but he gave each of them a turnip, for which they were grateful.

The words spoken by the voice reproached him repeatedly throughout the day. Whenever they erupted in his mind, he flinched in horror and desired to weep.

Where was Christ? Where was the great Heart? Why had he departed?

By closing time Pawel was crying out continuously in silent entreaty, but he could hear no answer, feel no reassurance.

"If only Father Andrei were here! He would know what it means. He would explain."

But Father Andrei was gone, safe in exile in North America.

"How many times in my life have I sinned against the will of God?" he thought. "How many times have I despaired? Yes, I have already betrayed him. Perhaps I am one of those not chosen. Surely I am lost. I am damned."

If this were so, did it any longer make sense to delay the satisfaction of the senses?

"No, no, no! Even if I am to fall forever into the pit that has no bottom, still I will ask that my little brother be saved. I will not endanger his progress toward the light."

But even this heroism, which was in fact no more than his duty, contained distortions. Why did he suppose, he asked himself, that there was the slightest inclination in the boy to what the temptation suggested? It was an absurdity heaped upon absurdities. Lies upon lies—all of it for the purpose of spinning him around and around in a spiral that bored ever downward into the imprisonment of self. And the method being used upon him was all too familiar: first a temptation, then a disappointment, then bitterness, then self-loathing, and finally despair.

That night, when he heard David sink into the whistle-breath of innocent sleep, Pawel got out of bed and knelt before the icon.

"Mother, please, speak to me. I will lose my mind. I am afraid."

*Do not be afraid.*

"The voice said I would betray your Son."

*I cannot speak to your heart if you will not trust. Your fear closes all doors.*

He calmed his breathing.

*All men are capable of betrayal.*

"The voice said I would, as if it were certain."

*There are many voices.*

After that there was no more communication, although there was now a small hole of light in his mind. It enabled him to fall into a troubled sleep from which he awoke before dawn.

That morning he found the old chaplain at the Visitation convent sitting in the confessional. After the introductory ritual, the priest said, "What do you wish to tell me, my son?"

Pawel was suddenly confused. There was nothing to tell him.

"Have you committed any mortal or venial sins since your last confession?"

Pawel surprised himself by saying what had not been obvious until this very moment: "No, I don't think so."

"You are unsure?"

"It is not clear. I do not know. There are many thoughts—evil thoughts—impure thoughts."

"Do you seek them?"

"No."

"When they appear in your mind, do you encourage them, take pleasure in them?"

"I do not encourage them, and though they surge upon me in pleasurable forms, they are a source of grief and shame."

"You resist them?"

"Yes."

"My son, have you not heard the old saying, 'A thousand temptations do not make a single sin'?"

"Yes, but still I am unsure. Am I depraved?"

"You are a human being."

"I am a very weak human being. I need an extraordinary grace to resist this evil."

"All the necessary graces are given, but you must ask our Lord for them. A guest comes to your door, but you must invite him into your home. "

"I ask and ask and ask, yet the temptations return."

"You are misunderstanding something, my son. Often we wish to make a little prayer and have a temptation or difficulty disappear. Presto! It is gone."

"Not for me. It returns."

"Yes, it returns. That is because grace is not a magician's trick. Grace is God's love flowing into you, and your response to grace must be love flowing back to him."

"Why does he not simply change me?"

"He *is* changing you, day by day."

"I see no change."

"Our eyes are so easily blinded by the darkness around us and within us. Listen, my son, perhaps this struggle against evil is God's gift to you."

"A gift?"

"Each day you go to the one who loves you, and each day you ask him for the grace to do good, only good. He gives it. Slowly, slowly—maybe a lifetime—deeper, deeper goes the understanding that he is there, he is your Father and Lord, he loves you with a total love, he will never abandon you. You and he make this union of trust together. Trust is not magic. Trust is built slowly, slowly, with patience and care."

"But there is a voice, Father. A voice is speaking to me. And it says a thing to me that destroys all trust."

"What does this voice say?"

"It says I will betray the Lord."

"One must be very cautious about voices. That message has been spoken before, as you know."

"To Judas."

"To all the apostles. Do you remember the passage where Jesus told them that one of them would betray him?"

"Yes."

"What was their response?"

"I do not remember."

"Each of them turned to Jesus and asked, 'Is it I, Lord?' Do you understand?"

"I am not sure."

"Each of them had recognized his own capacity for betrayal. Each knew in his heart that he could betray him, given the wrong circumstances. Even after the many miracles, the astounding signs, the words of God booming like thunder, they still doubted. Are we not also like this?"

"Yes."

"Of all the apostles, which one asked without sincerity, 'Is it I, Lord?'"

"Judas."

"That was because he had already set in motion the forces that would capture our Lord. He had *already* betrayed him in his heart, and there remained only the final act of betrayal. It was done, you see. That is the reason the Lord said it with such certainty."

"I had not thought of that."

"Judas *chose* to betray him. Have you chosen this thing, whatever it may be?"

"No."

"Cling to that."

"But the words. They are the most terrible words that could be spoken to me."

"That is probably why they were spoken to you."

"I was in despair after I heard it."

"That too is to be expected. And did not some temptation also follow in the wake of this despair?"

"Yes, it did. How do you know this?"

"It is an ancient device of the enemy. If he can trick you into believing you are lost, then he can seize everything in one stroke."

"Still, it is horrible. How can I be sure?"

"You are free. Your will is your own. At every moment choose the truth."

"But what if I do not know the truth in a situation? What if it becomes clouded?"

"I see that you are afraid of many things. Remember that perfect love casts out fear."

"How does one find perfect love in a time like this?"

"There never has been a perfect time for love. We choose it at every turn. Again and again we choose. That is how love grows strong."

"But for love to grow strong it takes a lifetime of choosing. It is too late for me."

"Begin now. At every moment the world begins again."

"I am too bent. I do not know how to love."

"Perhaps our Lord is teaching you a deep and difficult lesson—and teaching you swiftly, for the time may be short. He wishes you to conquer by faith, not by knowledge or by power or by success. You must learn to have confidence in him."

"He chooses a strange way to make me confident."

"Think of it as a shortcut to your soul. It is a hard path but a blessed one. A lifetime could be spent reassuring you, like a frightened child who must be held continuously. Do you have children?"

"No."

"Many family men come to me. If you were a father of children you would know that reassurance is necessary from time to time. But if one protects too much— if the child is not helped to learn his lessons, to overcome his fears—he will need a greater and greater dose of this medicine of consolations. He will not grow. Could it be that our Lord is asking you to grow very quickly? It seems he trusts you sufficiently to give you this test."

It was as if a candle had been lit in the well of Pawel's mind. Still, as he walked slowly back to the shop, the shadows of self-doubt began to close in again. Without the reassurance of the priest's voice speaking to him, the memory of the accuser's voice returned. But its power was now checked by a small light.

\* \* \*

After supper he went into the bedroom with some trepidation. The advent of nightfall, the excessive strain of the day, his worry over the recurring magnetism of his guest, the abiding fear that encroached around the little citadel of Sophia House—all cumulated in a desire to flee. Instead he prayed the prayers of the will and received no more voices and no consolations. He crawled under the blankets early. It was warm in the room. David had dismantled the last of the crates in the attic, and these, along with an ornamental door frame, had been smashed into a heap of kindling. The boy fed the firebox steadily with it for two hours. For this night, at least, they would be able to slide warmly into unthinking and unfeeling. As that moment approached, David read quietly from a large book without making comment.

Shortly before lights-out he looked up and said, "There is such an oil of gladness filling me."

"What is an oil of gladness?"

"A spirit of anointing. It came just as I read the words in this passage."

"In which book?"

"The Book of Zechariah. May I read it to you?"

"If you wish."

David sat upright on the chair and began reciting aloud in a steady voice that was neither child's nor man's:

*"Then he showed me Joshua the high priest standing before the angel of the Lord, while Satan stood at his right hand to accuse him. And the angel of the Lord said to Satan, 'May the Lord rebuke you, Satan; may the Lord who has chosen Jerusalem rebuke you! Is not this man a brand snatched from the fire?'*

*"Now Joshua was standing before the angel, clad in filthy garments. The angel spoke and said to those who were standing before him, 'Take off his filthy garments and clothe him in festal garments.'*

"Beautiful, is it not?" asked David, looking up.

Pawel admitted that it was and closed his eyes.

"Like the artist's model", the boy added, feeding the fire its last pathetic fuel. That done, he turned out the light, burrowed under his covers, and was soon dreaming.

Pawel stared into the darkness for a time that seemed beyond measure. He could not sleep, though he desperately desired it. Day and night he longed for rest, and once again it would not come. By day he depended on tea to give him energy. By night the tea churned in his veins and refused him even this licit form of escape.

"I will speak into the void", he whispered. "I do not *know* if you think of me as your son. But I tell you, God, though I cannot see you, cannot hear you, cannot touch you—yes, and even if in the end I be cast away from you forever—even so, I believe that you are beautiful. My sins are filthy rags, and my qualities and virtues and intelligence—they too are nothing compared to the splendor of your being."

The wells of his eyes were strangely full and began to brim over. His hands of their own volition raised toward the ceiling.

"This is the bottom. I see no sky above me, only the pinhole of light through which comes the faintest promise. A brand snatched from the burning? I do not know if it refers to me. I do not know if it refers to this little brother. It may even refer to us both. Or to neither of us. Nothing is certain."

No voice replied.

"O absent father, O silence. I hope in you, you whom I cannot see. Yet I ask, will light ever return? This fugitive you have placed into my hands, I must carry him, even though I do not have the strength to carry myself. I call to you. I call and call. But the night does not speak. When will we reach the distant land? When will the mountains fill our eyes? And if we arrive there, will the angels rush out to greet us? Or will we come to the edge of other pits and fall forever into fire?"

Before the coming of unconsciousness he heard a word, like the touch of a mother whispering, *Sleep.*

\* \* \*

David Schäfer is teaching me many things.

I have learned that my mind is capable of deceiving me. I have long recognized this about myself, but never before has it been so starkly revealed. I have projected upon him an image of what I perceive an ideal beloved to be. He is a very good soul, but he is not the icon I created in my interior. This is a great puzzle to me. What does it mean? Could it be that I am searching for a person who is beyond all creatures, and of whom this boy is but a reflection?

Mature love sees the beloved as he is and loves him for the reality of his being. Few come to this mature love with ease. In my play, for example, does Andrei love the romance of beauty more than the Being whom all beauty represents? Does he love Kahlia because of the intoxications of love itself, or does he love her for herself? Can he love her when she has become ancient and ugly Masha?

David has also taught me that within my own heart is the vertigo that pulls man toward darkness and possession. To seek to possess another is to become possessed. To use another human being as an object, even within the privacy of one's own thoughts, is to degrade the being of that person. It is to dehumanize oneself as well as the other. So far I have not fallen in this regard. Daily I struggle against it. But resistance is not enough. There must be a vision of how to love in a positive way. How to strengthen him to face the trials of an evil age.

And still, and still, the yearning does not depart. Though it declines, it does not cease. Hence the painful dialogue, because never can such desire bring about true union or any kind of ultimate good.

"Why is that so?" the flesh cries. "Is it really so?"

Yes, it is so. And even though the root of this love is good, as is the root of every other human love, yet its trunk and branches have been bent. I do not know why I am drawn to disordered desire. I grieve over it. But I refuse to call the bent tree a straight one. Smokrev has lost his right to the truth because he chooses just such a lie. And thus he has lost his ability to love creatures for themselves.

The pain of it is deep. The bent tree resists the wind that would push it straight. It suffers. I have come to believe that this pain is good. And with my very life I cling to the promise that in paradise everything that is genuine love will find fulfillment. Every sacrifice will find a reward far surpassing earthly consolations. There, love will be in full flower, a joy and a splendor beyond measure. This is my only hope.

## 16

Night after night he wrestled with exhaustion. Words and signs came and went like wild birds, like windblown leaves, like paper angels. Prayer arose like incense. The ideas of many writers were consumed in copious amounts, along with tea and sleep. Tea and sleep—his new obsessions.

Late one evening, after throwing a useless book into the fire, and the one he was reading onto the mattress, David leaned his head back against the wall and stared into space.

"The only thing one can give to another is what he truly is", he declared.

"And if one doesn't know what he truly is?" Pawel replied.

The boy's brows furrowed.

"That is an unfortunate person", he murmured pensively.

"I have just described most of mankind", Pawel said with nearly detectable irony.

"Do you really think so?"

Pawel left this unanswered, but David seemed not to notice, or else his question had been rhetorical. He turned his gaze to the window and became lost in thought.

As Pawel observed him, he realized that a sense of timelessness had captivated his guest and that a churning process was quietly under way within him. He let it be and engaged upon some musing of his own.

*There he sits*, Pawel said to himself. *This David Schäfer, this youth barely out of childhood pondering the imponderable like an ancient sage.*

Where had this incongruous presence come from? What had formed him? Why was he here? The first line of explanation was obvious—the causality clear enough. But if an invisible hand was upon both their lives, surely it had brought them together for a purpose. What purpose? And how could such a purpose be fulfilled?

That they were imprisoned together was never in doubt. Not so clear was the character of their imprisonment. Was it a case of sharing the same cell and speaking different languages unintelligible to each other? Or were they enclosed in two different cells and speaking the same language? There were times when it seemed the former, other times when it seemed the latter.

I believe in Christ, Pawel thought. I believe in the New Covenant, which his people rejects. Why has God permitted the Jews to remain for so many centuries without the light of our faith? Surely God has the power to tell them, show them, prove himself to them?

It struck Pawel suddenly that he too had lived for a period without faith during his years in Paris and after his return from France. What had been the state of his mind at the time? The memory of it had grown dim, though he recalled the bridges over the Seine, the Spree, and the Vistula, the humiliations and despair. The beliefs of his childhood had faded like a dying candle and flickered into darkness like a smoldering wick without enough oxygen. How had it happened? Not by choice, surely, or at least not by a choice based on full knowledge of the factors and consequences. No, he had reached that state through a series of ignorant steps made by himself and by others. By himself mostly—his bitterness, his inability to communicate, and his refusal to let anyone come close. Why? Why had he become like that? How had he so easily, so steadily, lost his faith? At the time, he had thought he was discovering reality—a harsh reality but a true one—a world purged of the false myths of family, homeland, God. Initially there had seemed to be no negative results, simply a relief from the intolerable tension of sustaining religious activities that were

405

no longer meaningful for him. He had become a free man—
so he had supposed. But the consequences had been nearly
disastrous.

For years he did not pray, did not think about God. He had
not missed it in the least. But from the vantage point of experience, he now saw that his consciousness had changed during
that period; certain faculties of seeing and feeling had declined
until one after another they shut down. Then he had forgotten
them, barely recalled how real they had once been for him. If
they had come to mind from time to time, he had dismissed
them as the residue of Christian indoctrination, emotionalism,
pietism, the naïveté of childhood. He had been blinded by his
lack of belief, and worse, had not known he was blind.

Was it the same for this boy sitting across the room from him
earnestly digging his way through rational and spiritual concepts? No, David's condition was radically different, for he had
never known Christ. Yet he possessed something else, something alien to Pawel's experience. Was it a quality unique to this
individual person, regardless of his race and religion? Or was it
common to all Hasids? Was it fundamentally alien, or was it a
cultural dialect of the universal human condition? While it was
true that whatever faculties of the soul Christian faith awakened
in a believer were dormant within this boy, other gifts were
functioning in him full force. *Flowing*, he called it. But what
exactly was this flowing?

The pursuit of wisdom? Yes, he actively sought it at every
turn, in scholarly research, private thought, and discussion. But
this was common to many religions.

Love? But what kind of love? Love of life, love of being? An
appetite for that mysterious dimension he called *communion*?
But this was also universal, was it not?

And where was God in all of this? If the Jews were his chosen
people, why had he left a majority of them without belief in the
true Messiah?

Looking up, David broke into Pawel's train of thought.

"Sometimes I feel as if a veil covers my eyes."

"A veil?"

"It is like a thin cloth, which hides a part of reality from me. It should not be this way."

"What do you mean? Surely no man can know all things."

"I am not referring to the realm of knowledge."

"Then what do you mean by the part of reality hidden from you?"

"I mean that there should be no divisions between the sacred world and the things of this world. There should be no veils between man and his Creator. This is what the Ba'al Shem Tov taught us."

"Who is the Ba'al Shem Tov?"

"A spiritual teacher of my people. The founder of our faith. He said that a man's every act must worship the Creator. In this way we find communion with the Most High."

"It is the same in my faith."

"Is it?"

They regarded each other in silence.

"We must have childlike hearts", David continued. "Joy is essential to *devekus*, clinging to him at all times with constant devotion."

"That too is like my faith," Pawel said, "but perhaps not in the way you mean it."

"But how do you mean it, when you speak of joy? For us it is *hislahavus*, like bursting into holy flame—singing and dancing flame."

"A flame that does not burn you, does not hurt you?"

"It does not hurt. It is a sweet burning. It is the spiritual exultation we feel as the soul rises toward the Most High and all the while is within him."

Pawel nodded. "For us it is the same."

"Truly? The same?"

"I do not know if it is exactly the same. But our saints and mystics speak of this."

Pawel withdrew into his own thoughts, reflecting on the fact that saints and mystics also spoke of suffering, darkness, and the agony of interior crosses. For a Christian, these were an indispensable part of the rising toward God.

David closed his eyes and reached his hands forward like a blind man groping his way along an unknown road.

"What is this veil I feel? I know there is something beyond it, but I cannot see what it is. Never before have I sensed its presence."

"Never before?"

"Since I have lived in this house, it has grown and grown. The Most High has given me to know that great changes will occur in my life and that they will surely come to pass if I abide by the Torah and entrust myself to his care."

"He has told you that much, but not told you what is beyond the veil?"

"The veil is thin, yet its weave is strong. The threads are like steel."

"Why does not the Most High simply lift the veil and show you?"

"Perhaps I am not ready to see it, for with one breath the Most High could easily dissolve the threads."

"Why does he not breathe on it?"

"I do not know."

David opened his eyes, exposing the puzzlement and sadness he felt. "I do not know", he said again.

Staring into the distance, he continued to strain for vision, until at last it seemed the effort had exhausted or dispirited him. He sighed, looked at Pawel, and asked:

"Do you see the veil?"

"I have my own veils."

"Ah", he nodded, then fell silent again.

"You began by saying that the only thing one can give to another is what he truly is. Does the presence of a veil not indicate that a person is more than what he seems to be at any given moment?"

"What do you mean, Pawel?"

"Does not the veil imply that you will become something else?"

"Become something else? That is a very strange thought. No, we never become something else. But I believe we can become something more, something better."

"On this, I think we can agree."

"Good!" The boy smiled suddenly, jumped up, and hastened off to the kitchen to make tea.

After drinking their cups of faintly flavored hot water, they turned out the lights and tried to sleep. The cold made it nearly impossible. In the dark, David chose to appeal a closed case.

"I do not understand", came a voice from the floor.

"What do you not understand?"

"Why you do not want me to read the story you wrote."

"My play? The German has taken it away and has not returned it."

"The German. You let a stranger read it, but you would not let me read it?"

"It happened that way by accident. Besides, I think it is probably just one more piece of poorly written literature."

"I believe I mentioned before, Pawel," David said politely, "that I am interested in the soul of a work, not in its literary qualities."

"You are amazing."

"Why am I amazing?"

"You are so different from a man I once knew in Paris. He was a novelist. He liked to quote Flaubert, who said that language is a cracked kettle on which writers beat out tunes for bears to dance."

"Did this man teach you to write, Pawel? Was he a good friend?"

"He was not a good friend. But he told me something useful once. He said that bad literature is often written with noble sentiments. My play is about noble sentiments."

"Is it bad literature?"

"I do not know."

"Does it matter? Perhaps it is necessary only that your play be full of wisdom."

"I do not think so. Answer me this: When your zaddiks tell a story *beautifully*, do they not plant the story more deeply?"

"Yes. It is stronger."

"How does a zaddik learn to tell a tale beautifully?"

"It is an art."

"How does he learn this art?"

"At one time, when I was a child, I thought it was simply given to this or that man. He did not have to learn it."

"You no longer think so?"

"I no longer think so, Pawel."

"What, then, is the secret of the teller of tales?"

"He observes. He reflects upon what he has seen. He suffers because of this. And from his suffering he makes a story. The soul of his listener recognizes that it is a true story, even if it is about a deer leaping on clouds or children dancing on the waves of the sea. It is not merely entertainment. It is food."

"Here is a great puzzle. You say the zaddik becomes strong in his gift because of suffering. Where then is his joy?"

No reply was forthcoming. However, the boy got up and turned on the bedside lamp.

"Do you mind, Pawel? We need light. It seems we are in discussion."

"It seems we are."

David burrowed under his blankets again, frowning and thinking. "You ask me where is his joy, the zaddik who suffers.

I believe this kind of zaddik finds *hislahavus* by converting the raw material of his sorrows into a tale that spreads happiness—as wood when it is consumed gives heat so that others may live."

"But is his suffering not a form of weakness?"

"Such weakness makes others strong."

"Only a wise man knows this. You are a zaddik, David."

"Do not say such a thing! I am not wise."

"Ah, yes, all the true zaddiks say that."

"You are learning to use my tactics, Pawel."

"You have taught me well."

"You are embarrassing me."

"Why are you embarrassed?"

Casting his eyes down, David said, "When I was twelve years of age, I studied Torah continuously. People began to say foolish things of me. They called me a prodigy. The most foolish called me a zaddik."

"Ah, then, I apologize for adding to your embarrassment. Let me ask you this, David Schäfer: When a man is a true zaddik is he embarrassed when people say he is wise?"

"In the truly humble man there should be neither pride nor shame. He knows only that he is a man with a message to bear. I am not humble. Therefore, I am not wise."

"What is wisdom?"

"It is holy fear of the Most High. It is devotion to him. It is knowledge of the Torah, understanding of his ways, ability to counsel others according to his mind, fortitude to do battle against his enemies. Is it not the same in your teachings?"

"Yes. We have the same pillars of wisdom."

"But your face is confusing me. Your face is telling me that you think there is more than this."

"The house of wisdom is a sacred mystery. One cannot become master in this house by memorizing a formula."

"Or by ignorance of the formula, Pawel."

"I agree. The formula is true. But it is not everything."

"Then what are you trying to say?"

"I think that the pillars of the house are not made of stone, nor of will, nor of strength, nor of intelligence."

"Of what are they made?"

"The pillars of wisdom are these: humility, powerlessness, poverty, loneliness, sickness, rejection, and abandonment."

"Those are sad things."

"Yes, they are."

"It is a hard saying."

"There is a secret joy in it."

"I cannot accept this entirely, Pawel. It is too dark."

"It contains pain, but a passing pain."

"Man was created for joy!" the boy protested. "He was made to dance!"

"Yes, and to know in his marrow that he is a creature. That he is not God."

"But he rejoices in this knowledge. He dances for love of it."

"Does the dance come before this knowledge?"

"For some people, *yes*", David said emphatically. "The knowledge grows *with* the dancing. *With* the rejoicing."

"But not for all people. For a few only. Most human beings learn the difficult lessons only by suffering. If they persevere, they will in time find joy."

"What you say is puzzling to me. I have found only the joy of the Most High."

"Only the joy? You, who have nothing?"

David pondered this, then covered his eyes with a hand.

"I have said too much", Pawel murmured.

The boy shook his head. "It is true that I have lost everything. Even so, it is not the end."

"You are right. It is not the end. And where life will take you in the years to come is not yet certain. You are not locked in a prison of fate."

"Yes", David replied, looking up, brightening a little. "I have not lost everything, for I *have* myself, and I *am* myself. And in paradise I will see my family again."

Pawel nodded sympathetically. Taking a deep breath, he said, "Perhaps that is all I really meant: you have your joy, but you also have your grief."

"Yet suffering should not paralyze us. It *must* not, for then we would have no place for joy."

"Yet without suffering, would we understand the joy? Would we value it?"

"Pawel, I am sorry, but I no longer understand this conversation."

"It is too obscure for both of us. We are attempting to know what can be seen only with the heart."

"With a whole heart."

"With a broken heart", Pawel said with finality.

\*   \*   \*

Little discussion occurred on the following nights, as both were exhausted by short and fitful sleeps. On the third night, they drifted off under the dull red glow of the vigil candle. For once the city was completely silent. Pawel was almost asleep when David stirred, sat up, and said:

"Suppose that I am a man with one eye and you are another one-eyed man. Suppose we have only seen separately. Each knows the meaning of the world as seen through his one eye. He is convinced that he is the master of true seeing. Suppose the Most High brings the two one-eyed men together and they meet and befriend each other. Let us say that there is a respect between them that grows and grows. They do not understand one another. But gradually they begin to see as if they had two eyes."

"Two eyes?" Pawel mumbled. Recognizing David's tone, he raised himself on an elbow and sighed.

"They see farther and deeper because of it. And this seeing is love, I believe. Yes, there is love."

"That is a pleasant thought. But few human beings know how to love."

"That is a dark saying, Pawel."

"You have come from the ghetto and you think my words are dark? Think of the darkness beyond that wall. Think of the killers."

"That is the darkness of the men with no eyes."

"You are young. Few people know how to love. All are killers and do not know it."

"All? I think you are wrong in this. There are two races on this earth."

"Only two?"

"Yes. Killers and victims."

"That is a dark saying, David."

"It is dark only when the victim refuses to dance."

"You are a philosopher and very, very young."

"I have seen much love."

"I have seen little since my childhood."

"You do not believe in love?"

"I believe in it. But in the country of blind men, there is little love."

"I do not understand. I see your love every day."

"Whatever you admire in me is no more than my longing for sight."

"What is love?" said David, astonished.

"Love takes nothing for itself."

"Every day you feed me. Each day you keep death away from this door. In return I sweep dust and make glasses of tea. I do not understand what you mean."

"You are young."

"Please stop saying that."

"I am sorry. I will never again remind you of your youth."

"There is another thing I do not understand."

"Again! You do not understand! What do you not understand?"

Silence followed this rebuke.

"Tell me."

"The bed", David said meekly.

"The bed?"

"It is not fair! I have three blankets and you have two. Yet you are the head of this household. You own everything."

"It is easy to understand. I simply wish it to be this way. That is all there is to it."

"No. There is a hidden reason. And I know what it is."

"You know what it is?" Pawel said slowly.

"I have suspected for a long time. And now I am certain why you do not want me to come into your bed."

A stab of fear pierced Pawel's heart.

"Now you are certain."

"Now I understand it, this dark thing."

"Now you understand it", Pawel replied coldly. "How splendid. Well, then, if you wish to come into my bed, why don't you come!"

In no sense did he intend this to be an invitation. He meant it as a bitter irony, or rather an actual sarcasm. Sure that the secret had been stripped bare, he knew the boy would now move away from him as far as possible and would seek a means of escape.

*And so*, Pawel said to himself, *in the end, even sacrificial love is nothing more than an alternative romance!* All that he had painfully endured for the sake of this boy's freedom was effortlessly demolished by an ugly revelation. Shame, guilt, fear—the great levelers. Yes, one whiff of it and everything collapsed!

To Pawel's utter amazement, David climbed into bed beside him and pulled his blankets over their bodies.

"Thank you, Pawel", he said. "Five blankets are better than two. Now at last we will have a warm sleep."

The radiant heat was inches away. Employing every gram of will, Pawel flung back the covers and got out. He pulled two blankets off the top of the bed and lay down under them on the mattress on the floor.

For several minutes a terrible silence ensued, so freighted with tension that the very air seemed filled with inarticulate shouts of confusion and pain. Both man and boy felt utterly incapable of breaking the silence, but the pressure of what had occurred and what remained unspoken soon became unendurable.

"It is true", said David in a choked voice. "I see now that I guessed correctly. You do not need to hide the reason. I understand."

*Understand?* Pawel raged to himself. *What can this angelic youth, this sterling soul, this prodigy, possibly understand of my condition!*

David Schäfer wept. At first it was a groaning sound, muffled by the arm he cast across his face. Then it increased in volume, erupting into sobs. He covered his face with cold, white, trembling hands and gave full vent to it, shattering his perpetual dignity.

Pawel was shocked. At first he thought the boy had seen into his soul and was weeping over it. Then he wondered if David was weeping for his own predicament, hurt and disillusioned by the tentative friendship that was now revealed as something dangerous, even sinister. He was trapped in a place of refuge that had proved to be no refuge at all, held captive by a protector who was suddenly unmasked as a monster.

Hating the condemnation implicit in the outburst, Pawel snapped, "Why are you crying?"

David did not answer, though the sobbing declined.

"What is the matter?" he demanded. "Why do you cry?"

When David had finally choked back his tears, he said, "Now I see what I am to you. I am the artist's model, the child who became Judas. I know now that you are the kind of man who would give shelter even to one whom you consider to be the lowest creature on earth."

"What? What are you saying?"

"Yes, even to a Jew. Why does the world hate us? Why? Even you, Pawel, you who are the best of men! Do you hate me?"

"Hate you—?"

"It was wrong of me to think that I should be permitted to share your bed—me, a Jew—as if I were your family. For this I am sorry. You have risked your life to protect me, and because of it I presumed too much. How could I have been so foolish! To think that you felt for me as a father feels for his child! I have been blind. I should have seen that I was a blight upon your life. I am defilement for you. Come back to your bed. I will return to the attic."

"Stay there. Do not move, and I will explain."

"Explain?" David murmured in a broken voice. "How can this pain between us be explained? Our two peoples—"

"David, David, be silent. For me, a man's value is measure-less. Every man. It is no less if he is a Jew or if he is a Gentile. My brother's wife is a Jew. My lawyer, who has disappeared, is a Jew. The woman of that icon is a daughter of Zion, a Jew of the New Covenant. My God and Savior is a Jew. That is how I see it. There is no defilement in your presence. Not in any way."

"Then I am returned to not-understanding!"

"When I was young I wished to be a monk. Do you know what a monk is?"

Sitting upright, drying his eyes, David looked at Pawel with perplexity. "A *monakh*? He is a *prister* who goes away alone, is he not?"

"He is a man of prayer. He seeks no earthly consolations. He listens in the darkness for God."

"Like Elijah on Mount Carmel?"

"Yes. Like that. When I went to the place where young men become monks, they said I was not strong enough. Later, much later, after many strange experiences, I returned to this house. I became a solitary in the world, living here, praying and working alone. It turns out that I was not strong enough for this, either."

"I never understand when you speak of this not-strongness, Pawel. You are the strongest man I have ever known. After my father, that is."

"Even so, it is what I felt, and still feel."

"But I do not see how this connects to the bed."

"I made a promise to God that I would forgo any consolations that men usually expect from life. I asked only that I be an instrument for placing good books into people's hands, so that their lives would be enriched by truth. I asked only for enough income to survive. I was content to be a poor man." He paused and sighed. "God has taken me at my word, you see. I am a poor man not only in my possessions but in my very self. I live in this poverty and I make it my offering to him, like the boy who gave away the whole book on the Day of Atonement. Long ago I took the solitary path, and I cannot depart from it."

"It is difficult to grasp. Are you saying that you *like* the cold floor?"

"No. I do not like it. But it is teaching me to love."

"Teaching you to love?"

"It helps me to turn toward the Most High in search of *his* warmth."

"I too believe that he is there, Pawel. But it is not necessary for me to be cold to seek him."

"The difference between us is impossible to describe. I can say only that it is difficult for me to search for the sound of his beating Heart. I must use every opportunity."

"Not being warm is a training?"

"Yes, it is."

"It seems a very cold religion."

"Things are warmer on the inside than the outside. There are moments when the face of the Beautiful One is before us, in the eyes of the heart. There is an embrace that is all Love. It is worth everything—everything."

"Such a thing I have not experienced."

"Thus, you will give me your kind permission to sleep on the floor. And you will keep my bed."

"It is not right."

"In time you will understand."

"I will never understand."

"David Schäfer, was it not you who once told me that the man who has nothing is the man who has everything?"

There was no reply to this, merely a deep sigh of incomprehension. Before long, David rolled over, and Pawel pulled the blankets around his own shoulders.

"You ask everything of me", he said to the image of the Mother.

*Yes, everything.*

\*     \*     \*

19 March 1943

Dear Monsieur Rouault,

Where are you at this moment? Are you in Versailles or Paris, or in some other place hidden from the *kultur* of the enemy, awaiting a better day? Are your friends the Maritains with you? O to be with you! O to retrace the steps of my past and take a better path! To have conquered my fear and to stand among you as one of the poor, a damaged man, yet bearing glory in his heart, defending the glory of paradise with his freedom.

Why did I run from you? Was it because I thought there was nothing in me of any worth? Or was it because I desired to be the Christ Child and could not bear the revelation that Judas is also within me? I believed that if I could not be the Child in God's great work of art, then I could be only be the Judas. By such little lies are we so often defeated!

You have not read my play about an obscure historical figure from Russia. Perhaps some day you will read it, if you and this manuscript survive the war. It is about an artist. Andrei Rublëv was broken open, and in that breaking he knew himself to be a son of the Father. Knew at last that the maker of icons was himself the icon.

You wrote to me once that the rejected Christ cannot be viewed without prejudice and that only the eye freed by suffering can gaze upon the face of the mutilated Christ and truly see it. For many years I fled this face, terrified that it is our definitive portrait, that we are no more than animals easily degraded, easily snuffed out. You spoke of the majesty of a God who suffers with us and in us, and you spoke of his embrace of the broken image within us. You said that he goes down into the darkest places on earth in search of the lost, so that we might know our own true face and be taken up by him into the place where we are restored to what we were intended to be from the beginning. I did not understand, and I ran from it. Like Judas, I could not believe in forgiveness. You tried to tell me, Monsieur, that the face of Judas can be restored to the face of the Child, if we would only accept mercy. The scarred icon restored by a master.

I pray that we meet some day, you and I.

Pawel Tarnowski

\*   \*   \*

With these thoughts uppermost in his mind, his heart gathered strength throughout the next day. He pondered again and again the junctions in his past at which he had made departures, falling or rising, veering into the darkness, swerving back to a path that had never presented itself as anything other than obscure. It now seemed to him that this very obscurity was more a problem of interpretation—the mirror or the window that he had discussed with David. For too many years he had read only the grievous messages of his reflected image, and had translated these according to his hurt. He had, as a result, felt locked into a course that had seemed inescapable, determined, hopeless. He now felt certain that forgiveness was the key, as Father Andrei had told him at Czestochowa. And a key implied that a door existed. It was the reality of the door, more than the constellation of new insights, that he now found most important.

That evening he sat down at his private desk in the shop and reread his letter to Rouault. Contrary to his expectation, the truth in it had not been blown away by the habitual instability of his emotions, nor had it faded into abstractions. He folded the paper, inserted it into an envelope, and sealed it. After writing the name, *Georges Rouault, Versailles, France,* on the front, he held it in his hands a while, gazing at it, musing. If he survived the war, God willing, he would mail it and attempt to reestablish a dialogue with the man who had knocked on his door at a time when he had not believed in doors.

Better still, he would go to Paris and deliver it in person. And though it seemed a hope beyond hope, perhaps he would even paint again.

Pawel put the envelope into the tin box in the desk's bottom drawer and shut it. He turned off the desk lamp and sat in the dark. The night was no longer fearful to him. Why this should be, he could not say. Sophia House was hushed, its stillness unbroken by gunfire, sirens, or the screams of the chorus, yet the quieting of his interior noise struck him as more significant. In this hiatus between the past and the future, he experienced a taste of the peace he had known only in childhood. It was brief, yet it added to his newfound sense that a future larger than he had supposed was still possible. On an impulse, not knowing why he did it, he went upstairs to the apartment and entered the bathroom.

This was the room in which only a few months before he

had come within a hair of slashing the pulsing vein in his neck. This was the mirror into which he had stared with loathing, the face in it returning and amplifying its message. An infinity of mirrors that could end only in madness. A locked cell from which the only apparent escape had been self-destruction.

Now he forced himself to look into his face, striving to see through it as one would seek a glimpse of a fairer world beyond a window glass. At first it was difficult, for the immediate truth was that Pawel the Beautiful had gone forever. Sweet Pawel had grown old before his time. He saw a haggard man who had failed at everything, his eyes full of grief, confusion, longings that he was unable to articulate even to himself. He saw a history of losses, an exposed archive of tales that, if not futile, were full of sorrows.

For once he did not recoil in fear or strike out at his image in rage. He stood still and waited.

"This is what I am", he said at last.

Then, one by one, unsummoned, the faces of many people came before him—those who had betrayed him, or had despised him, or had tried to bend him into the objects they wanted to consume.

First came Photosphoros, the man of God, raging and condemning. This old blow had lost some of its power, though not all. Pawel exhaled, seeking what lay on the other side of his own reflected eyes.

"Forgive me", said the priest. "I did not know you, I did not understand you."

"I forgive you", Pawel growled, and though his will was in these words, his heart was not.

"Forgive me", pleaded the priest again.

"I forgive you, I forgive you", Pawel said, his lips tightening, his eyes narrowing.

"Please forgive me", said the priest once more, in the voice of a child. "On the day I hurt you, I felt as you do now. It was not you whom I desired to strike, but all the ignorance that lay on the world and had robbed me of my home."

"I forgive you", Pawel whispered. "I release you, and no longer do I hold it against you. I will pray for you, and if you are no longer in this world, I ask you to pray for me."

The priest nodded his assent and disappeared.

Immediately in his place there stood Achille Goudron.

"Forgive me, Pawel."

"I forgive you", Pawel muttered.

"Do you think I fail to see my guilt? Do you think a day has passed in which I have not remembered what I did to you?"

"I trusted you."

"I saw your trust, and your need. And for more than a year I sheltered you."

"You built my trust only so that you could take from me what you wanted."

"That was not my intention in the beginning. In you I saw myself when I was young. You, who had lost your way, bearing the treasure of your gifts, not knowing how to use them, you sought refuge and guidance. Refuge I gave. But I did not know how to guide you, for I too was adrift, without a hand upon my life, with no father's voice to speak my own true name and tell me what I was for. And thus did the love of a friend become mingled with the desire of a despoiler. It was at war within me."

"You tried to seize what was not yours, and in doing so you swept aside my very self."

"I was tempted and I fell. Forgive me."

"I forgive you."

"Please forgive me", pleaded Goudron once again.

"I have forgiven you!" Pawel snarled.

And in the sound of his reply he knew that he had not forgiven.

"A kiss", Goudron cried, "was all I asked—"

"You wanted all of me. You would have taken it, if I had let you, at the price of my own true self."

"As I would have done in that time of darkness, so others had done to me. Just as you feel now, so I felt then."

Startled, Pawel now understood what he had not seen until this very moment: once he had been David, and Goudron had been Pawel.

"Forgive me, for I dwell in the realm of shame and have need of your mercy."

Bowing his head in silence for a time, Pawel replied at last: "I do forgive you. I release you. No longer can I hold this against you, for I too would seize what is not mine, if darkness were to engulf me. I too have need of mercy."

Looking up, he saw that Goudron was gone. In his place came more human forms, and behind them more again, ranks upon ranks, the lesser and the greater.

He balked at this, for it seemed that with every forgiveness beseeched of him, he must face his unforgiveness and ask forgiveness.

"Is it so?" he said to the crowd awaiting his answer. "Am I to beg from you—you who have robbed me?"

He was repelled at first, flaring with anger, clinging to his bitterness, yet he allowed it to fall from his hands again—and let it go. He saw that freedom was always latent within the human heart and that he could choose. For the first time in his life he understood that he was like all men, and all were like him. They too were called to love, and they too feared love. Germans, Russians, and Poles, Gentiles and Jews, good men and bad, rich and poor—all clinging to their weapons of defense, all dwelling in terror of absolute nakedness.

He had been stripped and seen his nakedness, which was man's common inheritance. Of his many fears, this had been the greatest, for he had thought that if he were to see his abject poverty, he would collapse into nonbeing; if he were to meet

Love face-to-face, Love itself would turn away from him. Yes, with great dedication he had sought to turn himself to stone, thinking that love was just a variation of entertainments in a Berlin nightclub, a pleasure for the paying customers. Such was the lie that had found a home in him for so long.

Pawel now saw that the beggar who forgave the thief possessed a greater wealth. The humiliated who forgave the one who had degraded him rose to higher dignity. He looked at each face in the crowd and gave each mercy. He let what each one had done or not done go away on the wind forever.

All but two shadows disappeared, though these did not come forward. Who they were, he did not know, for try as he might he could not see their faces. And with that, his sight receded from what lay beyond the glass and rested on the surface of the mirror.

There he saw the face that Rouault had desired to paint—the face of Christ humiliated, in agony, despised and rejected. At first it frightened him, for though Christ was within him, in this world it was yet possible that he would fail him.

*This too is what I am*, Pawel said to the icon of Christ. *I need mercy.*

"Forgive me", he whispered.

Then, peering once more through the window of memory, he saw one of the two shadow figures step forward.

*"Dziecko*, my child", whispered the shadow, its face lifting into the light, that it might be seen. "*Mój synu*, my little son."

Pawel turned from it, gripping the sides of the sink with both hands.

"O my father, why did you leave me?"

"I did not want to leave you."

"Why did you not love me when you returned?"

The light increased, revealing the battle dress of a soldier whose eyes were like empty wells. "I did love you, but you did not know the language of my heart."

"Could you not read the language of a child's heart?"

"If I had understood . . ."

"Why didn't you?"

"I had fallen in combat, yet that combat and that falling I endured for your sake, though you did not know it."

"Why did you not tell me, explain to me?"

"I did tell you. The little knight and dragon were my word, which I gave you in remembrance of me. I thought it would be enough for you."

"Never can a word be enough for a child. He needs many words, and not least of these are those of hands and heart."

"With my heart, which had suffered its own blows, I sought to speak with you, but you would not come to me. With my hands I reached for you, but you turned from me."

Then Papa bowed his head, and though he wept he continued to offer his hands. Pawel turned away and looked no more.

"Forgive me, my Pawelek." Again and again the shadow cried, his voice receding into the past. Trembling, Pawel left the room and spent the night staring into the darkness above, until dawn crept in accompanied by a series of dull explosions in the streets to the northwest.

For four days the forces of nature conspired with the forces of war to press down on the people of Warsaw. The thermometer plunged to a new low, just when spring seemed to have arrived on the doorstep. It was winter's last gasp, but the weather was arctic. Following her own inscrutable dictates, Baba Yaga appeared on each of these days, once with a message from Bronek, once with scraps of information about the depleted resources of the city (grimacing with satisfaction, ever glad to be the bearer of ill tidings), and once with a few books for his assessment. She would not divulge the sources of these volumes and seemed content with anything he gave her by way of payment. There were only a few meager *groszy* at hand, but it did not strike her as useful to return on a day when he would have more solid cash to pay, even though he suggested it. The chance to sit on his shop chair, sip tea, eat a crust of bread, and issue her cryptic remarks was sufficient reward.

He knew without a doubt that she was "a tiny patriot", as Bronek called her, but he wondered nevertheless if she contained a vein of genuine madness. Try as he might, he could not pry open her mind to read her personal hoard of secret thoughts. She seemed uneducated and crude, yet there was a keen intelligence in her eyes. Perhaps it was mere craftiness. It was impossible to know if she was a split personality or an actress of surpassing genius. In the end he concluded that she was a mixture of both.

On the afternoon of the fourth day, she entered the shop with rime on her upper lip and two white spots of frostbite on her blue cheeks. When Pawel pointed them out to her, she began to hop around, holding her face with yelps of dismay. He brought her a glass of tea but she put it on the floor, where it sat cooling for twenty minutes while she stomped and groaned. Tears of pain dribbled from her eyes.

"It hurts, Pani?" he asked sympathetically.

"It stings like hell. But that's life, eh? If you want no pain, then go ahead and freeze! You won't feel a thing. If you want to be alive, let it hurt."

Feeling helpless, he watched her for some minutes while she wrestled with her flesh.

"There, that's better. Now it feels hot and good. Thank you. Nice boy."

When she stooped to pick up the glass he had brought her, she growled, "Och, this tea is cold!"

Pawel went upstairs to make more, and when he returned he found her slumped in the chair at his desk, sleeping.

He sat for a while at the book-mending table and pondered the wheezing bundle of rags.

*Poor soul,* he thought, *do you belong to anyone? Were you once a little girl in a lace dress parading to church? Were you once the most endearing creature in the world? You must have been the apple of your father's eye. Did he hold you close in his arms and rock you to sleep at night, singing to you? Did he marvel at your smallness? Did he wonder if you contained the womb of many generations? Pani? What is your name?*

An hour later she shook herself, glanced at the clock, glared at him, and said in a threatening voice, "Why didn't you wake me?"

"You looked so tired."

"When have I not been tired? Life is tiredness. Now I'm late for a meeting."

"What meeting is that?"

"You don't need to know."

"I am sorry. It was rude of me to ask."

"You think your kindness allows you liberties? You think it makes you superior to me—a stupid old ragwoman who smells?"

"Not in the least, Pani."

"And stop calling me Pani. I am a Panna. A *panienka*, a sweet little *miss!*"

Well, that was that. The apple of the eye had long ago soured.

"*Panna*, then. If you have missed your meeting, may I bring you another glass?"

"Forget that!"

He wondered if she would sit all day at his desk—*his* desk, mind you—punishing him for not behaving as badly as the Germans.

"It is you who are rude", he said.

She shot him a black look, then smiled—a bad-tempered badger caught in a snare of humor.

"Nice boy. You're a nice boy."

"Stop calling me Nice Boy. I am Pan Tarnowski."

She laughed.

"Nice Boy, I like you very much."

"Why do you speak that way, if you like me?"

"I don't like pity."

"Obviously you find it useful enough."

"True, when I'm in control of the one who pities me, and when it's necessary."

"You are not what you appear to be, *panienka!*"

"Nor are you, *kruliczyk.*"

*Little rabbit!* He was tempted to lash back but let it go.

"You know, if you weren't such a nice rabbit, I'd think of asking you to join us."

"Join you?"

"Bronek has come in."

"Come in to what?"

She sighed. "Should I trust you, *kruliczyk*?"

"Fear not, *panienka*."

"The future is being made at this very moment."

"A philosophy of history with which I have no disagreement."

"Don't be smart. Listen to me. It's hammer and anvil all the way. The Germans can't win this war. They will continue to do big damage. It's going to be bad. They may succeed in murdering millions more. They may even destroy Warsaw. Himmler was here in January. I saw him get into a car at the Brühl palace. They're brewing something big, I tell you. The underground knows it too."

"You *know* it or *suspect* it?"

"I didn't say I."

"I don't understand."

"I'm not with the underground, at least not as you think of it."

"You're confusing me. Bronek is—"

"Ah yes, dear Bronek. He was in the regular underground. But he has come in with us."

He wondered if the panienka's madness was reasserting itself. In a flash he caught a glimpse of her life, a destitute old woman roving about the city cultivating shopkeepers with her mystique, her stories, and her intrigues. It might be a practical way to keep warm and feed oneself.

"Come upstairs", he said. "Let me make you a meal."

She had no argument against that. He led the way up the staircase, slowly and noisily, allowing David time to hide. When she had eased herself onto a kitchen chair, the lectures continued between mouthfuls of boiled cabbage.

"They will destroy the ghetto, of course", she declared with a wave of her hand.

"Why would they?"

"The Jews are fighting back. The Germans will go through

430

the ghetto, building by building, until they catch every one—what's left of them. Then, *boom!*—down it all goes!"

"Why would they go to such trouble for a handful of fugitives? It's only a few square kilometers of tenements."

"Don't ask me, I'm not a German. They hate Jews, and hatred has top place. After that comes us. We're next."

"No, no, that is too fantastic."

"Ten years ago people thought a war like this couldn't happen. But here we are in the middle of it. And it's turning out to be worse than we could have imagined."

"That is true."

"Pawel Tarnowski, when this big German bogeyman goes home, what do you think will be left in its place?"

"We will rebuild Poland."

"With a Soviet army inside our borders?"

"We have driven them out before."

"We won't this time. They'll let the Germans demolish us, and when that's done they'll come in to clean up. Poland will be communist."

"It could never happen."

"Have you seen Treblinka? Have you seen Majdanek, Chelmno, Belzec, Oświęcim? Listen, anything can happen. Anything."

"When the British and Americans land in Europe, they will liberate us. They would never let Stalin swallow half of Europe."

"You think so? They'll be so grateful to the Soviets for throwing ten million Russians in front of German guns, they'll *give* them half of Europe. You'll see. Because of this we must prepare now. We're forming a socialist front that will make our own kind of communism. I'm an officer in the People's Guard."

Pawel controlled a smile.

"General Panienka?" he said.

"Joke if you will. It's coming."

She sat there drinking and chattering until without warning a thump sounded on the ceiling above them. Pawel forced himself not to look up. He watched the woman. She did not look up. Nor did she look at him. Nothing changed in her expression. There was not the slightest indication that she had noticed. But the flow of her conversation ceased, and she sat brooding, staring at the floor.

He was growing uncomfortable when she said for no apparent reason, "A man like you, such a prince. You should have a girlfriend."

"It's a difficult time for love."

She grunted. "No invader has ever stopped love between the boys and the girls."

"The Germans are the worst we have ever endured."

"Yes, yes, the Germans, the Germans. They're bastards, all right. They're sending lots of Poles up the smokestacks, too. But at least they're scouring Poland clean of Jews."

"Don't say such things", he said vehemently. "The Jews are *people*!"

She did not immediately answer but gave him one of her badger looks.

"People? Who said they weren't people?"

"But if it is true what they say—killing millions of people! Think of it!"

"It *is* true."

"But that is impossible!"

"Don't you believe your own brother? Bronek told you all this a long time ago."

"Yes, he did, but it was too incredible. No civilized nation would do such a thing."

"What is civilization?" she snorted. "Just a little village that got too big and too bold. So the enemy village comes along and rams pointed sticks into all the babies and takes the women back for slaves. And the men run away, except the foolish boys who

432

throw themselves on the invader's knives. Then the winner steals all the useful things, burns the houses and temples, and goes back to his own village for a big supper and a big sleep. After raping somebody for a nightcap, of course. That's civilization, boy."

"You have a pessimistic view of existence."

"Speak simple. I'm not smart like you."

"I think you're saying that nothing changes."

"That's right. Nothing! Instead of a band of a hundred stupid savages, we have a million smart savages. What's the difference in that, I ask you? Millions and millions of people killed—and lots more to die before they're finished—hell, doesn't that tell you something? When they kill millions by a signature on a paper, what's one little dumb life worth, eh? Life is cheap."

"We must show them that *we* are not savages. We must live by the conviction that each human life—even the humblest—is of infinite worth. Every soul is an icon of Christ."

"God, you idealists! You'd save even the Jews."

"Yes. And I would save a German if he were an innocent victim."

"Are the Jews innocent? Look, they're rich. They stick by themselves. They smell. Those pampered Jewesses seduce our Polish boys. Their men chase after our girls—"

"Enough", said Pawel in disgust. "In my entire life I have not once seen anything like that—except, on occasion, the smell. Their tanners smell bad because hides smell. Our tanners smell bad, too. If one Jew smells bad you say all Jews smell bad; but if a Pole smells bad you say, 'That man should take a bath.' If one Jew is rich you say all Jews are rich; if a Pole is rich you say, 'What a lucky fellow!' Don't you see how full of contradictions your mind is?"

Baba Yaga brushed his arguments aside.

"You know, I like it when you're rude. It means there's a man inside those pants."

"By such reasoning you must think the Germans are the best of men, the real men! For they are very rude indeed."

"Ah, you intellectuals!"

She sighed, slapped her hands on her knees, and heaved herself upright.

"Time to go, Nice Boy."

Exasperated, he said, "It has been a pleasure, General."

She gave him a sardonic grimace.

Pausing by the stairwell, she turned and peered straight up at the ceiling over the kitchen table, then stared at Pawel and raised her eyebrows. Without another word she creaked and groaned her way downstairs and disappeared.

\*   \*   \*

Archive, 24 March 1943

Beneath her sneering there is a legitimate question: What is a real man?

The distinction between male and female is fundamental to the human species. Yet within the male principle there is a broad variety of expression. The differences between souls is greater than the differences between faces. David and me, for example.

How strange it seems to me that God has placed him in my life, and me in his—if indeed this dwelling together under a single roof is the divine will. Last autumn it seemed to me that only the madness of the world, or the tyranny of the meaning-less, could have arranged it. Now I sense that there is more at work in this than I had first supposed.

Even so, it is a grief to me that this best of souls—the fruit of all that is good in Judaism—is dependent on one such as me, a most disordered representative of Christianity.

What, really, is God doing here?

\*   \*   \*

No one else came into the shop that week. No human shadows passed the windows. Not even patrol trucks went by at the end of the street. After dark, Pawel went out surreptitiously to cut, break, and tear dead limbs off the solitary lime tree in the courtyard. Tadeusz's rusty saw was employed with great expenditure of energy to portion the branches into short logs. For two days they kept the bedroom warm this way. On the third day the last *sitra ahra* book had gone up into the sky, and the solid fuel was entirely gone. The chill settled into the apartment with alarming speed.

An uncomfortable chair was broken up and burned, but this was hardly enough to push back the invading cold. The hot plate was kept on steadily, but it only just prevented the water pipe from freezing.

"What will we do, Pawel?" David asked.

"I keep hoping that one of our *benefactors* will appear soon. I suspect they're biding their time until I'm desperate enough to unbury some rare treasures for them."

"Could it be they are not even thinking of you? Maybe they are huddling in their own apartments."

"Possibly. But wherever he is, I do not think the count is suffering from the cold. No, he is manipulating the effects of this winter just as he manipulates everything that comes under his influence."

"You have mentioned him before, this man. Why is his face in my mind, though I have never seen him? A twisted face."

"It is a plain enough face. He is completely ordinary. It is the inside of the man that is twisted."

"Of course, in a sense we are all twisted", David pointed out in a philosophical tone. "The loss of our metaphysical—"

"Yes, in one way or another we are all damaged."

"What is it that has damaged him?"

"It has names. But it is more accurate to say that he is the kind of person who turns people into things—things that he uses."

435

"Is he a fascist?"

"Only for the sake of expedience. If the communists were in power, he would be a communist. If democracy, you would never find a better democrat. Of course, before the war, he was a nobleman. The latter still provides him some status with the Germans. They are a strange blend of pragmatism and romance. They have not lost their love of titles."

"Let us talk about him no more, Pawel. It is a bitter day."

"Unless we find some coal, it will be a bad night."

"Are there no other blankets? Could we search? There are trunks in the attic."

"There is nothing of worth in them."

"Are you certain?"

"When I took over the shop, I opened them up and found my grandmother's letters, embroidered handkerchiefs, and mounds of invoices from the days of the House of Wisdom. Useless things. Nothing that would help us now. I doubt you will find a blanket or a cabbage in all those dusty old wrecks. I shut it up years ago and looked no deeper."

"Perhaps we should look. We might find things to burn."

"Go ahead, if it will pass a few hours. I am going down to the shop in case one of our benefactors happens to think of us."

The shop windows were frosted heavily. He had obtained another *Hamman* for Haftmann, and spent a quarter hour opening it here and there at random. When he spoke the printed words aloud, white clouds of vapor came from his lips:

"*True poetry is a natural form of prophecy.*"

He was watching the vapor dissipate when shouts came through the ceiling.

"Pawel, Pawel, Pawel!"

He bolted up the staircases and within seconds was in the attic, standing panting before David.

"Silence!" he said angrily. "Have you lost your mind? You could kill us "

436

"I'm sorry", David said, looking anything but repentant. He moved excitedly from trunk to trunk.

"Look, look!"

On the floor, beside a battered wooden case decorated with Galician folk art, lay a white satin gown unwrapped from its oilcloth covering. What woman ancestor had owned it? At how many dress balls had it been worn?

"This was beneath it!"

A hand-stitched coverlet, deep blue with white flowers embroidered around the edges, and in the center a heart, a cross, and his name, *Pawelek*, stitched in light-blue thread.

"I remember this", said Pawel, musing, stroking the azure border.

"There are feathers inside, I think", said David. "Very warm. And it smells strange."

The trunk was lined with cedar, and sachets of lavender and sage were tucked in the four corners, which accounted for the smell. Apart from that it was empty.

"No cabbage, Pawel, but look over here. It is like finding buried treasure!"

Lying on the floor beside a steamer trunk were bundles of receipts tied with string.

"Look inside", said the boy triumphantly.

Halfway down was a block of something that looked like white marble wrapped in wax.

David broke off a piece and said, "Close your eyes."

The man obeyed.

"Open your mouth."

When he did so, a shard of almond-flavored rock was placed on his tongue and began to melt.

"Wedding cake!" Pawel exclaimed. "This must have been my grandmother's. See, the icing is like Roman architecture. It is unbelievable—so well preserved."

This trunk, like the other, was dry and lined with cedar. The

437

cake had long ago fallen from the icing; the crumbs were stale sand. Beneath it they found a sealed tin that contained candies resembling red and green Venetian glass beads fused into a single clump. When broken up and sucked, they were a great delight.

At the bottom of the trunk, they found a metal casket containing photographs yellowed with age. Pawel did not recognize many of the people in them, although there were some little boys whose faces looked familiar, for they resembled his brothers. They were in fact his uncles. They had been dressed by nannies in the constraining, ornate "best" of the day, platinum hair slicked down, lips curved like scimitars, and Slavic eyes glaring into the cyclops eye of the camera.

There indeed was Tadeusz, scowling with arms crossed on his chest—at ten years of age already a curmudgeon. And here his own father looking extremely sensitive and pained. Pawel had never seen the man look so, and was shocked to find his own face reflected back through a lens of sixty years' depth. Two of Papa's brothers resembled Jan and Bronek. The rest of the uncles he had never met. The only other identifiable figure was Masha's mother, Aunt Irma, a sweet princess surrounded by a troop of fierce little militarists pledged to protect her.

Holding up another photograph, David asked, "Who is this boy dressed in white?"

"That is me at my First Holy Communion."

He remembered walking home from church in a luminous cloud, carrying within himself the first experience of sacred Presence, a passion flower bursting hotly in his heart. It was the happiest moment of his childhood.

In the photograph, he wore a white shirt, short white pants, a white jacket with a white carnation in the lapel, a white armband with gold lettering, white knee-stockings, and white shoes. He was holding a long white candle. Black eyes. Black lips. Black hair slicked sideways.

"You look serious."

"Yes, David, I took life so seriously it nearly killed me."

Serious? Yes. As the photographer pressed the shutter button, one of his brothers said, "Pawel looks just like a *girl*!" and Jan and Bronek rolled giggling around the floor like two wrestling chipmunks.

"So do you, Jan and Bronek, so do you!" growled Grandfather, which did not help matters. In fact, Jan and Bronek had inherited their burly frames and their blunt faces from Grandfather himself.

For many years after, Pawel avoided glimpses of himself in mirrors and cringed at the thought of photographs. Fortunately, at some point in history he sprouted shoulders and grew a jaw. His eyebrows ceased to be arched pencil lines, and his lips turned from the color of wet, overripe berries to a more manly hue. But it happened far too late to be of much help.

Gazing at a photograph of smiling nuns, he said, "When I was a child we often went to the church of the Visitation. The sisters were so good to us. My mother loved them because she had wanted to enter their convent when she was a girl. But she met my father in the Catholic Youth Movement and that was that. When he died my mother went to live with relatives at Mazowiecki. She had so little of her own. My father left us nothing."

"My family too has suffered want", David said. "Even so, we have been blessed. King Stephan protected us from the Cossacks and gave us many rights. In the seventeenth century our family took up the textile trade. We have been scholars and rabbis and singers, but always the labor of our hands has been with cloth. I too will one day be a tailor."

"You should be a philosopher. You have an inquiring mind. I must say it is like a bear-trap."

David smiled. "One can be a philosopher and still labor by the sweat of his brow. It is a good thing to work. Philosophy is pleasure."

"It feels like work to me."

The boy looked pensive. "Sometimes I have a longing to go to *Eretz Yisrael*. Oranges and pomegranates grow on trees there. One is never cold. I would like to be a person who digs up the ancient places."

"An archaeologist? Yes, you would be good at that. You would read ruins as you read books."

David laughed.

Picking up a photograph of a wealthy country house, Pawel said, "This was my grandfather's original home. It's in the Tatras."

"Was your family rich, Pawel?"

"No. We only appeared to be rich. An ancestor of mine, an army officer, was given a few hundred hectares of forest and upper pastures by King Stephan in the sixteenth century. He built it into an estate that grew steadily for two hundred and fifty years after his death. One of his descendants became a count."

"Then *you* are a count!" David declared.

Pawel waved this away. "We are all counts. Everyone in Poland is a count."

"Not everyone", David replied. For an instant their eyes met, then looked away.

In silence they sifted through more pictures—deer hanging from trees, a dance in the palace ballroom, a religious procession, a tilting hay wagon on top of which children grinned at the camera.

"What happened to your family after you became nobility?" David asked.

"During my great-grandfather's lifetime our holdings began to decline. My family forgot their connections to peasant stock and entertained dreams of grandeur. They borrowed too much money and wasted it. The Russians and the Hungarians came and went. We never really recovered. We lost our strength. And then we lost our nerve. The estate was sold before I was born. The family scattered. My father and his brother were living in Warsaw. None of the other brothers could take on the enormous debts that had accumulated."

"What did your father and your uncle do here?"

"My uncle inherited our huge library and brought it up to the city and opened this shop. My father was working in a law firm and had already anchored himself here. You know, my father once said that in his youth he wanted to be a historian and write books about Poland. He loved our country very much. But he was told that there was no future in history—"

"A strange idea—"

"Well, he believed it and became a clerk. He worked in an office over on a side street, off Krakowskie, near Holy Cross church, which contained the heart of Chopin. Many wealthy people were my father's regular customers. It was a suffering for him, because he had grown up in a 'palace'. My father and uncle often talked of it as if it were the estate of a prince. I first saw it when I was driven past it in a carriage as a child. I was surprised to see that it was only a big house—a very big house, mind you—surrounded by a prosperous farm. The new owners waved at us from the terrace. My grandmother wept. Once, I looked inside its windows—a splendid place. Then I understood why my grandparents grieved for it. They were living in a rented house on their old estates. We visited it every summer."

"And in winter, where did you live?"

"I grew up in an apartment near the Saski Gardens."

"Near the Saski Gardens?" David said with a wondering look. "So did I. What street?"

"Zielna."

"We lived on Wielka. My father was born there and so was I. We moved to Zamenhofa Street when I was ten."

"Wielka, you say. That is right across the wall from Zielna."

441

Man and youth now stared into the past, saying nothing for a time.

At last David picked up another photograph.

"And who is this, Pawel? A *prister*?"

Looking closely at the photo, so aged it was sepia brown, he saw a tall young man in a cassock, very handsome, standing by the front door of the "palace" at Zakopane. His arms were crossed, the expression of his face grave and ascetic.

"Yes, a priest", Pawel said. "A friend of our family, he must have been. Or perhaps the local parish priest."

He turned the photo over and found written on the back: *Fr. Nicholas Tarnowski*.

Startled, Pawel's heart began to hammer. Added to this was a surge of terror.

His eyes flaring, his chest heaving, he tore the photo into small pieces and flung them away.

David stared at him in amazement. "Why did you do that?"

"I don't know", Pawel gasped.

"Was that man not a good person?"

"I don't know," Pawel whispered, "I don't know."

"Did he hurt you?"

"No. Yes. He frightened me once when I was a child."

Pawel stood and walked to the attic window, where he spent several minutes gazing out at the night. Staring into his past as if through lens after lens of telescoping significance, he saw in stark clarity the meaning of so much that he had witnessed as a child, and not understood until this moment.

If Great-Uncle had abandoned his high calling in favor of alcohol and indolence, what had been the reason? He had spent time in prison. Why? The secret shame, known by the elders of the family, had been shrouded always in cryptic references.

*It is for the best*, Babscia whispered as she walked from the grave of the one-eyed man.

*He was my brother*, Ja-Ja replied. *He was not always like that.*

442

Then Ja-Ja sobbing, *It devoured everything! Everything!*

What was *it*? The failure? The alcohol? The prison?

Or was it the playing? The stripping and forcing and smothering play. The devouring play. Was the dream reality and reality the dream, inverted in Pawelek's mind as the paws pulled his limbs from their protective knot and nailed him to the cruciform of that pleasure? Slowly, the priest fell and fell and fell into the mouth of Wrog, and played as he fell, the priest reshaping himself into the red-eyed bear in a series of small choices that became bigger and bigger as he plunged to the bottom of the pit.

*This is when he is most dangerous*, said the Child to the boy with a new name. *For that which seems harmless but is not harmless leads downward to the bottomless pit.*

As Great-Uncle's jaws had closed over Pawelek, the bear was eaten even as it ate the child.

The unknown shadow he had seen in the mirror days before stepped forward and lifted its face, seeking to meet his eyes, the hands held out in supplication, the mouth open but unable to plead, the single eye sightless, sickly fire flickering in the other socket.

Now Pawel knew—knew conclusively what had happened. He saw for the first time many things about his world, and about himself, that he had not understood until this moment. Throughout these torturous revelations he remained motionless, as if mesmerized, staring through the attic window into the darkness. All the while, David regarded him with a sober, reflective look, listening to his soul-speech—the anguish and horror pouring from the man without a sound.

At last the boy got up.

"Pawel?"

There was no response.

"Pawel", he said again, touching the man's arm.

Pawel shuddered, his eyes still staring into the well of the past.

443

"Speak to me, Pawel."

"Speak?" The word was a long exhalation.

"Are you all right?"

"I am all right", he replied, wiping a hand across his brow, a measure of awareness returning to his eyes, as if he were coming home from a long journey.

"You saw something?"

"I saw something."

"About the past?"

Pawel nodded.

"It was pain?"

"It was pain."

They stood side by side for some minutes, saying nothing, until Pawel shook himself and turned to David.

"Thank you."

"For what are you thanking me, Pawel?"

"For your presence here."

"I am happy to be here."

Then, in a youthful and not altogether inappropriate effort to change the mood of the evening, David grinned and declared, "I have saved the best for last! There are more surprises! Very great and delightful surprises! You will laugh when you see them! You will dance!"

"I do not think so", Pawel whispered.

In answer, the boy merely hopped across the room, clownlike, toward a jumble of cartons. So buffoonish was this—indeed, so completely out of character—Pawel could not help but produce a feeble smile.

David lifted a circular box papered with a design of purple irises.

"The surprises", he announced theatrically. "Come, look."

Inside they found small toy trumpets and glass angels.

"I remember these from my childhood", Pawel murmured. "They were old even then—Christmas decorations from the attic of my grandfather's last home. It seems my Uncle Tadeusz inherited them. They have been buried here for years, and I didn't realize . . ."

Pawel's eyes widened as he picked up an angel and revolved it carefully in his fingers.

"I remember now", he breathed.

"What do you remember?" David pressed.

"Nothing."

"No, tell me, Pawel, tell me. I want to know."

"Why do you want to know?" said Pawel, half-listening, fighting the suction of the ancient dread.

"I want to know because you are my friend", David insisted. "And because I have given you the key to my house, and now you must give me the key to your house."

"What?" Pawel stared at the boy, trying to make sense of this. At last he recalled scraps of their dialogues and looked down at the angel in his hand.

"It was a hot summer day", he began slowly. As the memory took him, color returned to his face and his voice steadied. "The grownups had gone to Zakopane for ice, and I was left alone with my great-uncle. It was easy to escape him. Easier as I grew older. He never went to the attic. I was safe there. The angels were like soldiers, holy and brave. I loved them so. They were my brothers, my friends. I spent whole days lining them up row upon row. The light through the attic window was gold. The dust on the sunbeams dropped slowly through the air like snow falling on retreating armies. The angels were victorious and the invisible devils fled. When they were gone, utterly defeated, I blew the little tin horns."

"Like this", David declared with a bright smile, picking up a green one and blowing a sharp atonal note.

"Yes, like that."

"Then what did you do?"

"Then I blew another."

445

David picked up another horn and blew into it. The second note was higher. He picked up a third instrument, which was gold and emblazoned with the image of a white hart, and handed it to Pawel.

"Show me."

Pawel put it to his lips and forced a lower note from it.

David laughed like a child.

"There was a little drum too", said Pawel, casting his eyes about the floor. "A real drum with red and white braided ropes and a skin top."

David picked up the candy tin and rapped it.

"Boom, boom, boom!" he said with a grin. He chose a red whistle and blew it.

*Tweet, tweet, tweet!*

*Boom, bam, boom!*

*Trill, trill, tweet!*

*Rat, tat, tat!*

"What then?"

"Then I marched around the attic."

"Yes? You were leading your troops?"

"I was leading my angels against the forces of darkness", Pawel murmured, his tone implying the futility of such childish fantasies.

"To the east you pushed them back!" David declared. "To the west you pushed them back! To the north and to the south you pushed them back into the regions of darkness from which they came!"

"A dream, a dream . . ."

"You were *very* brave!"

"Brave? Though I thought I was, I was not."

"But you were, Pawel! You were!" David cried. "For it is in the attics and the cellars of life where we must be bravest of all. It is in the fiery furnace that the three young men dance their praises of the Most High! So too in the furnace of life's afflic-

446

tions! Yes, I can see you now! Little Pawel blew his trumpet and rapped his drum. He marched around the attic of his palace, smiling ecstatically!"

David began to march about the room, blowing a horn, rapping the tin. So ridiculous was this behavior that Pawel was momentarily distracted from his pain.

"Boom, boom, boom", said David.

As he passed Pawel he grabbed him by the arm.

"Like this! Do as I do!"

But Pawel could not force himself to follow for more than a few steps. David continued to march in a circle around the attic, pounding his feet, tramping along the tops of trunks slammed closed, *bang*, up and down, up and down, round and round, *tweet, boom, bam*.

David threw his arms in the air, and his body whirled. He stumbled, righted himself, laughing, and spun himself again.

"Come, Pawel, like this. Just dance!"

Pawel sat down upon a trunk and continued to observe as the boy twirled about the room, creating spiral wakes in the dust, inarticulate cries spilling from his lips. And it seemed that his feet moved upon waters, and his wings beat upon currents of wind, soaring as angels do when they dance through infinite space.

Pawel saw with a seeing beyond all words that this was the true story told by saints and zaddiks. Though he did not join in the dance, he was enthralled and for the duration of this extraordinary performance remained entirely entranced.

David suddenly stopped and said with a worried look, "The noise!"

"The noise", said Pawel, stricken with a bolt of realism. He went to the window, drew back the curtain, and looked out.

"Nothing!"

David pulled off his shoes, tiptoed to the stairwell, and peered down, cupping his ear.

447

"Nothing!"

He dropped his arms and grinned, holding the candy drum in one hand and the tin flute in the other. His chest heaved beneath the heavy felt coat. The fringes of his prayer shawl dangled unevenly. The cuffs of his pants had fallen over his ankles during the dance. The bare feet on the floor were white marble. His lips were blue, cheeks and ears bright red, eyes flashing.

Pawel gazed at him as if he were an apparition, a blade of fire, a symmetry of light, a form that occupied space like revelation itself. A solid word that had unfolded from the chrysalis of metaphor.

Shattered phrases careened through his mind: *Image! Language! Dialect! Love! Gift! Deny! Console! Desolate! Father! Son! Beloved! Elijah!*

A galaxy of angels descended about the boy, swords drawn, eyes fixed left and right, above and below—guardians, messengers, warriors, and a fiery six-winged seraph vibrating the air with sacred ardor.

*Elijah*, said the seraph.

Pawel stared.

*Elijah?*

"Why are you troubled, Your Majesty? Do not look so worried! We are safe!" The boy wiped away droplets of perspiration that had appeared on his brow despite the cold. Bursts of frosty breath came from his lips.

Blinking rapidly, shaking his head free of the hallucination, Pawel mumbled, "We should go down to the kitchen. We will freeze to death here."

## 18

They made a supper feast of cabbage and icing, and ate the meal slowly, savoring each bite. To sweeten the last of the tea, they dropped candies into the glasses of pale brown liquid. Whenever David looked up, he found Pawel considering him with an unfathomable expression.

In the early evening there came a loud insistent rapping on the shop door, and Pawel went down to answer it. Haftmann stood on the step, stamping his feet from the cold. Beyond him, a car rumbled at idle, clouds of exhaust spewing from its tailpipe.

"May I come in?"

Without waiting for a reply, Haftmann removed his officer's hat and stepped inside.

Pawel closed the door behind him and cast a look to the ceiling, hoping that David would make no noise.

"Excuse me, please, for disturbing you after hours. It has been a hideous week. Many Poles are being evacuated . . . the labor shortage, you know. Not that it is any affair of mine. Some have approached us with a view to buying their art collections. I have been in Lodz and Krakow tracking down some priceless paintings that the underground, in their haste, almost permitted to be destroyed. I have saved them."

As Pawel remained without speaking, staring at him, Haftmann cleared his throat, adjusted his body to a more official bearing, and said, "I suppose you are going to ask about your manuscript. Unfortunately, there has been a delay. My secretary has been ill for weeks. I am severely understaffed. But I promise you I will bring it back at the earliest opportunity."

Haftmann opened the door and gestured. A soldier carried a heavy coal sack through the entrance and threw it down on the floor.

"Severe weather these days. I thought perhaps you might be suffering from the fuel shortage."

"I am grateful", Pawel replied in a subdued tone. "Thank you."

Though he would not have thought it possible, something close to affection for Haftmann arose within him. He went to his desk and returned with a book.

"This is for you. A gift."

"Hamman!" said Haftmann, visibly moved. "This is really too kind. I will not forget it."

When Haftmann had gone, Pawel dragged the sack down to the cellar and started a fire in the furnace. There was enough coal for more than a week if used sparingly. But for one night he would indulge in a blast of glorious heat. He got it roaring, and soon he could hear the water in the boiler rumbling with a delicious sound. He unbent his aching bones. He opened his coat and undid the scarf. He smelled bad. Tonight he was surely due the opulent luxury of a bath. As he mounted the staircase, he heard the radiators clanking all the way up to the third floor.

"It is wonderful", the boy said. "What happened?"

"A benefactor."

"I hope it was not the twisted one. In any event, bless him."

"It was the half-twisted one. Bless him doubly!"

The room was so warm they began to sweat. David removed his coat and scarf, two sweaters Pawel had given him, and his sockless shoes and sat wiggling his toes beside the kitchen radiator.

He sniffed.

"I do not smell pleasant? No? It has been too long between baths."

"I do not smell very polite myself. This is a good opportunity to wash. You go ahead. I will keep myself occupied eating more Roman architecture."

"*Tak!*"

It had been their custom during the warmer weather, or when there was fuel, to take turns bathing once a week. The bathroom contained only a sink and a tub designed for someone the size of Baba Yaga. During the cold snap the waterlines to the bath had frozen and burst, and Pawel had been forced to shut them off at the source. The pipe to the kitchen still worked, however, and before the situation became too miserable for cleanliness he and David had established a routine of warming a cauldron of water on the hot plate for cursory wash-downs. This they now set out to do.

When David went into the bathroom, Pawel sat down at the table to nibble the chips of icing that remained. The heat made him extremely drowsy. He had not slept the night before, nor had he slept properly for weeks. His eyes closed against his will, and when he awoke a few minutes later he thought he must have dozed for hours.

There was no sound from the bathroom, and he concluded that David was finished and had gone up to the attic for one reason or another, perhaps to rummage for more "treasure".

He opened the bathroom door, rubbing his eyes.

David looked up, surprised, his mouth open, his eyes like black pools. He was stripped to the waist and soaped along his arms and neck.

Pawel turned away and mumbled, "Excuse me. I thought you were finished."

"I'm almost done", David said in a bantering tone. "Be patient!"

Pawel entered the bedroom and stood by the window, trying to gaze out into the opaque night, out beyond the image burned onto the screen of his consciousness.

A few minutes later the boy appeared.

"Your turn", he said and stood by the door, wrapped in a towel, grinning.

Pawel's brow furrowed, and his eyes took in the exposed landscape in a glance. He nodded and swiftly turned his gaze to the floor. David cast a curious look at him, then went back to the kitchen.

"This desire is not good", Pawel whispered. "But where do I go to escape it?"

*The man you seek is within you, my little son.*

"When will this end?"

*They are not long, the days of your purification. When they are completed, you will understand.*

He put his head in his hands. The power of the image was cut in half, then by halves again as the minutes ticked over. Distant gunshots competed with a bell.

Later, when David was sleeping soundly on the mattress by the wood stove, Pawel drew over him the hand-stitched quilt with the heart and the cross and the name. The boy's breath was like the wind coursing through wheat fields or a child sighing in dreams. Pawel did not switch on the light for fear of waking him. Instead, he groped blindly toward the staircase and went up to the attic.

It was cooler there, and he shivered. Going by touch he found a candle and lit it with a match. The light was blinding, the shadows leaping up to the peak of the roof.

He blew a trumpet softly, just above the level of silence.

The future was a wall into which he could not run, and the present a cage in which he was permitted to run only in circles. Was the past the only door through which he might go? Could he return to it and not be trapped in it? Could he undo what had been done to him?

In the tin trunk, he found a red-and-white national flag. A card with his name on it was pinned to the silk.

*To my grandson Pawel Casimir Tarnowski*

He held the square of cloth in his hands for a time, then unfolded it. Wrapped inside was a large silver medallion attached to a stained crimson-and-white ribbon. Embossed on the metal were the words:

## + PROWADZ NAS BOZE + [1]

Above the words was an image of an angel. He turned it over.

## + MADROSC + [2]

Above this was an image of the Mother of God of Czestochowa.

\* \* \*

He woke early. The dawn was near. The streets were still silent. David stirred on the mattress by the wood stove but did not wake.

The electricity was off. Pawel dressed himself in his business suit and put the medal in the jacket pocket. Going by touch in the semidarkness, he went down to the ground floor and seated himself at his desk.

There, in a circle of candlelight he wrote:

*Archive in a tin box*

He crossed it out and began again:

*My dearest—*

After some hesitation, he addressed it to Elzbieta, but this did not seem to be exact. To whom, then, was he writing?

*My dearest Kahlia—*

---

[1] "Lead us, God!"
[2] "Wisdom!"

No, this also was inexact.

*My dearest Sophia*—

He shook his head and crossed it out. Then after some minutes of concentration, he leaned over the desk and penned the following:

A note to myself.

Pawel,

Last night I held my grandfather's legacy in my hand, its word purchased by countless martyrdoms over nearly two millennia. As I held it and prayed, I offered my heart totally to God. The image of David Schäfer came before me then, and I saw his goodness, his belovedness in the eyes of God. I saw too (though I cannot explain how it came to me or in what language I understood it) that he is a word of love, though an imperfect love—as all human love is—a word spoken to me for a reason that I cannot yet comprehend.

As I lay my desire for human love upon the altar of God, I felt fire touch my heart. It was a burning. Like dying. Yet I knew that in this dying I am being born.

This is my final entry in the archives. No longer do I need these mirrors, for all around me are windows and doors.

He looked up, hearing sounds in the kitchen above. David was making their meager breakfast. He must go stoke the fire in the furnace and complete the letter later.

\*   \*   \*

David cleared away the dishes from the table and brought glasses of tea for them both. He sat on the edge of his chair and waited for Pawel to meet his eyes.

"Pawel, you are angry?"

"Angry?"

"Yes, you are angry with me."

"No, I am not angry."

"You have not looked at me this morning. You have not spoken. Once again I have offended you."

"I have been thinking of many things. Forgive me, I did not mean to exclude you."

"I have offended you."

"You have not offended me."

"Pawel, there are many things that differ in our cultures. Sometimes I am not sensitive."

"It is nothing you have done."

"My habits, perhaps?"

"No, nothing."

"I can tell there is something. I can read hearts."

"Can you?" Pawel smiled.

"I can!"

"I believe you."

"You do not believe me; that much I read in your eyes."

"Then please read the passage in my eyes states you are without fault in any matter whatsoever."

"Yes, I read it, but there is something else. Its meaning is hidden from me."

They sipped from their glasses of tea.

"Pawel, you wish me to leave. It is time for me to go."

"That is not in my thoughts."

"I endanger your life. This is true."

"This has been true from the moment you arrived. But you have been a great help to me."

"Now my work is finished and it is time for me to go."

"The work is finished, yes, but you may stay as long as you wish."

"I do not want to go, yet I feel in my soul that my presence is a great burden to you."

Pawel shook his head, unable to speak. How could words ever explain this gift? How could fire be translated into the language of men? *If I were to tell you, David, that I am dying because of you, and I am also being born because of you, could you understand it?*

"I am the burden," said Pawel quietly, "not you, my friend."

David was completely surprised by this and watched the man go to the kitchen sink to splash cold water on his face.

"Have you considered the possibility that a person might serve another in ways that are not visible?"

"Yes, Pawel, I think it may be so." Then, considering it further: "Yes, it's certainly so."

"I'm glad you understand."

"I did not say I understand. I only say I believe it's this way. Why is it this way?"

"You will have to ask someone wise."

"You looked at me. Just now, you looked at me."

"What do you mean? I often look at you."

"It was the look my father sometimes gave me."

"Oh."

"Am I like a son to you, Pawel?"

"Yes, a little like a son."

"And a friend?"

"Yes, that too."

"But a young friend who says childish things."

"Sometimes it is so. But I see the man you are becoming. A good man who will walk with me beside the Vistula, when this war is over, telling me wise things and correcting my poor philosophy."

David smiled. "I see now that you are not angry with me."

"You should have believed me from the beginning. I am not angry with you. I have never been angry with you."

Furrowing his brow, more perplexed than ever, David said, "But there is that thing—I see it in your heart. It remains."

"Someday, on a spring morning when the invaders have

gone, we will walk in the sun beside the river, and then we will speak of this thing."

"Is it a thing that makes you unhappy?"

"Yes."

"Is it *sitra ahra*?"

"Part of it is good, and part of it is a wound inflicted by the *sitra ahra*."

"This wound, it hurts you?"

"Yes. It hurts me."

"Is it like a stone in your heart? Like the prince?"

"Yes, like that."

"Can you not remove the stone and throw it away?"

"You are very young, David."

"Sometimes the young see things the old do not see."

"More often the old see things the young do not see."

David regarded Pawel for some moments.

"Would you like me to sweep the shop now?"

"That is a good idea."

Pawel was left alone staring at the window, where sunlight was returning earlier each day. Spring was not far off. It seemed to him now that he could gaze very far above the confines of Sophia House, above the broken rim of Stare Miasto, and as Warsaw's battered horizon receded below, there opened before him the curve of the earth.

Destruction had fallen upon everyone, yet the passage of the sun and moon remained constant, the seasons and the tides continued to fulfill their tasks, and even in the islands of life scattered among fires of hatred the trees furled and unfurled their transient palette of color, bearing witness to death and rebirth. Their leaves were waving goodbye to him, though he did not know where he was going. Soaring up over the cities of the night, across the broad earth, he knew that he must float down again among the peoples of the world, for he was one of them.

He remained without moving, watching the sunlight slowly pour across the kitchen floor toward him. He prayed for grace. He asked for wisdom.

It felt like an old Sunday, the kind he had known a long time before the war, before Papa went away. His father and mother would rise early and take his hands, one on each side, and walk through the sleeping city to the earliest Mass as the convent bells tolled the dawn.

"Papa," he would say, "are the bells happy?"

"Oh yes, they are happy."

"Why are they happy?"

"Because they do not ask themselves if they are unhappy. Because they are content to be bells."

Papa was wise.

After Mass the sisters sang, *Non nobis, Domine, non nobis, sed nomini tuo da gloriam*, and Mama wakened Pawel from the slumber induced by glory and incense. Sometimes Papa would carry him home on his shoulders and call out to the cats and the squirrels, "Hear ye, hear ye, all creatures! Bow down before the young prince Pawel Casimir, heir of all Tarnowski titles, scion of the family fortunes."

And Pawel would ride high on his shoulders, one arm wrapped around Papa's forehead, the other hand holding out the little red airplane with four wings and a propeller spinning in the wind, making engine noises with his lips, making Mama and Papa laugh.

Papa would squeeze his ankles tenderly, and they would go home under the chestnut trees to eggs and sausages and chocolate in the parlor. Afterward, Mama would spread out her needlework on her knees and Papa read the newspapers. Pawel would lie on the rose-colored rug in the patches of sunlight streaming through the leaded window panes. He would watch the progress of light. He would kiss the paper angels and listen to the sound of a room where no one is missing.

Down in the shop he found David sweeping the floor.

"To be a father in the realm of the soul", Pawel said. "I would like to be this for you. May I be this for you?"

"Yes, Pawel", David said in a tone of calm deliberation. "This would be good."

As if standing on a threshold of radical departure, they faced each other without speaking, gazing now into a dimension that seemed for both to be wholly undiscovered. This sense of embarkation into a fathomless mystery was in no way daunting; neither was it fraught with emotion. It was a moment of perfect stillness.

At last the boy said, "It is a blessed gift to be a son in the realm of the soul. May I be this for you?"

"Yes", Pawel nodded.

"It is a thing we can make alive between us."

"It is possible. It is that which I doubted."

"The doubting made a darkness. A fear. I saw it there in you. We will remove the stone and throw it into the river."

The angle of the morning sun filled the shop with light. At that moment the door to the street moved slowly on its hinges and opened wide.

## 19

Count Smokrev entered and closed the door.

He surveyed the shop with pleasure, and his eyes lingered on David.

David went white, dropped the broom, and stepped backward toward the staircase.

"You will remain where you are", said Smokrev.

"The shop is closed", said Pawel.

Smokrev turned slowly toward him.

"You have saved the best till last, my dear fellow. Where did you find this exquisite piece of Jewish porcelain?"

"I will go up, Pawel", David murmured.

"You will stay", said Smokrev with effeminate severity, then resumed his saccharine expression.

"Leave my shop."

"I do not think you are in any position to give me commands. Consider your words carefully."

"I am considering. You are invading my place of business."

"One telephone call and your life is over. You will be on your way to the *Umschlagplatz.*"

"You would not do that. You are not a traitor, Count."

"Do not mock me", he said. "I am already a traitor in your eyes and you know it. You fool! In the larger scheme of things *you* are the real traitor, if only you realized it."

"This is not the place for a debate. You will leave."

Smokrev threw his head back and laughed aloud, his mouth open wide, revealing many gold fillings.

"You underestimate me", he said.

"If you choose to betray us, go do it now, but do not play with us."

Smokrev walked about the shop slowly, regally, entertaining a flickering smile, slapping his kid gloves in the palm of one hand.

"There is, of course, another possibility."

"Yes, there is. You can simply leave and go home to enjoy your day of rest. And you can forget what you see here. That is what any decent human being would do."

"I have never pretended to be a decent human being. I am not a hypocrite!"

He went over to Pawel and put his face too close.

"Do you think I am blind? Do you think I cannot see exactly what the situation is here? You are as corrupt as me, you *tapette*. Yes, Goudron told me many things about you, your perversities, your conquests, the way you toyed with his affections only to throw him in the gutters of Berlin with all the world watching!"

"That is not true", Pawel stammered. "It is a lie."

"*It is a lie!*" Smokrev mimicked.

"It *is* a lie."

"Oh, yes, yes, such a very big lie! Goudron had no reason to lie."

"His life was riddled with lies. You know it. So is your life."

The count drew back and struck Pawel a stinging blow on the face with his gloves. More startled than hurt, Pawel did not retaliate.

"Listen to me, you merchant", Smokrev hissed. "You are a failure. You were a mediocre artist and a joke in society—oh, how we used to laugh about you. Nothing has changed. You could not for an instant survive without me and Haftmann providing for you like a kept boy. You have wasted your life and you are grubbing for your furtive pleasures just as we do."

"Even if it were true—which it is not—why would it be of any interest to you?"

Smokrev was taken aback for a few seconds.

"I am not an evil man," he said with a toss of his head, "though of course it must appear to you that I am. I have a jealous temperament. I wish only for freedom to live according to my nature."

"Let *us* be free, then. Be on your way."

"It is not so simple. Let me continue."

Smokrev's mood had changed. He sat down in the captain's chair by the desk, facing Pawel and David.

The boy had never looked more Jewish. The skullcap askew, the tassels of the *tallis* dangling below the hem of his sweater, the sockless shoes—as if he had just arrived from the *shtetl*.

"As you see, I am an impetuous man. If you will overlook my slap, I will forget your vicious criticisms."

As Pawel did not reply, the count went on:

"Let us determine what we have in common, Tarnowski. We are both Poles. We are both men of the world. We have similar pasts."

He held up a hand swiftly to silence Pawel's protest.

"We are both *sympathique* to the cause of culture. We both appreciate . . . beauty."

He cast a subtle glance across the room at David.

"What are you saying? What do you want?"

"This brings me back to the point I raised a minute ago."

"Which is?"

"There is another possibility."

"What is it?"

Smokrev did not immediately respond. He sat gazing at David. The boy stared at the floor.

The count lowered his voice. "He is a danger to you."

"A cost I am willing to bear."

"I can relieve you of your burden. Here you are too close to the ghetto. Eventually they will dig through every closet in this city. I will hide him in my townhouse near the palace. It is an excellent neighborhood. They will not search there. My association with the Reich Culture Chamber protects me."

Pawel was momentarily overwhelmed by the count's suggestion. It was an offer that could not be dismissed without consideration. In this decaying house, water and food and fuel were sporadic at best. Could he and David hope to outlast the occupation when it was entirely possible that the Germans would never leave? It was only a matter of time before the boy was caught.

"David, would you please go make tea for us", Pawel said.

"Thank you, *David*", said the count unctuously.

When the boy had disappeared up the staircase, Pawel turned a cold eye on Smokrev.

"You can speak plainly."

Smokrev crossed his legs and folded his hands on his knees. He began to play with a ring on his forefinger, revolving it again and again, as if musing on what he would say next.

Pawel waited, standing before the count in an attitude of total tension.

"Relax", Smokrev smiled. "Have a seat."

Pawel suppressed his irritation at this reversal of authority and seated himself like an obedient employee.

As the two men regarded each other face-to-face, the sun passed from the shop windows. The blinds turned from gold to gray, casting the room into gloom.

"I am not a cruel man", Smokrev said. "I do not *like* what the Germans are doing. It is not a *pleasure* for me to see so many beautiful young people go up in smoke. I am offering you and the boy a chance to live. Under certain conditions you might be able to continue your *relationship* uninterrupted."

"I do not understand."

"Come, come, you said plain talk."

"What exactly are you proposing?"

"He is your lover. I will save him."

"He is not my lover."

Smokrev threw up his hands. "An impossible man!"

"How would you save him?"

"I will take him to my home in my official car. I am never stopped. To walk there would be too dangerous, even with the proper papers. That wonderful face is unmistakably Jewish. So many eyes watching in the streets. Always they watch—Polish eyes and German eyes. The Resistance hates me, the Germans hate all Jews—a recipe for trouble."

"And then?"

Smokrev smiled, opening wide his arms. "Then, nestled in the bosom of my home, he will be safe. Indeed, we all shall be much safer." The count resumed fidgeting with his rings. "You would be able to see him. I would give you the necessary permits to deliver books of quality to my house, after curfew. You and he can spend the night together there if you wish. I have lovely rooms, a big place; really a pity that it's empty. Before the war we had such enchanting parties. I live only with my servants now—but of course they are most *sympathique*. One visit per month would be about right."

"Once a month?"

"We must not arouse suspicion, you see. Of course, I realize that once a month is not enough for two young people in love. But I'm sure you are no stranger to deprivation."

Pawel did not allow his expression to change.

"How would you arrange his escape?"

"I did not say *escape*. I offer sanctuary. Then, in a few years from now, after Europe has been pacified, there will come a time to reassess the situation. He may even choose to remain with me. I have a country house where he would be happy. There are horses, my orchards, my borzois—I *adore* borzois—and a lovely pond I made for boating on summer nights."

"Give me your word that you will not touch him."

Smokrev drew back, much offended. "Do you think my touch is poison?" he snarled.

Pawel stared at him.

Smokrev huffed and glared. "I offer you life, you idiot!"

464

"Why? What is the cost?"

"Cost?"

"Life has a cost. What is the price you ask?" Pawel insisted.

"Ah, at last you are speaking plainly, Tarnowski", he snorted. "I knew you were a sensible businessman underneath the tortured Catholic conscience. The price is not much. Do you think I do not know what I am—a nobleman living on the last scraps of a dying era—though I still possess a certain charm. The boy has been initiated, has he not? I ask only a share."

Pawel stared at him in disgust.

"Is it a problem that he be shared, Tarnowski? He might like it."

"Get out", Pawel said in a low voice.

"If you cannot bargain on that plane, let us discuss things bluntly. I will give you a great deal of money if you convince the boy to come with me."

"Leave now", said Pawel rising.

"Do not play the outraged idealist with me. Every man on this planet can be bent or bought. Name the price, but spare me your hypocrisy."

Pawel grabbed the count by the lapels of his coat, shook him, and dragged him to the front entrance. Smokrev struggled and lashed back with his gloves, shrieking, "Stop! You will obey me or I will call the SS!"

Pawel let go of his coat and reached over and grabbed Uncle Tadeusz's walking stick. With bared teeth, he lifted it high and was about to bring it down hard on Smokrev's shoulder. The count staggered back, eyes wild with fright. Suddenly Pawel stopped himself and threw the cane to the floor. Smokrev wheeled, scrambled for the door, and went running away down the street.

"Are you all right?" said David, staring at Pawel, who stood by the open door looking as if he had seen death, his eyes snapping, lips curled back, chest heaving. Buttons had popped where his shirt was torn open, his jacket askew across his shoulders.

David put a tray onto the desk, the glasses rattling.

"Where is that man?"

"He has gone."

"Is he the twisted one?"

"Yes."

Pawel slammed the door shut and locked it.

"Upstairs, quickly."

When they stood catching their breath in front of the fortress, Pawel, still enraged, looked this way and that, uncertain about what to do—hide, flee, barricade?

"What happened?" David pleaded, fearing the worst.

The question jolted Pawel out of his confusion.

"He is going to report you to the Germans."

"Are you certain?"

"I have offended his pride. In his need for revenge, he will want no less than our deaths." Pawel paused. "At least he will want my death. He may have other plans for you. We must get away."

"Where will we go?"

"To my cousin's farm. East of the city, about thirty kilometers. We can travel cross-country. She will hide us. But you cannot go anywhere looking like that." He pointed to the *tallis* and the *yarmulke*. "You must leave those."

The boy stared at the fringe of his tallis, and fingered it, frowning, thinking.

"Quickly", Pawel urged. "Please. There may not be much time."

David folded his shawl and removed his cap with a pained expression, and placed them on the lid of a trunk.

Pawel raced downstairs. In the cellar he found his dirty work clothes—the overalls he wore when shoveling coal, a felt hat, a greasy jacket—and ran with them back to the apartment. He closed the door, locked it, and shoved the kitchen table against it. He heaped as many heavy things as he could find on top. Then he careened into his bedroom closet, went through to the attic door, shot the bolt behind him, and stumbled up heavily. He threw the bundle of clothing at David.

"Hurry."

David dressed himself.

"Good, you look like a laborer."

"What about you, Pawel? You can't run across fields and ditches in a business suit. They would know."

"I'll find something else to wear. I need a few minutes to write Masha a note and draw a map for you. If we are separated you won't have any way of finding her."

He was finishing these tasks when a crash echoed two floors below in the shop.

"They're here", Pawel said.

The sound of smashing glass came upon the heels of another crash.

"They're destroying the door. Quickly, now, get out the window. Crawl along the roof to the wall. Then across to the apartments on the other side. Keep low. Do not let anyone see you. Go along the rooftops as far as you can. Then down to the street and head toward the river. When you get there, walk south along the bank. Anyone who sees you will think you're a worker going for a stroll on Sunday. Keep moving until you're out of the city. Then look for a way to cross the river. After that, head northeast to Mazowiecki. Do not hurry. Appear as if you have all the time in the world. Here, take these."

He crammed the note and the map into David's pocket.

"You're coming, Pawel. I cannot go without you."

"I will distract them for a while—enough time for you to get away."

"No!" David cried.

Pawel went to the window. The courtyard was deserted.

"They have not yet thought to surround the building."

Boots hammered on the staircase, followed shortly by battering on the apartment door.

"You *must* leave now!"

David came to Pawel and stood before him motionless, his face contorting in pain.

"*Un az du vest kumen iber a groysn fayer,*" he groaned, "*far groys tsores zoltsu zikh nit farbrenen.*"

"What are these words?"

"A song we sang in the ghetto", David said in a broken voice. "*If you should come across a great fire, do not burn for sorrow.*"

The boy raised his arms toward the man.

"Go!" Pawel said sternly, pushing him away.

David's face crumpled, and he turned toward the window.

"Go", Pawel said again.

The boy climbed onto the boxes. With a final look back into the room, he was out the window and gone.

Pawel immediately began to stack trunks and boxes up the wall until the window was hidden.

He waited patiently for the Germans to find the closet and to break down the attic door. He held a glass angel in one hand and a tin trumpet in the other. He was afraid. But it was not a great fear. When the soldiers and two men in trench coats came up the steps, at the end of the muzzles of their guns they found a thin, tired man sitting on a trunk, looking at them without emotion.

"Where is the Jew?" one of them barked.

Pawel put the prayer shawl over his shoulders and the skullcap on his head.

He stood up.

"Here", he said and pointed a finger at his heart.

468

## 20

After they kicked him down the stairs they took him to join the streams of humanity converging toward the railway station. These people, hounded and frightened, had trailed through the streets carrying children or pushing carts on which their old people and trunks were rocking. At the *Umschlagplatz* the trunks and the dead were pulled from their grasp and left in heaps for sorting.

Flowing by in one such stream, Pawel passed Haftmann, who was inspecting luggage, searching for cultural treasure. In a moment of half-hope he shouted, "Doktor!" But the German looked up to see only an exhausted face sweeping past, indistinguishable from the tide of numbers and names that had no meaning. Haftmann turned away.

With thousands of others, Pawel was packed into a freight train.

In his boxcar there were two hundred.

It was impossible to sit down. The latrine bucket in the corner was already overflowing. The stench of terror was choking.

Trainmen went by on the platform and stopped to light cigarettes. Through a crack in the boards Pawel could see their round red cheeks and the ritual peasant gestures of humorous exchange.

"Trouble on the Byalistok line", one said. "This lot will never see Treblinka."

"Where is it going?"

"Oświęcim."

"Does Krakow know unexpected guests are arriving for lunch?"

Then the trainmen were pulled back into history as the car jerked and banged forward, forward, forward, and the freight groaned and cried. The wailing of the babies and the small children was the worst. And the arguments. The pleading and lamentation. At times it was totally silent, though never for long. Cold and stench ruled everything. People tried to maneuver closer to the breathing hole at the roof-line. Old men and women fainted but could not collapse because of the press of bodies that held everyone upright. Families that had become separated cried out names, seeking to know if a loved one was in the car.

Mama!    Zdenka!    Babscia!    Papa!    Marta!
Leonhard!    My God, My God, why have you forsaken me!
Tsipora!    *Shtiler, shtiler. Shhhhhh!*    Eugene!
Pappa!    Be still, be still.    Mamma!
*Shtiler, kind mayns, veyn nit, veyn nit.*
My child! My child!
*Hear, O Israel, the Lord is our God, the Lord is One!*
Anna!    Grandfather!
Berthe!    Gunther!    Ruth!    Mama!    Papa!
*Israel, my firstborn, is my son.*
We shall rise like incense to the Lord!
Please, please do not imply such things.
Do not frighten the children!
Do not cry.    Do not cry.
*Israel, my firstborn, is my son.*
*Adonai, Adonai!*
*Adonai!*

And so it went, hour after hour. Long past nightfall the train rolled to a stop on a siding, and the people huddled together like a frozen mass.

"Mr. Edelman is dead", someone said.

470

"Mrs. Koz also!"

"It is unclean!" cried others.

"What are we to do? What are we to do?"

"Nothing, nothing can be done!"

"*Sh'ma Yisrael . . .*"

Others yelled and pounded the walls, calling for help.

Pawel was pressed into the corner beneath the breather hole. He found a foothold on a bulging plank and pulled himself up. Outside, the world was deserted. Far ahead the engine hissed and steamed. There was fire in the sky.

"What do you see?" many voices cried.

"The sky is glowing red", said Pawel. "A rain of sparks is rising from tall chimneys on the horizon."

A clamor of speculation broke out all around:

"It's heavy industry. You see, they're going to use us for cheap labor."

"The smell is terrible."

"It could be a slaughterhouse."

"No, we stopped beside a garbage dump."

"No, no, a canning factory."

"Will they make us stay here long?"

"They cannot possibly. More people will die tonight if they keep us out in this weather."

"Mama! Papa!"

Again the cries rose and fell like waves on an eternal beach.

Two German guards strolled by, laughing in the crisp night air.

"Ask them, ask them, young man."

"What are those chimneys over there?" Pawel shouted through the hole.

The guards exchanged a look and one of them answered, "They are baking bread for you. Night and day they bake bread."

But no one knew if this should be taken seriously.

471

By morning, more people had died, and others were coughing and shaking with chill. Many wept. Some were in hysterics—their mouths opened, but no sound emerged.

Pawel had been awake all night. He looked continuously at the square of red light until it turned to the color of grease. The sky was heavily overcast. In his jacket pocket he found a stub of pencil and an old receipt from Sophia House. It was the invoice for the paper he had purchased to print Soloviev's tale of the Antichrist. On its back he wrote:

David,
My son, my friend. Never have I wanted to live so much as I do now. I go down into darkness in your place. I give you my life. I carry your image within me like an icon. This is my joy. I go down at last to sleep, but my heart is awake.
                                            Pawel

When he had finished, he took the red-and-white ribbon from around his neck and the heavy medallion to which it was attached. He wrapped the medallion in the sheet of paper and bound the package with the ribbon. Carefully, he printed the name *David Schäfer* on the outside.

Sometime later a group of Polish trackmen came grumbling along beside the rails with tamping bars across their shoulders. As the last one approached, Pawel hurled the package through the breather hole, and it landed at his feet.

The man stooped and picked it up.

"Please", Pawel called. "Please, I beg you to find the person whose name is on this package."

"Am I a Jew?" the man scowled.

"I beg you to take this to my cousin at Mazowiecki, east of Warsaw. Or send it there later on. The war will not last forever."

He told him Masha's name and where the farm could be found.

"I beg you, in the name of the Mother of God of Czesto-chowa", he pleaded.

"What's this about Czestochowa?" said the man, hesitating.

"For the sake of our Savior."

"Are you a Catholic?"

"Yes."

"Lots of Catholics go to the vacation spot where you're going."

"I am one."

"It's warm there. It's so nice, no one returns from it."

"Can you do me this great favor?"

"People sometimes throw messages out of the trains. But never before has a Catholic tossed me a message addressed to a Jew. Is it gold?" he asked, shaking the package.

"I beg you. You will be rewarded. God sees everything."

The trackman turned his hard eyes to the chimneys.

"Does God see that? Where is God?"

"Poselski, you idiot!" his comrades shouted. "Who are you talking to? Let's get going!"

The trackman walked away carrying the package.

Not long after, the train lurched and rolled with sickening slowness toward the source of the stench.

Pawel fell down into the crowd below.

"Watch out! Be careful! Oh, he's heavy!"

When he was standing again, he rested against the wall, feeling dizzy and sick to his stomach. There was ringing in his ears.

An arm grabbed him, then another arm, and he found himself compressed in a vise of human anguish. An old man in tattered rags and a peasant's cap. The smell of him was overwhelming even among the odors in the car. The eyes ran with yellow fluid, and a mouth full of rotten teeth exuded corruption.

"Mottele, my son, my son, I have found you!" the old man screamed.

473

"Excuse me, sir", Pawel said, prying the other's arms away from himself. "I am not your son."

"Mottele, do not say such things! It *is* you! It *is* you!"

"I am not Mottele. My name is Pawel. I am not your son!" He tried to push the creature away decisively, without hurting him.

His assailant burst into tears.

"When they took you away I hid in the coal cellar. But they found me. I had no strength to fight them. You're a young man. You're strong. I prayed. I asked the All-Powerful One to spare you. Is it beyond the strength of him who determines the courses of the planets and the stars to guard the life of my boy, my son, my beloved? Oh, yes, I said to myself, the Lord of the Universe will protect him. If there is justice in the world, he will deliver him into my arms. Who will sing *Kaddish* for me if my son perishes? Who? Tell me, who?"

"Please, sir, I am not your son. You are mistaken."

The press of bodies was so great that it was impossible to remove himself from the vicinity of the old man. Once again he wrapped his arms around Pawel's chest and sobbed, "I love you, my son. Do not cast me aside!"

Pawel looked down upon the skull mashed against his chest. The embrace was completely repulsive. The stench and the ugliness of the face made him retch.

"I know it is you, I know it is you", whimpered the old man with a look of haunting and hunger.

Pawel put his arms around him. At first he felt only nausea. Then the nausea eased and the creature's trembling subsided into sighs and meek cries of gratitude.

"It *is* you. It *is* you. I knew it."

"Soon they will let us out", said Pawel. "Soon you will have rest and food. I will help you."

"Moitteleh, how kind you are to me."

"It won't be long. Don't be afraid!"

"Not long. I won't cry."

474

Pawel's eyes burned. He kept them closed. In his arms was a father, a child, a beloved, disguised in the many disguises of man. As he held the creature it ceased to be just that—a creature, an *it*, wretched, unlovely, invasive of his privacy. He no longer felt afraid of him nor disgusted by his lack of beauty. The being he held in his arms was, indeed, beautiful.

It seemed to him now in this inexplicable moment of vision, that his own father was the child and he, Pawel, the father. Had not every father once been a child, each suffering in turn those blows and absences that chained all souls, link by link, back into the shadows of time? What, then, would break the link? What would turn a man's vision from the dictates of the past toward the future?

"*Mój synu*", he whispered into the old man's ears, and kissed his forehead.

He held him for a long time, and eventually the old man slept. But when there came a gap in the crowd and Pawel bent to lay him against a wall, he saw that he was dead. He did not know the Hebrew words for *Kaddish*. He whispered the Latin prayers of intercession for the souls of the departed.

"I forgive", he exhaled. "I forgive everything."

For another hour the train crept onward, and this eternal creeping toward the unknown incited a form of madness in many. Some began to shriek from frustration and terror.

"*Shtiler, shtiler*, quiet, quiet!" men and women shouted.

"Do not be afraid, children."

"Do not let them degrade us!"

"Pray! Do not lose hope!"

Pawel tried to encourage those around him. "We are not alone", he said, but there were many people raving, and no one listened.

Nearby, a young mother carrying a two-year-old gazed steadily at Pawel. Her face was like a thousand faces, ten thousand faces. Her child was like a thousand children, a thousand times ten thousand children. In her eyes there was perfect still-ness. The child pressed his cheek against the mother's cheek as he played with the patch of her yellow star, and he too was looking at Pawel. The woman's face was not unusually pretty, though it was tender and good. Neither was the child's face extraordinary. Yet Pawel found it impossible to turn his eyes away from them. They regarded each other for what seemed a very long time. No words were spoken, no emotions crossed their faces. In the end the little boy raised a small, white butterfly hand and waved at him. The palm of the hand was bandaged with a dirty piece of linen, stained with blood.

At that moment the car screeched to a halt and all its inhabitants fell against each other in a jumble. When Pawel was again upright, he looked around but could not find the woman and her child.

Within minutes the shouting of harsh voices and the barking of dogs erupted outside.

As he waited for the doors to open, Pawel understood what was about to happen. He saw that a life is a word spoken. It cannot be taken back once uttered. It is a seed launched upon the wind for a brief flight, then planted in the soil, where it sleeps for a time. Many are the elements that make the harvest: sun and rain, heat and cold, plowing and sowing, the season of bounty and the season when creation dies.

If he were to tell the people this, his voice would disappear in the vortex of words swirling and plunging and flying to heaven and to hell. In their pain, they could not see the glory of his discovery. Few would hear him, fewer would comprehend. Perhaps only the mother with her child, the father with his son, and the writer with his grief. They understood the end of words. Their lives had been spoken, and so shifted, a little, the balance of the world.

Falling slowly into the mouth of Wrog, Pawel was unafraid for the first time in his life. He was rising, his eyes shining, his arms lifting to greet the messages the angels were pouring out over the world.

The doors of the wagon opened, and the shouting soldiers and barking dogs surged forward.

"Snow", he whispered.

# Epilogue

The bodyguards crashed through the doorway. Behind them came Lev.

"Hurry, or you'll miss your flight!" he roared, fuming with irritation. He glared at the old woman. "Why is this ridiculous creature so important?"

Ewa Poselski rose slowly from her chair and fumbled in her purse. She took something from it, kissed it, and pressed it into the hands of the politician. Then, blindly, with big sighs, she walked out the door and was gone from his life.

They caught their flight at LaGuardia on time and connected in Paris with the El Al flight to Tel Aviv. The aircraft's VIP lounge was practically empty. The politician's secretary went back to first class to discuss the next election with other members of the entourage, leaving him alone with Lev. Lev doubled as executive assistant and campaign manager. His agitation, barely restrained beneath his cool demeanor, alerted the politician that he was about to receive a lecture on strategy and style. A steward brought them drinks, and they sat facing each other.

"What's the matter with you? It was a great talk. The *New York Times* will have a complete transcript on page four tomorrow. You should be ecstatic. It's that old lady, isn't it?"

"It's more than her."

"What's it all about?"

"A piece of history."

"The *Shoah*?"

He nodded and looked down into the palm of his hand.

His manager glanced there too.

"What's that?"

"A medallion wrapped in a letter. A message hurled over a wall."

"From someone you knew?"

"Yes."

Lev reached out and tapped the medallion. "We missed an important meeting because of this distraction. We can't afford self-indulgence. We have a struggle ahead. We've survived these past twenty years because of clearheadedness and nerves of steel. Please, no more sentimentalism."

"This is not sentimentalism."

"Tell me what it is, then, because you look like you've seen a ghost."

"Not a ghost", said the politician, shaking his head. "A window into the past. Isn't it strange how one sees the future best by looking into the past?"

"What are you talking about?"

"I'm not going to run for election, Lev."

"What the hell! Don't say that! Not now!"

"Yes, now. If I wait, it will soon be impossible for me to choose."

"That's insane! Don't do this to the Party and don't you dare do it to the People! Not because of a moment of nostalgia or whatever that woman said to you."

"She was just a messenger."

Lev grew silent and watched.

"Did you ever love anything, Lev? Yes, of course, you love your wife and your children and a kibbutz-full of grandchildren. I mean love something you can't see, but when it's gone you feel its absence? That kind of thing."

"Sure. How about the spirit of a nation? How about a promise that was made to a lot of people who believe in you?"

"Should a man sell his soul for the good of the people?"

"Take a week's vacation. You're worn out. Don't make any rash decisions. Damn it, man, the country's yours on a platter.

You'll have a chance to change things, to make peace in the world."

"No one can do that single-handedly. If he tries, he'll become a tyrant, just like the ones who made the Shoah. Do you want that for me?"

"You're talking nonsense. You're overwrought."

"No, I feel peace for the first time in decades. I don't have to keep climbing for power just so that when I get enough of it I can make the world a safe place. It's a lie, my friend."

"You believe that?"

"I remember a poem my father taught me when I first learned to sing. Shall I sing it?"

Lev looked over his shoulder. "No", he said dryly. "Please do *not* sing it."

The politician sang in Yiddish:

> "*Poor men want to be rich,*
> *rich men want to be kings,*
> *and kings are not satisfied until they rule everything.*"

He looked out the window at the stars.

"I haven't sung in so many years. It is good to sing. It feels very, very good. Do you know what would happen if a ruler should ever arrive at the point of absolute power? In the end he would become as much a monster as the Hitlers and the Stalins."

Lev took a long drink, emptying his glass.

"I thought you were a realist."

"A realist? What is a realist? I no longer know the answer to that."

"Yesterday you knew. Yesterday you were willing. You always claimed you were doing it for your family, and for all the others who perished."

"Yes", he replied slowly. "Yes, it was for them."

"And for Ruth", Lev said carefully.

481

"And for Ruth."

"When they killed her, I thought they had killed you too—killed your spirit."

"It almost did. Do you know how many times I sat up all night in the dark during the last two years with a loaded pistol in my hand, telling myself I should put the barrel in my mouth and pull the trigger? Do you know how hard it was not to?"

"You fought it. You fought harder than any man I've ever known. Why are you giving up now?"

"I'm not giving up. The nature of the war is changing. My role on this front has ended."

Leaning forward, Lev put a hand on his arm. "She's dead", he said. "The ones who killed her are dead. But it's still a fresh memory—a terrible memory. Give it time. You need this work. And we need you."

"No."

Lev sat back, exasperated. "Taking into consideration the possibility that you're not joking, I must ask what you're thinking of doing?"

"I'm giving the Prime Minister my resignation tomorrow morning. And then I'm going away."

"Where?"

"I might go to Warsaw. Everything was destroyed, you know. But the streets are the same. I'll walk around them and look at the cobblestones. And I'm going to Treblinka. My family died there. And to Auschwitz. A man I knew died there—or at least he may have died. He saved my life. I have to go to the places where they suffered. I need to be still. I need to listen."

"The Soviets would never let you into Poland."

"Perhaps not. This has happened so fast. I need time to think. There has been so little time, hasn't there. Why are we always galloping toward some undefined end?"

"Time is a luxury we can't afford."

"Time is a necessity. Time and silence. Otherwise we repeat

the past, find ourselves doing the very things our oppressors once did."

"Don't be absurd. We're not evil men."

"Is anyone immune? Tell me, Lev, how do evil men become what they become?"

Lev eyed him coldly. The politician knew him well enough to see that he was struggling to find the trail of logic.

"There are other things I'd like to do. When I was young I wanted to unearth the past. Maybe I'll go to the digs at Jericho—there's a *tel* nearby that no one has touched yet—maybe they'll let me help sift for pottery. I might go to the desert, camp on Massada, look at the stars. Or build a little boat and sail it around Kinneret. Or hike on Carmel. One thing for certain, I won't be coming back in search of power."

"How do you know that?"

"I know it."

"What do you mean, you *know* it! How can you be so sure?"

"The only thing I know is that if I ignore this little coin, I will never find my own true name."

Lev snorted discreetly. "Your own true name? What's that supposed to mean? I'll tell you your own true name: You were born to power. You have style, you have strength, and you have that clever mind of yours. You're ethical and the country is in love with you. You could lead this whole damn world if you really wanted it!"

Lev turned away and stared at his reflection in the window.

David Schäfer faltered. He felt an invisible force tearing him from the medallion. Conflicting ideologies raced through his mind. Foremost among them was the lure of the good he could achieve if he were to bless the earth with a philosopher-king.

For a moment he looked away from the little word in his palm, and in the turning he felt for the first time in his life the presence of an intelligence far greater than his own. In it there was malice. It was another being, invisible but *there*, demanding entrance. And it was exulting, for its influence over him, which had been weakened by the coming of the messenger, was now about to be restored. It was forcing him to think of the medallion as a trinket, a memento of the past, and his rise to political power as a destiny that could not be rejected. The pressure from this dark presence was . . . evil. Yes, why not use the word, he thought. There was good and there was evil. The evil presence hated. The good presence loved, just as the Torah said it did. An old mythology. But there it was.

With a great effort of the mind, he acknowledged that he too had hated. Yes, he had hated the ones who killed his parents, brothers, sisters. They had killed his wife and child. They had killed everybody. They had killed his feelings. He hated the ones who let it happen almost as much as he hated the ones who had done it. And the hatred had flowered full force after Ruth's murder, as if hatred were the only antidote to despair.

He had wanted to make it so they could never do it again. For most of his life he had desired this, and when she died the desire had become a consuming obsession beneath the surface of his admirable public image. The thing had fed on this passion. It had relentlessly pushed him toward power, and all the while it had ripened a dull, black seed within his heart. Now he understood how close he was to the abyss.

The thing spat a thought into his mind: *If not you, then another!*

Then his manager turned to him and said bitterly, "If not you, then another!"

"Not me, Lev. Not ever. And I hope there won't be any other."

"There are many like you. We'll find one instantly."

"Do you know what a *shammash* is?"

"Of course I know what a *shammash* is."

"I am more sure than ever", he said finally. "My name is David Schäfer. I wish to be poor."

484

\* \* \*

Twenty years later, a man lay dying at his home in a suburb of an East German city. He was suffering the last stages of cancer and was in great pain. One of his sons, a physician, administered an additional dose of morphine and he began to feel some relief. His other children, middle-aged and prosperous, were sitting in armchairs arranged around the walls of the expansive bedroom, talking quietly among themselves. A brother consoled a weeping sister. Some of their children's children skipped in noisily and were quickly hushed. An aunt escorted them out.

"Hans", said the dying man.

A portly, balding man approached the bed.

"Yes, Father."

"Will you do something for me?"

"Anything. What is it?"

"You must promise me."

"I promise you, Father."

"You must not interfere with a project I have undertaken with my publishers. Go to the safe behind the Monet. In it you will find a folder. It contains the original manuscript of *Andrei Rublëv*."

"Your play?"

The man did as directed then returned with the folder.

"It is not my play", said his father.

Several voices uttered protests, and eyes exchanged glances.

"My mind is perfectly clear."

The son removed a sheaf of papers. He read the title page.

"Who is Pawel Tarnowski?" he asked.

"The person who wrote this play."

Various members of the family hastened over to reassure the old man that he was, in fact, who he was, and to remind him that the sickness or the medication was disorienting his thoughts.

"The morphine . . ."

He waved them away.

"I stole this play", he said.

"*Nein, Vati, nein . . .*"

"Yes, your dear Papa. A fraud who sat for a quarter century in the chair of literature at the university. I have lived all this time on its reputation. Not an immortal play, they said, but a significant footnote to the times. Professor Haftmann is a genuine artist of the postwar reconstruction, they said. And of course it was so useful when the Soviets closed us off from the West. They saw in it a metaphor of Russian unity, resistance to the Chinese."

His son passed the manuscript around to the others.

"I regret that I have ruined your memory of me. Not a kind legacy to leave to one's children. But there are things in the heart that cannot be taken to the grave. There are things in each of your hearts that my failure has made in you. You must look into these shadows. Truth is the power that will liberate us."

The son took his father's hand.

"It was so long ago. It is better to forget the past."

"It was just this morning, it seems, that I took the soul of another man and called it my own. Was it because, Hans, I had lost my own?"

"No, no, no . . ."

"A manuscript has been smuggled out to *Neumann Buchverlag* on the other side of the wall. Were I an honest man and a courageous one, I would have done this long ago. The book will be republished in the spring, with a full explanation, under the name of its true author."

A flurry of discussion and emotion swept through the room.

"I realize how humiliating this will be for you all. I beg you to forgive me. Forgive me . . ."

\*     \*     \*

Over the northern bushlands of British Columbia the stars were so brilliant that many people who had fallen into the habit of not seeing them looked up. The Milky Way was a river of pale blue light. The visible planets were at their brightest. Jupiter's moons could be seen through binoculars. Venus was sharp and Mars an angry eye just above the horizon. Meteors fell from time to time.

In the parish church of a remote Indian reserve the lights went out, and a figure emerged from the front door. It was the pastor, an elderly Polish man.

The night was one of the coldest that winter, trees cracking like gunshots in the surrounding forest, smoke rising straight up from the chimneys of the village. The priest stood a while until his eyes adjusted to the darkness. As he observed the motions in the heavens, he pondered, as he had so often during his life, the question of why people had ceased to look upward. The people of his times had once again begun to think that there was no *lebensraum*—no room in the world, no room in the material universe, and no infinity in which to discover immortal room.

He had met so many like that in the camps, in universities, in seats of power, and even in the place where he now lived. All of them felt compelled to seek solutions, and in doing so they tried to force their will upon others. The worst would try to force it upon mankind. They would make space for humanity by destroying a portion of humanity. Like their forerunners, they would in the end make the world more bereft of space and time. They looked at the sky, but it was meaningless to them, empty and flat. They killed hope because they had no true hope.

The priest sighed and gazed in wonder at the wheeling cosmos.

He shook himself. "Enough! To bed, old man!"

He must be strong for tomorrow. There were confessions to be heard in the morning. Not many came anymore, but a few children, the elderly, and the dying would be there. Later in the afternoon he would go by snowmobile to the other villages down-river. A long day. Three Masses for possibly a hundred souls.

Looking back to the earth, he turned and limped toward the log cabin that was his rectory, feeling only a little pain in an ancient wound.